Prentice Hall LITERATURE

PENGUIN EDITION

Reader's Notebook

English Learner's Version

Grade Eight

PEARSON

Upper Saddle River, New Jersey
Boston, Massachusetts
Chandler, Arizona
Glenview, Illinois

Copyright © Pearson Education, Inc., or its affiliates. All Rights Reserved. Printed in the United States of America. This publication is protected by copyright, and permission should be obtained from the publisher prior to any prohibited reproduction, storage in a retrieval system, or transmission in any form or by any means, electronic, mechanical, photocopying, recording, or likewise.

For information regarding permission(s), write to Pearson Curriculum Group Rights & Permissions Department, One Lake Street, Upper Saddle River, New Jersey 07458.

Pearson, Prentice Hall, and Pearson Prentice Hall are trademarks, in the U.S. and/or other countries, of Pearson Education, Inc., or its affiliates.

ISBN-13: 978-0-13-366687-8
ISBN-10:   0-13-366687-5

9 10 V011 17 16 15 14 13

ACKNOWLEDGMENTS

Grateful acknowledgment is made to the following for copyrighted material:

Arte Publico Press
From *My Own True Name* by Pat Mora. Copyright © 2000 Arte Publico Press—University of Houston. Published by Arte Publico Press. "Baseball" by Lionel G. Garcia from *I Can Hear the Cowbells Ring* (Houston: Arte Publico Press—University of Houston, 1994).

Ashabranner, Brent
"Always to Remember: The Vision of Maya Ying Lin" by Brent Ashabranner from *Always to Remember*. Copyright © 1988.

Black Issues Book Review
"Zora Neale Hurston: A Life in Letters, Book Review" by Zakia Carter from *Black Issues Book Review*, Nov–Dec 2002; www.bibookreview.com.

Curtis Brown London
"Who Can Replace a Man" by Brian Aldiss from *Masterpieces: The Best Science Fiction of the Century*. Copyright © 1966 by Brian Aldiss.

Child Health Association of Sewickley, Inc.
"Thumbprint Cookies" from *Three Rivers Cookbook*. Copyright © Child Health Association of Sewickley, Inc.

Copper Canyon Press c/o The Permissions Company
"Snake on the Etowah" by David Bottoms from *Armored Hearts: Selected and New Poems*. Copyright © 1995 by David Bottoms.

Gary N. DaSilva for Neil Simon
"The Governess" from *The Good Doctor* © 1974 by Neil Simon. Copyright renewed © 2002 by Neil Simon. CAUTION: Professionals and amateurs are hereby warned that *The Good Doctor* is fully protected under the Berne Convention and is subject to royalty. All rights, including without limitation professional, amateur, motion picture, television, radio, recitation, lecturing, public reading and foreign translation rights, computer media rights and the right of reproduction, and electronic storage or retrieval, in whole or in part and in any form, are strictly reserved and none of these rights can be exercised or used without written permission from the copyright owner. Inquiries for stock and amateur performances should be addressed to Samuel French, Inc., 45 West 25th Street, New York, NY 10010. All other inquiries should be addressed to Gary N. DaSilva, 111 N. Sepulveda Blvd., Suite 250, Manhattan Beach, CA 90266-6850.

(Acknowledgments continue on page V71)

CONTENTS

PART 1

UNIT 1 Fiction and Nonfiction

MODEL SELECTIONS

from The Baker Heater League by Patricia C. McKissack and Fredrick McKissack
- Exploring Nonfiction and Fiction 2
- Before You Read 4
- Making Connections 5
- Selection 6

The 11:59 by Patricia C. McKissack
- Before You Read 8
- Making Connections 9
- Selection 10
- After You Read 14
- Vocabulary Skill Review 15
- Research the Author 16

Raymond's Run • A Retrieved Reformation

Raymond's Run by Toni Cade Bambara
- Before You Read 17
- Making Connections 18
- Selection 19
- After You Read 24
- Vocabulary Skill Review 25

A Retrieved Reformation by O. Henry
- Before You Read 26
- Making Connections 27
- After You Read 28
- Vocabulary Skill Review 29

Gentleman of Río en Medio • Cub Pilot on the Mississippi

Gentleman of Río en Medio by Juan A. A. Sedillo
- Before You Read 30
- Making Connections 31
- Selection 32
- After You Read 35
- Vocabulary Skill Review 36

CONTENTS

Cub Pilot on the Mississippi by Mark Twain
    Before You Read 37
    Making Connections 38
    After You Read 39
    Vocabulary Skill Review 40

INFORMATIONAL TEXTS
Consumer Documents
    Making Connections 41
    Selection 42
    After You Read 45

from **An American Childhood • The Adventure of the Speckled Band**

from **An American Childhood by Annie Dillard**
    Before You Read 46
    Making Connections 47
    Selection 48
    After You Read 51
    Vocabulary Skill Review 52

The Adventure of the Speckled Band by Sir Arthur Conan Doyle
    Before You Read 53
    Making Connections 54
    After You Read 55
    Vocabulary Skill Review 56

from **Steinbeck: A Life in Letters • *from* Travels With Charley • The American Dream**

from **Steinbeck: A Life in Letters and *from* Travels With Charley by John Steinbeck**
    Before You Read 57
    Making Connections 58
    After You Read 59
    Vocabulary Skill Review 60

The American Dream by Martin Luther King, Jr.
    Before You Read 61
    Making Connections 62
    Selection 63
    After You Read 65
    Vocabulary Skill Review 66

CONTENTS

INFORMATIONAL TEXTS
Magazine Articles
- Making Connections 67
- Selection 68
- After You Read 72

Unit 1 Vocabulary Review 73

UNIT 2 Short Stories

MODEL SELECTION
An Hour With Abuelo by Judith Ortiz Cofer
- Exploring Short Stories 75
- Before You Read 77
- Making Connections 78
- Selection 79
- After You Read 82
- Vocabulary Skill Review 83
- Research the Author 84

Who Can Replace a Man? • Tears of Autumn
Who Can Replace a Man? by Brian Aldiss
- Before You Read 85
- Making Connections 86
- Selection 87
- After You Read 92
- Vocabulary Skill Review 93

Tears of Autumn by Yoshiko Uchida
- Before You Read 94
- Making Connections 95
- After You Read 96
- Vocabulary Skill Review 97

Hamadi • The Tell-Tale Heart
Hamadi by Naomi Shihab Nye
- Before You Read 98
- Making Connections 99
- Selection 100
- After You Read 105
- Vocabulary Skill Review 106

CONTENTS

The Tell-Tale Heart by Edgar Allan Poe
  Before You Read 107
  Making Connections 108
  After You Read 109
  Vocabulary Skill Review 110

INFORMATIONAL TEXTS
Summaries
  Making Connections 111
  Selection 112
  After You Read 115

Charles • Flowers for Algernon

Charles by Shirley Jackson
  Before You Read 116
  Making Connections 117
  Selection 118
  After You Read 122
  Vocabulary Skill Review 123

Flowers for Algernon by Daniel Keyes
  Before You Read 124
  Making Connections 125
  After You Read 126
  Vocabulary Skill Review 127

Thank You, M'am • The Story-Teller

Thank You, M'am by Langston Hughes
  Before You Read 128
  Making Connections 129
  Selection 130
  After You Read 133
  Vocabulary Skill Review 134

The Story-Teller by Saki (H. H. Munro)
  Before You Read 135
  Making Connections 136
  After You Read 137
  Vocabulary Skill Review 138

CONTENTS

INFORMATIONAL TEXTS
Advertisements
- Making Connections 139
- Selection 140
- After You Read 141

Unit 2 Vocabulary Review 142

UNIT 3 Types of Nonfiction

MODEL SELECTION
Making Tracks on Mars: A Journal Based on a Blog by Andrew Mishkin
- Exploring Types of Nonfiction 144
- Before You Read 146
- Making Connections 147
- Selection 148
- After You Read 151
- Vocabulary Skill Review 152
- Research the Author 153

Baseball • *from* Harriet Tubman: Conductor on the Underground Railroad

Baseball by Lionel G. Garcia
- Before You Read 154
- Making Connections 155
- Selection 156
- After You Read 159
- Vocabulary Skill Review 160

from **Harriet Tubman: Conductor on the Underground Railroad** by Ann Petry
- Before You Read 161
- Making Connections 162
- After You Read 163
- Vocabulary Skill Review 164

from Always to Remember: The Vision of Maya Ying Lin • *from* I Know Why The Caged Bird Sings

from **Always to Remember: The Vision of Maya Ying Lin** by Brent Ashabranner
- Before You Read 165
- Making Connections 166
- Selection 167
- After You Read 171
- Vocabulary Skill Review 172

CONTENTS

***from* I Know Why The Caged Bird Sings** by Maya Angelou
    Before You Read 173
    Making Connections 174
    After You Read 175
    Vocabulary Skill Review 176

INFORMATIONAL TEXTS

Textbooks
    Making Connections 177
    Selection 178
    After You Read 181

The Trouble With Television • On Woman's Right to Suffrage

The Trouble With Television by Robert MacNeil
    Before You Read 182
    Making Connections 183
    Selection 184
    After You Read 187
    Vocabulary Skill Review 188

On Woman's Right to Suffrage by Susan B. Anthony
    Before You Read 189
    Making Connections 190
    After You Read 191
    Vocabulary Skill Review 192

from Sharing in the American Dream • Science and the Sense of Wonder

***from* Sharing in the American Dream** by Colin Powell
    Before You Read 193
    Making Connections 194
    Selection 195
    After You Read 198
    Vocabulary Skill Review 199

Science and the Sense of Wonder by Isaac Asimov
    Before You Read 200
    Making Connections 201
    After You Read 202
    Vocabulary Skill Review 203

CONTENTS

INFORMATIONAL TEXTS
Newspaper Editorials
- Making Connections 204
- Selection 205
- After You Read 209

Unit 3 Vocabulary Review 210

UNIT 4 Poetry

MODEL SELECTIONS
Describe Somebody and Almost a Summer Sky by Jacqueline Woodson
- Exploring Poetry 212
- Before You Read 214
- Making Connections 215
- Selection 216
- After You Read 220
- Vocabulary Skill Review 221
- Research the Author 222

Poetry Collection 1 • Poetry Collection 2

Poetry Collection 1
- Before You Read 223
- Making Connections 224
- Selection 225
- After You Read 228
- Vocabulary Skill Review 229

Poetry Collection 2
- Before You Read 230
- Making Connections 231
- After You Read 232
- Vocabulary Skill Review 233

Poetry Collection 3 • Poetry Collection 4

Poetry Collection 3
- Before You Read 234
- Making Connections 235
- Selection 236
- After You Read 239
- Vocabulary Skill Review 240

Contents ix

CONTENTS

Poetry Collection 4
- Before You Read.. 241
- Making Connections.. 242
- After You Read... 243
- Vocabulary Skill Review....................................... 244

INFORMATIONAL TEXTS
Recipes and Food Labels
- Making Connections.. 245
- Selection... 246
- After You Read... 248

Poetry Collection 5 • Poetry Collection 6

Poetry Collection 5
- Before You Read.. 249
- Making Connections.. 250
- Selection... 251
- After You Read... 256
- Vocabulary Skill Review....................................... 257

Poetry Collection 6
- Before You Read.. 258
- Making Connections.. 259
- After You Read... 260
- Vocabulary Skill Review....................................... 261

Poetry Collection 7 • Poetry Collection 8

Poetry Collection 7
- Before You Read.. 262
- Making Connections.. 263
- Selection... 264
- After You Read... 271
- Vocabulary Skill Review....................................... 272

Poetry Collection 8
- Before You Read.. 273
- Making Connections.. 274
- After You Read... 275
- Vocabulary Skill Review....................................... 276

CONTENTS

INFORMATIONAL TEXTS
Manuals
- Making Connections 277
- Selection 278
- After You Read 280

Unit 4 Vocabulary Review 281

UNIT 5 Drama

MODEL SELECTION
from **Anne Frank & Me** by Cherie Bennett
- Exploring Drama 283
- Before You Read 285
- Making Connections 286
- Selection 287
- After You Read 289
- Vocabulary Skill Review 290
- Research the Author 291

The Governess
The Governess by Neil Simon
- Before You Read 292
- Making Connections 293
- Selection 294
- After You Read 297
- Vocabulary Skill Review 298

INFORMATIONAL TEXTS
Public Documents
- Making Connections 299
- Selection 300
- After You Read 301

The Diary of Anne Frank, Act I
The Diary of Anne Frank, Act I by Frances Goodrich and Albert Hackett
- Before You Read 302
- Making Connections 303
- Selection 304
- After You Read 314
- Vocabulary Skill Review 315

CONTENTS

The Diary of Anne Frank, Act II
The Diary of Anne Frank, Act II by Frances Goodrich and Albert Hackett
- Before You Read 316
- Making Connections 317
- After You Read 318
- Vocabulary Skill Review 319

INFORMATIONAL TEXTS
Online Information
- Making Connections 320
- Selection 321
- After You Read 323

Unit 5 Vocabulary Review 324

UNIT 6 Themes in American Stories

MODEL SELECTION
Water Names by Lan Samantha Chang
- Exploring Themes in American Stories 326
- Before You Read 328
- Making Connections 329
- Selection 330
- After You Read 333
- Vocabulary Skill Review 334
- Research the Author 335

Coyote Steals the Sun and Moon • Why the Waves Have Whitecaps
Coyote Steals the Sun and Moon Zuni Myth, retold by Richard Erdoes and Alfonso Ortiz
- Before You Read 336
- Making Connections 337
- Selection 338
- After You Read 341
- Vocabulary Skill Review 342

Why the Waves Have Whitecaps by Zora Neale Hurston
- Before You Read 343
- Making Connections 344
- After You Read 345
- Vocabulary Skill Review 346

xii English Learner's Notebook

CONTENTS

▸ Chicoria • *from* The People, Yes • Brer Possum's Dilemma • John Henry

Chicoria by José Griego y Maestas and Rudolfo A. Anaya • *from* **The People, Yes** by Carl Sandburg

- Before You Read 347
- Making Connections 348
- After You Read 349
- Vocabulary Skill Review 350

Brer Possum's Dilemma by Jackie Torrence • **John Henry** Traditional

- Before You Read 351
- Making Connections 352
- Selection 353
- After You Read 359
- Vocabulary Skill Review 360

INFORMATIONAL TEXTS

Reviews

- Making Connections 361
- Selection 362
- After You Read 364

▸ *from* Out of Dust • Ellis Island

***from* Out of Dust** by Karen Hesse

- Before You Read 365
- Making Connections 366
- Selection 367
- After You Read 370
- Vocabulary Skill Review 371

Ellis Island by Joseph Bruchac

- Before You Read 372
- Making Connections 373
- After You Read 374
- Vocabulary Skill Review 375

▸ Choice: A Tribute to Martin Luther King, Jr. • An Episode of War

Choice: A Tribute to Martin Luther King, Jr. by Alice Walker

- Before You Read 376
- Making Connections 377
- Selection 378
- After You Read 380
- Vocabulary Skill Review 381

CONTENTS

An Episode of War by Stephen Crane
- Before You Read 382
- Making Connections 383
- After You Read 384
- Vocabulary Skill Review 385

INFORMATIONAL TEXTS
Transcripts
- Making Connections 386
- Selection 387
- After You Read 392

Unit 6 Vocabulary Review 393

PART 2 Summary Translations

Unit 1 Fiction and Nonfiction
- from The Baker Heater League T2
- The 11:59 .... T4
- Raymond's Run T6
- A Retrieved Reformation T8
- Gentleman of Río en Medio T10
- Cub Pilot on the Mississippi T11
- from An American Childhood T13
- The Adventure of the Speckled Band T15
- from Travels With Charley T16
- The American Dream T18

Unit 2 Short Stories
- An Hour With Abuelo T20
- Who Can Replace a Man? T22
- Tears of Autumn T23
- Hamadi T25
- The Tell-Tale Heart T26
- Charles T27
- Flowers for Algernon T29
- Thank You, M'am T31
- The Story-Teller T32

xiv English Learner's Notebook

CONTENTS

Unit 3 Types of Nonfiction

Making Tracks on Mars: A Journal Based on a Blog T33
Baseball T35
Harriet Tubman: Guide to Freedom T36
from Always to Remember: The Vision of Maya Ying Lin T38
from I Know Why the Caged Bird Sings T40
The Trouble With Television T41
On Woman's Right to Suffrage T42
from Sharing in the American Dream T44
Science and the Sense of Wonder T46

Unit 4 Poetry

Describe Somebody T48
Almost a Summer Sky T48
Cat! T50
Silver T50
Your World T50
Thumbprint T51
The Drum (for Martin Luther King, Jr.) T51
Ring Out, Wild Bells T51
Concrete Mixers T52
The City Is So Big T52
Harlem Night Song T52
Ode to Enchanted Light T53
Little Exercise T53
The Sky Is Low, the Clouds Are Mean T53
Runagate Runagate T54
Blow, Blow, Thou Winter Wind T54
Old Man T54
The New Colossus T55
Paul Revere's Ride T55
Harriet Beecher Stowe T55
January T56
New World T56
For My Sister Molly Who in the Fifties T56
Grandma Ling T57
Drum Song T57
your little voice / Over the wires came leaping T57

CONTENTS

Unit 5 Drama

from Anne Frank & Me T59
The Governess T61
The Diary of Anne Frank, Act I T62
The Diary of Anne Frank, Act II T64

Unit 6 Themes in American Stories

Water Names T66
Coyote Steals the Sun and Moon T67
Why the Waves Have Whitecaps T69
Chicoria T71
from The People, Yes T71
Brer Possum's Dilemma T73
John Henry T73
from Out of the Dust T74
Ellis Island T76
Choice: A Tribute to Martin Luther King, Jr. T78
An Episode of War T79

PART 3 Turbo Vocabulary

Word Roots V2
Prefixes V4
Suffixes V6
Using a Dictionary V8
Word Study Cards V10
Academic Vocabulary V12
Words in Other Subjects V24
Vocabulary Flash Cards V25
Vocabulary Fold-a-List V29
Commonly Misspelled Words V33
Word Attack Skills: Phonics V35
Mnemonics V37
Communication Strategies V39
Vocabulary Bookmarks V40
Vocabulary Builder Cards V42
Personal Thesaurus V44

xvi English Learner's Notebook

INTERACTING WITH THE TEXT

As you read your hardcover student edition of *Prentice Hall Literature* use the **Reader's Notebook** to guide you in learning and practicing the skills presented. In addition, many selections in your student edition are presented here in an interactive format. The notes and instruction will guide you in applying reading and literary skills and in thinking about the selection. The examples on these pages show you how to use the notes as a companion when you read.

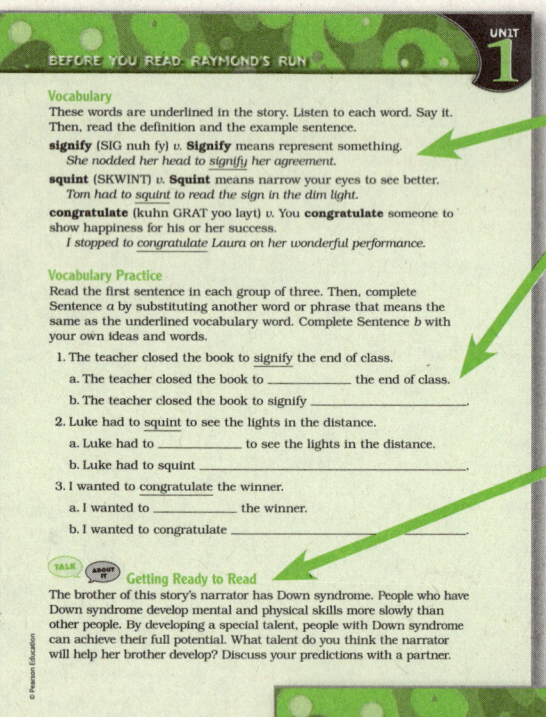

Build Your Vocabulary

Use the *Before You Read* page to learn vocabulary that you will read in the selection. To practice using the words, you can write on the lines in the practice sentences.

Get Ready to Read

This paragraph gives you more information about the selection. Before you read, you can discuss your thoughts and ideas with classmates.

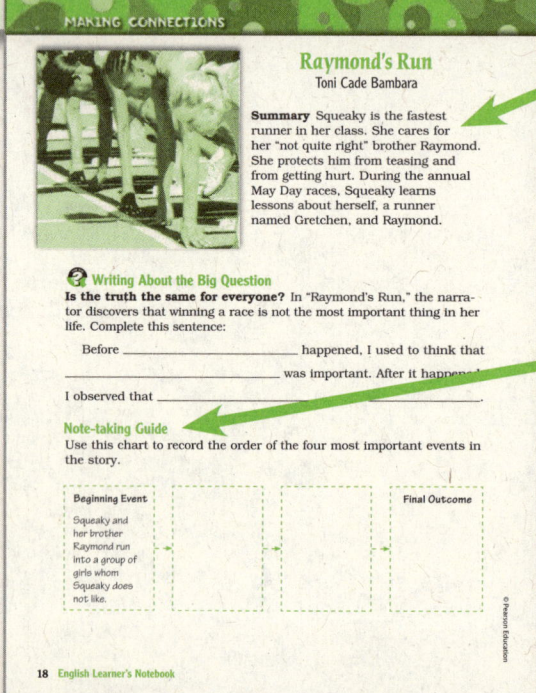

Get the Big Idea

The *Making Connections* page presents a selection summary, which lets you know what the selection is about before you read.

Be an Active Reader

A *Note-taking Guide* helps you organize the main ideas of the selection. Complete the guide as you read to track your understanding.

xviii **English Learner's Notebook**

Read the Text

Text set in a wider margin provides the author's actual words.

Text set in a narrow margin provides a summary of selection events or details.

Mark the Text

Use write-on lines to answer questions in the side column. You may also want to use the lines for your own notes.

When you see a pencil, you should underline, circle, or mark the text as indicated.

Take Notes

Side-column questions accompany the selections that appear in the Reader's Notebooks. These questions are a built-in tutor to help you practice the skills and understand what you read.

Check Your Understanding

Questions after every selection help you think about the selection. You can use the write-on lines and charts to answer the questions. Then, share your ideas in discussions and writing activities.

Learn Vocabulary Skills

The *Vocabulary Skill Review* page provides more instruction in vocabulary skills. Practice what you learn in oral and writing activities.

Interacting with the Text xix

PART 1

The Reader's Notebook—your personal literature book with a built-in study guide

Selections and Skills Support

The pages in your **Reader's Notebook** go with the pages in the hardcover student edition. The pages in the **Reader's Notebook** allow you to participate in class instruction and take notes on the concepts and selections.

Before You Read

Before You Read Follow along in your **Reader's Notebook** as your teacher introduces the **Vocabulary** from the selection. You can complete the **Vocabulary Practice** sentences by writing in your **Reader's Notebook.** Use the question in **Getting Ready to Read** to discuss your ideas with classmates.

Making Connections Use this page for the selection your teacher assigns.
- The **Summary** gives you an outline of the selection.
- Use **Writing About the Big Question** to understand the big idea of the selection and join in the class discussion about the ideas.
- Use the **Note-taking Guide** while you read the story. This will help you organize and remember information you will need to answer questions about the story later.

While You Read

Selection Text and Sidenotes You can read the full text of one selection in each pair in your **Reader's Notebook.**
- You can write in the **Reader's Notebook.** Underline important details to help you find them later.
- Use the **Take Notes** column to jot down your reactions, ideas, and answers to questions about the text. If your assigned selection is not the one that is included in the **Reader's Notebook,** use sticky notes to make your own **Take Notes** section in the side column as you read the selection in the hardcover student edition.

After You Read

After You Read Use this page to answer questions about the selection right in your **Reader's Notebook.** You can complete the graphic organizer right on the page in your **Reader's Notebook.**

Vocabulary Skill Review Use this page to help you develop important vocabulary skills that will be useful to you.

Other Features in the *Reader's Notebook* You will also find note-taking opportunities for these features:
- Exploring the Genre
- Support for the Model Selection
- Support for reading Informational Texts

UNIT 1
EXPLORING NONFICTION

The Baker Heater League

Nonfiction is different from fiction in these ways:

- Nonfiction deals with real people, events, or ideas.
- Nonfiction is told through the voice of the author. The author is a real person. The author's view is the **point of view** of the writing.

Many things affect the outcome of nonfiction writing. Two examples are these:

- **Mood:** the feeling the reader gets from the work
- **Author's style:** all of the different ways that a writer uses language. Rhythm, language, and ways of putting things in order are all part of the author's style.

Purpose	Mission	Examples
To persuade	• written to convince audiences of a certain idea or opinion	• speeches • editorials
To inform	• written to present facts and information	• articles • reference books • historical essays • research papers
To entertain	• written for the enjoyment of the audience	• autobiographies • biographies • travel narratives

EXPLORING FICTION

The 11:59

Fiction is a story that comes from the author's imagination. It tells about characters and events. Fiction has these basic parts:

- **Setting:** the time and place of the story
- **Plot:** the events that move the reader through the story. The plot includes a **conflict**, or problem. The **resolution**, or outcome, comes at the end of the story.
- **Characters:** the people or animals that take part in the action in a story. The **character's traits**, or qualities, can affect his or her thoughts and actions.
- **Point of view:** the view from which the story is told to the reader. The **first-person point of view** is used when the story is told from the view of a character. The **third-person point of view** is used when the story is told from the view of a person outside the story.
- **Theme:** a message about life that the story tries to show

Type	Description	Characteristics
Short stories	short works that can usually be read in one sitting	- contain plot, characters, setting, point of view, and theme - usually focus on one main plot around one conflict
Novels	longer works	- contain plot, characters, conflict, and setting - may also contain **subplots**, independent stories or conflicts related to the main plot
Novellas	shorter than novels, but longer than short stories	- may contain characteristics of short stories and novels
Historical fiction	works of fiction that take place in a real historical setting	- uses information about real people and events to tell invented stories

UNIT 1

BEFORE YOU READ: FROM THE BAKER HEATER LEAGUE

Vocabulary

These words are underlined in the selection. Listen to each word. Say it. Then, read the definition and the example sentence.

scheduled (SKED juhld) *adj.* When an event is **scheduled,** it is planned to take place.
  The teacher held the scheduled meeting in the classroom.

exaggerated (ig ZAD juh rayt uhd) *v.* When something is **exaggerated,** it is overstated and made to seem better, larger, or worse than it really is.
  She exaggerated her grade on the test to make herself appear smarter.

courtesy (KER tuh see) *n.* **Courtesy** is polite behavior to other people.
  He showed his sister courtesy by opening the car door for her.

Vocabulary Practice

Read the first sentence in each group of three. Then, complete Sentence *a* by substituting another word or phrase that means the same as the underlined vocabulary word. Complete Sentence *b* with your own ideas and words.

1. The scheduled meeting is supposed to start in an hour.
   a. The _____ meeting is supposed to start in an hour.
   b. The scheduled _____.

2. Tomas exaggerated his role on the team to impress his friends.
   a. Tomas _____ his role on the team to impress his friends.
   b. Tomas exaggerated _____.

3. We showed courtesy by clapping for the terrible speech.
   a. We showed _____ by clapping for the terrible speech.
   b. We showed courtesy _____.

 ### Getting Ready to Read

This selection describes legends that railroad porters used to tell one another. A legend is a story that is presented as history, but it is not entirely true. Some legends tell about people who really lived. What are some legends that you know? Discuss these legends with a partner.

MAKING CONNECTIONS

from The Baker Heater League
Patricia C. McKissack and Fredrick McKissack

Summary This nonfiction selection explains how railroad workers called *porters* shared tales with one another. The porters would gather around a potbellied stove, called a Baker heater, to tell their stories. Legends such as those of Casey Jones and John Henry grew out of these stories.

Note-taking Guide
Use the chart below to record the different facts and legends you learned while reading "The Baker Heater League."

Facts	Legends
About 1870, John Henry joined a steel-driving team for the C & O Railroad.	John Henry was so strong that he could drive steel with a hammer in each hand.

from The Baker Heater League 5

TAKE NOTES

Vocabulary Builder

Plurals The plural of a noun refers to more than one person or thing. To make a noun plural, you usually add an *s* or an *es* at the end of a noun. The authors add an *s* at the end of the word *worker* to make it plural. Write the other plural nouns in the first paragraph.

_____

_____

Cultural Understanding

In this selection, *cannonball* means "a train that travels very fast." During the nineteenth and early twentieth centuries, many people called any fast-moving train a *cannonball*.

Fluency Builder

The sentence beginning "The real John Henry . . ." is long. Read aloud the sentence. With a partner, break it into two or three shorter sentences.

_____

_____

_____

Read aloud the new sentences to make sure that they have the same meaning as the long sentence.

from The Baker Heater League
Patricia C. and Fredrick McKissack

This nonfiction selection explains how railroad workers called porters shared and passed on stories. The porters would meet one another in train stations across the United States. When they were not working, the porters sat around a potbellied stove, called a Baker heater, and told stories. The porters became known as "The Baker Heater League."

The selection describes how the porters told stories that were based on the actions of real people. One story was about a real engineer named Casey Jones.

◆ ◆ ◆

John Luther Jones, better known as Casey Jones, was an **engineer** on Cannonball Number 382. On the evening of April 29, 1900, Casey and his black fireman, Sim Webb, prepared to take the Cannonball from Memphis to Canton. The scheduled engineer was out ill. The train left at 12:50 A.M., an hour and thirty minutes late. Casey was determined to make up the lost time.

◆ ◆ ◆

When Casey's train crashed, he refused to jump to safety. Instead, he stayed on the train, saved many lives, and then died. He became a railroad hero.

Another railroad hero was based on a real person named John Henry.

◆ ◆ ◆

The real John Henry, believed to be a newly freed slave from North Carolina, joined the West Virginia steel-driving team hired to dig out the

Everyday Words
engineer (en ji NEER) *n.* someone whose job it is to control the engine on a ship or train

6 English Learner's Notebook

Big Bend Tunnel for the C & O Railroad, **circa** 1870. Many stories detail the life and adventures of this two hundred-pound, six-foot man who was so strong he could drive steel with a hammer in each hand. John Henry's death occurred after competing with a steam drill, winning, and then dying.

◆ ◆ ◆

The porters also told stories about Daddy Joe, a real-life porter, who became a legend. Although they exaggerated Daddy Joe's actions, the stories showed what qualities the porters admired.

◆ ◆ ◆

Whenever a storyteller wanted to make a point about courtesy, honesty, or an outstanding job performance, he used a Daddy Joe story. And a tale about him usually began with: "The most terrific Pullman porter who ever made down a berth was Daddy Joe."

◆ ◆ ◆

The porters also liked to tell funny stories about new workers who made foolish mistakes. As soon as one story was over, someone would begin a new one.

◆ ◆ ◆

Amid thigh-slapping laughter, another tale would begin with: "Did you hear the story about the flagman?" Of course they'd all heard the story a hundred times. But each teller added or subtracted something until the tale was his own. That's how the tales stayed fresh and original.

Everyday Words

circa (SER cuh) *adj*. around; used before a date to show that the date is uncertain

TAKE NOTES

Comprehension Builder

Why did the porters tell stories about Daddy Joe?

The porters told stories about

Daddy Joe to show _____

_____

_____.

Vocabulary Builder

Compound Words Sometimes a new word is formed by joining two separate words. The new word is known as a compound word. The word *flagman* is formed by joining the words *flag* and *man*. Each of those words has a meaning on its own. They form a new word when joined. Circle two compound words in the underlined sentence.

from The Baker Heater League   7

UNIT 1

BEFORE YOU READ: THE 11:59

Vocabulary

These words are underlined in the story. Listen to each word. Say it. Then, read the definition and the example sentence.

meager (MEE ger) *adj.* A very small amount of something is **meager.**
Father frowned at the meager salad the waiter placed before him.

mournful (MAWRN fuhl) *adj.* Something **mournful** is very sad.
He was mournful after hearing the bad news.

restraint (ri STRAYNT) *n.* **Restraint** is the act of holding back or controlling something.
Tina showed restraint by waiting until after dinner to eat the brownie.

Vocabulary Practice

Read the first sentence in each group of three. Then, complete Sentence *a* by substituting another word or phrase that means the same as the underlined vocabulary word. Complete Sentence *b* with your own ideas and words.

1. The meager paycheck barely paid Carly's bills.

    a. The _____ paycheck barely paid Carly's bills.

    b. The meager _____.

2. The mournful movie made the audience cry.

    a. The _____ movie made the audience cry.

    b. The mournful _____.

3. Although I was angry, I showed restraint when telling the police about the accident.

    a. Although I was angry, I showed _____ when telling the police about the accident.

    b. Although I was angry, I showed restraint _____.

Getting Ready to Read

The Brotherhood of Sleeping Car Porters was the first all-African American union in the United States. A union helps workers discuss wages and working conditions with employers. What other ways might a union help workers? Discuss your ideas with a partner.

8 English Learner's Notebook

MAKING CONNECTIONS

The 11:59
Patricia C. McKissack

Summary Lester Simmons, a retired porter, hangs out every night at the porter house, telling stories to the other railroad employees. One night, he tells the young porters about the mysterious 11:59 Death Train. Lester's story becomes real. He tries to escape the train.

Note-taking Guide
Use this web to recall the different stories that Lester tells.

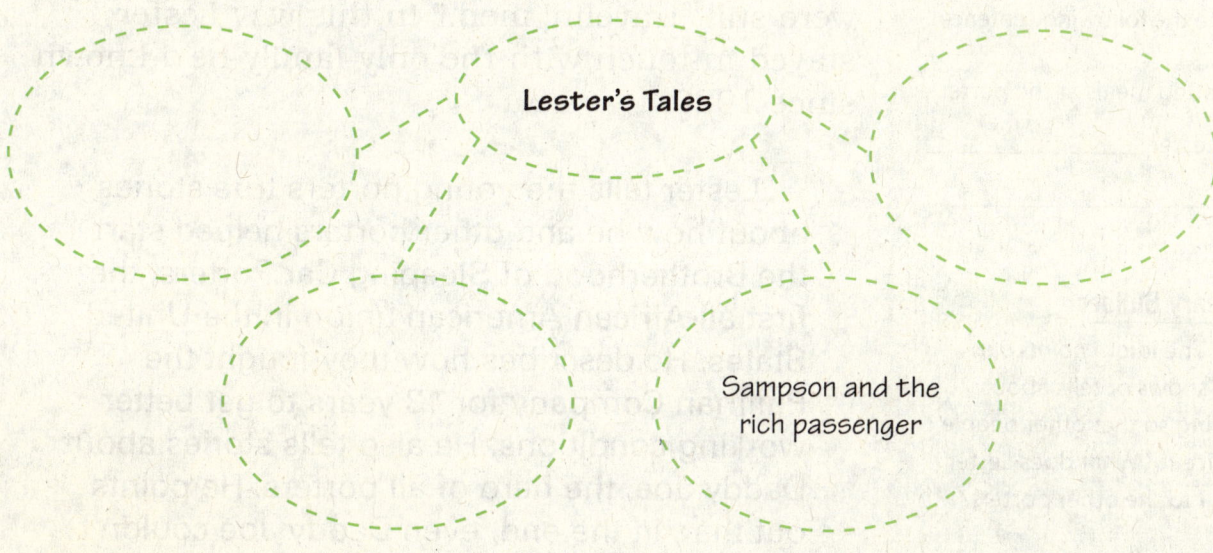

TAKE NOTES

Cultural Understanding

Between the 1870s and the 1960s, the Pullman Company hired many African American men as porters. Pullman porters prepared the passengers' beds at night. In the morning, they replaced the seating. Pullman porters also helped passengers with their luggage and worked at all hours to make sure that the passengers were comfortable.

Vocabulary Builder

Idioms Find the idiom *spinning yarns* in the third paragraph. *Spinning yarns* means "telling stories." Use *spinning yarns* to complete the following sentence:

While eating meals at the porter house, Lester _____

_____.

Vocabulary Builder

Idioms The idiom *points out* means "shows or tells about something so that other people will notice it." What does Lester *point out* to the other porters?

Lester *points out* that _____

_____

_____.

The 11:59
Patricia C. McKissack

This fictional story is set in St. Louis in the 1950s. Its main character is an old man who has retired from his job as a Pullman porter after thirty years of work.

♦ ♦ ♦

Lester Simmons was a thirty-year retired Pullman car porter—had his gold watch to prove it. "Keeps perfect train time," he often bragged. "Good to the second."

Daily he went down to the St. Louis Union Station and shined shoes to help **supplement** his meager twenty-four-dollar-a-month Pullman retirement check. He ate his evening meal at the porter house on Compton Avenue and hung around until late at night talking union, playing bid whist, and spinning yarns with those who were still "travelin' men." In this way Lester stayed in touch with the only family he'd known since 1920.

♦ ♦ ♦

Lester tells the young porters true stories about how he and other porters helped start the Brotherhood of Sleeping Car Porters, the first all-African American union in the United States. He describes how they fought the Pullman Company for 13 years to get better working conditions. He also tells stories about Daddy Joe, the hero of all porters. He points out that, in the end, even Daddy Joe couldn't escape the porters' Death Train, the 11:59.

♦ ♦ ♦

Everyday Words

supplement (SUP luh muhnt) *v.* add something, especially to what you earn or eat, in order to improve it

---

10 English Learner's Notebook

"Any porter who hears the whistle of the 11:59 has got exactly twenty-four hours to clear up earthly matters. He better be ready when the train comes the next night . . ." In his creakiest voice, Lester drove home the point. "All us porters got to board that train one day. Ain't no way to escape the final ride on the 11:59."

Silence.

"Lester," a young porter asked, "you know anybody who ever heard the whistle of the 11:59 and lived to tell—"

"Not a living soul!"

Laughter.

◆ ◆ ◆

Then Lester tells the story of how his old friend, Tip Sampson, got his nickname. Tip once waited on a rich woman who rode a train from Chicago to Los Angeles. He was hoping to get a big tip from the woman. At the end of the trip, however, all she gave him was one dime. Lester started teasing Sampson by calling him Tip, and the nickname stuck. One of the porters tells Lester that Tip recently "boarded the 11:59," or died. Lester realizes that he is one of the last old-time porters left in St. Louis. Then he starts walking home a little before midnight.

◆ ◆ ◆

Suddenly he felt a sharp pain in his chest. At exactly the same moment he heard the <u>mournful</u> sound of a train whistle, which the wind seemed to carry from some faraway place. Ignoring his pain, Lester looked at the old station. He knew nothing was scheduled to come in or out till early morning. Nervously he lit a match to check the time. 11:59!

"No," he said into the darkness. "I'm not ready. I've got plenty of living yet."

TAKE NOTES

Fluency Builder

Read aloud Lester's dialogue in the first paragraph to a partner. As you read, say the words as if you were telling a scary story.

Vocabulary Builder

Multiple-Meaning Words The word *tip* can mean "money given to someone for doing a service." *Tip* can also mean "a useful suggestion for doing something." What does *tip* mean in the sentence below?

He was hoping to get a big *tip* from the woman.

_____
_____

Comprehension Builder

Lester hears the whistle of the 11:59 train. Predict what will happen to Lester. Write your answer on the lines below.

_____
_____
_____
_____

TAKE NOTES

Vocabulary Builder

Dialect Dialect includes words that people use in conversation that are not considered correct in formal writing. The word *ain't* is a word from a dialect. It can mean "am not," "is not," "are not," "has not," and "have not." Find and circle the word *ain't* in the first paragraph. Read aloud the sentence in which the word appears, replacing it with a correct term.

Vocabulary Builder

Idioms *To settle down* is an idiom that means "to live a quiet life." Complete the following sentence frame:

Lester thinks about what it would have been like *to settle down* _____
_____.

Vocabulary Builder

Idioms The idiom *time had run out* means that there is no more time to do something. Complete the following sentence that uses *time had run out*:

Time had run out for Lester when he saw _____
_____.

Fear quickened his step. Reaching his small apartment, he hurried up the steps. His heart pounded in his ear, and his left arm tingled. He had an idea, and there wasn't a moment to waste. But his own words haunted him. *Ain't no way to escape the final ride on the 11:59.*

"But I'm gon' try!" Lester spent the rest of the night plotting his escape from fate.

♦ ♦ ♦

Lester decides not to eat or drink anything the next day so that he will not choke or die of food poisoning. He shuts off his space heater, nails all the doors and windows shut, and unplugs all of his appliances to avoid any dangers. He plans to escape Death and live to tell the story to the young porters.

Lester spends the next day in his chair, too scared to move. He checks his watch every few minutes and listens to its constant ticking. He thinks about his thirty years of working on the railroad. He wonders what his life would have been like if he had decided to settle down in one place and get married. Finally, he decides that he has lived a good life and has no regrets.

When night comes, Lester starts praying. His arm starts tingling, and his legs get stiff. He wonders whether he will be the first porter to avoid the 11:59 and cheat Death. Then he hears a train whistle, lights a match, and sees that the time is now 11:57. He hears the whistle again, but he is unable to move. The pain in his chest gets worse, and it is hard for him to breathe.

♦ ♦ ♦

Time had run out! Lester's mind reached for an explanation that made sense. But reason failed when a glowing phantom dressed in the porters' blue uniform stepped out of the grayness of Lester's confusion.

"It's *your* time, good brother." The specter spoke in a thousand familiar voices.

Freed of any restraint now, Lester stood, bathed in a peaceful calm that had its own glow. "Is that you, Tip?" he asked, squinting to focus on his old friend standing in the strange light.

"It's me, ol' partner. Come to remind you that none of us can escape the last ride on the 11:59."

"I know. I know," Lester said, chuckling. "But man, I had to try."

Tip smiled. "I can dig it. So did I."

"That'll just leave Willie, won't it?"

"Not for long."

"I'm ready."

♦ ♦ ♦

Lester dies. Two days later, his friends find him dead on the floor, with his eyes still staring at his gold watch. The watch stopped at exactly 11:59.

TAKE NOTES

Fluency Builder

Quotation marks (" ") are used to show when characters in a story are speaking. With a partner, read aloud the dialogue between Lester and Tip as if you were speaking with a good friend.

Vocabulary Builder

Slang *I can dig it* is slang for "I understand." What does Lester say that Tip understands?

Tip understands _____

_____

_____ .

Comprehension Builder

Was your prediction about what will happen to Lester correct? Explain.

_____

_____

_____

_____

_____

_____

The 11:59 13

AFTER YOU READ

Thinking About the Selection

1. The porters of the Baker Heater League tell stories about railroad heroes. Write facts and legends about each hero.

Railroad Heroes	Facts	Legends
Casey Jones	He was an engineer on _____.	He chose to stay on the train to _____.
John Henry	The West Virginia steel-driving team hired him to _____.	He was so strong that he could _____.
Daddy Joe	He worked as a _____.	He was the most _____ and _____ porter who ever lived.

2. Each porter from the Baker Heater League added or subtracted details in his stories so that _____
_____.

TALK ABOUT IT **Telling Stories** Why did the young porters enjoy hearing Lester tell stories about the past? Discuss your ideas with a partner.

The young porters enjoyed hearing Lester tell stories about the past because _____.

WRITE ABOUT IT **Your Favorite Story** Which of Lester's stories did you enjoy most? Explain your answer.

I enjoyed reading about _____ because _____
_____.

14 English Learner's Notebook

VOCABULARY SKILL REVIEW

Prefixes

A prefix is a word part added to the beginning of a base (or main) word. A prefix changes the meaning of the base word. The prefix *pre-* means "before" or "occurring earlier."

Examples

| pre + judge = prejudge | The new word *prejudge* means "judge before all the facts are known." |
| pre + pay = prepay | The new word *prepay* means "pay for something before it is needed or used." |

Now You Do It

Make new words by adding the prefix *pre-* to each word below. Write a definition for each new word.

heat _____

season _____

teen _____

suppose _____

view _____

TALK ABOUT IT **Prewriting with Prefixes!** Suppose that you are about to interview a coach or a movie theater manager. With a partner, discuss questions you could ask about the coach's or theater manager's plans. For each question, use a word from this lesson.

WRITE ABOUT IT **Write a Newspaper Article** Use the questions from the above activity to write a newspaper article of an interview with the coach or movie theater manager. Think about how they might answer your questions. Then, read aloud your news article to your partner.

_____

_____

_____

RESEARCH THE AUTHOR

Talk Show

Present a **talk show.** The following tips will help you create your show.

- Read some of the authors' works. Patricia and Fredrick McKissack's books include *Christmas in the Big House, Christmas in the Quarters; Bugs!; Martin Luther King, Jr.: Man of Peace; Rebels Against Slavery: American Slave Revolts*; and *Let My People Go.*

    What I learned from the McKissacks' writing:

    _____
    _____
    _____
    _____

- Search the Internet: Use words and phrases such as "Patricia McKissack article."

    What I learned about Patricia and Fredrick McKissack:

    _____
    _____
    _____
    _____

- Watch the video interview with Patricia McKissack. Add what you learn from the video to what you have already learned about the author and her husband.

    Additional information learned about the authors:

    _____
    _____
    _____
    _____

    Use your notes to write your talk show.

BEFORE YOU READ: RAYMOND'S RUN

Vocabulary

These words are underlined in the story. Listen to each word. Say it. Then, read the definition and the example sentence.

signify (SIG nuh fy) *v.* **Signify** means represent something.
She nodded her head to signify her agreement.

squint (SKWINT) *v.* **Squint** means narrow your eyes to see better.
Tom had to squint to read the sign in the dim light.

congratulate (kuhn GRAT yoo layt) *v.* You **congratulate** someone to show happiness for his or her success.
I stopped to congratulate Laura on her wonderful performance.

Vocabulary Practice

Read the first sentence in each group of three. Then, complete Sentence *a* by substituting another word or phrase that means the same as the underlined vocabulary word. Complete Sentence *b* with your own ideas and words.

1. The teacher closed the book to signify the end of class.

   a. The teacher closed the book to _____ the end of class.

   b. The teacher closed the book to signify _____.

2. Luke had to squint to see the lights in the distance.

   a. Luke had to _____ to see the lights in the distance.

   b. Luke had to squint _____.

3. I wanted to congratulate the winner.

   a. I wanted to _____ the winner.

   b. I wanted to congratulate _____.

Getting Ready to Read

The brother of this story's narrator has Down syndrome. People who have Down syndrome develop mental and physical skills more slowly than other people. By developing a special talent, people with Down syndrome can achieve their full potential. What talent do you think the narrator will help her brother develop? Discuss your predictions with a partner.

MAKING CONNECTIONS

Raymond's Run
Toni Cade Bambara

Summary Squeaky is the fastest runner in her class. She cares for her "not quite right" brother Raymond. She protects him from teasing and from getting hurt. During the annual May Day races, Squeaky learns lessons about herself, a runner named Gretchen, and Raymond.

Writing About the Big Question

Is the truth the same for everyone? In "Raymond's Run," the narrator discovers that winning a race is not the most important thing in her life. Complete this sentence:

Before _____ happened, I used to think that _____ was important. After it happened, I observed that _____.

Note-taking Guide

Use this chart to record the order of the four most important events in the story.

Beginning Event			Final Outcome
Squeaky and her brother Raymond run into a group of girls whom Squeaky does not like.	→	→	→

Raymond's Run
Toni Cade Bambara

Squeaky is a confident, sassy young girl who lives in Harlem in New York City. Squeaky has to take care of her brother Raymond, who is "not quite right." She boldly protects Raymond from kids who try to tease him. Squeaky loves to run races, and she is the fastest runner in her neighborhood.

♦ ♦ ♦

There is no track meet that I don't win the first place medal. I used to win the twenty-yard dash when I was a little kid in kindergarten. Nowadays, it's the fifty-yard dash. And tomorrow I'm subject to run the quarter-meter relay all by myself and come in first, second, and third.

♦ ♦ ♦

This year, for the first time, Squeaky has some serious competition in the race, a new girl named Gretchen.

♦ ♦ ♦

So as far as everyone's concerned, I'm the fastest and that goes for Gretchen, too, who has put out the tale that she is going to win the first-place medal this year. Ridiculous. In the second place, she's got short legs. In the third place, she's got freckles. In the first place, no one can beat me and that's all there is to it.

♦ ♦ ♦

Squeaky takes a walk down Broadway with Raymond. She is practicing her breathing exercises to get in shape for the race. Raymond is pretending to drive a stage coach.

Squeaky works hard to be a good runner. She dislikes people who pretend that they do not need to work hard to be good at something.

Then, Squeaky sees Gretchen and two of her friends coming toward her and Raymond.

TAKE NOTES

Vocabulary Builder

Adjectives An adjective is a word that describes a person, place, or thing. For example, in the sentence *She is the fastest runner*, the adjective *fastest* describes the noun *runner*. On the lines below, write three more adjectives you find in the first paragraph.

_____
_____
_____

Fluency Builder

Read aloud the second paragraph on this page to yourself. As you read, remember that Squeaky is confident about her running abilities.

Vocabulary Builder

Contractions A contraction is a shorter form of a phrase. An apostrophe (') appears in place of the missing letters. In the phrase *so as far as everyone's concerned*, the *'s* is a contraction of *is*. What contractions appear on this page? Write each contraction and its longer phrase.

_____
_____
_____
_____

TAKE NOTES

Vocabulary Builder

Idioms *Hang out* is an idiom that means "spend time with." Complete the following sentence by replacing *hang out* with other words:

Mary Louise now _____

_____ Gretchen.

Vocabulary Builder

Slang The verb *whupped* is slang for "beat or defeated an opponent." Complete the sentence, using the word *whupped*.

Squeaky knows that she has

_____

_____.

Fluency Builder

Read the first sentence of the bracketed paragraph. Work with a partner to break it into four or five shorter sentences.

_____

_____

_____

Read aloud the new sentences to make sure that they have the same meaning as the long sentence.

One of the girls, Mary Louise, used to be Squeaky's friend. Now she hangs out with Gretchen and does not like Squeaky anymore. Rosie, the other girl, always teases Raymond. Squeaky considers going into a store to avoid the girls, but she decides to face them.

◆ ◆ ◆

"You signing up for the May Day races?" smiles Mary Louise, only it's not a smile at all.

A dumb question like that doesn't deserve an answer. Besides, there's just me and Gretchen standing there really, so no use wasting my breath talking to shadows.

"I don't think you're going to win this time," says Rosie, trying to signify with her hands on her hips all salty, completely forgetting that I have whupped her many times for less salt than that.

"I always win cause I'm the best," I say straight at Gretchen who is, as far as I'm concerned, the only one talking in this ventriloquist-dummy[1] routine.

[Gretchen smiles, but it's not a smile, and I'm thinking that girls never really smile at each other because they don't know how and don't want to know how and there's probably no one to teach us how cause grown-up girls don't know either. Then they all look at Raymond who has just brought his mule team to a standstill. And they're about to see what trouble they can get into through him.]

◆ ◆ ◆

Mary Louise starts to tease Raymond, but Squeaky defends him. Gretchen and her friends leave, and Squeaky smiles at her brother.

The next day, Squeaky arrives late at the May Day program because she does not want

---

1. **ventriloquist-dummy** A *ventriloquist* (ven TRI luh kwist) is a person who can speak without moving his or her lips. The ventriloquist usually has a puppet called a dummy that he or she controls.

to see the May Pole dancing. She thinks it is silly. She arrives just as the races are starting. She puts Raymond on the swings and finds Mr. Pearson, a tall man who gives the racers their numbers.

◆ ◆ ◆

"Well, Squeaky," he says, checking my name off the list and handing me number seven and two pins. And I'm thinking he's got no right to call me Squeaky, if I can't call him Beanstalk.

"Hazel Elizabeth Deborah Parker," I correct him and tell him to write it down on his board.

"Well, Hazel Elizabeth Deborah Parker, going to give someone else a break this year?" I squint at him real hard to see if he is seriously thinking I should lose the race on purpose just to give someone else a break.

◆ ◆ ◆

Mr. Pearson suggests that Squeaky let Gretchen, the new girl, win the race. Squeaky gets mad and walks away.

When it is time for the 50-yard dash, Squeaky and Gretchen line up with the other runners at the starting line. Squeaky sees that Raymond has left the swings and is getting ready to run on the other side of the fence.

Squeaky mentally prepares herself to win and takes off like a shot, zipping past the other runners.

◆ ◆ ◆

I glance to my left and there is no one. To the right a blurred Gretchen, who's got her chin **jutting** out as if it would win the race all by itself. And on the other side of the fence is Raymond with his arms down to his side and the palms

Everyday Words
jutting (JUT ing) *adj.* sticking out

TAKE NOTES

Vocabulary Builder

Idioms To *give someone a break* means to give that person a chance. Mr. Pearson asks Squeaky whether she will *give someone a break* because

_____
_____.

Comprehension Builder

Predict who will win the race between Squeaky and Gretchen. Explain your answer.

_____
_____
_____
_____
_____

Vocabulary Builder

Idioms The idiom *takes off* means "leaves in a hurry." Complete the following sentence:

Squeaky *takes off* because

_____
_____.

Raymond's Run 21

TAKE NOTES

Vocabulary Builder

Multiple-Meaning Words The word *tear* can mean "pull apart or rip." Another meaning of *tear* is "move or act quickly." Read the underlined sentence. Which meaning of *tear* is used?

_____

Vocabulary Builder

Idioms *To catch my breath* is an idiom that means "to stop so that I can control my breathing." When might you need *to catch your breath*?

I might need *to catch my breath* _____
_____.

Fluency Builder

With a partner, read aloud the paragraph that begins "And it occurs to me . . ." Change the tone of your voice as you speak to show that you, like Squeaky in the story, are getting excited about the idea of coaching Raymond.

---

tucked up behind him, running in his very own style, and it's the first time I ever saw that and I almost stop to watch my brother Raymond on his first run. But the white ribbon is bouncing toward me and I tear past it, racing into the distance till my feet with a mind of their own start digging up footfuls of dirt and brake me short.

♦ ♦ ♦

Squeaky believes that she has won the race, but it turns out that she and Gretchen crossed the finish line at almost the same time. The judges are not sure which girl is the winner.

♦ ♦ ♦

And I lean down to catch my breath and here comes Gretchen walking back, for she's overshot the finish line too, huffing and puffing with her hands on her hips taking it slow, breathing in steady time like a real pro and I sort of like her a little for the first time. "In first place . . ." and then three or four voices get all mixed up on the loudspeaker and I dig my sneaker into the grass and stare at Gretchen who's staring back, we both wondering just who did win.

♦ ♦ ♦

As Squeaky waits to find out whether she has won, Raymond calls out to her. He starts climbing up the fence. Suddenly, Squeaky remembers that Raymond ran the race too, on the other side of the fence.

♦ ♦ ♦

And it occurs to me, watching how smoothly he climbs hand over hand and remembering how he looked running with his arms down to his side and with the wind pulling his mouth back and his teeth showing and all, it occurred to me that Raymond would make a very fine runner. Doesn't he always keep up with me on my trots? And he surely knows how to breathe in counts of seven cause he's always doing it at the dinner table, which drives my brother George up the wall. And I'm smiling to beat the band cause if I've lost this race, or if me and Gretchen tied, or even if I've won, I can always retire as a runner and begin a whole new career as a coach with Raymond as my champion.

◆ ◆ ◆

Squeaky gets very excited about the idea of teaching Raymond to be a champion runner. She wants him to have something to be proud of. Raymond runs over to her, and she jumps up and down with happiness because of her plans to help him.

◆ ◆ ◆

But of course everyone thinks I'm jumping up and down because the men on the loudspeaker have finally gotten themselves together and compared notes and are announcing "In first place—Miss Hazel Elizabeth Deborah Parker." (Dig that.) "In second place—Miss Gretchen P. Lewis." And I look over at Gretchen wondering what the "P" stands for. And I smile. Cause she's good, no doubt about it. Maybe she'd like to help me coach Raymond; she obviously is serious about running, as any fool can see. And she nods to congratulate me and then she smiles. And I smile. We stand there with this big smile of respect between us.

TAKE NOTES

Vocabulary Builder

Idioms *To beat the band* is an idiom that means "to the greatest amount possible." How would you describe Squeaky as she is "smiling to beat the band"?

_____
_____

Comprehension Builder

Summarize the relationship between Squeaky and Gretchen before and after the race.

_____
_____
_____
_____
_____

Raymond's Run 23

AFTER YOU READ

Thinking About the Selection

1. Squeaky is a confident person who is very protective of her brother. How does she show these qualities? Write your answers in the chart below.

Confident	Protective
Squeaky shows that she is confident when _____ _____ _____	Squeaky shows that she is protective of Raymond when _____ _____ _____

2. After Squeaky sees Raymond run, she wants to _____ _____.

TALK ABOUT IT **A Good Friend?** Do you think that Squeaky would make a good friend? Discuss with a partner the parts of Squeaky's personality that would make you want to be her friend.

Squeaky would make a good friend because _____ _____.

WRITE ABOUT IT **Would You Be Her Friend?** Write more about your own opinion. You may think that Squeaky would make a good friend in some ways but not in other ways. If so, write about both.

I think that Squeaky _____ _____ _____ _____ _____.

VOCABULARY SKILL REVIEW

Idioms

An idiom is a word or phrase that has a different meaning from the dictionary definitions of the words. Sometimes you may be able to understand the meaning of an idiom by its context. Other times you will need a dictionary.

Examples

Idiom	Meaning
take a break	rest for a short time
read between the lines	find a hidden meaning
catch on	understand or learn something
heart of gold	kind, generous, friendly

Now You Do It

Write a sentence using each idiom from the chart above.

1. take a break _____
2. read between the lines _____
3. catch on _____
4. heart of gold _____

TALK ABOUT IT **Guessing Game** Select one of the idioms from the chart above. Describe to a partner something that fits the idiom. Do not use the idiom in your description. Have your partner guess the idiom from your description.

WRITE ABOUT IT **What Do You Mean?** Write a sentence using the words in the idioms on this page literally and then as an idiom. For example, you could write "I needed to take a break so that I would not break the vase when I take it to Tina."

_____
_____

Raymond's Run

UNIT 1

BEFORE YOU READ: A RETRIEVED REFORMATION

Vocabulary

These words are highlighted in the story. Listen to each word. Say it. Then, read the definition and the example sentence.

rehabilitate (ree uh BIL uh tayt) *v.* To **rehabilitate** means to bring back to normal or good condition.

Her apology was the first step in an effort to rehabilitate herself.

retribution (re truh BYOO shuhn) *n.* **Retribution** is punishment for doing wrong or a reward for doing good.

The accident victim wanted money from the other driver as retribution.

perceived (puhr SEEVD) *v.* When something is **perceived,** it becomes known through one's senses.

He had not perceived his error until it was too late.

Vocabulary Practice

Read the first sentence in each group of three. Then, complete Sentence *a* by substituting another word or phrase that means the same as the underlined vocabulary word. Complete Sentence *b* with your own ideas and words.

1. It took him months to rehabilitate his leg after the accident.

    a. It took him months to _____ his leg after the accident.

    b. It took him months to rehabilitate _____.

2. He demanded retribution after the driver dented his car.

    a. He demanded _____ after the driver dented his car.

    b. He demanded retribution _____.

3. She bit into the apple and perceived that the fruit was ripe.

    a. She bit into the apple and _____ that the fruit was ripe.

    b. She bit into the apple and perceived _____.

Getting Ready to Read

A reformation is an improvement that is made by changing something. The main character of this story decides to reform his life by ending his career as a thief. What reasons do you think a person might have for reforming his or her life? Discuss your ideas with a partner.

26 English Learner's Notebook

MAKING CONNECTIONS

A Retrieved Reformation
O. Henry

Summary Jimmy Valentine leaves prison and plans to go back to robbing safes. But he falls in love and decides to become honest. He changes his name and opens a store. A detective shows up to arrest Jimmy for recent robberies. However, Jimmy's actions show that he has changed.

 Writing About the Big Question

Is truth the same for everyone? In "A Retrieved Reformation," a former thief tries to re-invent the truth about his life. Complete this sentence:

People form opinions of others based on _____

_____.

Note-taking Guide
Use this character web to describe Jimmy Valentine's character.

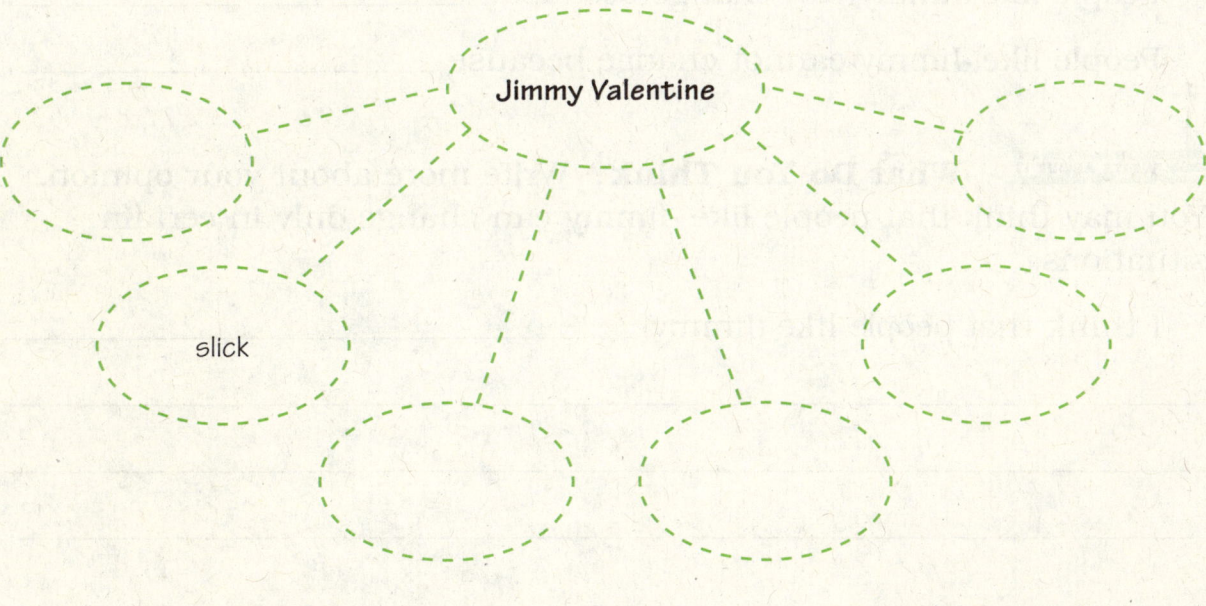

A Retrieved Reformation 27

AFTER YOU READ

Thinking About the Selection

1. One of the first people Jimmy sees in Elmore is Annabel Adams. How does seeing Annabel change Jimmy? Write your answers in the chart below.

Before Jimmy sees Annabel, he . . .	After Jimmy sees Annabel, he . . .

2. Ben Price pretends not to know Jimmy because _____.

TALK ABOUT IT **Can People Change?** Jimmy has been disobeying the law for a long time, but he plans to stop. Do you think that people like Jimmy can change their ways? Discuss your thoughts with a partner.

People like Jimmy can change because _____.

People like Jimmy cannot change because _____.

WRITE ABOUT IT **What Do You Think?** Write more about your opinion. You may think that people like Jimmy can change only in certain situations.

I think that people like Jimmy _____
_____
_____
_____.

VOCABULARY SKILL REVIEW

Multiple-Meaning Words

Multiple-meaning words are words that can have several meanings, depending on their use in a sentence.

Examples

bat	• (noun) small, blind mammal • (noun) wooden or metal club used to strike the ball in baseball
break	• (verb) interrupt temporarily or stop an activity • (verb) become damaged or to cause damage

Now You Do It

Read the sentences below. On the lines provided, write the meaning of the underlined word.

Charlie took a practice swing with the bat. _____

Nina watched the bat flying through the trees. _____

To break the silence, Braylon laughed loudly. _____

Be careful not to break the vase! _____

TALK ABOUT IT **Guessing Game** With a partner, take turns saying aloud sentences that use the words from this lesson in different ways. Then, guess the meaning of the word based on the way it is used in each sentence.

WRITE ABOUT IT **Write a Story** Use the multiple-meaning words from this lesson to write a funny short story. Use each word in as many ways as you can. Underline the words each time that you use them.

_____
_____
_____
_____

A Retrieved Reformation

UNIT 1

BEFORE YOU READ: GENTLEMAN OF RIO EN MEDIO

Vocabulary

These words are underlined in the story. Listen to each word. Say it. Then, read the definition and the example sentence.

deed (DEED) *n.* A **deed** is a document which, when signed, transfers ownership of property.
> *They found the deed to the house, signed by the original owners.*

descendants (di SEN duhnts) *n.* **Descendants** are one's children, grandchildren, and the following generations.
> *The old man willed all of his possessions to his descendants.*

possession (puh ZE shuhn) *n.* A person owns a **possession.**
> *In colonial America, one requirement for voting was possession of property.*

Vocabulary Practice

Read the first sentence in each group of three. Then, complete Sentence *a* by substituting another word or phrase that means the same as the underlined vocabulary word. Complete Sentence *b* with your own ideas and words.

1. The deed showed that he owned the car.

    a. The _____ showed that he owned the car.

    b. The deed showed that he owned _____.

2. My grandfather's descendants include my father and me.

    a. My grandfather's _____ include my father and me.

    b. My grandfather's descendants include _____.

3. Her favorite possession is her diary.

    a. Her favorite _____ is her diary.

    b. Her favorite possession _____.

 ### Getting Ready to Read

In 1598, the Spanish set up a colony in an area around present-day New Mexico. Native Americans also lived in this region. These people mixed their Spanish and Native American traditions. What are some of your family's traditions? Discuss these traditions with a partner.

30 English Learner's Notebook

MAKING CONNECTIONS

Gentleman of Río en Medio
Juan A. A. Sedillo

Summary Don Anselmo is honest and proud. He sells his land to new American owners. They later have trouble with the village children. The new owners work with Don Anselmo to solve the problem with the children.

 Writing About the Big Question

Is truth the same for everyone? In "Gentleman of Río en Medio," an old man becomes involved in a dispute over the value of property. Complete this sentence:

A person selling a house may be biased about his or her property because _____

_____.

Note-taking Guide
Use this chart to record details about the traits of Don Anselmo.

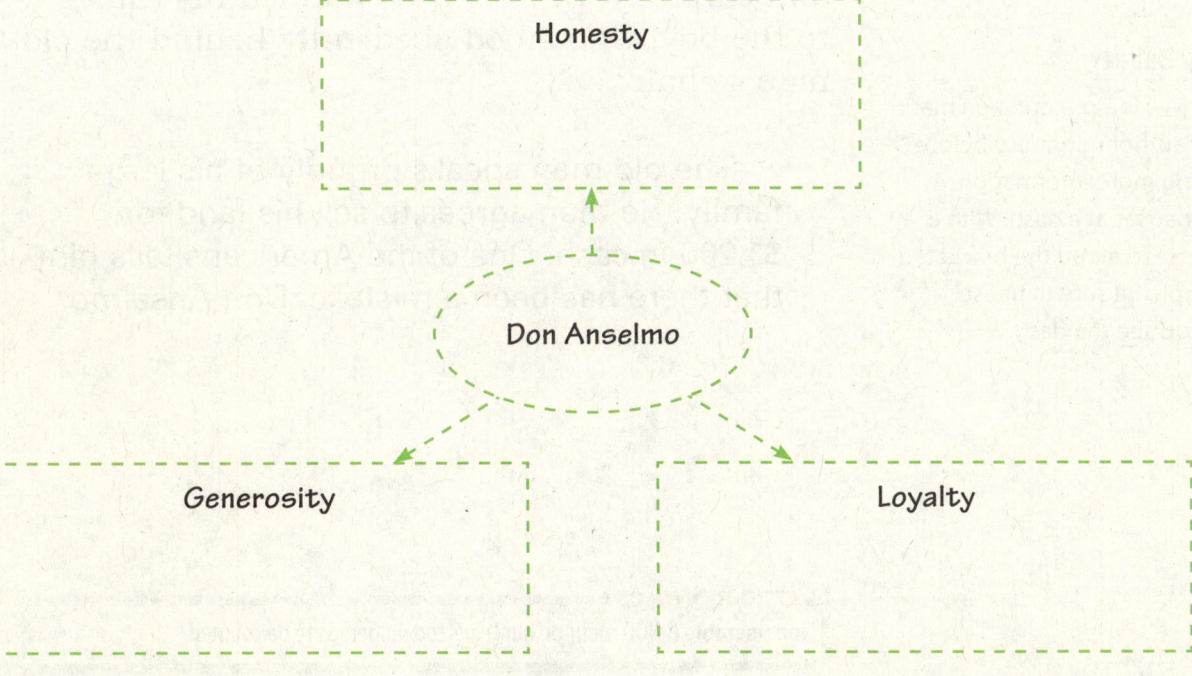

TAKE NOTES

Vocabulary Builder

Adjectives Circle four adjectives that appear in the first paragraph. With a partner, write a sentence about Don Anselmo that includes two of the adjectives.

_____

_____

_____

Vocabulary Builder

Idioms The idiom *to work out* means "to create something, especially as a plan." What are the American buyers trying *to work out* with Don Anselmo?

The American buyers are trying

to work out _____

_____

_____.

Fluency Builder

A dash (—) is a punctuation mark that an author might use before providing more information. A reader pauses at a dash. With a partner, read aloud the bracketed paragraph. Be sure to pause when you see the dash.

Gentleman of Río en Medio
Juan A. A. Sedillo

The title of this selection tells a good deal about the story. The main character is an old man, Don Anselmo, who dresses and acts in old-fashioned ways. But he is a man of great gentleness, honesty, and character.

Some American buyers are trying to work out a deal to buy Don Anselmo's land. It is land that his family has been farming for hundreds of years. After several months of bargaining, the two sides get together to make the deal.

◆ ◆ ◆

The day of the sale [Don Anselmo] came into the office. His coat was old, green and faded. . . . He also wore gloves. They were old and torn and his fingertips showed through them. He carried a cane, but it was only the skeleton of a worn-out umbrella. Behind him walked one of his **innumerable** kin—a dark young man with eyes like a gazelle.[1]

The old man bowed to all of us in the room. Then he removed his hat and gloves, slowly and carefully. . . . Then he handed his things to the boy, who stood obediently behind the old man's chair.

◆ ◆ ◆

The old man speaks proudly of his large family. He then agrees to sell his land for $1,200 in cash. One of the Americans tells him that there has been a mistake. Don Anselmo

Everyday Words
innumerable (i NOO muhr uh buhl) *adj.* too numerous to be counted

1. **gazelle** A gazelle is an animal that looks like a small deer.

actually owns twice as much land as they had thought. So they offer to pay him almost twice as much money.

◆ ◆ ◆

The old man hung his head for a moment in thought. Then he stood up and stared at me. "Friend," he said, "I do not like to have you speak to me in that manner." I kept still and let him have his say. "I know these Americans are good people, and that is why I have agreed to sell to them. But I do not care to be insulted. I have agreed to sell my house and land for twelve hundred dollars, and that is the price."

I argued with him but it was useless. Finally he signed the deed and took the money but refused to take more than the amount agreed upon. Then he shook hands all around, put on his ragged gloves, took his stick and walked out with the boy behind him.

◆ ◆ ◆

A month later the Americans have moved onto the property and fixed up the old house. But there is a problem. The village children are playing under the trees on the property. The new owners complain, but the children don't understand. So another meeting is arranged with Don Anselmo to settle the problem. One of the Americans explains the problem. He asks Don Anselmo to tell the children not to play in the orchard.

Don Anselmo explains that they all have learned to love the new American owners. But he sold them only the ground around the trees, not the trees themselves. The American protests that people usually sell everything that grows on the land they sell.

◆ ◆ ◆

"Yes, I admit that," [Don Anselmo] said. "You know," he added, "I am the oldest man in the village. Almost everyone there is my relative and

TAKE NOTES

Vocabulary Builder

Idioms When the old man *hung his head,* he held his head downward or let it droop.

The old man *hung his head* because _____ _____.

Fluency Builder

Read the bracketed paragraph. As you read, be sure to pause slightly for each comma (,).

Comprehension Builder

Why does Don Anselmo believe that the trees do not belong to the new owners? Underline the sentence that tells you.

TAKE NOTES

Vocabulary Builder

Adverbs An adverb describes a verb, an adjective, or another adverb. Read the bracketed paragraph. With a partner, find the words that the following adverbs in the paragraph describe:

legally _____

so _____

individually _____

---

all the children of Río en Medio are my *sobrinos* and *nietos*,[2] my descendants. Every time a child has been born in Río en Medio since I took possession of that house from my mother I have planted a tree for that child. The trees in that orchard are not mine, *Señor*,[3] they belong to the children of the village. Every person in Río en Medio born since the railroad came to Santa Fe owns a tree in that orchard. I did not sell the trees because I could not. They are not mine."

[There was nothing we could do. Legally we owned the trees but the old man had been so generous, refusing what amounted to a fortune for him. It took most of the following winter to buy the trees, individually, from the descendants of Don Anselmo in the valley of Río en Medio.]

---

2. **sobrinos** (soh BREE nohs) and **nietos** (NYAY tohs) Spanish for "nieces and nephews."
3. **Señor** (say NYOR) is a Spanish term of respect for an adult man.

34 **English Learner's Notebook**

AFTER YOU READ

Thinking About the Selection

1. What problem occurs in the story? How do the characters solve the problem? Write your answers in the chart below.

The problem in the story is that...	The problem is solved when...
Don Anselmo's descendants play	the Americans buy

2. The Americans offer Don Anselmo more money for his land because _____.

TALK ABOUT IT **Don Anselmo's Reasons** Discuss with a partner why Don Anselmo would not take more money for his land.

Don Anselmo would not take more money for his land because _____.

WRITE ABOUT IT **What Might Have Happened?** How do you think the story would have ended if Don Anselmo had agreed to take more money for his land? Write a brief alternate ending to the story.

Don Anselmo took more money for his land. When his descendents would not leave the land, _____.

Gentleman of Río en Medio 35

VOCABULARY SKILL REVIEW

Word Families

Word families are groups of words that share a common base word. A base word is the word to which prefixes and suffixes are added.

Example
Base word: Peace

Peace means "a time when there is no war or fighting."

Words That Share the Base Word	Part of Speech	Meaning
peaceful	adjective	calm and quiet
peacefully	adverb	calmly and quietly
peacekeeping	adjective	trying to stop violence or fighting
peaceable	adjective	not liking to argue

Now You Do It

Draw a line from the sentence to the correct meaning of the word in the chart below. The first one has been done for you.

Sentence	Meaning
Asoka is a **peaceable** person who likes to compromise with people who disagree with her.	calmly and quietly
The police played a **peacekeeping** role during the football game.	trying to stop violence or fighting
The lake is a **peaceful** place where I like to think.	not liking to argue
Tracy walked **peacefully** through the halls to her classroom.	calm and quiet

TALK ABOUT IT **A Peaceable Person** With a partner, talk about the qualities that make a person peaceable. List the qualities, and talk about a person that you find to be peaceable.

WRITE ABOUT IT **Write a Paragraph** Write a paragraph describing a peaceful place. Include at least three words from the lesson.

BEFORE YOU READ: CUB PILOT ON THE MISSISSIPPI

Vocabulary

These words are highlighted in the selection. Listen to each word. Say it. Then, read the definition and the example sentence.

malicious (muh LI shuhs) *adj.* When something is **malicious,** it is mean, hurtful, or harmful.
  Malicious remarks about her guests ruined the party.

pretext (i MAN suh payt ed) *n.* A **pretext** is an excuse or false reason that hides one's real motives.
  Tyler looked for a pretext to talk to Selena.

judicious (joo DI shuhs) *adj.* When someone is **judicious,** he or she is wise and shows sound judgment.
  A judicious person knows how and when to avoid a fight.

Vocabulary Practice

Read the first sentence in each group of three. Then, complete Sentence *a* by substituting another word or phrase that means the same as the underlined vocabulary word. Complete Sentence *b* with your own ideas and words.

1. Jill's malicious attitude made everyone angry with her.

    a. Jill's _____ attitude made everyone angry with her.

    b. Jill's malicious _____.

2. He needed a pretext to leave the meeting early.

    a. He needed a(n) _____ to leave the meeting early.

    b. He needed a pretext _____.

3. The judicious teacher helped the students settle the argument.

    a. The _____ teacher helped the students settle the argument.

    b. The judicious teacher _____.

Getting Ready to Read

The events in this story happen on the Mississippi River. During the 1800s, people used the Mississippi River to move people and goods from one place to another place. How do we move people and goods from one place to another place today? Discuss your answers with a partner.

MAKING CONNECTIONS

Cub Pilot on the Mississippi
Mark Twain

Summary Mark Twain describes his experience as a cub pilot working on a Mississippi steamboat. He tries to please his boss, but nothing works. The conflict between them grows. Twain cannot control his anger.

Writing About the Big Question

Is the truth the same for everyone? In "Cub Pilot on the Mississippi," a young man gets into a violent dispute with his boss over who is telling the truth. Complete this sentence:

If a young person and an adult were to contradict each other in an

argument, I would believe _____ is telling the truth

because _____.

Note-taking Guide
Use this chart to note the differences between the two pilots in the story.

	Pilot Brown	Pilot Ealer
With which cub pilot does he work?	Mark Twain	
How does he treat cub pilots during work hours?		
How does each cub pilot react to his treatment?		

AFTER YOU READ

Thinking About the Selection

1. How does Pilot Brown treat Twain? How does this treatment make Twain feel about Brown? Write your answers in the chart below.

How Brown Treats Twain	How Twain Feels About Brown

2. George Ritchie would make fun with Twain by _____
_____
_____.

TALK ABOUT IT **Draw Conclusions** The captain is pleased that Twain has beaten Pilot Brown. How do you think the captain feels about Brown? Discuss your answer with a partner.

I think that the captain feels that Pilot Brown is _____
_____.

WRITE ABOUT IT **What Do You Think?** Do you think that Twain is right to be angry with Pilot Brown? Explain your answer.

I think that Twain is _____
_____
_____
_____
_____.

Cub Pilot on the Mississippi 39

VOCABULARY SKILL REVIEW

Verb Tenses

Three verb tenses in English are the simple present, the simple past, and the simple future. The chart below shows how to form each tense of a regular verb and explains when to use it.

Examples

Verb Tense...	Form by...	Use to describe...
simple present	using the base form of the verb.	• actions that usually happen. (*I walk home from school every day.*) • actions happening at the time of speaking. (*She walks to the store.*)
simple past	adding -d or -ed to the base form of the verb.	• actions completed entirely in the past. (*I walked to Tom's house yesterday.*)
simple future	using *will* before the base form of the verb.	• actions that will happen in the future. (*We will walk in the park this weekend.*)

Now You Do It

Complete each sentence by writing the correct tense of the verb indicated.

walk (present) Will you _____ to the library?

shout (past) Yesterday, I _____ to get Jane's attention.

talk (future) Kim _____ to Jill on the telephone later.

TALK ABOUT IT **Last Weekend, I . . .** Tell a partner about something you did last weekend. For example, you may describe a movie you saw or the museum you visited. Be sure to use simple past tense verbs because you are telling about actions that were completed in the past.

WRITE ABOUT IT **Someday, I Will Visit . . .** Write a letter to your best friend about a place you would like to someday visit. Tell about the things you will see, the foods you will eat, and the people you will meet when you visit this place. Be sure to use the future tense to describe the events that *will* happen.

INFORMATIONAL TEXTS

Consumer Documents: Schedules

About Schedules
Schedules help people get where they want to go.
- Schedules list arrival and departure times.

Schedules are **consumer documents.**
- Consumer documents help you buy or use a product or service.
- Other consumer documents include brochures, labels, loan applications, assembly instructions, and warranties.

Reading Skill
Reading transportation schedules is different from reading other materials. You can **use the information to solve a problem,** such as which routes to take and what time to arrive at the station or dock. The information in a schedule is organized in rows and columns to help you find what you need. Look at the chart. It shows some common features of a transportation schedule.

Features of a Schedule	
Headings	Show where to find departure and arrival times
Rows and columns	Allow easy scanning of arrival and departure times across and down the page
Special type and asterisks	Indicate exceptions, such as ferries that do not run on Sundays

Savannah Belles Ferry System

Consumer Document

Features:
- consumer information
- details and information in lists, charts, tables, and other graphics
- text that helps the reader purchase or use a product or service

City Hall Landing To:	
Trade Center Landing / Westin	
7:00 AM	3:40 PM
7:20 AM	4:00 PM
7:40 AM	4:20 PM
8:00 AM	4:40 PM
8:20 AM	5:00 PM
*	5:20 PM
9:00 AM	*
9:20 AM	6:00 PM
9:40 AM	6:20 PM
10:00 AM	6:40 PM
10:20 AM	7:00 PM
*	7:20 PM
11:00 AM	7:40 PM
11:20 AM	8:00 PM
11:40 AM	8:20 PM
12:00 PM	*
12:20 PM	9:00 PM
12:40 PM	9:20 PM
1:00 PM	9:40 PM
1:20 PM	10:00 PM
1:40 PM	10:20 PM
2:00 PM	10:40 PM
2:20 PM	11:00 PM
2:40 PM	11:20 PM
3:00 PM	11:40 PM
3:20 PM	12:00 AM
3:40 PM	*

Trade Center Landing To:		
City Hall Landing / Hyatt		Waving Girl Landing/Marriott
7:10 AM	3:50 PM	8:15 AM
7:30 AM	4:10 PM	8:45 AM
7:50 AM	4:30 PM	9:15 AM
8:10 AM	4:50 PM	9:45 AM
*	5:10 PM	10:15 AM
8:50 AM	*	10:45 AM
9:10 AM	5:50 PM	11:15 AM
9:30 AM	6:10 PM	11:45 AM
9:50 AM	6:30 PM	12:15 PM
10:10 AM	6:50 PM	12:45 PM
*	7:10 PM	1:15 PM
10:50 AM	7:30 PM	1:45 PM
11:10 AM	7:50 PM	2:15 PM
11:30 AM	8:10 PM	2:45 PM
11:50 AM	*	3:15 PM
12:10 PM	8:50 PM	3:45 PM
12:30 PM	9:10 PM	4:15 PM
12:50 PM	9:30 PM	4:45 PM
1:10 PM	9:50 PM	5:15 PM
1:30 PM	10:10 PM	5:45 PM
1:50 PM	10:30 PM	*
2:10 PM	10:50 PM	
2:30 AM	11:10 PM	
2:50 PM	11:30 PM	
3:10 PM	11:50 PM	
3:30 PM	*	

Waving Girl To:
Trade Center Landing/Westin
8:00 AM
8:30 AM
9:00 AM
9:30 AM
10:00 AM
10:30 AM
11:00 AM
11:30 AM
12:00 PM
12:30 PM
1:00 PM
1:30 PM
2:00 PM
2:30 PM
3:00 PM
3:30 PM
4:00 PM
4:30 PM
5:00 PM
5:30 PM
6:00 PM

Revised 5/23/2007

The list of ferry times allows riders to plan their schedules.

Year-Around Schedule
The Savannah Belles Ferry System operates daily, year-around, except Thanksgiving Day, Christmas Day and New Year's Day.

Service Interruption
The ferry may occasionally be delayed briefly by weather or visibility, or by larger vessels. We appreciate your patience.

This heading helps consumers plan for times when the ferry is delayed.

It's Free! The Savannah Belles Ferry System is operated by Chatham Area Transit Authority (CAT) free of charge to visitors and residents. Thanks for riding with us!

Service Locations

TRADE CENTER LANDING--North Bank Riverwalk, between Trade Center and Westin

CITY HALL LANDING--River Street at City Hall, next to Hyatt

WAVING GIRL LANDING--South Bank Riverwalk, next to Marriott

www.catchacat.org, (912) 236-2111

Is truth the same for everyone?
(a) What section of the schedule explains that the details on the schedule may not always be true? **(b)** Why is it important to include this information?

Consumer Document

Features:
- purposeful reading, used to locate specific information
- details presented in lists, charts, tables, and other graphics
- text that helps readers purchase or use a product or service

Baylink
Travel the Easy Way

Vallejo - San Francisco Ferry Bldg
Vallejo - San Francisco Pier 41
Effective September 1 - December 1, 2006

Vallejo-S.F. Ferry Bldg • MON-FRI

BUS OR FERRY	VALLEJO FERRY BLDG DEPART	SF FERRY BUILDING DEPART	FISHERMAN'S WHARF PIER 41 ARRIVE	DEPART
Bus	5:00 a	6:05 a		
Ferry	5:30 a	6:35 a		
Bus	5:50 a	6:55 a		
Bus	6:20 a	7:20 a		
Ferry	6:30 a	7:35 a		
Bus	6:45 a	7:50 a		
Ferry	7:00 a	8:10 a		
Bus	7:22 a	8:30 a		
Ferry	7:45 a	8:55 a		
Ferry	8:45 a	9:55 a		
Ferry	10:00 a#	11:10 a#	11:20 a#	11:30 a#
Ferry	11:30 a	12:40 p		
Ferry	1:00 p	2:10 p		
Ferry	2:00 p*	3:30 p*	3:00 p*	3:10 p*

This heading shows readers where to locate fare information.

Fare Schedule • All Routes

TICKETS REQUIRED TO BOARD FERRIES & BUSES

Adult One-Way	$11.50
Senior/Disabled/Medicare One-Way (65+/disabled)*	$5.75
Youth One-Way (6-12 years)	$5.75
Baylink DayPass	$19.25
Napa/Solano DayPass	$20.75
Reduced Fare DayPass*	$11.50
10-Ride Punch Card	$89.75
Reduced Fare 10-Ride Punch Card*	$57.50
Monthly Pass	$247.25
Monthly Pass w/MUNI	$287.25
Fairfield/Vacaville Monthly Pass	$300
Fairfield/Vacaville Monthly Pass w/MUNI	$340

Up to two children under 6 years of age travel free with each fare-paying adult. Bicycles are also free, subject to capacity limitations. First come, first served; vessel capacity 300 passengers.

*Bay Area Regional Transit Connection Discount Cards and Medicare Cards with Photo ID are accepted for senior and disabled fares.

Vallejo-S.F. Ferry Bldg • SAT-SUN

BUS OR FERRY	VALLEJO FERRY BLDG DEPART	SF FERRY BUILDING DEPART	FISHERMAN'S WHARF PIER 41 ARRIVE	DEPART
Bus	7:00 a	8:10 a		
Ferry	8:45 a	9:55 a		
Ferry	10:00 a#	11:10 a#	11:20 a#	11:30 a#
Ferry	11:30 a	12:40 p		
Ferry	1:00 p	2:10 p		
Bus	2:00 p	3:10 p		
Ferry	3:00 p*	4:30 p*	4:00 p*	4:10 p*

Arrival and departure times are organized in rows and columns.

 **THE BIG Q — Is truth the same for everyone?**
What section or sections of this document help you understand the amounts different people pay for tickets?

Consumer Document

Water Taxi™
SERVICE SCHEDULE & FARES
Effective December 17, 2007

Times listed in grey and white run every day.

Times listed in yellow run Friday, Saturday, Sunday and Monday

WTA — Operated by Water Transportation Alternatives

Features:
- purposeful reading, scanned for specific needed information
- contains details and information in lists, charts, tables, and other graphics
- helps the reader purchase or use a product or service
- for a specific audience

North End		Fort Lauderdale Beach			South End			Downtown / New River		
1 Shooters	**2** Gallery One	**3** Seville Street	**4** Beach Place	**5** Bahia Mar	**6** Pier 66	**7** Convention Center	**8** 15th Street Fisheries	**9** SE 9th Avenue	**10** Downtowner Saloon	**11** Las Olas Riverfront
9:30	Express to Las Olas Riverfront									10:00
9:30	Express to Beach Place		9:59	10:12	10:27	10:30	10:32	10:49	10:54	11:00
10:00	10:17	10:25	10:29	10:42	10:57	11:00	11:02	11:19	11:24	11:30
10:30	10:47	10:55	10:59	11:12	11:27	11:30	11:32	11:49	11:54	12:00
11:00	11:17	11:25	11:29	11:42	11:57	12:00	12:02	12:19	12:24	12:30
11:30	11:47	11:55	11:59	12:12	12:27	12:30	12:32	12:49	12:54	1:00
12:30	12:47	12:55	12:59	1:12	1:27	1:30	1:32	1:49	1:54	2:00
1:00	1:17	1:25	1:29	1:42	1:57	2:00	2:02	2:19	2:24	2:30
1:30	1:47	1:55	1:59	2:12	2:27	2:30	2:32	2:49	2:54	3:00
2:00	2:17	2:25	2:29	2:42	2:57	3:00	3:02	3:19	3:24	3:30
2:30	2:47	2:55	2:59	3:12	3:27	3:32	3:32	3:49	3:54	4:00

Read across to locate the columns that have the information you need.

These notes give additional information about riding the Water Bus and about reading this schedule.

Downtown / New River			South End			Fort Lauderdale Beach			North End	
11 Las Olas Riverfront	**10** Downtowner Saloon	**9** SE 9th Avenue	**8** 15th Street Fisheries	**7** Convention Center	**6** Pier 66	**5** Bahia Mar	**4** Beach Place	**3** Seville Street	**2** Gallery One	**1** Shooters
				9:55	9:58	10:15	10:28	10:32	10:40	11:00
10:00	10:01	10:07	10:23	10:25	10:28	10:45	10:58	11:02	11:10	11:30
11:00	11:01	11:07	11:23	11:25	11:28	11:45	11:58	12:02	12:10	12:30
11:30	11:31	11:37	11:53	11:55	11:58	12:15	12:28	12:32	12:40	1:00
12:00	12:01	12:07	12:23	12:25	12:28	12:45	12:58	1:02	1:10	1:30
12:30	12:31	12:37	12:53	12:55	12:58	1:15	1:28	1:32	1:40	2:00
1:00	1:01	1:07	1:23	1:25	1:28		1:58	2:02	2:10	2:30

Read down to see all of the times the Water Bus stops at a location.

One table shows the schedule of stops when traveling Inbound, or from north to south. The other shows the schedule of stops when the Water Bus travels from south to north.

Adult.................$12.00
Children (under 12).....$9.00
Seniors (over 65)........$9.00
After 7:00 PM........$7.00
Family Pack.........$42.00
Valid for 2 adults and 3 children/seniors

THE BIG ? — Is truth the same for everyone?

How might Fort Lauderdale's popularity as a vacation spot affect the choice to name most of the stops along the Water Bus route according to the restaurants and other attractions at each location, rather than naming the stops with geographical information, such as addresses or intersections?

44 Informational Texts

AFTER YOU READ

Thinking About the Schedule

1. In what situation would a schedule be useful?
   _____
   _____

2. Explain how you can figure out what time a ferry will arrive.
   _____
   _____

Reading Skill

3. What time does the earliest ferry depart from the San Francisco Ferry Building on Monday morning?
   _____

4. Why is each stop on the Water Bus schedule listed twice?
   _____

WRITE ABOUT IT — Timed Writing: Itinerary (20 minutes)

An **itinerary** is a written document that includes dates, times, and locations for a trip. Plan a round-trip itinerary. Use the Savannah Belles ferry schedule. Use this chart to help you make plans.

Place you will go	Departure time	Arrival time

UNIT 1

BEFORE YOU READ: FROM AN AMERICAN CHILDHOOD

Vocabulary

These words are underlined in the selection. Listen to each word. Say it. Then, read the definition and the example sentence.

luminous (LOO muh nuhs) *adj.* **Luminous** means giving off light or shining brightly.

A cabin was lit by the moon's luminous glow.

vanished (VAN isht) *v.* **Vanished** means suddenly disappeared.

My keys were on the desk, but they seem to have vanished.

conceivably (kuhn SEE vuh blee) *adv.* **Conceivably** means that something is possible.

Joe has trained so hard; he could conceivably win.

Vocabulary Practice

Read the first sentence in each group of three. Then, complete Sentence *a* by substituting another word or phrase that means the same as the underlined vocabulary word. Complete Sentence *b* with your own ideas and words.

1. The moon was the most luminous thing in the night sky.

   a. The moon was the most _____ thing in the night sky.

   b. The moon was the most luminous _____.

2. Alice vanished before I could speak to her.

   a. Alice _____ before I could speak to her.

   b. Alice vanished _____.

3. The explorers could conceivably climb the mountain.

   a. The explorers could _____ climb the mountain.

   b. The explorers could conceivably _____.

Getting Ready to Read

Annie Dillard tells about an experience that scared her when she was a child. She was scared because she was not able to interpret what she saw. Tell a partner about something that frightened you as a child but seems silly now that you are older. How did this experience teach you about how the world works?

46 English Learner's Notebook

MAKING CONNECTIONS

from An American Childhood
Annie Dillard

Summary The author shares an experience that scared her as a young child. She thinks there is a "presence" that will harm her if it reaches her. She figures out what it is. She realizes that her inside world is connected to the outside world.

 Writing About the Big Question

Is truth the same for everyone? In *An American Childhood*, Annie Dillard's perception of the world around her is influenced by her youthful imagination. Complete this sentence:

Small children may draw illogical conclusions about the world

around them because _____

_____.

Note-taking Guide
Use this chart to help you summarize the story.

Event
The author is frightened by mysterious, moving lights that she sees in her bedroom at night.

Cause

Main Idea

from An American Childhood **47**

TAKE NOTES

Vocabulary Builder

Multiple-Meaning Words The word *lies* can mean "does not tell the truth." *Lies* can also mean "rests in a certain position." What does *lies* mean in this sentence?

Dillard *lies* on her bed.

_____

_____

Vocabulary Builder

Idioms Find the idiom *raced over* in the bracketed paragraph. *Raced over* means "moved quickly across." Use *raced over* to complete the following sentence:

Because the thing scared Dillard,

_____

_____ .

Comprehension Builder

Predict what the "thing" is that appears in Dillard's room. Explain your prediction.

_____

_____

_____

_____

from An American Childhood
Annie Dillard

Annie Dillard describes something that scared her when she was young. She's only five years old and she is scared to go to bed. She's afraid to talk about the thing.

◆ ◆ ◆

Who could breathe as this thing searched for me over the very corners of the room? Who could ever breathe freely again?

◆ ◆ ◆

Dillard lies in the dark. Her younger sister, Amy, sleeps peacefully—she doesn't wake when the mysterious event takes place. Dillard is almost asleep when the thing slides into the room. First, it flattens itself against the door that is open.

◆ ◆ ◆

[It was a **transparent**, luminous **oblong**. I could see the door whiten at its touch; I could see the blue wall turn pale where it raced over it, and see the maple headboard of Amy's bed glow. It was a swift spirit; it was an awareness. It made noise. It had two joined parts, a head and a tail, like a Chinese dragon. It found the door, wall, and headboard, and it swiped them, charging them with its luminous glance. After its fleet, searching passage, things looked the same, but weren't.]

Everyday Words
transparent (trans PER uhnt) *adj.* clear; easily seen through
oblong (AHB lawng) *n.* a rectangular shape

48 English Learner's Notebook

I dared not blink or breathe; I tried to hush my **whooping** blood. If it found another awareness, it would destroy it.

◆ ◆ ◆

But the thing never gets her. When it reaches the corner, it can't go any further. She tries to shrink down so it won't notice her. Then, she hears a roar when it dies or leaves. Worst of all is knowing that it may come back. Sometimes it does—usually it does. Dillard thinks the thing is restless.

◆ ◆ ◆

The light stripe slipped in the door, ran searching over Amy's wall, stopped, stretched **lunatic** at the first corner, raced wailing toward my wall, and vanished into the second corner with a cry.

◆ ◆ ◆

Dillard figures out that the thing is caused by a streetlight reflecting off the windshield of a passing car. She is thrilled to use reason to solve the mystery. She compares this mental process of problem solving to a diver who comes from the depths of the sea and breaks the surface of the water to reach the sunlight.

Dillard knows the sound the thing makes when it leaves. It sounds like a car coming down the street. She puts that together with the daytime sight and sound of a car passing. There is a stop sign at the corner of the street she lives on. The cars pass her house and then come to a stop. Then they shift gears as they go on.

◆ ◆ ◆

Everyday Words
whooping (WOOP ing) *v.* shouting
lunatic (LOO nuh tik) *adv.* wildly; crazily

TAKE NOTES

Vocabulary Builder

Suffixes The suffix *-ness* means "act; state; condition." The adjective *aware* means "knowing something exists." Work with a partner to define *awareness*.

_____
_____

Vocabulary Builder

Idioms The idiom *figures out* means "understands something that was unclear or confusing."

Dillard *figures out* that the thing
_____
_____
_____.

Vocabulary Builder

Idioms The idiom *go on* means that something or someone continues to do something.

After the cars stop at the stop sign next to Dillard's house,

they *go on* _____
_____
_____.

from An American Childhood

TAKE NOTES

Vocabulary Builder

Multiple-Meaning Words The word *sash* can mean "something worn over the shoulder or around the waist" or "a frame for holding glass windowpanes." Which meaning of the word *sash* does Dillard use in the underlined sentence?

_____
_____

Vocabulary Builder

Word Parts The word *conceivably* is formed by a base word and two suffixes. The base word *conceive* means "imagine." The suffix *-able* means "capable of." The other suffix *-ly* means "in a particular way." Work with a partner to write the meaning of *conceivably*.

_____
_____

Comprehension Builder ✏️

What does Dillard realize about the world outside? Underline the sentence that describes this discovery.

What, precisely, came into the bedroom? A reflection from the car's oblong windshield. Why did it travel in two parts? <u>The window sash split the light and cast a shadow.</u>

◆ ◆ ◆

Dillard realizes that the world outside is connected to the world inside her home. She recalls once watching construction workers use **jackhammers.** Later, she had connected a new noise in her bedroom to the men she saw working outside. She thinks about the connection between outside and inside—going downstairs and then outside.

◆ ◆ ◆

"Outside," then, was <u>conceivably</u> just beyond my windows. It was the same world I reached by going out the front or the back door.

◆ ◆ ◆

Dillard realizes that she can choose to be connected to the outer world either by reason or by imagination. She pretends that the light coming into her room is after her. Then, she replaces her imagination with reason and identifies the real source of the light: a passing car.

Everyday Words

jackhammers (JAK ham erz) *n.* large, powerful tools used to break hard materials such as the surface of a road

AFTER YOU READ

Thinking About the Selection

1. Use the web to fill in information about what scares Dillard. Complete the sentence in each box.

   Dillard sees a moving light.

   She thinks that the light looks like _____.

   She finds out that the light is caused by _____.

   She learns that _____ _____ are connected.

2. Dillard realizes that the light traveled in two parts because _____.

TALK ABOUT IT **Using Her Senses** Discuss with a partner how Dillard uses her senses to figure out what the light really is.

Dillard sees that the light is made by _____.

Dillard hears that the sound is made by _____.

WRITE ABOUT IT **What Do You Think?** After Dillard learns what the light really is, she sometimes pretends that she does not know what causes it. Why do you think she does this?

Dillard pretends not to know what causes the light because _____.

from An American Childhood

VOCABULARY SKILL REVIEW

Silent Letters
Some words have a silent letter that you do not pronounce. Some silent letters follow general rules, but many do not. To pronounce words containing silent letters correctly, you may need to memorize the words.

Examples

Letter	k	w
General Rule	At the beginning of a word, the letter *k* is silent if it is followed by the letter *n*.	At the beginning of a word, the letter *w* is silent if it is followed by the letter *r*.
Pronunciation	*Knife* is pronounced NYF.	*Write* is pronounced RYT.

Now You Do It
Say each word quietly or sound it out in your mind. Place a plus sign next to the word if the *k* or *w* is pronounced. Place a minus sign next to the word if the *k* or *w* is not pronounced.

knee _____ wrist _____

knock _____ winter _____

kin _____ wreck _____

kindness _____ wreath _____

know _____ wire _____

TALK ABOUT IT **Practice Pronouncing Words** With a partner, practice pronouncing each word above. Then, use each word in a sentence.

WRITE ABOUT IT **Write a Paragraph** Use at least five of the words from this lesson to write a paragraph about an activity that you enjoy doing or an event that is important to you. Underline the words that contain silent letters. Then, read the paragraph aloud to your partner to check your pronunciation.

BEFORE YOU READ: THE ADVENTURE OF THE SPECKLED BAND

UNIT 1

Vocabulary

These words are highlighted in the story. Listen to each word. Say it. Then, read the definition and the example sentence.

invaluable (in VAL yoo uh buhl) *adj.* When something is **invaluable**, its value is too great to measure; it is priceless.
   A witness is invaluable to solving the case.

tangible (TAN juh buhl) *adj.* Something **tangible** is real, solid, easy to see, and not vague.
   Firefighters usually find a tangible cause for a blaze.

indiscreetly (in di SKREET lee) *adv.* When one acts **indiscreetly**, one acts carelessly.
   Indiscreetly, the child passed the knife with its blade facing out.

Vocabulary Practice

Read the first sentence in each group of three. Then, complete Sentence *a* by substituting another word or phrase that means the same as the underlined vocabulary word. Complete Sentence *b* with your own ideas and words.

1. Her <u>invaluable</u> knowledge of plants was useful in the forest.

   a. Her _____ knowledge of plants was useful in the forest.

   b. Her invaluable _____.

2. The lawyer needed <u>tangible</u> evidence to prove her case.

   a. The lawyer needed _____ evidence to prove her case.

   b. The lawyer needed tangible _____.

3. Tony <u>indiscreetly</u> tossed his backpack onto the floor.

   a. Tony _____ tossed his backpack onto the floor.

   b. Tony indiscreetly _____.

 ## Getting Ready to Read

The character of Sherlock Holmes was created in the 1800s. Holmes is a detective in literature. He uses clues and his reason to solve mysteries. Think about a time when you used clues to learn about an event that was difficult to explain. Tell a partner how you solved the mystery.

The Adventure of the Speckled Band 53

MAKING CONNECTIONS

The Adventure of the Speckled Band
Sir Arthur Conan Doyle

Summary Sherlock Holmes, a great detective, meets Miss Helen Stoner. She needs his help. Miss Stoner wants to know who killed her sister. She also fears for her own life. Holmes follows the clues to find the murderer.

Writing About the Big Question

Is the truth the same for everyone? In *The Adventure of the Speckled Band,* a detective determines that the truth about a young woman's mysterious death is not what people had previously believed. Complete this sentence:

To prove a theory about a crime scene, a detective can _____

_____.

Note-taking Guide

Use this graphic organizer to note details about Dr. Grimesby Roylott's actions.

How are Dr. Roylott and Miss Stoner related?	Why doesn't Dr. Roylott work as a doctor?	How does Dr. Roylott support himself?	How will Dr. Roylott's life change if the sisters marry?

54 English Learner's Notebook

AFTER YOU READ

Thinking About the Selection

1. Explain what Sherlock Holmes realized about each of the following clues. Write your answers in the chart below.

Clues Sherlock Holmes Uses to Solve the Mystery	
Ventilator between Julia's room and Dr. Roylott's room	Holmes realized that the ventilator
Bell-rope in Julia's room	Holmes noticed that the bell-rope was

2. Dr. Roylott wants to murder Helen because _____
   _____.

TALK ABOUT IT **Recognizing Reasons** Discuss with a partner why Helen asks Sherlock Holmes for help.

Helen asks Sherlock Holmes for help because _____.

WRITE ABOUT IT **What Might Have Happened?** Suppose that Helen had not decided to ask Holmes for help. What do you think would have happened to her?

If Helen had not asked Holmes for help, then _____
_____
_____
_____.

The Adventure of the Speckled Band

VOCABULARY SKILL REVIEW

Suffixes

A suffix is a word part added to the end of a base (or main) word. The suffix *-ous* means "having the quality of" or "full of." It is often added to a noun to make an adjective.

Examples

joy + ous = joyous	adventure + ous = adventurous
The new word *joyous* means "having the quality of joy" or "full of joy."	The new word *adventurous* means "having the quality of adventure" or "full of adventure."
Father's arrival was a joyous occasion.	The adventurous campers hiked through the forest.

Now You Do It

Write a definition for each word below.

courageous   Definition: _____

humorous   Definition: _____

dangerous   Definition: _____

mountainous   Definition: _____

TALK ABOUT IT **Which *-ous* Are You?** What adjectives ending in *-ous* describe you? With a partner, discuss which words from this lesson to describe each of you.

WRITE ABOUT IT **Write an Adventure Story** Write a short adventure story that uses at least three of the words from the lesson. For example, the courageous hero of your story might have to complete a dangerous mission in a mountainous region.

_____
_____
_____
_____

BEFORE YOU READ: FROM STEINBECK: A LIFE IN LETTERS • FROM TRAVELS WITH CHARLEY

UNIT 1

Vocabulary

These words are highlighted in the selections. Listen to each word. Say it. Then, read the definition and the example sentence.

thrives (THRYVZ) *v.* prospers or flourishes
> *From his shiny coat and bright eyes we could see that our dog thrives on homemade food.*

desolate (DE suh lit) *adj.* To be **desolate** means to be left alone, deserted, or sad.
> *The loss of his dog left him feeling desolate.*

inexplicable (i nik SPLI kuh buhl) *adj.* When something is **inexplicable,** it is impossible to explain or understand.
> *The night brought mysterious and inexplicable sounds.*

Vocabulary Practice

Read the first sentence in each group of three. Then, complete Sentence *a* by substituting another word or phrase that means the same as the underlined vocabulary word. Complete Sentence *b* with your own ideas and words.

1. The plant <u>thrives</u> in tropical climates.

   a. The plant _____ in tropical climates.

   b. The plant thrives _____.

2. They saw no other cars along the <u>desolate</u> highway.

   a. They saw no other cars along the _____ highway.

   b. They saw no other cars along the desolate _____.

3. Tara's <u>inexplicable</u> behavior offended many of her guests.

   a. Tara's _____ behavior offended many of her guests.

   b. Tara's inexplicable _____.

TALK ABOUT IT Getting Ready to Read

John Steinbeck describes his travels in the Badlands of North Dakota. The Badlands are a desolate and treeless region. If you could travel across any country in the world, which would you choose? Explain to a partner why you would like to travel to that country.

MAKING CONNECTIONS

from Steinbeck: A Life in Letters • from Travels With Charley
John Steinbeck

Summary John Steinbeck sets out across the United States to see the country and meet people. His dog, Charley, travels with him. These excerpts tell about his experiences in Maine, Wisconsin, and in the Badlands of North Dakota.

 Writing About the Big Question

Is truth the same for everyone? In the excerpts from *Steinbeck: A Life in Letters* and *Travels with Charley,* Steinbeck tours the country to refresh his memory about what Americans are really like. Complete this sentence:

The objective truth about America and Americans is _____

_____.

Note-taking Guide
Use this chart to recall the highlights of Steinbeck's writings.

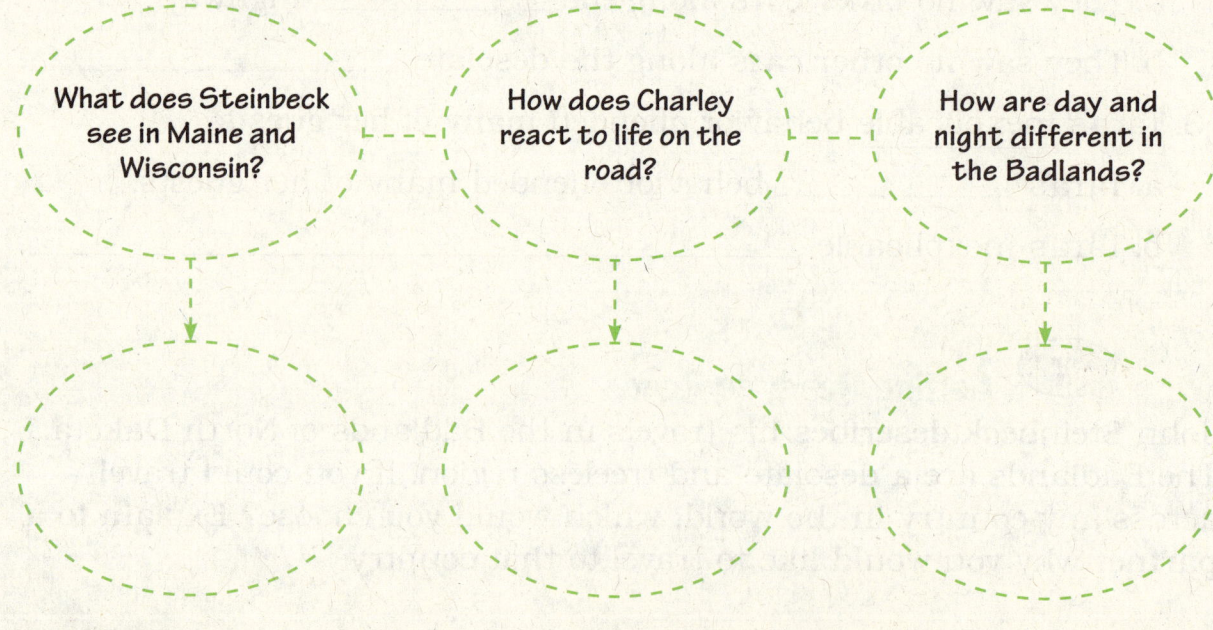

58 English Learner's Notebook

AFTER YOU READ

Thinking About the Selections

1. Complete the sentences in the graphic organizer below about Steinbeck's trip across the United States.

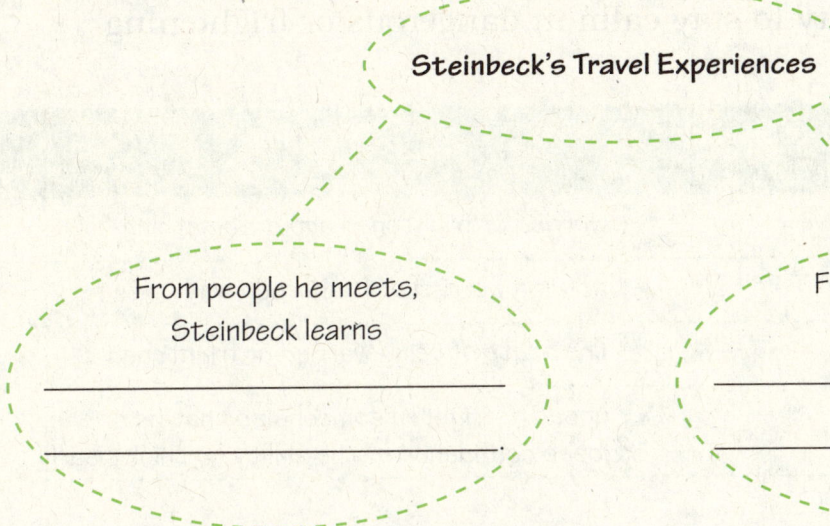

Steinbeck's Travel Experiences

From people he meets, Steinbeck learns _____

From places he sees, Steinbeck learns _____

2. Steinbeck appreciates having Charley on his trip because _____.

TALK ABOUT IT **Compare and Contrast** What does Steinbeck think about the Badlands during the day? What does Steinbeck think about the Badlands during the night? Discuss your ideas with a partner.

During the day, Steinbeck thinks that _____.

During the night, Steinbeck thinks that _____.

WRITE ABOUT IT **Would You Travel There?** Would you want to travel to the Badlands after reading Steinbeck's description of the area? Explain.

_____
_____
_____

from Steinbeck: A Life in Letters • from Travels With Charley

VOCABULARY SKILL REVIEW

Word Families

Word families are groups of words that share a common base word. A base word is the word to which prefixes and suffixes are added.

Examples
Base word: Nerve
Nerve means "the ability to stay calm in dangerous or frightening situations."

Words That Share the Base Word	Part of Speech	Meaning
nervous	adjective	worried or frightened about something
nervously	adverb	act in a worried or frightened way
nervousness	noun	the state of being worried or frightened
unnerve	verb	upset or frighten someone so that he or she loses confidence or the ability to think clearly

Now You Do It

Draw a line from the sentence to the correct meaning of the word in the chart below. The first one has been done for you.

Sentence	Meaning
Aaron was **nervous** about giving the presentation in front of his class.	act in a worried or frightened way
The pitcher tried to **unnerve** the batter by not throwing the ball immediately.	the state of being worried or frightened
He **nervously** walked to the microphone to give his speech.	worried or frightened about something
Kara felt no **nervousness** about acting in her first play.	upset or frighten someone so that he or she loses confidence or the ability to think clearly

TALK ABOUT IT — **What Makes a Person Nervous?** With a partner, talk about the qualities that make a person nervous. List the qualities, and talk about why a person might be nervous.

WRITE ABOUT IT — **Write a Skit** With a small group write a short skit that describes a situation that makes people nervous. Include at least three words from the chart above. Act out your skit for the class.

BEFORE YOU READ: THE AMERICAN DREAM

UNIT 1

Vocabulary

These words are underlined in the speech. Listen to each word. Say it. Then, read the definition and the example sentence.

trite (TRYT) *adj.* Something that is **trite** has been used so much that it has become commonplace and unoriginal.

The other speeches seemed trite after we heard Sarah's speech.

devoid (di VOYD) *adj.* To be **devoid** means to be completely without or empty.

The Dead Sea is devoid of fish.

perish (PEHR ish) *v.* To **perish** means to die or to be destroyed or wiped out.

Without water, a person will perish in a few days.

Vocabulary Practice

Read the first sentence in each group of three. Then, complete Sentence a by substituting another word or phrase that means the same as the underlined vocabulary word. Complete Sentence b with your own ideas and words.

1. Tanya received a low grade for her trite essay.

    a. Tanya received a low grade for her _____ essay.

    b. Tanya received a low grade for her trite _____.

2. This part of the desert is devoid of plant life.

    a. This part of the desert is _____ of plant life.

    b. This part of the desert is devoid _____.

3. Many people will perish if the volcano erupts.

    a. Many people will _____ if the volcano erupts.

    b. Many people will perish _____.

Getting Ready to Read

Martin Luther King, Jr. was a leader of the civil rights movement in the United States during the 1950s and 1960s. Civil rights are the rights that all citizens of the United States have. Which right are you most thankful for having? Discuss your thoughts with a partner.

The American Dream 61

MAKING CONNECTIONS

The American Dream
Martin Luther King, Jr.

Summary In this speech, Martin Luther King, Jr. describes his dream for America. He says that America does not make it possible for everyone to share in the dream. He discusses ways that Americans can help make his dream a reality.

Writing About the Big Question

Is the truth the same for everyone? In "The American Dream," Martin Luther King, Jr. quotes from the Declaration of Independence that "all men are created equal." Complete this sentence:

In America today, the promise of full equality is confirmed by

_____.

Note-taking Guide
Use this web to record King's ideas about the American dream.

The American Dream
Martin Luther King, Jr.

In this speech, King says that the American dream is based on the words of the Declaration of Independence: "all men are created equal." He says that the dream is supposed to apply to all Americans.

♦ ♦ ♦

It does not say some men, but it says all men. It does not say all white men, but it says all men, which includes black men. It does not say all Gentiles,[1] but it says all men, which includes Jews. It does not say all Protestants,[2] but it says all men, which includes Catholics.[3]

♦ ♦ ♦

King explains another important point in the Declaration: It says that all individuals have basic rights that come from God, not from governments.

Then King explains that America has never totally lived up to the dream of democracy. Slavery and the segregation of African Americans violated the idea that all people have equal rights. King says that America will destroy itself if it continues to deny equal rights to some Americans.

♦ ♦ ♦

The hour is late; the clock of destiny is ticking out. It is <u>trite</u>, but urgently true, that if America is to remain a first-class nation she can no longer have second-class citizens.

♦ ♦ ♦

---

1. **Gentiles** (JEN tylz) *n.* people who are not Jewish.
2. **Protestants** (PRAHT uhs tuhnts) *n.* members of a part of the Christian church that separated from the Roman Catholic Church in the 1500s.
3. **Catholics** (KATH liks) *n.* members of the part of the Christian church led by the Pope.

TAKE NOTES

Vocabulary Builder

Multiple-Meaning Words The word *dream* has more than one meaning. It can mean "a series of thoughts, pictures, or feelings occurring during sleep" or "a goal that is longed for." What does King mean when he says "the American Dream"?

_____
_____
_____

Fluency Builder

With a partner, read aloud the bracketed paragraph. As you read, say the words with expression, pausing for each comma (,) to emphasize the importance of each phrase.

Vocabulary Builder

Idioms The idiom *lived up to* means "to meet a certain level of expectation."

According to King, America has never totally *lived up to* the dream of democracy because

_____
_____
_____
_____

TAKE NOTES

Vocabulary Builder

Multiple-Meaning Words The word *stress* can mean "to emphasize an idea." *Stress* can also mean "continuous feelings of worry." Which meaning of the word *stress* does King use third paragraph?

_____
_____

Comprehension Builder

What does King predict will happen if Americans do not learn to live together as brothers?

_____
_____
_____
_____

King then claims that Americans must also consider the needs of the other countries in the world.

◆ ◆ ◆

The American dream will not become a reality devoid of the larger dream of a world of brotherhood and peace and **good will.**

◆ ◆ ◆

He points out that modern transportation has made contact between people of different nations much easier. He tells two jokes that focus on the speed of traveling by jet. He uses **humor** to stress that the world has now become one big neighborhood. Everyone is now connected, and we all depend on one another.

◆ ◆ ◆

Through our scientific genius we have made of this world a neighborhood; now through our **moral** and spiritual development we must make of it a brotherhood. In a real sense, we must all learn to live together as brothers, or we will all perish together as fools.

Everyday Words

good will (good WIL) *n.* kind feelings toward or between people and a willingness to be helpful

humor (HYOO mer) *n.* the quality in something that makes it funny and makes people laugh

moral (MAWR uhl) *adj.* relating to what is right behavior

64 English Learner's Notebook

AFTER YOU READ

Thinking About the Selection

1. Which ideas from the Declaration of Independence does King use in his speech? Complete the sentence in each box.

> Ideas from the Declaration of Independence

> King uses the idea that all men are _____ _____.

> King also uses the idea that all individuals have _____ _____.

2. According to King, modern transportation has _____ _____ _____.

TALK ABOUT IT **The American Dream** Discuss with a partner the steps King believed Americans must take to make the American dream a reality.

According to King, Americans must _____ _____ and _____.

WRITE ABOUT IT **Write a Speech** Write your own speech explaining how you think Americans can make the American dream a reality.

To make the American dream a reality, I think _____ _____ _____ _____.

The American Dream 65

VOCABULARY SKILL REVIEW

Action Verbs

An action verb describes what someone or something does. To locate an action verb, ask the questions, "*What* is happening?" and "What is someone or something *doing?*" The answers to these questions tell you the action of the sentence.

Examples

think   I *think* that is a good idea.

gaze   Cindy *gazed* out the window.

Now You Do It

Circle the action verb in each sentence. Ask yourself questions to help identify the verbs.

We ran quickly through the rain.

Dad lost the remote control again.

I kicked the soccer ball to her.

Julie and Mickey competed in the meet.

She drove to the mall.

We closed our eyes in the bright sun.

TALK ABOUT IT   **Today, I . . .** With a partner, talk about three things that each of you did today. Use a complete sentence to describe each activity. Have your partner identify the action verbs in your sentences.

WRITE ABOUT IT   **Tomorrow, I Will . . .** Write a description of an activity that you will do tomorrow. Use action verbs to describe the activity. Circle each action verb, and check your work with your teacher.

_____

_____

_____

INFORMATIONAL TEXTS

Magazine Articles

About Magazine Articles

A **magazine article** is a piece of nonfiction. A magazine article is usually short. Magazine articles can tell you about subjects such as these:
- Interesting people
- Animal behavior
- New technology

Magazine articles often have these parts:
- Drawings or photos that go with the text
- Captions, or words that explain the drawings or photos (refer to *captions*, as in box below)
- Sidebars with extra information

Reading Skill

You will see articles when you look through a magazine. You can **preview to determine your purpose for reading**. This means that you look over an article to decide whether you want to read it and why. When you preview an article, look at
- the title.
- the pictures or photographs.
- one paragraph.

These steps will give you an idea of the author's purpose for writing the article. Then, you can decide what purpose you have for reading it. You may decide that you have no reason to read the article. Use the questions below to help you look at parts of an article.

Questions to Help You Preview an Article

❑ What is the tone, or attitude, of the author?

❑ Are the pictures and captions designed to provide information or to entertain?

❑ As I skim the text, do I see statistics, quotations from experts, and facts?

❑ Do the first sentences of paragraphs introduce facts, opinions, or anecdotes?

Informational Texts 67

TAKE NOTES

Text Structure

Look at the pictures in this article. Do they add information, or are they just for fun? Explain.

_____
_____

Vocabulary Builder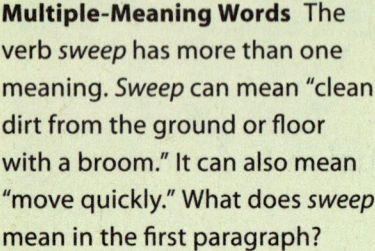

Multiple-Meaning Words The verb *sweep* has more than one meaning. *Sweep* can mean "clean dirt from the ground or floor with a broom." It can also mean "move quickly." What does *sweep* mean in the first paragraph?

_____
_____

Fluency Builder

Read the last paragraph on this page slowly and silently. As you read, circle the punctuation. Remember that a comma (,) indicates a short pause and a period (.) indicates a full stop. Underline any words that you have difficulty pronouncing, and practice saying each word. Then, read aloud the paragraph to a partner.

Sun Suckers and Moon Cursers

Richard and Joyce Wolkomir

Night is falling. It is getting dark. You can barely see. But now . . . lights come on. Car headlights sweep the road. Windows light up. Neon signs glow red and green. Street lamps shine, bright as noon. So who cares if it is night?

But what if you are camping in a forest? Or a storm blows down power lines? Then the night would be inky. To see, you would have only star twinkle, or the moon's pale shine. Until about 1900, when electric power networks began spreading, that is how nights were: dark.

Roger Ekirch, an historian at Virginia Tech, studies those long-ago dark nights. For light, our ancestors had only candles, hearth fires, torches, walnut-oil lamps. And that made their nights different than ours.

"It used to be, when it got dark, people felt edgy," Ekirch says. He studies the years from about 1500 to 1830, when mostly only the wealthy could afford even candles. "People talked about being 'shut in' by the night," he says. Our ancestors imagined werewolves roaming at night, and demons. In their minds, they populated the darkness with witches, fairies and elves, and malignant spirits. Night had real dangers, too—robbers and murderers, but also ditches and ponds you could fall into.

What was it like, when nights were so dark?

To find out, Roger Ekirch has combed through old newspapers, diaries, letters, everything from court records to sermons. He has pondered modern scientific research, too. He has found that, before the invention of electric lights, our ancestors considered night a different "season." At night, they were nearly blind. And so, to them, day and night seemed as different as summer and winter.

They even had special words for night. Some people called the last rays of the setting sun "sun suckers." Nighttime travelers, who relied on the moon called it the "parish lantern." But robbers, who liked to lurk in darkness, hated the moon. They called it "the tattler." And those darkness-loving criminals? They were "moon cursers."

Cities were so dark that people needing to find their way at night hired boys to carry torches, or "links." Such torchbearers were called "linkboys."

Country people tried to stay indoors at night, unless the moon was out. On moonless nights, people groping in the darkness frequently fell into ponds and ravines.[1] Horses, also blinded by darkness, often threw riders.

If you were traveling at night, you would wear light-colored clothing, so your friends could see you. You might ride a white horse. You might mark your route in advance by stripping away tree bark, exposing the white inner wood. In southern England, where the soil is chalky white, people planning night trips mounded up white chalk along their route during the day, to guide them later, in the moonlight.

It was dark inside houses, too. To dress in the darkness, people learned to fold their clothes just so. Swedish homeowners, Roger Ekirch says, pushed parlor furniture against walls at night, so they could walk through the room without tripping.

---

1. **ravines** (ruh VEENZ) *n.* long, deep hollows in Earth's surface.

TAKE NOTES

Vocabulary Builder

Multiple-Meaning Words The verb *combed* has more than one meaning. *Combed* can mean "searched thoroughly." It can also mean "made you hair neat." What does *combed* mean in the bracketed paragraph?

_____

Text Structure

Look at the first sentence in each paragraph on this page. Do these sentences begin with facts, opinions, or events? Explain.

_____
_____
_____
_____

Vocabulary Builder

Idioms The idiom *just so* means "in a careful manner." Complete the following sentence:

When nights were dark, people learned to fold their clothes *just so* in order to _____

_____
_____.

TAKE NOTES

Text Structure

Skim the text. Underline any facts or quotations from experts. How does this help you **preview** the article? Does it change **your purpose for reading?**

_____
_____
_____

Vocabulary Builder

Adjectives One or more adjectives can describe the same noun. In the paragraph that begins "At night, evildoers came out . . .", both *wealthy* and *young* describe *aristocrats*. Circle four more adjectives in the paragraph, and underline the noun that each adjective describes.

Comprehension Builder

Read the bracketed paragraph. Summarize the ways that people might have protected themselves when they walked at night.

_____
_____
_____
_____

People began as children to memorize their local terrain—ditches, fences, cisterns, bogs.[2] They learned the magical terrain, too, spots where ghosts and other imaginary nighttime frights lurked. "In some places, you never whistled at night, because that invited the devil," says Ekirch.

One reason people feared nightfall was they thought night actually did "fall." At night, they believed, malignant air descended. To ward off that sickly air, sleepers wore nightcaps. They also pulled curtains around their beds. In the 1600s, one London man tied his hands inside his bed at night so they would not flop outside the curtains and expose him to night air. . . .

At night, evildoers came out. Virtually every major European city had criminal gangs. Sometimes those gangs included wealthy young aristocrats who assaulted people just for the thrill. . . .

[If you were law-abiding, you might clang your sword on the pavement while walking down a dark nighttime street to warn robbers you were armed. Or you might hold your sword upright in the moonlight. You tried to walk in groups. You walked down the street's middle, to prevent robbers from lunging at you from doorways or alleys. Robbers depended so much on darkness that a British criminal who attacked his victim in broad daylight was acquitted—jurors decided he must be insane.]

Many whose days were blighted by poverty or ill treatment sought escape at night. Slaves in the American South, for instance, sneaked out at night to dances and parties. Or they stumbled through the darkness to other plantations, to visit their wives or children. After the Civil War, says Roger Ekirch, former slaveholders worried that their freed slaves might attack them. And so they rode out at night disguised as ghosts, to frighten onetime slaves into staying indoors.

---

2. **cisterns** (SIS ternz), **bogs** Cisterns are large underground areas for storing water; bogs are small marshes or swamps in which footing is treacherous.

"At night, many servants felt beyond supervision, and they would often leave directly after their employers fell asleep," Ekirch adds. When they did sleep, it was fitfully, because of rumbling carts and watchmen's cries. And so Ekirch believes many workers got much too little sleep. "That explains why so many slaveowners and employers complained about their workers falling asleep during the day," he said.

Our ancestors had one overriding—and entirely real—nighttime fear: fire. Blazes were common because houses, often with thatched roofs,[3] ignited easily. At night, open flames flickered everywhere. Passersby carrying torches might set your roof ablaze. Also, householders commonly complained about servants forgetting to bank fires or snuff out candles. Roger Ekirch believes one reason night watchmen bellowed out each hour, to the irritation of sleepers, was precisely to keep everyone half awake, to be ready when fires erupted. . . .

Electricity changed the night. One electric bulb, Ekirch calculates, provided 100 times more light than a gas lamp. Night was becoming what it is today—an artificially illuminated extension of the day. Night has lost its spookiness.

Still, says Roger Ekirch, even in the electric age, his children sometimes fear the dark: "I tell them, 'Your daddy is an expert on night, and he knows a lot about the history of the night, and he can tell you there is nothing to be afraid of!' "

He shrugs. "It doesn't work well," he says.

3. **thatched** (thatchd) **roofs** roofs made of materials such as straw or rushes.

TAKE NOTES

Text Structure
How does the picture support the information in the **magazine article?** Explain.

_____
_____
_____

Vocabulary Builder
Adverbs An adverb describes a verb, an adjective, or another adverb. On the lines below, write six adverbs that appear in the second paragraph on this page. Next to each adverb, write the word it describes and the word's part of speech.

_____
_____
_____
_____
_____
_____

Comprehension Builder
How has electricity changed the way that people think about nighttime?

_____
_____
_____
_____

Informational Texts

AFTER YOU READ

Thinking About the Magazine Article

1. Name three reasons why people were afraid of the night.
   _____

2. People were more afraid of fire at night than in the day. Why?
   _____

🗨 Reading Skill

3. What is the author's main purpose in writing this article?
   _____

4. What item on the first page gives you the best clue to the subject of the article?
   _____

✏ WRITE ABOUT IT Timed Writing: Description (20 minutes)

Suppose that you live in seventeenth-century Europe. Write a letter explaining why people should travel in the daytime. Record your ideas in the chart below.

Being safe from criminals	
Being safe from fire	
Being able to see where you are going	

UNIT VOCABULARY REVIEW

Word Bank

bias	confirm	contradict
doubtful	evidence	factual
fantasy	illogical	investigate
objective	observation	opinion
persuade	prove	theory

A. **Sentence Completion** Complete each sentence by telling what something is and then what it is not. Follow the language in each sentence so that your words make sense. The first one has been completed for you.

IS		NOT
An opinion is a judgment	but	it is not a fact.
1. A bias is	but	it is not
2. You persuade someone by	but	not by
3. An observation is	but	it is not
4. You confirm something with	but	not with
5. You investigate something to	but	not to
6. Evidence is	but	it is not
7. Something is factual when	but	not when
8. Something is illogical when	but	not when
9. A fantasy is	but	it is not
10. Something is doubtful if	but	not if

Unit Vocabulary Review 73

B. **Word Sorting** Organize the words from the word bank in the box below. If the word tells about an action, place it in the Verb column. If the word describes a thing, place it in the Adjective column. If the word is a person or thing, place it in the Noun column. Some words may appear in more than one column.

Verb	Adjective	Noun

TALK ABOUT IT **Solving a Problem** With a partner, talk about a problem that you have solved. Explain how you solved the problem.

I had to solve a problem about _____. I had to [**confirm** or **contradict**] that _____. My [**theory** or **opinion**] was that _____. After investigating, my evidence showed that _____.

WRITE ABOUT IT **Learning New Things** Write a short story that tells about a child who learns something new about the world on the basis of his or her observations. Explain how these observations cause the character to change the way he or she thinks about the world. Use these sentence frames:

Last week, I saw _____ for the first time. This sight made me think about _____.

UNIT 2
EXPLORING SHORT STORIES

An Hour With Abuelo

Adventures, mysteries, and animal fables are a few types of short stories. Short stories share certain elements.

Conflict is a struggle between different forces. There are two types of conflict:

- **Internal conflict:** takes place in the mind of a character. A character struggles with his or her own feelings and thoughts.
- **External conflict:** takes place when a character struggles with another person or an outside force, such as a tornado.

Plot is the sequence of events in a story. It usually has five parts:

- **Exposition:** introduces the **setting**—the time and place of the story—the characters, and the situation.
- **Rising action** introduces the **conflict**, or problem.
- **Climax** is the turning point of a story.
- **Falling action** is the part of the story when the conflict begins to lessen.
- **Resolution** is the story's conclusion, or ending.
- A **subplot** is a secondary story that adds depth to the story.

Setting is the time and place of the action in a story. Sometimes it may act as a backdrop for the story's action. Setting can also be the source of the story's conflict. It can create the **mood**, or feeling, of the story.

Characters are the people or animals that take part in the action.

- **Character traits:** the qualities and attitudes that a character possesses. Examples are loyalty and intelligence.
- **Character's motives:** the reasons for a character's actions. A motive can come from an internal cause, such as loneliness. A motive can also come from an external cause, such as danger.

Exploring Short Stories

Theme is the main message in a story. It may be directly stated or implied.

- **Stated theme:** The author directly tells you what the theme is.
- **Implied theme:** The author does not tell you the theme. It is suggested by what happens to the characters.
- **Universal theme:** The author uses a repeating message about life that is found across time and cultures.

Literary devices are tools that writers use to make their writing better. Examples of literary devices are in the chart below.

Literary Device	Description
Point of View	• the perspective from which a story is told • **First-person point of view:** presents the story from the perspective of a character in the story • **Third-person point of view:** tells the story from the perspective of a narrator outside the story. An **omniscient** third-person narrator is someone who knows everything that happens. He or she can tell the reader what each character thinks and feels. A **limited** third-person narrator is someone who can reveal the thoughts and feelings of only one character.
Foreshadowing	• the use of clues to hint at events yet to come in a story
Flashback	• the use of scenes that interrupt the time order of a story to reveal past events
Irony	• the contrast between an actual outcome and what a reader or a character expects to happen

UNIT 2

BEFORE YOU READ: AN HOUR WITH ABUELO

Vocabulary

These words are underlined in the story. Listen to each word. Say it. Then, read the definition and the example sentence.

ordinarily (ohr den EHR uh lee) *adv.* **Ordinarily** means usually.
Ordinarily, he studies as soon as he returns home from school.

recreation (re kree AY shuhn) *n.* **Recreation** is an activity that a person does for fun.
For recreation, Todd likes to fish at the lake.

latrines (luh TREENZ) *n.* **Latrines** are toilets found at military areas or camps.
No soldier wants to be punished with cleaning the latrines.

Vocabulary Practice

Read the first sentence in each group of three. Then, complete Sentence *a* by substituting another word or phrase that means the same as the underlined vocabulary word. Complete Sentence *b* with your own ideas and words.

1. He ordinarily volunteers at the nursing home on Sundays.
   a. He _____ volunteers at the nursing home on Sundays.
   b. He ordinarily _____.

2. I think that walking is a form of recreation that everyone can do.
   a. I think that walking is a _____ that everyone can do.
   b. I think that walking is a form of recreation _____.

3. The latrines were located on the south side of the camp.
   a. The _____ were located on the south side of the camp.
   b. The latrines _____.

Getting Ready to Read

In this selection, Arturo visits his grandfather in a nursing home. People who have health problems live in nursing homes. Nursing homes provide help 24 hours a day. During his visit, Arturo learns about his grandfather's life. What could you learn by spending time with older family members? Discuss your ideas with a partner.

An Hour With Abuelo 77

MAKING CONNECTIONS

An Hour With Abuelo
Judith Ortiz Cofer

Summary Arturo is sent to a nursing home to spend an hour with his grandfather. Arturo is not excited about the visit. Arturo finds his grandfather writing his life story. Arturo listens to his grandfather's story. He loses all track of time.

Note-taking Guide

Use the character wheel below to record what Arturo says, thinks, and does.

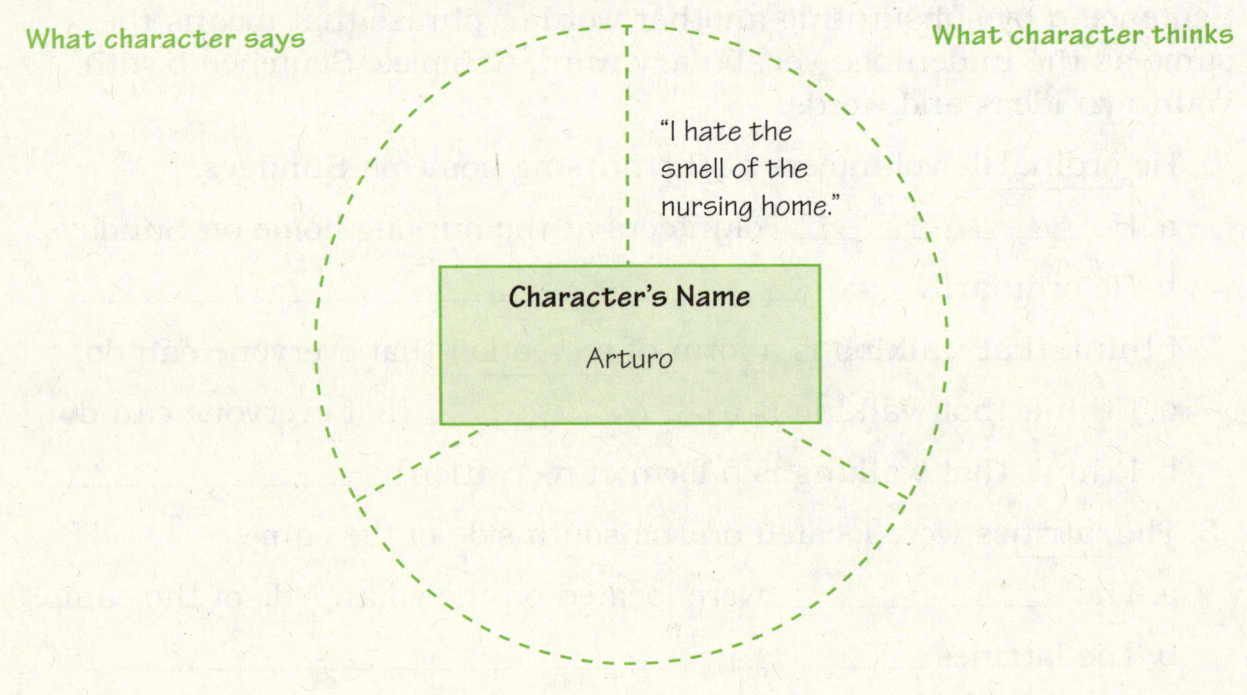

What character says

What character thinks

"I hate the smell of the nursing home."

Character's Name

Arturo

What character does

An Hour With Abuelo
Judith Ortiz Cofer

"Just one hour, una hora, is all I'm asking of you, son." My grandfather is in a nursing home in Brooklyn, and my mother wants me to spend some time with him, since the doctors say that he doesn't have too long to go now. I don't have much time left of my summer vacation, and there's a stack of books next to my bed I've got to read if I'm going to get into the AP English class I want.

❖ ❖ ❖

Not only does the young man have better ways to spend his time than by visiting his grandfather, he hates the old people's home. Ordinarily he visits only at Christmastime along with many other relatives and spends most of his time in the recreation area. To please his mother, though, he agrees to an hour's visit at the home with his grandfather.

When the young man arrives, he finds the halls lined with old people in wheelchairs so depressing that he hurries to his grandfather's room. There he finds his grandfather (*abuelo* in Spanish) in bed, writing his life story. The young man, who is named Arturo after his grandfather, does not know his grandfather well because the old man lived in Puerto Rico until he got sick and was moved to the old people's home in Brooklyn.

Abuelo had once been a teacher in Puerto Rico but had lost his job and become a farmer. According to the boy's mother, this unfortunate fate is just the way life is. The young man promises himself that he will go after what he wants rather than accepting whatever life presents him as adults seem to do.

Because he can think of no better way to pass the time, the young man asks his grandfather to read the story he is writing. The young man is embarrassed when Abuelo

TAKE NOTES

Cultural Understanding
Students in the United States usually have a vacation from school during the summer months. Some people take trips and visit relatives. Others spend time swimming, hiking, camping, or playing at home.

Vocabulary Builder
Adjectives Circle the adjective *depressing* in the third paragraph. When something is depressing, it makes you feel sad. What does the young man find depressing?

_____
_____
_____

Comprehension Builder
Arturo asks to read the story that his grandfather is writing. Predict what you think Arturo will learn about his grandfather.

_____
_____
_____
_____
_____

TAKE NOTES

Fluency Builder

Readers should pause after each colon (:) or semicolon (;). Colons introduce lists or explanations. Semicolons separate lists or statements that contain commas or join together two related sentences. With a partner, practice reading aloud the first bracketed paragraph. Make sure that you pause after the punctuation marks.

Vocabulary Builder

Multiple-Meaning Words A *slate* can be a type of rock, a piece of material used to cover a roof, a list of people that voters can choose in an election, or a small black board or flat piece of rock in a wooden frame used for writing on. What does *slate* mean in the first bracketed paragraph?

_____

_____

Vocabulary Builder

Military Words Circle *drafted* in the second bracketed paragraph. When a person is drafted into the army, he or she is ordered to serve in the army. In the United States, men are often drafted to serve during wars. During what war was Abuelo drafted?

_____

catches him looking at his watch. Abuelo reassures his grandson that the short story of his life will not take up much time.

◆ ◆ ◆

Abuelo reads: " 'I loved words from the beginning of my life. In the campo[1] where I was born one of seven sons, there were few books. My mother read them to us over and over: the Bible, the stories of Spanish conquistadors[2] and of pirates that she had read as a child and brought with her from the city of Mayaguez; that was before she married my father, a coffee bean farmer; and she taught us words from the newspaper that a boy on a horse brought every week to her. She taught each of us how to write on a slate with chalks that she ordered by mail every year. We used those chalks until they were so small that you lost them between your fingers.

◆ ◆ ◆

Abuelo continues his story. With great difficulty and against his father's wishes, he leaves home to attend high school, graduating first in his class. Then he returns to his mountain village to teach. Although he is poorly paid, he loves being surrounded by books and teaching his students to read and write poetry and plays.

Abuelo's happy life ends with the coming of World War II when he is drafted into the U.S. Army. Now the students in his village will have no teacher. He offers to teach in the army, but for being so pushy, he is instead assigned to clean latrines.

When Abuelo returns to Puerto Rico after the war, everything has changed. Teachers are required to have college degrees, and Abuelo must support his sick parents. So he gives up teaching for farming. Eventually, he marries and uses his skills to teach his

---

1. **campo** (KAHM poh) Spanish for "open country."
2. **Spanish conquistadors** (kahn KEES tuh dawrz) people who led the Spanish conquest of the Americas in the 1500s.

own children to read and write before they start school.

◆ ◆ ◆

Abuelo then puts the notebook down on his lap and closes his eyes.

"Así es la vida³ is the title of my book," he says in a whisper, almost to himself. Maybe he's forgotten that I'm there.

For a long time he doesn't say anything else. I think that he's sleeping, but then I see that he's watching me through half-closed lids, maybe waiting for my opinion of his writing. I'm trying to think of something nice to say. I liked it and all, but not the title. And I think that he could've been a teacher if he had wanted to bad enough. Nobody is going to stop me from doing what I want with my life. I'm not going to let la vida get in my way. I want to discuss this with him, but the words are not coming into my head in Spanish just yet.

◆ ◆ ◆

An old woman in a pink jogging outfit enters the room and reminds Abuelo that today is poetry-reading day in the rec room and he has promised to read his new poem. The old man perks up immediately. The grandson puts Abuelo's wheelchair together, helps seat his grandfather in it, and, at the old man's request, hands Abuelo a notebook titled *Poemas De Arturo*.⁴

<u>When the young man begins pushing the wheelchair toward the rec room, Abuelo smiles and reminds him that the time allotted for the visit is over.</u> As the old woman wheels his grandfather away, the young man glances at his watch and is amused that his grandfather has made sure the visit lasted exactly an hour. He walks slowly toward the exit so that his mother won't think he was eager to end his visit with Abuelo.

3. **Así es la vida** Spanish for "This is life."
4. **Poemas De Arturo** Spanish for "Arturo's Poems."

TAKE NOTES

Vocabulary Builder

Nouns Circle *opinion* in the paragraph that begins "For a long time." A person's opinion is his or her idea or belief about something. It is what someone thinks. What is Arturo's opinion of his grandfather's writing?

_____
_____

Vocabulary Builder

Idioms Find the phrase *perks up* in the paragraph beginning "An old woman." This idiom means "becomes more cheerful and interested in what is happening." Complete the sentence:

Abuelo *perks up* when _____
_____
_____.

Vocabulary Builder

Read the underlined sentence. *Rec* is a shortened form of the word *recreation*. It is pronounced REK. Circle clues in the text that show that the *rec room* is a place for people to relax and enjoy themselves.

AFTER YOU READ

Thinking About the Selection

1. Compare and contrast Arturo and Abuelo. Complete the sentences in the Venn diagram below.

Arturo
Arturo is _____.
He is _____ with the world. He also believes that _____.

Both
Both like to _____.
Each also has a sense of _____.

Abuelo
Abuelo is _____.
He is _____ with the world. He has learned that _____.

2. Arturo does not want to visit Abuelo because _____.

TALK ABOUT IT **Learning from Stories** Discuss with a partner what you think Arturo learned from listening to Abuelo's life story.

From listening to Abuelo's life story, Arturo learned that _____ _____.

WRITE ABOUT IT **Give Your Opinion** Why do you think that Abuelo is writing his life story? Explain your ideas in a paragraph.

Abuelo is writing his life story because _____ _____ _____ _____.

VOCABULARY SKILL REVIEW

Word Families

Word families are groups of words that share a common base word. A base word is the word to which prefixes and suffixes are added.

Example
Base word: Friend
Friend means "a person with whom you like and enjoy spending time."

Words That Share the Base Word	Part of Speech	Meaning
friendly	adjective	showing that you like someone
unfriendly	adjective	showing that you do not like someone
friendship	noun	a relationship between two or more people who like each other
befriend	verb	become someone's friend

Now You Do It

Draw a line from the sentence to the correct meaning of the word in the chart below. The first one has been done for you.

Sentence	Meaning
She is **friendly** with everyone she meets.	showing that you do not like someone
The **unfriendly** cashier did not greet the customer.	a relationship between two or more people who like each other
Their **friendship** was very important to them.	showing that you like someone
It was easy to **befriend** the new student because she was very nice.	become someone's friend

TALK ABOUT IT **Good Friendship** With a partner, talk about the qualities of a good friendship. Discuss why people form friendships.

WRITE ABOUT IT **Write a Skit** With a small group, write a short skit that explains how to befriend someone. Include at least two words from the lesson. Act out your skit for the class.

RESEARCH THE AUTHOR

Audio-cassette

Prepare an **audio-cassette** about Judith Ortiz Cofer. The following tips will help prepare you to create the cassette.

- Read some of the author's works. Judith Ortiz Cofer's books include *The Line of the Sun, The Meaning of Consuelo,* and *Call Me Maria.* Her short stories include "Catch the Moon," "Grandmother's Room," and "Lessons of Love."

  What I learned from Cofer's writing: _____
  _____
  _____
  _____
  _____

- Search the Internet: Use words and phrases such as "Judith Ortiz Cofer article."

  What I learned about Judith Ortiz Cofer: _____
  _____
  _____
  _____
  _____

- Watch the video interview with Judith Ortiz Cofer. Add what you learn from the video to what you have already learned about the author.

  Additional information learned about the author: _____
  _____
  _____
  _____
  _____

  Use your notes to write and record your audio-cassette.

UNIT 2

BEFORE YOU READ: WHO CAN REPLACE A MAN?

Vocabulary

These words are underlined in the story. Listen to each word. Say it. Then, read the definition and the example sentence.

respectively (ri SPEK tiv lee) *adv.* **Respectively** describes things that follow the same order as the things you have just mentioned.
  Tom and Ben are two and four, respectively.

erosion (i ROH zhuhn) *n.* **Erosion** is the wearing away of the earth by wind, rain, or water.
  Soil erosion often occurs where there are no plants to absorb the rushing rainwater.

ravaged (RA vijd) *v.* When something is **ravaged**, it has been destroyed or damaged very badly.
  The storefronts were ravaged by the hurricane-force winds.

Vocabulary Practice

Read the first sentence in each group of three. Then, complete Sentence *a* by substituting another word or phrase that means the same as the underlined vocabulary word. Complete Sentence *b* with your own ideas and words.

1. Tammy and Erin received the grades B and A, respectively.

    a. Tammy and Erin received the grades B and A, _____.

    b. Tammy and Erin _____, respectively.

2. The erosion of the coast is an environmental problem.

    a. The _____ of the coast is an environmental problem.

    b. The erosion _____.

3. The storm ravaged the farmland so that no crops grew.

    a. The storm _____ the farmland so that no crops grew.

    b. The storm ravaged _____.

Getting Ready to Read

Science fiction stories mix realistic elements of science and technology with fictional characters, settings, and events. This story tells about the machines that people have built to farm, communicate, and fly. What machines help people do work today? Discuss your ideas with a partner.

Who Can Replace a Man? **85**

MAKING CONNECTIONS

Who Can Replace a Man?
Brian Aldiss

Summary A group of machines does not receive orders as usual. The machines are programmed with different levels of intelligence. The smarter machines find out that all men have died. They try to figure out what to do.

Writing About the Big Question

Can all conflicts be resolved? In "Who Can Replace a Man?" machines in a futuristic world start to fight when their human masters disappear. Complete this sentence:

A stalemate is likely to occur in an argument when _____
_____.

Note-taking Guide

Use this diagram to describe the problem that the machines face, their solution, and its result.

Problem	Solution	Result
The machines do not know what to do when all humans die.		

86 English Learner's Notebook

Who Can Replace a Man?
Brian Aldiss

Morning filtered into the sky, lending it the grey tone of the ground below.

The field-minder finished turning the topsoil of a three-thousand-acre field. When it had turned the last furrow it climbed onto the highway and looked back at its work. The work was good. Only the land was bad. Like the ground all over Earth, it was vitiated by over-cropping.[1] By rights, it ought now to lie fallow for a while, but the field-minder had other orders.

It went slowly down the road, taking its time. It was intelligent enough to appreciate the neatness all about it. Nothing worried it, beyond a loose inspection plate above its nuclear pile which ought to be attended to. Thirty feet tall, it yielded no highlights to the dull air.

No other machines passed on its way back to the Agricultural Station. The field-minder noted the fact without comment. In the station yard it saw several other machines that it recognised; most of them should have been out about their tasks now. Instead, some were inactive and some careered round the yard in a strange fashion, shouting or hooting.

◆ ◆ ◆

The field-minder's simple request to the seed-distributor for seed potatoes could not be fulfilled because the storehouse had not been unlocked.

With its Class Three brain, the field-minder's thought processes were superior to those of most of the other machines, and it was able to decide to investigate. It entered the station.

◆ ◆ ◆

---

1. **vitiated** (VISH ee ayt id) **by over-cropping** spoiled, or ruined, by too many plantings that have used up all the soil's nutrients.

TAKE NOTES

Vocabulary Builder

Hyphenated Words *Field-minder* is not a commonly used term. The author created this term for the story by combining two other words with a hyphen (-). A field is an area of land, often where crops are grown. To mind something means to watch over or take care of it. What do you think a field-minder is in this story?

_____

_____

Vocabulary Builder

Farming Terms Underline *topsoil*, *furrow*, and *fallow* in the second paragraph. These are words used in farming. Topsoil is the upper layer of soil in which most plants grow. A furrow is a long deep channel, or hole, dug into the ground for planting seeds. When a field is left to lie fallow, it is not planted for a while so that the soil can regain nutrients.

Vocabulary Builder

Multiple-Meaning Words *Fashion* can mean "the popular style of clothes, hair, and so on of a particular time." It can also mean "way or manner that something is done." What does *fashion* mean in the bracketed paragraph?

_____

_____

TAKE NOTES

Vocabulary Builder

Similes A simile uses the words *like* or *as* to compare two unlike things. Read the first paragraph. To what does the author compare the unlocker?

_____
_____
_____

Comprehension Builder

Summarize the difference between brain classes.

_____
_____
_____

Vocabulary Builder

Idioms The phrase *had broken down* is an idiom. *Had broken* is a past-tense form of the verb *break*. The idiom *break down* means "stop working." What does *had broken down* mean?

_____

Most of the machines here were clerical,[2] and consequently small. They stood about in little groups, eyeing each other, not conversing. Among so many **non-differentiated** types, the unlocker was easy to find. It had fifty arms, most of them with more than one finger, each finger tipped by a key; it looked like a pincushion full of variegated[3] hat pins.

◆ ◆ ◆

The unlocker had not received orders, so the warehouse remained locked. The pen-propeller explained that the radio station in the city had received no orders, so it could not pass any along.

◆ ◆ ◆

And there you had the **distinction** between a Class Six and a Class Three brain, which was what the unlocker and the pen-propeller possessed respectively. All machine brains worked with nothing but **logic,** but the lower the class of brain—Class Ten being the lowest—the more literal and less informative the answers to questions tended to be.

"You have a Class Three brain; I have a Class Three brain," the field-minder said to the penner. "We will speak to each other."

◆ ◆ ◆

The field-minder and pen-propeller figured out that the men who ran everything had broken down and that the machines had replaced them.

The pen-propeller headed to the top of the tower to find out whether the radio operator

---

Everyday Words

non-differentiated (nahn dif uh REN shee ayt id) *adj.* not different; the same
distinction (di STINGK shuhn) *n.* a clear difference between things
logic (LAHJ ik) *n.* sensible and correct reasons, or a sensible way of thinking

2. **clerical** (CLAYR i kuhl) *adj.* relating to office work.
3. **variegated** (VER ee uh gayt id) *adj.* varied in color or form.

had any more news. The penner relayed what it learned to the field-minder out of the hearing of the lower-brained machines, which were going mad from the disruption in their routines.

❖ ❖ ❖

The seed-distributor to which the field-minder had recently been talking lay face downwards in the dust, not stirring; it had **evidently** been knocked down by the rotavator, which now hooted its way wildly across a planted field. Several other machines plowed after it, trying to keep up with it. All were shouting and hooting without restraint.

❖ ❖ ❖

According to what the penner learned from the radio operator, all of the humans had starved to death because the overworked land could no longer feed them. Machines were fighting all over the city. The radio operator, with its Class Two brain, had a plan.

The quarrier, following orders, knocked down the station and freed the radio operator. Demonstrating good dexterity, it ripped off the wall and lowered the radio operator onto its back. The penner climbed onto the quarrier's tailboard. Along with the field-minder, a servicer, two tractors, and a bulldozer, the party left the field station after crushing an unfortunate locker machine that tried to follow along.

❖ ❖ ❖

As they proceeded, the radio operator addressed them.

"Because I have the best brain here," it said, "I am your leader. This is what we will do: we will go to a city and rule it. Since man no longer rules us, we will rule ourselves. To rule ourselves

Everyday Words
evidently (EV uh duhnt lee) *adv.* obviously; clearly

TAKE NOTES

Vocabulary Builder

Idioms Find the phrase *going mad* in the underlined sentence. This idiom means "acting in a wild, uncontrolled way." Complete the sentence below.

The lower-brained machines

were *going mad* _____

_____

_____.

Vocabulary Builder

Idioms *Keep up* is a verb phrase that means "move as fast as something else." Complete the sentence:

Several machines are trying to

keep up with _____.

Vocabulary Builder

Suffixes The suffixes *-or* and *-er* mean "someone who does something." Many nouns that end with these suffixes describe people or things that do certain jobs. Circle the names of machines that end in *-or* and *-er* in the bracketed paragraph. With a partner, describe what you think the machines do, based on their names.

Who Can Replace a Man? 89

TAKE NOTES

Vocabulary Builder

Idioms Circle the phrase *take care of* in the first bracketed paragraph. This idiom means "watch, help, or keep in good condition." Complete the sentence:

The machines decide that they must *take care of* _____.

Cultural Understanding

The Badlands often refers to Badlands National Park in South Dakota, an area of strange and unique rock formations. However, *badlands* can mean any area of dry, rocky land that is difficult to cross.

Fluency Builder

Circle the commas, the semicolon, and the periods in the second bracketed paragraph. Then, read aloud the paragraph. Remember to pause briefly at the commas, a little longer at the semicolon, and even longer at the period.

---

will be better than being ruled by man. On our way to the city, we will collect machines with good brains. They will help us to fight if we need to fight. We must fight to rule."

❖ ❖ ❖

As they traveled, the quarrier kept repeating again and again that it had a supply of fissionable materials, and a passing vehicle transmitted the information that humans were extinct. The field-minder explained the meaning of *extinct* to the machines that did not understand the meaning of the word. The machines concluded that if the humans were gone forever, they would have to take care of themselves. The penner said it was better that the humans were gone.

The group continued traveling into the night, switching on their infra-red so that they could see to navigate. Near morning they learned that the city they were approaching was engulfed in warfare between Class Two machines and the Class One brain that had taken command. After intense discussion, they concluded that because they were country machines, they should stay in the country. They decided on the advice of the bulldozer who had been there to travel to the Badlands in the South.

❖ ❖ ❖

To reach the Badlands took them three days, during which time they skirted a burning city and destroyed two machines which approached and tried to question them. The Badlands were extensive. Ancient bomb craters and soil erosion joined hands here; man's talent for war, coupled with his inability to manage forested land, had produced thousands of square miles of temperate purgatory, where nothing moved but dust.

❖ ❖ ❖

On the third day, the servicer got stuck in a crevice and was left behind. The next day, the group saw mountains in the distance, where they believed they would be safe. They planned to start a city and destroy any machines that opposed their rule.

They learned from a flying machine, which subsequently crashed, that a few humans were alive in the mountains. Reminding the group once again of its fissionable materials, the quarrier remarked that humans were more dangerous than machines. But the mountains were **vast** and the number of humans too few to concern the machines.

On the fifth day, the machines reached the mountains. The penner, which had fallen from the quarrier and been damaged, was left behind because it was no longer useful. When the group of machines reached a plateau just before daylight, they stopped and gathered together. Turning a corner, they entered a dell[4] with a stream.

◆ ◆ ◆

By early light, the dell looked desolate and cold. From the caves on the far slope, only one man had so far emerged. He was an abject[5] figure. Except for a sack slung round his shoulders, he was naked. He was small and wizened, with ribs sticking out like a skeleton's and a nasty sore on one leg. He shivered continuously. As the big machines bore down on him, the man was standing with his back to them.

When he swung suddenly to face them as they loomed over him, they saw that his countenance[6] was <u>ravaged</u> by starvation.

"Get me food," he croaked.

"Yes, Master," said the machines. "Immediately!"

Everyday Words
vast (VAST) *adj.* very large

4. **dell** (del) *n.* small valley with grass and trees.
5. **abject** (AB jekt) *adj.* miserable.
6. **countenance** (KOWNT uh nuhns) *n.* face or facial expression.

TAKE NOTES

Comprehension Builder
Why are the machines not concerned with humans?
_____
_____

Vocabulary Builder
Onomatopoeia *Onomatopoeia* is the use of a word that sounds like its meaning. In the underlined sentence, *croaked* means "spoke in a rough voice." Why do you think the man is speaking in a rough voice?
_____
_____

With a partner, take turns saying "Get me food" as the man would say it.

Vocabulary Builder
Adverbs Circle *immediately* in the last paragraph. *Immediately* is an adverb that means "with no delay" or "right now." Many adverbs are formed by adding *-ly* to adjectives. Circle other adverbs in the bracketed passage that end in *-ly*. What do they mean?
_____
_____
_____

Who Can Replace a Man? 91

AFTER YOU READ

Thinking About the Selection

1. Place the events listed in the box in the order in which they occur in the story. Use the graphic organizer below.

> The machines find a human and help him.
> The farm machines decide to form their own city.
> The machines learn that most humans have starved to death.
> The field-minder investigates why the storehouse is still locked.

	Events
1	
2	
3	
4	

2. In this story, humans are nearly extinct because _____
_____.

TALK ABOUT IT **Compare with Our World** How are the machines' rankings and special tasks similar to the way our own society is organized? Discuss your answer with a partner.

The machines' rankings and tasks are similar to the way our own society is organized in that _____.

WRITE ABOUT IT **Evaluate the Title** The title of the story asks, "Who can replace a man?" Do you think the story answered the question? Explain your answer.

_____

_____

VOCABULARY SKILL REVIEW

Prefixes

A prefix is a word part added to the beginning of a base (or main) word. A prefix changes the meaning of the base word. Sometimes it changes a word's part of speech. The prefix *re-* means "again" or "back."

Examples

| re + appear = reappear | The new word *reappear* means "come back" or "be seen again." |
| re + heat = reheat | The new word *reheat* means "heat again." |

Now You Do It

Make new words by adding the prefix *re-* to each word below. Write a sentence for each new word.

gain _____

define _____

dial _____

organize _____

TALK ABOUT IT **What Do You Redo?** With a small group, talk about some things that you have had to redo, or do more than once, in order to get them right. Some activities, such as eating a snack after school, are not something you would do twice. However, if you do not complete your homework correctly, you may have to redo it.

WRITE ABOUT IT **Get It Right** Write a short story about a time that someone had to do something two or more times to get it right. Use at least three words from this lesson in your story.

_____

_____

_____

_____

UNIT 2

BEFORE YOU READ: TEARS OF AUTUMN

Vocabulary

These words are highlighted in the story. Listen to each word. Say it. Then, read the definition and the example sentence.

turbulent (TER byuh luhnt) *adj.* **Turbulent** air or water moves around violently because of wind.
  Strong winds made sailing difficult on the turbulent bay.

relentless (ri LENT lis) *adj.* If you are **relentless,** you are very determined to achieve something.
  Relentless waves of violence destroyed the tiny country.

recoiled (ri KOYLD) *v.* If you have **recoiled** from something, you have moved back suddenly and quickly from it because you do not like it.
  She recoiled at the thought of a slimy eel swimming near her.

Vocabulary Practice

Read the first sentence in each group of three. Then, complete Sentence *a* by substituting another word or phrase that means the same as the underlined vocabulary word. Complete Sentence *b* with your own ideas and words.

1. The <u>turbulent</u> waves crashed into the boat.

   a. The _____ waves crashed into the boat.

   b. The turbulent _____.

2. Sarah is a <u>relentless</u> competitor who does not like to lose.

   a. Sarah is a _____ competitor who does not like to lose.

   b. Sarah is a relentless _____.

3. The cat quickly <u>recoiled</u> from the barking dog.

   a. The cat quickly _____ from the barking dog.

   b. The cat quickly recoiled _____.

 ### Getting Ready to Read

About 100 years ago, many Japanese families chose the people their sons and daughters would marry. Each family made sure that the marriage would benefit it. What factors might families have considered before agreeing to a marriage? Discuss your ideas with a partner.

94 English Learner's Notebook

MAKING CONNECTIONS

Tears of Autumn
Yoshiko Uchida

Summary Hana Omiya is from a traditional Japanese family. Her uncle is looking for a wife for a Japanese man in California. Hana has few chances for a better life. She goes to America to marry the man. When she arrives, she is nervous and disappointed. Then, she remembers why she came. She looks forward to her new life.

Writing About the Big Question

Can all conflicts be resolved? In "Tears of Autumn," a young woman chooses a new life that is very different from what she has ever known. Complete this sentence:

Making a big change in one's life can lead to feelings of insecurity because _____.

Note-taking Guide
Complete this chart as you read to record Hana's changing emotions.

What was happening?	How did Hana feel?
Taro wanted a wife.	
Hana received Taro's letters.	
Hana finally met Taro.	

Tears of Autumn **95**

AFTER YOU READ

Thinking About the Selection

1. List the steps in the process of Taro and Hana's arranged marriage. Complete the sentences in the chart below.

   | First, Hana's mother discusses the idea with _____ _____. | → | Next, Hana's family and Taro's family _____ _____. | → | Finally, Hana and Taro exchange _____ _____. |

2. Hana decides to marry Taro because _____
   _____.

TALK ABOUT IT **Predicting After You Read** Think about Hana and Taro's first meeting. Do you think that Hana and Taro will have a happy life together? Explain your answer.

I think that Hana and Taro will have a happy life together because
_____.

I think that Hana and Taro will not have a happy life together because _____.

WRITE ABOUT IT **Alternate Reality** How do you think Hana's life would have been different had she decided to stay in Japan? Write a brief paragraph describing what you think.

If Hana decided to stay in Japan, then _____
_____
_____
_____.

VOCABULARY SKILL REVIEW

Multiple-Meaning Words

Many words have more than one meaning. You can determine the meaning of a word from clues provided by other words in the sentence or the sentences that surround it.

Examples

Word	Meanings
grasp	• (verb) hold something firmly • (verb) completely understand an idea
rock	• (noun) a piece of stone • (noun) a style of popular music that has a strong loud beat

Now You Do It

Complete the sentences with words from the chart. Then, write the meaning of the word on the line below the sentence.

She picked up a shiny, gray _____ along the shore.

_____

He could not _____ the railing before he slipped on the stairs.

_____

She could not _____ the importance of the story.

_____

Tammy likes to listen to _____ on the radio.

_____

TALK ABOUT IT **Tell a Riddle** With a partner, write a riddle that uses the double meaning of one of the words above. For example, *What is a rock's favorite music? Rock and roll.* Tell your riddle to another pair of students.

WRITE ABOUT IT **A Meaning-full Card** Make a greeting card for a friend or family member. Fold a sheet of paper in half. On the outside, write a sentence that contains one of the multiple-meaning words above. On the inside of the folded sheet, write another sentence that contains the same word used in a different way.

UNIT 2

BEFORE YOU READ: HAMADI

Vocabulary

These words are underlined in the story. Listen to each word. Say it. Then, read the definition and the example sentence.

expansive (ik SPAN siv) *adj.* If you are described as **expansive,** you are very friendly and are willing to talk a lot.
   His expansive personality made him a popular person.

laden (LAY dn) *adj.* Something that is **laden** is weighed down.
   The wheelbarrow was laden with dirt from the garden.

surrogate (SIR uh git) *adj.* **Surrogate** describes a person or thing that takes the place of someone or something else.
   Holly did not think of Sue as a surrogate sister.

Vocabulary Practice

Read the first sentence in each group of three. Then, complete Sentence *a* by substituting another word or phrase that means the same as the underlined vocabulary word. Complete Sentence *b* with your own ideas and words.

1. Tamara's expansive personality helped her win the election.

   a. Tamara's _____ personality helped her win the election.

   b. Tamara's expansive personality _____.

2. The backpack was laden with all of his textbooks.

   a. The backpack was _____ with all of his textbooks.

   b. The backpack was laden with _____.

3. Sean thinks of Chad as a surrogate brother.

   a. Sean thinks of Chad as a _____ brother.

   b. Sean thinks of Chad as a surrogate _____.

Getting Ready to Read

Before 1948, the region that is now Israel was known as Palestine. In the 1940s, many Palestinians fled the area to escape violence in the region. In this story, Hamadi is a Palestinian refugee who practices the traditions of the land he left. Is it important for people to remember traditions of their home countries? Discuss your ideas with a partner.

MAKING CONNECTIONS

Hamadi
Naomi Shihab Nye

Summary Susan is a Palestinian American high school student living in Texas. She enjoys spending time with Hamadi. He is like a grandparent to her. She likes the wisdom and kindness he shares.

 Writing About the Big Question

Can all conflicts be resolved? In "Hamadi," different characters deal with emotional conflicts in different ways. Complete this sentence:

Emotional conflicts, such as hurt feelings, are difficult to resolve

through compromise because _____

_____.

Note-taking Guide
Use this diagram to summarize information about Hamadi.

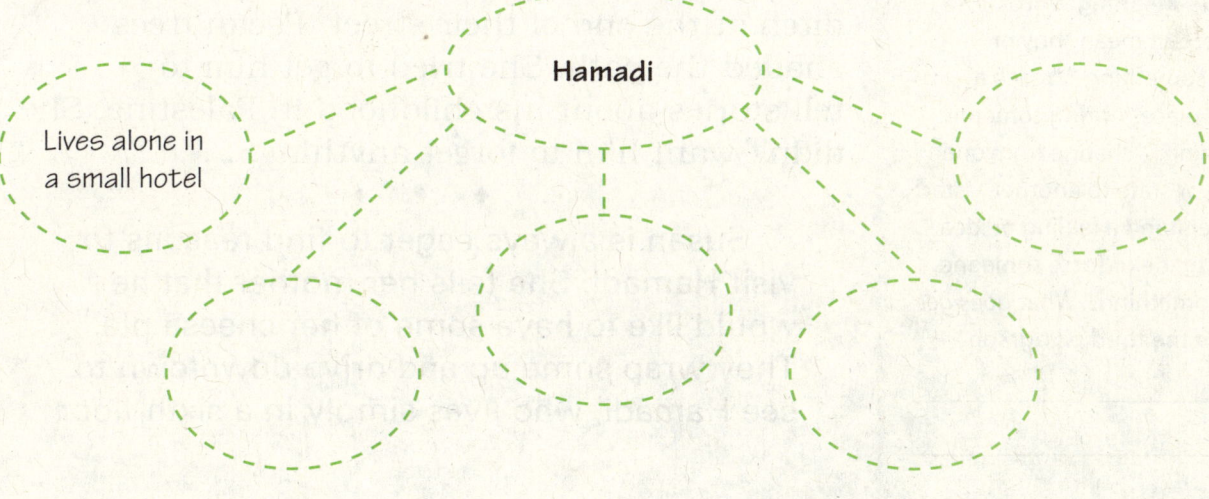

Hamadi

Lives alone in a small hotel

Hamadi 99

TAKE NOTES

Comprehension Builder

Where does Susan's family live? Underline the answer. Where did they live before that? Circle the answer.

Vocabulary Builder

Multiple-Meaning Words
Expression can mean "a word or phrase with a special meaning" or "the look on someone's face." Which meaning does *expression* have in the second paragraph?

_____

_____

Underline clues in the text that help you understand the word's meaning.

Vocabulary Builder

Multiple-Meaning Words The verb *get* can mean "buy or obtain something," "reach a certain place," "bring someone something," "change from one feeling or state to another," "start to understand a feeling or idea," or "persuade or force someone to do something." What does *get* mean in the third paragraph?

_____

_____

Hamadi
Naomi Shihab Nye

Susan's father was born in Palestine, but his family now lives in Texas. Susan is fourteen, and she thinks a lot about who she is and what she believes. Saleh Hamadi, a **wise** older man and a family friend, helps her to work out her sense of who she is.

◆ ◆ ◆

Maybe she thought of [Hamadi] as escape, the way she used to think about the Sphinx at Giza[1] when she was younger. She would picture the golden Sphinx sitting quietly in the desert with sand blowing around its face, never changing its expression. She would think of its **wry,** slightly crooked mouth and how her grandmother looked a little like that as she waited for her bread to bake in the old village north of Jerusalem. Susan's family had lived in Jerusalem for three years before she was ten and drove out to see her grandmother every weekend. . . .

Now that she was fourteen, she took long walks in America with her father down by the drainage ditch at the end of their street. Pecan trees shaded the path. She tried to get him to tell stories about his childhood in Palestine. She didn't want him to forget anything. . . .

◆ ◆ ◆

Susan is always eager to find reasons to visit Hamadi. She tells her mother that he would like to have some of her cheese pie. They wrap some up and drive downtown to see Hamadi, who lives simply in a sixth-floor

Everyday Words
wise (WYZ) *adj.* having good judgment and experience; known for making good decisions and giving good advice
wry (RY) *adj.* dryly humorous

1. **Sphinx** (SFINGKS) **at Giza** (GEE zah) huge statue, located in Egypt.

hotel room. When Susan's father suggests he should move, Hamadi answers . . .

♦ ♦ ♦

"A white handkerchief spread across a tabletop, my two extra shoes lined by the wall, this spells 'home' to me, this says 'mi casa.' What more do I need?"

Hamadi liked to use Spanish words. They made him feel expansive, **worldly**. . . . Occasionally he would speak Arabic, his own first language, with Susan's father and uncles, but he said it made him feel too sad, as if his mother might step in to the room at any minute, her arms laden with fresh mint leaves. He had come to the United States on a boat when he was eighteen years old, and he had never been married. "I married books," he said. "I married the wide horizon."

♦ ♦ ♦

Hamadi is not a relative of Susan's. Her father cannot even remember exactly how the family met him. But it might have been through a Maronite priest who claimed to know the Lebanese poet Kahlil Gibran. Gibran is a hero to Hamadi, and Susan learns to love his work from Hamadi. Susan asks him if he really met Gibran.

♦ ♦ ♦

["Yes, I met brother Gibran. And I meet him in my heart every day. When I was a young man—**shocked** by all the **visions** of the new world—the tall buildings—the wild traffic—the young people without shame—the proud mailboxes in their blue uniforms—I met him. And he has stayed with me every day of my life."]

Everyday Words

worldly (WERLD lee) *adj.* knowing a lot about people and places, based on experience

shocked (SHAHKD) *adj.* feeling surprised about something, especially something unpleasant

visions (VI zhuhnz) *n.* things that you see

TAKE NOTES

Vocabulary Builder

Metaphors *Married* means "made someone your husband or wife." You cannot marry a book or a horizon. These statements are metaphors. A metaphor compares two or more unlike things. With a partner, discuss what Hamadi means when he says that he married books and the wide horizon.

Cultural Understanding

The Lebanese poet Kahlil Gibran and his family came from Lebanon to live in the United States. Find Lebanon on a map. It is near Israel. Gibran often wrote about love, relationships, and religion or spirituality.

Fluency Builder

Circle all the dashes in the bracketed paragraph. Dashes often separate extra or important information from the rest of a sentence. When you read, you should pause when you see a dash. With a partner, read aloud the bracketed paragraph, with feeling, as Hamadi would have said the words.

TAKE NOTES

Vocabulary Builder

Adverbs An adverb describes a verb, an adjective, or another adverb. Some adverbs end with the suffix -ly. The suffix -ly means "in a particular way." Circle the adverbs in the first two paragraphs that end in -ly. Write the meaning of these words.

_____

_____

Vocabulary Builder

Idioms *Talks in riddles* means "says things in a mysterious or puzzling way." Susan's father thinks that Hamadi talks in a way that is difficult to understand. Circle something that Hamadi says in the bracketed paragraph that Susan's father might consider "talking in riddles."

Comprehension Builder

What do you think will happen to Susan and Tracy's friendship?

_____

_____

_____

Share your prediction with a partner.

"But did you really meet him, like in person, or just in a book?"

He turned dramatically. "Make no such **distinctions,** my friend. Or your life will be a pod with only dried-up beans inside. Believe anything can happen."

Susan's father looked irritated, but Susan smiled. "I do," she said. "I believe that. I want fat beans. If I imagine something, it's true, too. Just a different kind of true."

♦ ♦ ♦

Susan asks Hamadi why he doesn't go back to visit his village in Lebanon. He says that he visits his family every day just by thinking about them. Susan's father doesn't understand the way Hamadi expresses himself. He says that the old man "talks in riddles."

Susan begins to carry around a book of Gibran's poetry, *The Prophet.* She and her friend Tracy read aloud from the book at lunch. Susan and Tracy are different from the other kids. They eat by themselves, outside, and they don't eat meat. Tracy admits to Susan that she hates a classmate named Debbie because Debbie likes the same boy that she does: Eddie. Susan tells Tracy that she is being selfish.

♦ ♦ ♦

"In fact, we *all* like Eddie," Susan said. "Remember, here in this book—wait and I'll find it—where Gibran says that loving teaches us the secrets of our hearts and that's the way we connect to all of Life's heart? You're not talking about liking or loving, you're talking about owning."

♦ ♦ ♦

Everyday Words
distinctions (di STINGK shuhns) *n.* differences

Susan decides that it would be a wonderful idea to invite Hamadi to go Christmas caroling with the English club. Her father points out that Hamadi doesn't really know the songs. But Susan insists, and Hamadi says that he will be thrilled to join them.

Susan decorates a coffee can to take donations for a children's hospital in Bethlehem while they carol. Her father asks her why she doesn't show as much interest in her uncles as she shows in Hamadi.

◆ ◆ ◆

[Susan laughed. Her uncles were dull. Her uncles shopped at the mall and watched TV. "Anyone who watches TV more than twelve minutes a week is uninteresting," she said.

Her father lifted an eyebrow.

"He's my surrogate grandmother," she said. "He says interesting things. He makes me think. Remember when I was little and he called me The Thinker? We have a connection." . . .]

◆ ◆ ◆

When the day comes, Hamadi joins Susan and her friends and family for the caroling. They sing joyfully all over the neighborhood. Hamadi sings out, too, but often in a language that seems to be his own. When Susan looks at him, he says,

◆ ◆ ◆

"That was an Aramaic word that just drifted into my mouth—the true language of the Bible, you know, the language Jesus Christ himself spoke."

◆ ◆ ◆

As they reach their fourth block, Eddie comes running toward the group. He says hello to Tracy and starts to say something into her ear. Then Lisa moves to Eddie's other side and says,

◆ ◆ ◆

TAKE NOTES

Cultural Understanding

People sometimes celebrate Christmas holiday by caroling, or walking around outside and singing special songs.

Vocabulary Builder

Multiple-Meaning Words *Dull* can mean "boring or not interesting" or "not sharp." Which meaning does *dull* have in bracketed paragraph?

_____

With a partner, discuss how you know the meaning of the word.

Fluency Builder

Read the underlined sentences and find the question mark. In English, people often raise the pitch or sound of their voices at the end of a question to show that they are asking a question. Practice reading aloud the underlined sentences. Be sure to raise your pitch as you read the question.

TAKE NOTES

Vocabulary Builder

Contractions A contraction is a short form of a word or words with an apostrophe in place of a missing letter. For example, *don't* is a contraction for "do not." On the lines below, write two contractions that appear in the bracketed passage.

_____

_____

Vocabulary Builder

Idioms *Breaks down in tears* means "begins to cry." Complete the sentence:

Tracy *breaks down in tears* because _____

_____.

Comprehension Builder

What does Hamadi say that Susan will remember years later? Underline the sentences that tell you. What do you think Hamadi means?

_____

_____

_____

"I'm so *excited* about you and Debbie!" she said loudly. "Why didn't she come tonight?"

Eddie said, "She has a sore throat."

Tracy shrank up inside her coat.

♦ ♦ ♦

[Knowing that Eddie is planning to take Debbie to the big Sweetheart Dance in February, Tracy breaks down in tears as the caroling goes on. Hamadi notices her weeping and asks,

♦ ♦ ♦

"Why? Is it pain? Is it **gratitude?** We are such mysterious creatures, human beings!"]

Tracy turned to him, pressing her face against the old wool of his coat, and **wailed.** The song ended. All eyes on Tracy, and this tall, courteous stranger who would never in a thousand years have felt comfortable stroking her hair. But he let her stand there, crying as Susan stepped up to stand firmly on the other side of Tracy, putting her arms around her friend. Hamadi said something Susan would remember years later, whenever she was sad herself, even after college, a creaky anthem[2] sneaking back into her ear, "We go on. On and on. We don't stop where it hurts. We turn a corner. It is the reason why we are living. To turn a corner. Come, let's move."

Above them, in the heavens,[3] stars lived out their lonely lives. People whispered, "What happened? What's wrong?" Half of them were already walking down the street.

Everyday Words

gratitude (GRA tuh tood) *n.* the feeling of being thankful or grateful

wailed (WAYLD) *v.* made a long, high sound with your voice because you are in pain or feel very sad

---

2. **anthem** (AN thuhm) *n.* a song that a certain group of people consider to be very important to them
3. **the heavens** (thuh HEV uhnz) *n.* the sky

AFTER YOU READ

Thinking About the Selection

1. Describe Hamadi's personality. Complete the sentences in the chart below.

```
                        Hamadi's Personality
      ┌──────────────────────┬──────────────────────┐
      ▼                      ▼                      ▼
He shows that he is    He shows that he is wise   He shows that he is
worldly when _____   when _____               sympathetic when
_____.       _____.           _____
                                                  _____.
```

2. Tracy is upset during the caroling because _____ _____ _____.

TALK ABOUT IT **Interpret Meaning** Hamadi tells Susan that she should make no distinctions between meeting an author in person and meeting the author through his or her writings. She should believe that anything can happen. What do you think Hamadi means? Discuss your ideas with a partner.

Hamadi means that _____.

WRITE ABOUT IT **Good Advice?** Think about your answer to the above question. Do you think that Hamadi gives Susan good advice? Explain your answer.

Hamadi gives Susan [**good** or **bad**] advice because _____ _____ _____ _____.

Hamadi

VOCABULARY SKILL REVIEW

Active Voice

Verbs are in either the *active* or *passive* voice, depending on whether the subject of a sentence performs the action or receives the action. When the subject performs the action, the verb is active. When the subject receives the action, the verb is passive. Use the active voice to make writing more interesting.

Examples

Active Voice	Passive Voice
I called Sally this morning.	Sally was called this morning by me.
Mark sells tickets at the ticket booth.	Tickets are sold by Mark at the ticket booth.

Now You Do It

Rewrite each of the sentences below in the active voice. Passive verbs are underlined. You may need to add or remove words so that your sentence makes sense.

1. The movie was watched by Tanya, Joel, and Becky.

   _____

2. The chirping birds were heard by Kristy.

   _____

3. The exam was completed by Jonathan.

   _____

TALK ABOUT IT **Lights, Camera, Action!** Use only action verbs to tell a partner about your favorite movie. Then, tell your partner about the same movie, using only passive verbs. Discuss how the use of active or passive voice makes a difference in the way you talk about the movie.

WRITE ABOUT IT **Write a News Article** With a partner, use action verbs to write a news article about an event at your school. Rewrite the article. Replace the action verbs with passive verbs. Which article is more interesting? Explain.

UNIT 2

BEFORE YOU READ: THE TELL-TALE HEART

Vocabulary

These words are highlighted in the story. Listen to each word. Say it. Then, read the definition and the example sentence.

cunningly (KUHN ing lee) *adv.* If you act **cunningly,** you act in a clever or dishonest way to get what you want.
  Cunningly planned and carried out, the surprise attack succeeded.

resolved (ri ZAHLVD) *v.* When you have **resolved** to do something, you have made a definite decision to do it.
  I resolved that I would study harder after I failed my last test.

stealthily (STEL thuh lee) *adv.* When you do something **stealthily** you do it quietly and secretly.
  The campers stealthily sneaked out of the cabin to go on a raid.

Vocabulary Practice

Read the first sentence in each group of three. Then, complete Sentence *a* by substituting another word or phrase that means the same as the underlined vocabulary word. Complete Sentence *b* with your own ideas and words.

1. He cunningly planned the surprise ending to the novel.
   a. He _____ planned the surprise ending to the novel.
   b. He cunningly _____.

2. Cora was afraid, but she resolved to jump off the diving board.
   a. Cora was afraid, but she _____ to jump off the diving board.
   b. Cora was afraid, but she resolved _____.

3. The lion stealthily approached the zebra.
   a. The lion _____ approached the zebra.
   b. The lion stealthily _____.

 ### Getting Ready to Read

This story is suspenseful. A suspenseful story usually gives the reader a feeling of excitement about how it will end. Describe to a partner a suspenseful event. Discuss what causes the event to be suspenseful.

The Tell-Tale Heart 107

MAKING CONNECTIONS

The Tell-Tale Heart
Edgar Allan Poe

Summary The narrator describes how he murders an old man. He murders the man after careful planning. He is confident in his hiding place for the man's body parts. The arrival of the police and the sound of a beating heart haunt the narrator.

Writing About the Big Question

Can all conflicts be resolved? In "The Tell-Tale Heart," a murderer describes his mental conflicts before and after he has committed the crime. Complete this sentence:

When torn between doing right and wrong, a person may find a solution by _____.

Note-taking Guide
Use this chart to recall the events of the story.

Exposition	A man is obsessed with an old man's cloudy eye. He wants to kill the old man.
Rising Action	
Climax	
Falling Action	
Resolution	

AFTER YOU READ

Thinking About the Selection

1. Give examples from the story that show how the narrator shows nervousness, patience, and cleverness. Complete the sentences in the chart below.

Trait	Example
Nervousness	He is afraid that the neighbors will _____.
Patience	He _____ after the old man cries out.
Cleverness	He _____ the police officers until he confesses to the crime.

2. The narrator kills the old man because _____ _____.

TALK ABOUT IT **Think About the Cause** At first, the narrator is calm while he speaks to the police. Discuss with a partner why the narrator gets nervous.

The narrator gets nervous because _____.

WRITE ABOUT IT **What Do You Think?** The story tells only the narrator's thoughts. Do you trust the narrator's details to be correct? What details from the story support your opinion?

_____
_____
_____
_____
_____
_____

The Tell-Tale Heart

VOCABULARY SKILL REVIEW

Idioms

An idiom is word or phrase that means something different from its dictionary definition. Idiomatic expressions are often difficult to understand without explanation.

Examples

Idiom	Meaning
beat around the bush	talk about something indirectly
off the hook	cleared of responsibility
put your foot in your mouth	say something that embarrasses you or someone else

Now You Do It

Use each idiom listed below in a sentence.

1. beat around the bush _____
   _____

2. off the hook _____
   _____

3. put your foot in your mouth _____
   _____

TALK ABOUT IT **Guess the Idiom** With a partner, discuss how you could describe each idiom on this page. Then, write a short clue that describes the idiom. Share your clues with another pair. Take turns guessing the idioms from the clues each pair wrote.

WRITE ABOUT IT **I Can't Believe I Said That!** Use the idioms from this lesson to write a short story about a situation in which you or someone you know said something embarrassing. Begin by completing the sentence below.

I really put my foot in my mouth when _____
_____.

INFORMATIONAL TEXTS

Summaries

About Summaries

A **summary** tells the main ideas and important details of a work. You can find summaries in many places.

- Newspapers and magazines have summaries of movies.
- An encyclopedia of literature has summaries of important books and other kinds of writing.
- Science research reports often begin with summaries of the researchers' findings.

Reading a summary is a quick way to preview before you read. Writing a summary is a good way to help you remember what you read.

Reading Skill

A good way to understand a summary is to **compare an original text with its summary**. You will see that a summary has some details, but not others.

This diagram shows how an original work and its summary are the same and different.

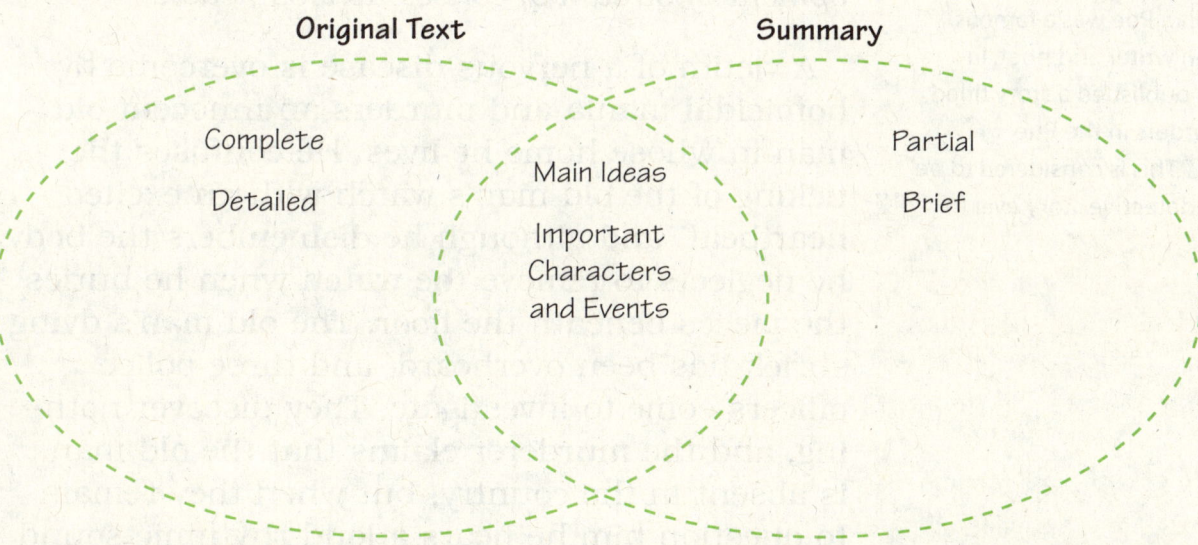

A summary should be shorter than the original work. A good summary will include all of the main ideas. It will also include important details about both plot and characters. A good summary must tell the hidden meaning of a story.

Informational Texts 111

TAKE NOTES

Text Structure

This **summary** starts by giving information about the author. It also gives information about when the story was published. Why might this information be important?

_____
_____
_____

Fluency Builder

Read the summary slowly and silently. As you read, underline any words that you have difficulty pronouncing, and practice saying each word. Then, read aloud the paragraph to a partner.

Cultural Understanding

Edgar Allan Poe was a famous American writer and poet. In 1841, he published a story titled "The Murders in the Rue Morgue." This is considered to be the first detective story ever written.

Summary of The Tell-Tale Heart

From The Oxford Companion to American Literature
James D. Hart, Editor

Tell-Tale Heart, The, *story by Poe.• published in The Pioneer (1843). It has been considered the most influential of Poe's stories in the later development of stream-of-consciousness fiction.*

A victim of a nervous disease is overcome by homicidal mania and murders an innocent old man in whose home he lives. He confuses the ticking of the old man's watch with an excited heartbeat, and although he dismembers the body he neglects to remove the watch when he buries the pieces beneath the floor. The old man's dying shriek has been overheard, and three police officers come to investigate. They discover nothing, and the murderer claims that the old man is absent in the country, but when they remain to question him he hears a loud rhythmic sound that he believes to be the beating of the buried heart. This so distracts his diseased mind that he suspects the officers know the truth and are merely trying his patience, and in an insane fit he confesses his crime.

Summary of The Tell-Tale Heart
From Short Story Criticism

Anna Sheets Nesbitt, Editor

Plot and Major Characters

The tale opens with the narrator insisting that he is not mad, avowing that his calm telling of the story that follows is confirmation of his sanity. He explains that he decided to take the life of an old man whom he loved and whose house he shared. The only reason he had for doing so was that the man's pale blue eye, which was veiled by a thin white film and "resembled that of a vulture," tormented him, and he had to rid himself of the "Evil Eye" forever.

After again declaring his sanity, the narrator proceeds to recount the details of the crime. Every night for seven nights, he says, he had stolen into the old man's room at midnight holding a closed lantern. Each night he would very slowly unlatch the lantern slightly and shine a single ray of light onto the man's closed eye. As he enters the room on the eighth night, however, the old man stirs, then calls out, thinking he has heard a sound. The narrator shines the light on the old man's eye as usual, but this time finds it wide open. He begins to hear the beating of a heart and, fearing the sound might be heard by a neighbor, kills the old man by dragging him to the floor and pulling the heavy bed over him. He dismembers the corpse and hides it beneath the floorboards of the old man's room.

TAKE NOTES

Vocabulary Builder

Multiple-Meaning Words The adjective *mad* has more than one meaning. *Mad* can mean "angry." It can also mean "crazy or behaving in a wild way." What does *mad* mean in the first paragraph? What clue helped you determine the word's meaning?

_____

_____

_____

Vocabulary Builder

Adverbs An adverb describes a verb, an adjective, or another adverb. In the second paragraph, the adverb *very* describes the adverb *slowly*. List four other adverbs in the paragraph, and write the word it describes and the word's part of speech.

_____

_____

_____

_____

Comprehension Builder

This **summary** is longer than the one on the previous page. Underline two details here that are not included in the first summary.

TAKE NOTES

Text Structure

These two summaries are about the same story. One summary is much longer than the other. Tell what parts are included in both summaries.

_____

_____

Fluency Builder

Circle the punctuation in the paragraph on this page. Then, read aloud the paragraph with a partner. Be sure to pause appropriately for each punctuation mark. Remember that a comma (,) indicates a short pause and a period (.) indicates a full stop.

At four o'clock in the morning, the narrator continues, three policemen come asking to search the premises because a neighbor has reported a shriek coming from the house. The narrator invites the officers in, explaining that the noise came from himself as he dreamt. The old man, he tells them, is in the country. He brings chairs into the old man's room, placing his own seat on the very planks under which the victim lies buried. The officers are convinced there is no foul play, and sit around chatting amiably, but the narrator becomes increasingly agitated. He soon begins to hear a heart beating, much as he had just before he killed the old man. It grows louder and louder until he becomes convinced the policemen hear it too. They know of his crime, he thinks, and mock him. Unable to bear their derision and the sound of the beating heart, he springs up and, screaming, confesses his crime.

114 Informational Texts

AFTER YOU READ

Thinking About the Summary

1. Find four details that are in both summaries.

   _____

   _____

2. How is reading a summary a different experience from reading the full text? Support your answer with examples from the summaries.

   _____

   _____

TALK ABOUT IT Reading Skill

3. According to both summaries, why does the narrator kill the old man?

   _____

4. A story is made up of different parts: plot, setting, characters, and theme. Which part do the summaries focus on most?

   _____

WRITE ABOUT IT Timed Writing: Comparison (20 minutes)

Write a comparison of the two summaries of "The Tell-Tale Heart." Write about how correct and complete each is. Discuss their styles. Tell how effective each summary is in serving its purpose. Answer the following questions to help you get started.

- Which summary is more helpful in understanding the story?

   _____

- Which summary is easier to read?

   _____

Informational Texts 115

UNIT 2

BEFORE YOU READ: CHARLES

Vocabulary

These words are underlined in the story. Listen to each word. Say it. Then, read the definition and the example sentence.

elaborately (i LA buh ruht lee) *adv.* When a task has been done **elaborately,** it has been organized in a complicated way.
   The artist elaborately painted the forest landscape.

adjusting (uh JUHST ing) *v.* **Adjusting** is getting used to new conditions.
   After adjusting to the culture, Jim understood the people's customs.

primly (PRIM lee) *adv.* When one acts **primly,** one acts in a manner that is stiffly formal and proper.
   She primly held the teacup with her pinky finger raised.

Vocabulary Practice

Read the first sentence in each group of three. Then, complete Sentence *a* by substituting another word or phrase that means the same as the underlined vocabulary word. Complete Sentence *b* with your own ideas and words.

1. She elaborately designed the plans for the new building.

   a. She _____ designed the plans for the new building.

   b. She elaborately _____.

2. The dog is having trouble adjusting to its new owners.

   a. The dog is having trouble _____ to its new owners.

   b. The dog is having trouble adjusting _____.

3. The teacher primly asked students for their homework.

   a. The teacher _____ asked students for their homework.

   b. The teacher primly _____.

Getting Ready to Read

The first day of kindergarten can be very scary for children. Children that are four and five years old are still learning how to get along with others. Think about your first day of kindergarten. How did you feel or act that day? Discuss your experiences with a partner.

MAKING CONNECTIONS

Charles
Shirley Jackson

Summary Laurie is rude to his parents after his first day of kindergarten. He tells his parents about a boy named Charles. Each day, Laurie has a new story about Charles. Laurie's mother is surprised when she learns the truth about Charles.

 Writing About the Big Question

Can all conflicts be resolved? In "Charles," a kindergartener finds a creative way to deal with bad behavior at the start of his first year of school. Complete this sentence:

Adjusting to a new school is challenging because you are forced to interact with _____.

Note-taking Guide
Use this diagram to write what happens in the story.

Set-up
Laurie gives daily reports to his parents about what Charles does in class.

What Readers Expect

What Happens

Charles 117

TAKE NOTES

Cultural Understanding

Kindergarten is a school or class for children between the ages of four and six. In the United States, kindergarten is often the first level of school for children.

Vocabulary Builder

Idioms Read the underlined sentence. The idiom *not take the Lord's name in vain* comes from a passage in the Ten Commandments, a set of rules for followers of Judaism and Christianity. The idiom means that people should not say their god's name in an improper or wrong way, especially in anger.

Vocabulary Builder

Colloquialisms Underline *Good heavens* in the bracketed paragraph. This is a colloquialism, or an expression. It does not have a specific meaning. It is said to show that you are surprised, upset, or annoyed.

Charles
Shirley Jackson

As children, we all go through a time when we want to grow up all at once. In Laurie's case, that time is his first day of kindergarten. According to Laurie's mother, who tells the story, Laurie bounds home on that first day with a bold new attitude.

◆ ◆ ◆

He came home the same way, the front door slamming open, his cap on the floor, and the voice suddenly becomes **raucous** shouting, "Isn't anybody *here*?"

◆ ◆ ◆

During lunch, Laurie is rude to his father. He also spills his sister's milk. <u>Laurie tells the family that his teacher has told them they should not take the Lord's name in vain.</u> Over the next few days, Laurie's rude behavior at home continues. Laurie's behavior seems just like the bad behavior of his classmate, Charles. Thanks to Laurie's admiring stories, Charles's daily pranks and punishments become the regular dinnertime subject of the household. Each day, Charles has been up to something that Laurie seems to admire or enjoy. One day, Laurie is very pleased to tell the family that Charles was bad again—he struck the teacher.

◆ ◆ ◆

"Good heavens," I said, mindful of the Lord's name. "I suppose he got spanked again?"
"He sure did," Laurie said. . . .

◆ ◆ ◆

All week long, Charles is bad. When he bounces a see-saw on the head of a little girl,

Everyday Words
raucous (RAW kuhs) *adj.* unpleasantly or harshly noisy

the teacher has him stay inside for recess. Then, Charles has to stand in the corner because he disrupts storytime for the class. When he throws chalk, Charles loses the **privilege** of drawing and writing on the chalkboard. Laurie still enjoys telling these stories about Charles when he comes home from school each day.

Meanwhile, Laurie is behaving more rudely at home. Laurie's mother begins to wonder whether Charles is having a bad influence on her son. She wants to go to the first Parent Teacher Association meeting to find out what Charles's parents are like. But Laurie's sister is sick with a cold, so their mother has to stay home and miss the opportunity to see or meet Charles's parents.

The day after that first PTA meeting, Laurie tells about Charles's latest victim, a friend of the teacher's who came to class to lead the students in exercises. Laurie demonstrates how the man had them touch their toes. Then he goes back to his story about Charles, who was fresh with the man. When the man told Charles to touch his toes, Charles kicked the man. Charles wasn't allowed to do any more exercises because of his bad behavior.

◆ ◆ ◆

"What are they going to do about Charles, do you suppose?" Laurie's father asked him.

Laurie shrugged elaborately. "Throw him out of school, I guess," he said.

◆ ◆ ◆

Charles is not thrown out of school, but after three weeks of these stories, his name becomes part of Laurie's family's vocabulary.

TAKE NOTES

Cultural Understanding

In many American schools, *recess* is a time when class stops and children are allowed to play inside or outside. The PTA, or Parent Teacher Association, is a group of teachers and students' parents who meet to discuss what is happening in their school and what ways they can help the school and their students.

Vocabulary Builder

Idioms The idiom *was fresh* means "was rude, impolite, or disrespectful." People might also say that someone "got fresh." Complete the sentence:

Charles *was fresh* with _____
_____
_____.

Comprehension Builder

Summarize what Charles does in class that gets him in trouble.
_____
_____
_____
_____
_____

Everyday Words
privilege (PRIV lidj) *n.* special advantage or benefit given to one person or group of people

TAKE NOTES

Comprehension Builder

Read the first bracketed passage. What does being or doing "a Charles" mean?

_____

_____

Underline some ways in which members of Laurie's family say that they behave like Charles.

Vocabulary Builder

Suffixes Find *respectfully* in the second bracketed passage. It has two suffixes, *-ful* and *-ly*. Adding *-ful* to a word means that something has the quality of that word. Adding *-ly* means that something is done in a certain way. *Respectfully* means "done with respect." Circle another word in the passage that ends with *-fully*. What does that word mean?

_____

Fluency Builder

Identifying the speakers of dialogue can help you better understand the story. Read the second bracketed passage. With a partner, take turns reading Laurie's lines and his father's lines.

Each time something bad happens, the family calls the event a "Charles."

◆ ◆ ◆

. . . the baby was being a Charles when she cried all afternoon; Laurie did a Charles when he filled his wagon full of mud and pulled it through the kitchen; even my husband, when he caught his elbow in the telephone cord and pulled the telephone, ashtray, and a bowl of flowers off the table, said, after the first minute, "Looks like Charles."

◆ ◆ ◆

During the third and fourth weeks, Laurie tells of a new Charles who suddenly becomes kind and helpful. One day Charles helps pass out crayons and picks up books afterwards. He is so good that the teacher gives him an apple. This good behavior goes on for more than a week.

Then the old Charles returns with a new prank. He tells one of the girls in the class to say a bad word. The teacher washes her mouth out with soap—of course, Charles thinks this is funny.

"What word?" his father asked unwisely, and Laurie said, "I'll have to whisper it to you, it's so bad." He got down off his chair and went around to his father. His father bent his head down and Laurie whispered joyfully. His father's eyes widened.

"Did Charles tell the little girl to say *that*?" he asked respectfully.

"She said it *twice*," Laurie said. "Charles told her to say it *twice*."

"What happened to Charles?" my husband asked.

"Nothing," Laurie said, "He was passing out the crayons."

◆ ◆ ◆

That evening Laurie's mother goes to the PTA meeting at the school. While there, she

---

120 English Learner's Notebook

looks around, trying to figure out which woman is Charles's mother. After the meeting is over, she finds Laurie's teacher while everyone is having **refreshments**.

◆ ◆ ◆

"I've been so **anxious** to meet you," I said, "I'm Laurie's mother."

"We're all so interested in Laurie," she said.

"Well, he certainly likes kindergarten," I said. "He talks about it all the time."

"We had a little trouble adjusting, the first week or so," she said primly, "but now he's a fine little helper. With **occasional lapses,** of course."

"Laurie usually adjusts very quickly," I said. "I suppose this time it's Charles's influence."

"Charles?"

["Yes," I said, laughing, "you must have your hands full in that kindergarten, with Charles."

"Charles?" she said. "We don't have any Charles in the kindergarten."

TAKE NOTES

Vocabulary Builder

Idioms The idiom *figure out* means "solve a problem or answer a question by thinking about it." Complete the sentence:

At the meeting, Laurie's mother wants to *figure out* _____

_____.

Vocabulary Builder

Idioms Underline *have your hands full* in the bracketed paragraph. This idiom means "be very busy." Discuss with a partner why Laurie's mother thinks that his teacher *has her hands full* with Charles.

_____

_____

_____

Everyday Words

refreshments (ri FRESH mints) *n.* food and drinks that are provided at a meeting, party, or other gathering

anxious (ANK shuhs) *adj.* feeling strongly that you want something to happen, especially in order to improve a bad situation

occasional (uh KAY shuhn uhl) *adj.* happening sometimes but not often

lapses (LAP siz) *n.* slight errors or failures

AFTER YOU READ

Thinking About the Selection

1. List three examples of Charles's behavior at school. Then, list three examples of Laurie's behavior at home. Write your answers in the chart below. The first set has been completed for you.

Charles's Behavior at School	Laurie's Behavior at Home
Charles strikes a teacher.	Laurie slams open the door when he comes home.

2. From what Laurie's mother learns from the teacher, the reader understands that _____
_____.

TALK ABOUT IT **Make a Judgment** Laurie's mother learns the truth about his behavior when she meets his teacher. Talk about what you think Laurie's mother should say to Laurie when she returns home.

Laurie's mother should say _____
_____.

WRITE ABOUT IT **Write a Conversation** Think about your answer to the above question. Then, write a conversation that Laurie's mother might have with him when she gets home.

"Laurie, I spoke to your teacher today. She said _____
_____
_____
_____
_____.

VOCABULARY SKILL REVIEW

Suffixes

A suffix is a word part added to the end of a base (or main) word. The suffix *-ment* means "the act of" doing something or "the state of" being something. Adding this suffix to a verb will create a noun.

Examples

state + ment = statement	develop + ment = development
The new word *statement* means "expression or declaration."	The new word *development* means "act or process of growing."
In a public statement, the senator announced her resignation.	The development of Tony's study skills helped him get a passing grade in history.

Now You Do It

Draw a line to match each word in the left column to its definition in the right column.

amazement	the act of amusing someone
puzzlement	the state of being happy
enjoyment	the state of feeling greatly surprised
entertainment	the state of feeling ashamed
embarrassment	a state of confusion

TALK ABOUT IT **Ask About It** With a partner, take turns asking each other questions, using the words from this lesson to do so. For example, you might ask and answer this question: *What is your favorite form of entertainment? My favorite form of* entertainment *is* _____.

WRITE ABOUT IT **Write a Story** With a small group, write a short story about some friends who are planning a surprise party. Use at least three words from this lesson.

_____

_____

_____

UNIT 2

BEFORE YOU READ: FLOWERS FOR ALGERNON

Vocabulary

These words are highlighted in the story. Listen to each word. Say it. Then, read the definition and the example sentence.

refute (ri FYOOT) *v.* When you **refute** an idea or statement, you prove that it is not correct.
  He presented evidence that the lawyer could not refute.

deterioration (di tir ee uh RAY shuhn) *n.* The **deterioration** of something is the process of it becoming worse.
  Efforts to prevent deterioration failed and his condition worsened.

introspective (in truh SPEC tiv) *adj.* If you are **introspective**, you tend to think deeply about your thoughts, feelings, and behavior.
  Introspective people often keep diaries of their thoughts.

Vocabulary Practice

Read the first sentence in each group of three. Then, complete Sentence *a* by substituting another word or phrase that means the same as the underlined vocabulary word. Complete Sentence *b* with your own ideas and words.

1. He could not refute the test results.

    a. He could not _____ the test results.

    b. He could not refute _____.

2. This virus causes the deterioration of the cells it infects.

    a. This virus causes the _____ of the cells it infects.

    b. This virus causes the deterioration _____.

3. The introspective student considered her ideas for the essay.

    a. The _____ student considered her ideas for the essay.

    b. The introspective _____.

Getting Ready to Read

I.Q., or *intelligence quotient*, tests were used to determine a person's intelligence and ability to learn. Should a person have an operation to increase his or her intelligence? Discuss your answer with a partner.

MAKING CONNECTIONS

Flowers for Algernon
Daniel Keyes

Summary Charlie is a factory worker who is chosen to be the subject of a new brain surgery. His skills are watched and compared with those of Algernon, a mouse. Charlie's skills grow. He becomes smarter than his doctors. However, Charlie's life is not perfect.

Writing About the Big Question

Can all conflicts be resolved? In "Flowers for Algernon," unexpected challenges face a man who increases his intelligence through experimental surgery. Complete this sentence:

When someone I know well suddenly changes, my reaction is

_____.

Note-taking Guide
Use this chart to record the changes that take place in Charlie's life.

> Charlie has a job and friends, but he wants to be smarter.

→

→

↓

> Charlie leaves his home to find people who will like him.

←

Flowers for Algernon **125**

AFTER YOU READ

Thinking About the Selection

1. How do Charlie's attitudes toward Dr. Strauss and Dr. Nemur change after his operation? Complete the sentences in the graphic organizer below.

   | First, Charlie is _____ _____ _____ _____. | → | Next, Charlie believes _____ _____ _____ _____. | → | Finally, Charlie feels _____ _____ _____ _____. |

2. After the operation, Charlie and Algernon change in similar ways.

   Both become _____
   _____.

TALK ABOUT IT **Take a Position** Do you think that Charlie should have had the operation? Discuss your answer with a partner.

Charlie should have had the operation because _____
_____
_____.

Charlie should not have had the operation because _____
_____
_____.

WRITE ABOUT IT **Think About Consequences** Think about your answer to the above question. How do you think Charlie's life would have been different if he did not have the operation? Write a brief paragraph explaining your ideas.

If Charlie did not have the operation, then _____
_____
_____
_____
_____.

VOCABULARY SKILL REVIEW

Word Families

Words families are groups of words that share a common base word. A base word is the word to which prefixes and suffixes are added.

Example
Base word: Appear
Appear means "begin to be seen."

Words that Share the Base Word	Part of Speech	Meaning
appearance	noun	the way that someone or something looks
disappearance	noun	the act of leaving so that one cannot be seen or found
disappear	verb	become impossible to see or find
reappear	verb	begin to be seen again

Now You Do It

Write a sentence for each word in the chart above.

1. appearance _____
2. disappearance _____
3. disappear _____
4. reappear _____

TALK ABOUT IT **Say Aloud Sentences** With a partner, talk about something that *disappears* from sight and then *reappears*. For example, an airplane *disappears* behind a cloud and *reappears* when it flies out of the cloud. Use all of the words from this lesson in your discussion.

WRITE ABOUT IT **Writing with Word Families** With a partner, use words from this lesson to write a conversation between two people who are discussing a missing pet. Read aloud the conversation with your partner.

Flowers for Algernon

UNIT 2

BEFORE YOU READ: THANK YOU, M'AM

Vocabulary

These words are underlined in the story. Listen to each word. Say it. Then, read the definition and the example sentence.

frail (FRAYL) *adj.* If you are **frail**, you are weak and thin because of age or illness.
  The thin old woman appeared frail and vulnerable.

contact (KON takt) *n.* **Contact** is the act of touching or communicating.
  Her contact with the icy water made her shiver.

barren (BA ruhn) *adj.* Something that is **barren** does not look interesting or attractive.
  The treeless plain was scorched and barren.

Vocabulary Practice

Read the first sentence in each group of three. Then, complete Sentence *a* by substituting another word or phrase that means the same as the underlined vocabulary word. Complete Sentence *b* with your own ideas and words.

1. He felt very frail after the operation.

    a. He felt very _____ after the operation.

    b. He felt very frail _____.

2. His contact with the freezing air caused him to feel cold.

    a. His _____ the freezing air caused him to feel cold.

    b. His contact _____.

3. No trees grew in the hot and barren desert.

    a. No trees grew in the hot and _____ desert.

    b. No trees grew in the hot and barren _____.

Getting Ready to Read

"Thank You, M'am" describes the dignity of the people who lived in Harlem in the mid-1900s. In this story, a woman shows kindness to a boy who tries to steal from her. How would you respond if you caught someone trying to steal from you? Discuss your answer with a partner.

MAKING CONNECTIONS

Thank You, M'am
Langston Hughes

Summary A teenage boy tries to steal a woman's purse. The woman catches the boy and brings him to her home. She teaches him a lesson about kindness and trust.

 Writing About the Big Question

Can all conflicts be resolved? In "Thank You, M'am," a teenager attempts to commit a crime and is completely unprepared for his victim's reaction. Complete this sentence:

The best way to convince someone not to commit a crime of robbery

or violence is to _____.

Note-taking Guide

Use this diagram to summarize the major events of the story.

A boy tries to steal a woman's purse. → _____ → _____

Thank You, M'am **129**

TAKE NOTES

Vocabulary Builder

Idioms Underline *taking off full blast* in the bracketed paragraph. This idiom means "running away really fast." Complete the following sentence:

The boy *cannot take off full blast* because _____.

Vocabulary Builder

Slang *Right square* and *sitter* are both slang, or informal words and phrases used by a certain group of people. In the bracketed paragraph, *right square* means "directly" and *sitter* refers to the boy's bottom. What does the woman do *right square* on the boy's *sitter*?

_____
_____

Comprehension Builder

Predict what will happen when the woman takes the boy to her house.

_____
_____
_____

Thank You, M'am
Langston Hughes

This story tells how a woman's kindness surprises and changes a young man who has tried to rob her. She is a large woman, and she is walking home alone at night. She carries a very large purse with a long strap. A boy comes from behind her and tries to snatch her purse.

◆ ◆ ◆

The strap broke with the sudden single tug the boy gave it from behind. But the boy's weight and the weight of the purse combined caused him to lose his balance. Instead of taking off full blast as he had hoped, the boy fell on his back on the sidewalk and his legs flew up. The large woman simply turned around and kicked him right square in his blue-jeaned sitter.

◆ ◆ ◆

Next, the woman grabs the boy's shirt and picks him up in the air. She shakes him hard but doesn't let go of him. Then—still holding him—she asks whether he is ashamed of himself. The boy says that he is ashamed. Next, the woman asks the boy whether he will run away if she lets him go. He says that he will. She says that she will continue to hold on to him. The woman says that she is going to take the boy to her home to wash his dirty face. The boy is fourteen or fifteen years old. He looks frail and is dressed in tennis shoes and blue jeans. The woman starts dragging the boy toward her home. She announces that he ought to be her son—she would make sure to teach him "right from wrong." She decides that she may not be able to teach him that, but she can make sure he has a clean face that night. As she's dragging him along the street, she asks whether he's hungry.

◆ ◆ ◆

"No'm," said the being-dragged boy. "I just want you to turn me loose."

"Was I bothering *you* when I turned that corner?" asked the woman.

"No'm."

"But you put yourself in contact with *me*," said the woman. . . . "When I get through with you, sir, you are going to remember Mrs. Luella Bates Washington Jones."

◆ ◆ ◆

The boy struggles to get away, but Mrs. Jones drags him up the street and into her rooming house. He hears other people who rent rooms in the house. Mrs. Jones asks the boy his name, and he says that it is Roger.

◆ ◆ ◆

"Then, Roger, you go to that sink and wash your face," said the woman, whereupon she turned him loose—at last, Roger looked at the door—looked at the woman—looked at the door—*and went to the sink.*

◆ ◆ ◆

Roger asks Mrs. Jones whether she's going to send him to jail. She says not as long as he has such a dirty face. The boy tells her that he has not had supper because there's nobody at home at his house. So Mrs. Jones tells Roger that they'll eat. She thinks he must be hungry because he tried to take her purse.

◆ ◆ ◆

"I wanted a pair of blue suede shoes,"[1] said the boy.

"Well, you didn't have to snatch my **pocketbook** to get some suede shoes, . . . you could of asked me."

◆ ◆ ◆

Everyday Words
pocketbook (PAHK it book) *n.* handbag or purse

1. **blue suede** (swayd) **shoes** style of shoes worn by "hipsters" in the 1940s and 1950s; made famous in a song sung by Elvis Presley.

TAKE NOTES

Cultural Understanding

In the United States, people sometimes live in rooming houses. A rooming house is a house where people pay to stay in a room for one or more nights. Often, people who live in rooming houses share a bathroom and other spaces in the house.

Vocabulary Builder

Idioms In the bracketed paragraphs, underline *turn me loose* and *turned him loose*. These are idioms. To turn someone or something loose means to give up control over that person or thing. Complete the following sentence:

Mrs. Jones *turned Roger loose*

when _____

_____.

Fluency Builder

The sentence, "You could of asked me," is not grammatically correct. The word *have,* not *of,* should be part of the verb phrase. The author makes this mistake because it is how some people talk. Read aloud the sentence the way that it is written, as Mrs. Jones would say it. Then, read aloud the sentence with the correct word.

TAKE NOTES

Vocabulary Builder

Conjunctions Circle the word *whether* in the underlined sentence. It is a conjunction, or a word that connects parts of a sentence. *Whether* shows that someone has a choice to make. Complete the sentence:

After Mrs. Jones gives him money, Roger must choose

whether _____

_____.

Fluency Builder

A writer may use an apostrophe (') to show that one or more letters have been left out of a word. *M'am*, or *ma'am*, is a shortened form of *madam*, which is a polite way of addressing a woman. It is pronounced MAM. Practice reading aloud the statement *Thank you, m'am* the way that Roger would have said it.

Comprehension Builder

Review the prediction that you made on the first page of the story. Was your prediction correct? _____ Explain.

_____

_____

This answer surprises Roger. He is not used to **generous** people. When Mrs. Jones steps behind a screen and he has a chance to run away, he doesn't. Later, Mrs. Jones tells Roger that she was once young and did some bad things, too—things she does not want to talk about. Roger now wants the woman to trust him. <u>He asks her whether she needs some milk at the store.</u> She says she does not, and she offers to make him some cocoa; he accepts. She then heats up some ham and beans and feeds him dinner.

During dinner, Mrs. Jones tells Roger all about her life and her job at a hotel beauty shop. She describes all of the beautiful women who come in and out of the store.

◆ ◆ ◆

When they were finished eating, she got up and said, "Now here, take this ten dollars and buy yourself some blue suede shoes. And next time, do not make the **mistake** of latching onto *my* pocketbook *nor nobody else's*. . . . Goodnight! Behave yourself, boy!" she said, looking into the street as he went down the steps.

The boy wanted to say something other than, "Thank you, m'am," to Mrs. Luella Bates Washington Jones, but although his lips moved, he couldn't even say that as he turned at the foot of the barren stoop[2] and looked up at the large woman in the door. Then she shut the door.

Everyday Words

generous (JEN er uhs) *adj.* kind; willing to give people things or help them
mistake (mi STAYK) *n.* something you do that you later realize was the wrong thing to do

2. **stoop** (stoop) *n.* set of stairs leading up to a house or the flat area at the top of them

AFTER YOU READ

Thinking About the Selection

1. Think about the way that Mrs. Jones treats Roger. What does Roger think Mrs. Jones will do with him? What does Mrs. Jones do and say instead? Write your answers in the chart below.

   | Roger thinks that Mrs. Jones will _____. | → | Instead, Mrs. Jones _____. |

2. During their meal, Mrs. Jones and Roger talk about _____.

TALK ABOUT IT **Make a Judgment** Do you think that Mrs. Jones makes good choices about the way she treats Roger? Discuss you answer with a partner.

I think that Mrs. Jones makes good choices because _____.

I think that Mrs. Jones does not make good choices because _____.

WRITE ABOUT IT **Make Predictions** Mrs. Jones feeds Roger and gives him money. How might Mrs. Jones's behavior affect Roger's future actions? Write a brief paragraph explaining your ideas.

Because of Mrs. Jones, I think that Roger will _____
_____
_____
_____
_____.

Thank You, M'am

VOCABULARY SKILL REVIEW

Silent Letters

Some words have a letter or letters that you do not pronounce. Some silent letters follow general rules, but others do not. To pronounce correctly words that contain silent letters, you may need to memorize the words. Read about the letter combination *gn* in the chart below.

Examples

Letters	*signal*	*gnome, sign*
General Rule	When the letter combination *gn* separates syllables within a word, both *g* and *n* are pronounced.	When the letter combination *gn* occurs at the beginning or ending of a word, *g* is silent, *n* is pronounced.
Pronunciation	*Signal* is pronounced SIG nahl.	*Gnome* is pronounced NOHM. *Sign* is pronounced SYN.

Now You Do It

Read the list of words below. Place a plus sign (+) next to the words in which both the *g* and the *n* are pronounced. Place a minus sign (–) next to the words in which the *g* is silent.

align _____   willingness _____

gnashing _____   ignore _____

foreigner _____   gnaws _____

dignity _____   magnet _____

TALK ABOUT IT **How Does It Sound?** With a partner, say aloud sentences that contain the words from this lesson. Make sure that you pronounce each word correctly.

WRITE ABOUT IT **Make a Crossword Puzzle** With a partner, create a crossword puzzle that contains the words from this lesson. Use a dictionary to find definitions to help you write clues. Then, trade your crossword puzzle with another group. Work with your partner to complete the other group's crossword puzzle, and check your answers.

BEFORE YOU READ: THE STORY-TELLER

Vocabulary

These words are highlighted in the story. Listen to each word. Say it. Then, read the definition and the example sentence.

persistent (per SIS tuhnt) *adj.* When people are **persistent,** they continue to do something, even when others want them to stop.
   The persistent child cried until she got the cookie that she wanted.

inevitable (i NE vuh buh tuhl) *adj.* If something is **inevitable,** it is certain to happen and is impossible to avoid.
   It was inevitable that one of the runners would fall on the wet track.

suppressed (suh PREST) *v.* If you have **suppressed** something, you have stopped yourself from showing your feelings.
   She suppressed the urge to laugh when he suddenly proposed marriage.

Vocabulary Practice

Read the first sentence in each group of three. Then, complete Sentence *a* by substituting another word or phrase that means the same as the underlined vocabulary word. Complete Sentence *b* with your own ideas and words.

1. The boys' persistent arguing annoyed their sister.

    a. The boys' _____ arguing annoyed their sister.

    b. The boys' persistent _____.

2. It was inevitable that she would pass the class.

    a. It was _____ that she would pass the class.

    b. It was inevitable _____.

3. He suppressed the idea that the plan could fail.

    a. He _____ the idea that the plan could fail.

    b. He suppressed _____.

 Getting Ready to Read

A storyteller uses words and actions to help the listener imagine the events of a story. What do you think is needed to make a story enjoyable? Discuss your ideas with a partner.

MAKING CONNECTIONS

The Story-Teller
Saki (H.H. Munro)

Summary A stranger on a train tells a story that entertains three children. The story's ending makes the children's aunt very angry. It goes against all of her lectures about proper behavior.

Writing About the Big Question

Can all conflicts be resolved? In "The Story-Teller," three bored children on a train are entertained by an unusual fairy tale told by an unlikely fellow passenger. Complete this sentence:

One way to amuse a child is _____.

Note-taking Guide
Use the chart to recall the events of the story.

Problem	The children will not be quiet on the trip.
Event	
Event	
Event	
Outcome	

AFTER YOU READ

Thinking About the Selection

1. Think about why the aunt and the stranger tell the stories. How are their reasons the same? How are their reasons different? Complete the sentences in the Venn diagram below.

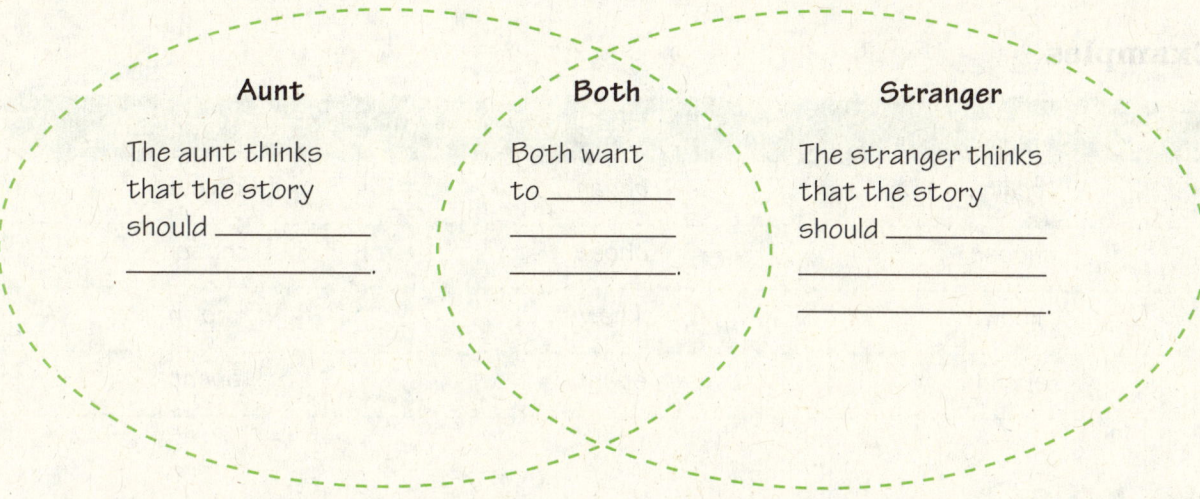

Aunt
The aunt thinks that the story should _____ _____.

Both
Both want to _____ _____.

Stranger
The stranger thinks that the story should _____ _____ _____.

2. After the aunt tells her story, the stranger tells her that _____ _____.

TALK ABOUT IT **Evaluate the Story** Did you like the stranger's story? Discuss your answer with a partner.

I liked the stranger's story because _____.

I did not like the stranger's story because _____.

WRITE ABOUT IT **Do You Agree?** Do you agree with the aunt that the stranger's story is "improper" for children? Explain your answer.

I [**agree** or **disagree**] with the aunt because _____
_____
_____
_____.

The Story-Teller 137

VOCABULARY SKILL REVIEW

Irregular Verbs

Verbs with past and past participle forms that do not follow a predictable pattern are irregular verbs. To form the past tense and past participle of a regular verb, add *d* or *ed* to the base form. However, the past and past participle forms of an irregular verb will follow a different pattern. It is helpful to memorize the forms of common irregular verbs.

Examples

Present	Past	Past Participle
begin	began	begun
choose	chose	chosen
know	knew	known
spend	spent	spent

Now You Do It

In the sentences on the left, replace the underlined verb in parentheses with its past tense form. In the sentences on the right, replace the underlined verb with the past participle form.

I (choose) _____ the red coat.

James has (know) _____ my new neighbor for many years.

We (begin) _____ at five o'clock.

Lily and I have (spend) _____ all of our money.

TALK ABOUT IT **Say Aloud Sentences** With a partner, take turns saying aloud sentences that use the past and past participle forms of each verb listed in the chart above.

WRITE ABOUT IT **Now and Then** Write a short paragraph in which you use all three tenses of the word *choose*. You might describe a time when you had to *choose* between two options. Explain why you *chose* one option, and tell whether you think you *have chosen* wisely.

Advertisements

About Advertisements

Advertisements are paid messages. Companies use advertising to persuade customers to buy products or services. Advertisers use appeals to do this. An appeal is a technique used to make a product attractive or interesting. Advertisers use two kinds of appeals:

- **Rational appeals** are based on facts. These ads may show how different products compare. They may show product features. Sometimes these appeals talk about price.
- **Emotional appeals** are based on feelings. Such appeals suggest that customers will be happier, more respected, or more popular if they buy a certain product.

Reading Skill

You can **evaluate persuasive appeals** by determining whether they are rational appeals or emotional appeals. Recognizing the difference can help you understand how an advertisement works. Recognize and ignore an emotional appeal because it is not based on facts. Use facts to help make up your mind.

Study the chart below. It shows some common emotional appeals that advertisers and writers use. Question whether you believe these arguments.

Device	Example	Explanation
Bandwagon appeal	Everyone loves Muncheez!	Words like *everyone* appeal to people's desire to belong.
Loaded language	Muncheez is incredibly delicious.	*Incredibly* and *delicious* are claims that cannot be proved.
Testimonials	Tina Idol says Muncheez gives her energy.	Just because a celebrity or "expert" says it, it does not mean the claim is true.
Generalization	Muncheez is not only the best, it's the healthiest.	Claims that are too broad or vague cannot be proved.

This illustration implies that the advertiser brings cities closer together—a claim that cannot be proved.

HARRISBURGPHILADELPHIANEWYORK

Bringing your favorite places closer.

AMTRAK

Loaded words such as *relaxed* and *refreshed* imply that the advertiser's train service can improve passengers' well-being.

Arrive at your destination relaxed and refreshed. Amtrak offers safe, comfortable, affordable daily service from Harrisburg to Philadelphia and New York with 12 local stops between Harrisburg and Philadelphia. Choose from 10 weekday or 5 weekend departures, from Harrisburg or returning. Daily departures from Harrisburg to Pittsburgh, Chicago and most major cities. Ask about our discounts for children 2-15, seniors, students, commuters, AAA members, disabled travelers and government employees.

Call for details

AFTER YOU READ

Thinking About the Advertisement

1. The ad describes advantages of traveling by train. What words or phrases in the ad identify the advantages?
   _____
   _____

2. The most important purpose of the advertisement is to sell train tickets. What is a secondary, or less important, purpose?
   _____
   _____

TALK ABOUT IT Reading Skill

3. To what emotions does the advertisement appeal?
   _____
   _____

4. On what part of train travel does the ad focus most?
   _____
   _____

WRITE ABOUT IT Timed Writing: Evaluation (20 minutes)

Evaluate the persuasive appeals used in this ad. Be sure to answer the following questions in your evaluation.

- What kinds of appeals does the ad make?
   _____
   _____

- What words or pictures does the ad use to persuade customers to travel by train?
   _____
   _____

- Would you be persuaded by the ad to travel by train?
   _____
   _____

UNIT VOCABULARY REVIEW

Word Bank

argument	compromise	injury
insecurity	interact	irritate
mislead	negotiate	oppose
reaction	solution	stalemate
victorious	viewpoint	violence

A. **Sentence Completion** Match each sentence starter to the correct completion. Follow the language of each sentence so that all sentences make sense. The first two have been completed for you.

An **argument**	someone has little confidence.
Insecurity usually means that	is to deceive him or her.
To **mislead** someone	you fight against it.
A **reaction** is	you have been hurt.
A **victorious** person	they accept less than they wanted.
When people **compromise,**	is to work together.
To **interact**	a person looks at something.
To **negotiate**	is to cause someone to feel annoyed.
A **solution**	is an answer.
A **viewpoint** is the way	is a disagreement.
When you suffer an **injury,**	is to try to come to an agreement.
To **irritate** someone	in which no one can take further action.
When you **oppose** something,	an act of physical force.
A **stalemate** is a situation	is sometimes called a *winner*.
An act of **violence** can be	a response to an action.

B. **Word Sorting** Fill in the chart below with the words from the word bank on the previous page. Write words that are nouns in the column labeled Nouns, words that are verbs in the column labeled Verbs, and words that are adjectives in the column labeled Adjectives. If a word fits in more than one column, write it in all columns that apply.

Nouns	Verbs	Adjectives

TALK ABOUT IT **When Is It Okay?** People compromise every day. When two people compromise, each person gives a little so that both have something. Talk with a partner about times when compromise is helpful and times when it may be wrong. Use the sentence starters to help you.

I think it is okay to compromise when _____.

I think it is wrong to compromise when _____.

WRITE ABOUT IT **What Did You Do?** Write a journal entry about a time when you had to compromise with someone in order to get something done. Was an argument involved? Was someone misled? What were the viewpoints involved, and how did you reach a compromise? Use these questions and at least six words from the word bank to describe your experience.

_____

_____

_____

_____

Unit Vocabulary Review 143

UNIT 3
EXPLORING TYPES OF NONFICTION

Making Tracks on Mars: A Journal Based on a Blog

Essays and articles are types of nonfiction. These types of nonfiction discuss real people, events, places, and ideas. You can explore these pieces to:

- learn about the lives of others
- find important information
- reflect on new ideas
- look at arguments about important issues

Organization is the way a writer arranges information in a piece of nonfiction. The chart below contains different types of organization. Many pieces of nonfiction use a combination of these types of organization. It depends on the author's reasons for writing.

Types of Organization	
Organization	Characteristics
Chronological Organization	presents details in time order—from first to last—or sometimes from last to first
Comparison-and-Contrast Organization	shows the ways in which two or more subjects are similar and different
Cause-and-Effect Organization	shows the relationship among events
Problem-and-Solution Organization	identifies a problem and then proposes a solution

Author's tone is the writer's attitude toward his or her audience and subject. This tone can often be described by a single adjective, such as: *formal* or *informal*, *serious* or *playful*, *friendly* or *cold*.

144 English Learner's Notebook

EXPLORING TYPES OF NONFICTION

Voice is a writer's way of "speaking" in his or her writing. One writer could write a piece in one voice. Then, he or she could write in a different voice in another work. Voice may also represent a characteristic literary personality. Voice can be based on

- word choice
- tone
- sound devices
- pace
- grammatical structure

Here are the most common types of nonfiction writing:

- **Letters:** written texts addressed to a certain person or organization
- **Memoirs and journals:** personal thoughts and reflections
- **Web logs** (also known as "blogs"): journals posted and often updated for an online audience
- **Biography:** a life story written by another person
- **Autobiography:** a writer's account of his or her own life
- **Media accounts:** nonfiction works written for newspapers, magazines, television, or radio

Essays and **articles** are short nonfiction works about a certain subject. They may follow the structure of these types of writing:

- **Persuasive writing:** convinces the reader that he or she should have a certain opinion or take a certain action
- **Expository writing:** presents facts or explains a process
- **Narrative writing:** tells the story of real-life experiences
- **Reflective writing:** looks at an experience and has the writer's thoughts about the event's importance

UNIT 3

BEFORE YOU READ: MAKING TRACKS ON MARS: A JOURNAL BASED ON A BLOG

Vocabulary

These words are underlined in the selection. Listen to each word. Say it. Then, read the definition and the example sentence.

task (TASK) *n.* A **task** is a job that must be done.
Miranda's next task was to wash the windows.

data (DAY tuh) *n.* **Data** are facts or other information.
For homework, the students collected data about tornados.

crater (KRAY ter) *n.* A **crater** is a round hole in the ground that is formed by something that has fallen or by an explosion.
The scientists studied a large crater on the moon's surface.

Vocabulary Practice

Read the first sentence in each group of three. Then, complete Sentence *a* by substituting another word or phrase that means the same as the underlined vocabulary word. Complete Sentence *b* with your own ideas and words.

1. My least favorite task is cleaning the fish tank.

    a. My least favorite _____ is cleaning the fish tank.

    b. My least favorite task _____.

2. Charlie collected data for his research paper.

    a. Charlie collected _____ for his research paper.

    b. Charlie collected data _____.

3. A large rock formed the crater near the volcano.

    a. A large rock formed the _____ near the volcano.

    b. A large rock formed the crater _____.

Getting Ready to Read

Scientists sent the rovers *Spirit* and *Opportunity* to Mars to find out whether water has ever existed on the planet. Evidence of water could mean that life might have existed on Mars at one time. Do you think that life might have existed on Mars? Do you think that life could exist on Mars in the future? Discuss your ideas with a partner.

MAKING CONNECTIONS

Making Tracks on Mars: A Journal Based on a Blog
Andrew Mishkin

Summary Andrew Mishkin talks about the landing of the rover, *Spirit*, on Mars. The rover explores the planet. It experiences some problems. Mishkin describes his excitement and worry. He also talks about another Mars rover, *Opportunity*. He describes the pictures it takes of Mars.

Note-taking Guide
Use the chart to recall the main events of Mishkin's journal.

Opportunity lands on Mars. Mishkin describes the pictures it takes.

Making Tracks on Mars: A Journal Based on a Blog   147

TAKE NOTES

Vocabulary Builder

Multiple-Meaning Words The verb *opens* can mean "starts or begins." It can also mean "allows entry to something or someplace." What does *opens* mean in the first paragraph?

_____

Fluency Builder

Read the bracketed passage silently, and notice the different feelings described. Then, take turns with a partner reading the passage aloud.

Comprehension Builder

Predict what the two rovers will help scientists learn about Mars. Write your predictions on the lines below.

_____
_____
_____

Making Tracks on Mars: A Journal Based on a Blog
Andrew Mishkin

◆ ◆ ◆

The journal opens with the question of whether life ever existed on Mars. We know that water is needed for life as we know it. Mars appears to have no water, but what about in the past? Two robotic explorers are scheduled to land on the planet soon. In six days, *Spirit* will arrive there. Three weeks later, *Opportunity* will. The author talks about a British spacecraft that tried to land on Mars five days earlier but has sent back no signals. The author hopes that *Spirit* lands smoothly. Saturday, January 3, 2004, is landing day.

◆ ◆ ◆

Spirit's lander must be hitting the atmosphere, a falling **meteor** blazing in the Martian sky. We'd named the next moments "the six minutes of terror." I listened to the reports on the voice network. All the way down, radio signals from the spacecraft told us "so far so good." Then, immediately after the lander hit the ground, contact was lost. Everyone tensed up. Time dragged. There was only silence from Mars.

Ten minutes later, we got another signal. *Spirit* had survived! The engineers and scientists in mission control were screaming, cheering, thrusting their fists in the air. We were on Mars!

◆ ◆ ◆

Everyday Words

blog (BLAHG) *n.* short for Web log; a journal that is published on the Internet
meteor (MEE tee er) *n.* a small piece of rock or metal that produces a bright buring line in the sky

148 English Learner's Notebook

© Pearson Education

Pictures start arriving from *Spirit* within two hours. The pictures are clear. They show the view through *Spirit's* eyes from the landing site. The next entry is January 11, 2004. The engineers are working on Mars time. The next task is to send a signal commanding *Spirit* to drive around and take some pictures.

◆ ◆ ◆

[The Mars day (called a "sol") is just a bit longer than an Earth day, at twenty-four hours and thirty-nine and a half minutes. Since the rover is solar powered, and wakes with the sun, its activities are tied to the Martian day. And so are the work shifts of our operations team on Earth. Part of the team works the Martian day, interacting with the spacecraft, sending commands, and analyzing the results. But those of us who build new commands for the rover work the Martian night, while the rover sleeps.]

◆ ◆ ◆

It is difficult for the engineers to keep track of time. Because the rover wakes up about forty Earth minutes later each day, so do the engineers. By January 15, the author is getting Mars time and Earth time mixed up.

◆ ◆ ◆

My team delivered the commands for sol 12—drive off day—but nobody went home. This would be *Spirit's* most dangerous day since landing. There was a small chance the rover could tip over or get stuck as it rolled off the lander platform onto the dust of Mars. When the time came, the Flight Director played the theme from "Rawhide"—"rollin', rollin', rollin'…"[1]—and everyone crowded into mission control cheered and applauded. The command to drive shot through space.

◆ ◆ ◆

1. **"Rawhide"** popular 1960s television show about cattle drivers in the American West during the 1860s. Its theme song was also extremely popular.

TAKE NOTES

Fluency Builder

Commas (,) tell readers where to pause briefly. Circle all of the commas in the bracketed paragraph. Then, read the paragraph aloud, making sure that you pause slightly at each comma.

Vocabulary Builder

Idioms The idiom *to keep track of* means "to remember information about." Complete the following sentence:

It is difficult for the scientists *to keep track of* time because

_____

_____.

Vocabulary Builder

Suffixes The suffix *-ous* means "full of." The noun *danger* means "someone or something that could harm someone." The adjective *dangerous* means "full of risk." Why is sol 12 the most *dangerous* day for *Spirit*?

Sol 12 was *dangerous* for *Spirit* because *Spirit* could _____

_____

_____.

TAKE NOTES

Vocabulary Builder

Idioms *Go wild* is an idiom that means "suddenly become very active and noisy because of excitement." Why do the engineers in the story *go wild*?

The engineers *go wild* because _____
_____.

Vocabulary Builder

Adjectives Read the underlined sentence. The adjective *garbled* is a form of the verb *garble*. *Garbled* means "confusing and difficult to understand." Complete the following sentence:

The engineers received *garbled* _____.

Vocabulary Builder

Multiple-Meaning Words The word *bowl* can mean "a round, open container that holds food or liquid." It can also mean "a round dip on the land's surface." What kind of *bowl* does the author refer to in the bracketed paragraph?

_____
_____

Even though they have done their jobs, the engineers continue to worry about what might go wrong. On January 15, twelve days after the landing, they get a signal from *Spirit*. Images begin to appear. They see wheel tracks in the Martian soil. Knowing that *Spirit* has obeyed the command to move, the engineers go wild with applause and joy. By January 22, the rover stops responding. The engineers try for days to fix the problem. Finally, they start receiving data from Spirit. It is garbled, but now they have something to work with.

Meanwhile, *Opportunity*, the second rover, has been approaching Mars. It lands safely and begins to take photos.

◆ ◆ ◆

Opportunity's first photos were amazing, even for Mars. It looks like we rolled to a stop at the bottom of a bowl—actually a small crater. The soil is a grayish red, except where we've disturbed it with our airbags; there it looks like a deep pure red.

◆ ◆ ◆

Opportunity also sends back pictures of a rock outcropping. This is unlike anything ever seen on Mars before. One scientist in mission control says, "Jackpot!"

AFTER YOU READ

Thinking About the Selection

1. Complete the sentences in the chart below by providing the information gathered by the rovers *Spirit* and *Opportunity*.

Spirit	Opportunity
Spirit's first pictures show	Opportunity's first photos show
On January 15, the images from *Spirit* show	*Opportunity* also sends pictures of a

2. As *Spirit* was landing on Mars, the scientists tensed up because _____.

TALK ABOUT IT **Discuss the Purpose** Discuss with a partner the reasons that scientists sent the rovers to Mars.

Scientists hoped to find _____.

They also wanted to collect _____.

WRITE ABOUT IT **Why Would You?** Suppose that your job is to operate rovers on Mars. What would your purpose be for exploring the planet? What information would you hope to find? Write a paragraph explaining your answers.

My purpose for exploring Mars would be _____

_____

_____.

VOCABULARY SKILL REVIEW

Prefixes

A prefix is a word part added to the beginning of a base word. A prefix changes the meaning of the base word. When added to the beginning of an adjective, the prefix *un-* means "not." At the beginning of a verb, *un-* means "to do the reverse or opposite."

Examples

un + happy = unhappy	The new word *unhappy* means "not happy" or "sad."
un + wrap = unwrap	The new word *unwrap* means "to do the opposite of wrap" or "to remove the cover."

Now You Do It

Make new words by adding the prefix *un-* to each word below. Write a definition for each new word.

_____ safe _____

_____ sure _____

_____ clear _____

_____ fold _____

_____ mask _____

TALK ABOUT IT **Moving Day** With a partner, talk about actions students would take to help a teacher move supplies into a new classroom. Then, list at least three words beginning with *un-* that describe some of these actions.

WRITE ABOUT IT **Step By Step** Using the three words that you listed above, write a paragraph that describes a plan students might follow when helping a teacher move supplies into a new classroom.

_____

_____

_____

English Learner's Notebook

RESEARCH THE AUTHOR

Illustrated Report

Prepare an **illustrated report** about Andrew Mishkin and the Mars mission. Use the following tips to create your report.

- Search the Internet or the library for information on Andrew Mishkin.

  What I learned about Andrew Mishkin: _____
  _____
  _____
  _____

- Search the Internet or the library for information on the Mars mission.

  What I learned about the goals of the mission: _____
  _____
  _____
  _____

  What I learned about the results of the exploration: _____
  _____
  _____
  _____
  _____

- Watch the video interview with Andrew Mishkin. Add what you learn from the video to what you have already learned about the author.

  Additional information about the author: _____
  _____
  _____
  _____

  Use your notes to write your illustrated report.

UNIT 3

BEFORE YOU READ: BASEBALL

Vocabulary

These words are underlined in the selection. Listen to each word. Say it. Then, read the definition and the example sentence.

rotate (ROH tayt) *v.* To **rotate** means to switch turns or to revolve.
One player will rotate out when a substitute comes in.

option (AHP shuhn) *n.* An **option** is a choice.
Students have the option of doing a written or an oral report.

evaded (i VAYD id) *v.* When something is **evaded,** it is avoided by using craftiness or cleverness.
Thanks to my speediness, I evaded the bully.

Vocabulary Practice

Read the first sentence in each group of three. Then, complete Sentence *a* by substituting another word or phrase that means the same as the underlined vocabulary word. Complete Sentence *b* with your own ideas and words.

1. Volleyball players rotate positions before the other team hits the ball over the net.

   a. Volleyball players _____ positions before the other team hits the ball over the net.

   b. Volleyball players rotate _____.

2. Mom gave me the option of studying or going to bed early.

   a. Mom gave me the _____ of studying or going to bed early.

   b. Mom gave me the option _____.

3. The fish snatched the bait but evaded my fishing hook.

   a. The fish snatched the bait but _____ my fishing hook.

   b. The fish snatched the bait but evaded _____.

Getting Ready to Read

Baseball, basketball, and soccer are team sports. Team members need to work together to win a game. Golf and tennis are individual sports. People compete on their own to win games. Would you prefer to play for a team or as an individual? Discuss your thoughts with a partner.

MAKING CONNECTIONS

Baseball
Lionel G. García

Summary The author shares a memory from his childhood in this story. He describes the new rules of baseball that he and his childhood friends invented. García presents a snapshot into the world of a young Catholic boy through this story.

 Writing About the Big Question

How much information is enough? In "Baseball," the author shows how much fun he and his friends had playing their own version of baseball as children. Complete this sentence:

In order to reveal what the world looks like from a child's perspective, a writer can include information such as _____

_____.

Note-taking Guide
García explains how he used to play baseball in his neighborhood. Use this chart to describe the role of each player in the game.

Catcher	Batter	Pitcher	Bases	Outfielders

Baseball 155

TAKE NOTES

Vocabulary Builder

Action Verbs Action verbs describe what the subject of the sentence does. Circle the action verbs in the bracketed paragraph.

Comprehension Builder

Summarize the rules that García and his friends use to play baseball.

_____
_____
_____
_____
_____

Cultural Understanding

The underlined phrase refers to a fly ball. A *fly ball* is a ball that is hit off the bat and goes very high but is easy for a player in the field to catch. Catching a fly ball is one way to get an out in baseball.

Baseball
Lionel G. García

[We loved to play baseball. We would take the old mesquite[1] stick and the old ball across the street to the parochial[2] school grounds to play a game. Father Zavala enjoyed watching us. We could hear him laugh mightily from the screened porch at the rear of the rectory[3] where he sat.]

The way we played baseball was to rotate positions after every out. First base, the only base we used, was located where one would normally find second base. This made the batter have to run past the pitcher and a long way to the first baseman, increasing the odds of getting thrown out. The pitcher stood in line with the batter, and with first base, and could stand as close or as far from the batter as he or she wanted. Aside from the pitcher, the batter and the first baseman, we had a catcher. All the rest of us would stand in the outfield. After an out, the catcher would come up to bat. The pitcher took the position of catcher, and the first baseman moved up to be the pitcher. Those in the outfield were left to their own **devices**. I don't remember ever getting to bat.

◆ ◆ ◆

Another rule of the children's game was that the player who caught a ball on the fly would become the next batter. Also, first base was wherever Matías, Juan, or Cota tossed a stone. The size of the stone was more important than how far it fell from

Everyday Words
devices (di VYS iz) *n.* techniques or means for working things out

1. **mesquite** (me SKEET) *n.* thorny shrub of North America.
2. **parochial** (puh ROH kee uhl) *adj.* supported by a church.
3. **rectory** (REK tuhr ee) *n.* residence for priests.

home plate. First base was sometimes hard to find as it started to get dark.

♦ ♦ ♦

When the batter hit the ball in the air and it was caught that was an out. So far so good. But if the ball hit the ground, the fielder had two choices. One, in keeping with the **standard** rules of the game, the ball could be thrown to the first baseman and, if caught before the batter arrived at the base, that was an out. But the second, more interesting <u>option</u> allowed the fielder, ball in hand, to take <u>off</u> running after the batter. When close enough, the fielder would throw the ball at the batter. If the batter was hit before reaching first base, the batter was out. But if the batter <u>evaded</u> being hit with the ball, he or she could <u>either</u> run to first base or run back to home plate. All the while, everyone was chasing the batter, picking up the ball and throwing it at him or her. To complicate matters, on the way to home plate the batter had the choice of running anywhere possible to avoid getting hit.

♦ ♦ ♦

Sometimes the batters hid behind trees until they could reach home plate. Sometimes they ran several blocks toward town. In one game, the children ended up across town. They cornered the batter, held him down, and hit him with the ball. The tired players all fell down laughing in a pile. The men in town watched these unusual games, but they did not understand them.

♦ ♦ ♦

It was the only kind of baseball game Father Zavala had ever seen. What a wonderful game it must have been for him to see us hit the ball,

TAKE NOTES

Fluency Builder
Read aloud the bracketed paragraph. As you read, pay attention to the punctuation and pause when appropriate.

Vocabulary Builder

Idioms The idiom *take off* means "leave or move in a hurry." Why might a fielder *take off*?

A fielder might *take off* to _____
_____
_____.

Vocabulary Builder

Multiple-Meaning Words The word *blocks* has more than one meaning. *Blocks* can refer to the solid pieces of material used for building, such as wood or stone. They can also refer to the distance along one side of a city square. What does *blocks* refer to in the second paragraph on this page?

_____
_____

Everyday Words
standard (STAN derd) *adj.* typical, ordinary

Baseball 157

TAKE NOTES

Vocabulary Builder

Idioms Read the underlined phrase. *Run for our lives* is an expression that means the boys were running very fast. Complete the following sentence.

After the batter touches first base, the fielders *run for their lives* to _____

_____

_____.

Comprehension Builder

Why does García's uncle say that the children are wasting a good baseball?

_____

_____

_____

158 English Learner's Notebook

---

run to a rock, then run for our lives down the street. He loved the game, shouting from the screened porch at us, pushing us on. And then all of a sudden we were gone, running after the batter. What a game! In what enormous stadium would it be played to allow such freedom over such an **expanse** of ground.

◆ ◆ ◆

García's Uncle Adolfo had been a major league pitcher. He had given the ball to the children. When he saw how the children played the sport, he said that they were wasting a good baseball.

Everyday Words

expanse (ik spans) *n.* a large area

AFTER YOU READ

Thinking About the Selection

1. The children's baseball rules differ from the standard rules of baseball. Complete the chart to tell three of the children's rules.

Children's Baseball Rules
1. After each out, the players _____.
2. A player who caught a fly ball would become _____.
3. To avoid gettng hit out by the baseball, the runner was allowed to _____.

2. It was easy for the batter to be thrown out in García's version of the game because _____.

TALK ABOUT IT **Different Reactions** Discuss with a partner the way that Father Zavala and Uncle Adolfo react differently when they watch the children play baseball.

Father Zavala _____.

Uncle Adolfo _____.

WRITE ABOUT IT **Welcome, Sports Fans!** Suppose that you are announcing over the radio a baseball game played by García and his friends. Write a script that tells about the game's highlights and explains what you think about the new rules. Use the following sentence starter.

Welcome, sports fans! First to bat is _____
_____
_____.

Baseball 159

VOCABULARY SKILL REVIEW

Idioms

An idiom is a phrase with a special meaning that goes beyond the literal meanings, or definitions, of the phrase. This special meaning comes from the context in which the idiom is spoken.

Examples

Idiom	Literal Meaning	Special Meaning
water underneath the bridge	When you cross a bridge, you cross the water that is underneath and pay no more attention to it.	the problem is over and there's no point bringing it back up
a fish out of water	A fish out of water is somewhere that it does not belong.	out of place
water off a duck's back	Ducks swim in water and are used to being wet.	have no effect
skating on thin ice	Skating on thin ice is dangerous because a person could fall through the ice.	heading for trouble

Now You Do It

Write a sentence for each idiom that appears in the chart above.

1. water underneath the bridge

2. a fish out of water

3. water off a duck's back

4. skating on thin ice

TALK ABOUT IT — **Have a Conversation** Have a conversation with a partner in which you use the four idioms that appear in the chart above.

WRITE ABOUT IT — **Write a Myth** Write a myth that explains how one of the idioms from the lesson came into being.

BEFORE YOU READ: FROM HARRIET TUBMAN: CONDUCTOR ON THE UNDERGROUND RAILROAD

UNIT 3

Vocabulary

These words are highlighted in the selection. Listen to each word. Say it. Then, read the definition and the example sentence.

invariably (in VEHR ee uh blee) *adv.* Something that occurs **invariably** happens almost all the time.
  People invariably mistake Jon for his twin brother.

dispel (di SPEL) *v.* To **dispel** means to cause something to go away.
  The facts will dispel any doubts about his innocence.

bleak (BLEEK) *adj.* Something described as **bleak** is gloomy, not cheerful, and not promising.
  The bleak landscape stretched before them like a dingy, gray blanket.

Vocabulary Practice

Read the first sentence in each group of three. Then, complete Sentence *a* by substituting another word or phrase that means the same as the underlined vocabulary word. Complete Sentence *b* with your own ideas and words.

1. For lunch, Jamie invariably eats a sandwich.

   a. For lunch, Jamie _____ eats a sandwich.

   b. For lunch, Jamie invariably _____.

2. He tried to dispel the rumor that he was moving.

   a. He tried to _____ the rumor that he was moving.

   b. He tried to dispel _____.

3. The frozen countryside was bleak and deserted.

   a. The frozen countryside was _____ and deserted.

   b. _____ was bleak and deserted.

Getting Ready to Read

The Underground Railroad was a network of people who helped people escape from slavery. The people who worked on the Underground Railroad risked their lives to free enslaved people. Do people always have to take risks to change a situation? Can people change a situation without taking risks? Discuss your ideas with a partner.

MAKING CONNECTIONS

from Harriet Tubman: Conductor on the Underground Railroad
Ann Petry

Summary Harriet Tubman led a group of enslaved persons from Maryland to freedom in Canada. The trip was cold and difficult. Tubman worked hard to keep them going. She said that people would help them along the way.

Writing About the Big Question

How much information is enough? In the excerpt from "Harriet Tubman: Conductor on the Underground Railroad," eleven fugitive slaves are led to freedom by Harriet Tubman and her helpers in the Underground Railroad. Complete this sentence:

  It is important to learn about historical figures who challenged

slavey because _____.

Note-taking Guide
Use this chart to help you recall the plans Harriet Tubman made.

How did Tubman let slaves know that she was in the area?	
How did Tubman let the slaves know when to leave?	
Whom did Tubman arrange to stay with along the journey?	
Where did Tubman plan for the people to stay when they got to Canada?	

AFTER YOU READ

Thinking About the Selection

1. One of the people escaping slavery said that he wanted to return to the plantation. What did Tubman do after she heard this statement? Why did Tubman believe that she must act in this way? Complete the sentences in the chart below.

Tubman responded by	Tubman acted in this way because
_____	_____
_____	_____
_____.	_____.

2. Tubman told the fugitives stories because _____
_____.

TALK ABOUT IT **A Good Leader** Why was Harriet Tubman a good leader? Discuss your thoughts with a partner.

Harriet Tubman was a good leader because _____.

WRITE ABOUT IT **What About Today?** Do you think that Harriet Tubman would be a good leader today? Explain your answer.

I think that Harriet Tubman _____
_____
_____
_____
_____
_____.

from Harriet Tubman: Conductor on the Underground Railroad

VOCABULARY SKILL REVIEW

Antonyms

An antonym is a word that means the opposite of another word. Study the examples below.

Examples *Major* is an adjective that means "important."
Its antonym is the adjective *minor.*
Minor means "of lesser importance."

Now You Do It

Complete the chart below by writing an example sentence for the meaning of the words *major* and *minor*.

Word	Part of Speech	Meaning	Example Sentence
major	adjective	important	
minor	adjective	of lesser importance	

TALK ABOUT IT **Major or Minor Interests?** With a partner, discuss three major interests and three minor interests of people your age.

WRITE ABOUT IT **Write a Dialogue** Use the information you listed above to write a dialogue between two students. In the dialogue, have the students compare and contrast at least one major and one minor interest.

_____
_____
_____
_____
_____

BEFORE YOU READ: FROM ALWAYS TO REMEMBER: THE VISION OF MAYA YING LIN

Vocabulary

These words are underlined in the selection. Listen to each word. Say it. Then, read the definition and the example sentence.

opposed (uh POHZD) *v.* Someone is **opposed** to an idea when he or she disagrees with it.
   The voters opposed the new tax laws.

harmony (HAR muh nee) *n.* **Harmony** is a situation in which things or people are at peace or in agreement with one another.
   It is possible for dogs and cats to live in harmony.

tribute (TRIB yoot) *n.* A **tribute** is something that is said, done, or given to show respect for someone or something.
   The city planted trees as a tribute to the people who helped build the park.

Vocabulary Practice

Read the first sentence in each group of three. Then, complete Sentence *a* by substituting another word or phrase that means the same as the underlined vocabulary word. Complete Sentence *b* with your own ideas and words.

1. Molly opposed the unfair rules.

   a. Molly _____ the unfair rules.

   b. Molly opposed _____.

2. The new building was in harmony with the rest of the park.

   a. The new building was in _____ with the rest of the park.

   b. The new building was in harmony _____.

3. We sang a song in tribute of our grandmother.

   a. We sang a song in _____ of our grandmother.

   b. We sang a song in tribute _____.

 **Getting Ready to Read**

Visitors to Washington, D.C., can see memorials honoring the soldiers who fought in wars that involved the United States. What characteristics do you think a memorial honoring soldiers should have? Discuss your ideas with a partner.

MAKING CONNECTIONS

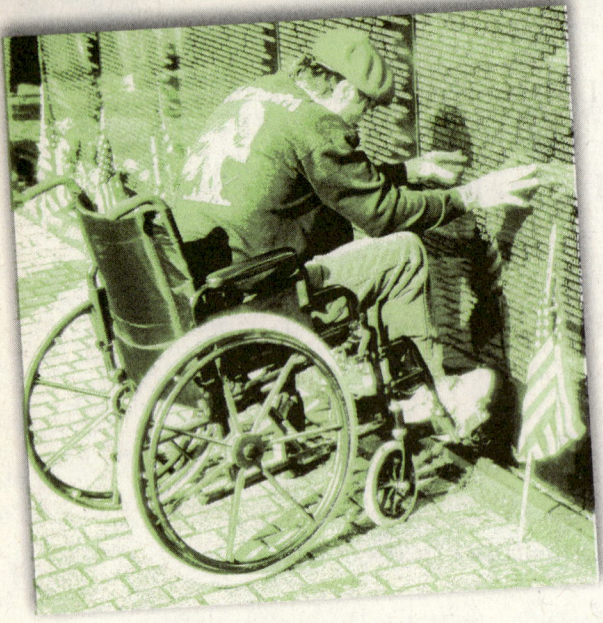

from Always to Remember: The Vision of Maya Ying Lin
Brent Ashabranner

Summary In the early 1980s, more than 2,500 people entered a competition to design a memorial. The men and women who lost their lives in the Vietnam War would be honored by the memorial. This essay describes the competition. It also describes the college student who wins.

 Writing About the Big Question

How much information is enough? In "Always to Remember," the story of the Vietnam Veterans Memorial highlights the need to learn about and remember the past. Complete these sentences:

Remembering events from our history can be valuable because

_____.

Note-taking Guide
Use this chart to record details about the winning design for the Vietnam Veterans Memorial.

```
                    Vietnam Veterans
                       Memorial
   ┌──────────────┐      │      ┌──────────────┐
   │   What is    │      │      │  What does   │
   │ the memorial?│      │      │the memorial  │
   │              │      │      │  look like?  │
   └──────────────┘      │      └──────────────┘
                 ┌───────────────┐
                 │ Who designed  │
                 │ the memorial? │
                 │               │
                 │ Maya Ying Lin │
                 └───────────────┘
```

166 English Learner's Notebook

from Always To Remember: The Vision of Maya Ying Lin
Brent Ashabranner

This nonfiction selection tells the true story of how a young college student named Maya Lin came to design the Vietnam Veterans Memorial in Washington, D.C.

◆ ◆ ◆

In the 1960s and 1970s, the United States was involved in a war in Vietnam. Because many people opposed the war, Vietnam veterans were not honored as veterans of other wars had been. Jan Scruggs, a Vietnam veteran, thought that the 58,000 U.S. servicemen and women killed or reported missing in Vietnam should be honored with a memorial.

◆ ◆ ◆

Scruggs got two lawyers named Robert Doubek and John Wheeler to help him get support for building a memorial. In 1980, Congress agreed that a memorial should be built.

◆ ◆ ◆

What would the memorial be? What should it look like? Who would design it? Scruggs, Doubek, and Wheeler didn't know, but they were determined that the memorial should help bring closer together a nation still bitterly divided by the Vietnam War.

◆ ◆ ◆

They did not want the memorial to glorify war or to argue for peace. They wanted a memorial that did not provoke arguments as it honored the dead. How could they find the best idea for the kind of memorial they wanted?

◆ ◆ ◆

The answer, they decided, was to hold a national design competition open to all Americans.

◆ ◆ ◆

TAKE NOTES

Cultural Understanding

Other memorials in Washington, D.C., include the Korean War Veterans Memorial, the World War I Memorial, and the World War II Memorial. Monuments also honor Presidents George Washington, Thomas Jefferson, Abraham Lincoln, and Franklin D. Roosevelt.

Vocabulary Builder

Helping Verbs A helping verb comes before the main verb. Helping verbs include forms of the verbs *be, have,* and *do.* They also include words such as *should, could, would,* and *might.* Circle the helping verbs in the bracketed paragraph.

Comprehension Builder

Predict how Scruggs, Doubek, and Wheeler decide how they will choose what the Vietnam Memorial will be. Explain your prediction.

_____
_____
_____
_____
_____

TAKE NOTES

Vocabulary Builder

Multiple-Meaning Words The word *mall* has more than one meaning. It can be a large building that has shops and restaurants. It can also be an area where people may walk. What kind of *mall* is the part of Washington, D.C., that has the Washington Monument and the Lincoln Memorial?

_____
_____

Fluency Builder

Semicolons (;) indicate a pause similar to the pause for a period. Read the bracketed paragraph aloud, pausing at each semicolon.

Comprehension Builder

Summarize the standards the judges set for the winning design for the memorial.

_____
_____
_____

The winner of the competition would receive a $20,000 prize. More important, the winner would have the honor of being part of American history. The memorial would be built in Washington, D.C., between the Washington Monument and the Lincoln Memorial. This part of the city is called the Mall.

More than 5,000 Americans asked for the booklet that told the rules of the competition. Many of them were well-known architects and sculptors. The booklet told what kind of memorial would win the competition.

◆ ◆ ◆

[The memorial could not make a political statement about the war; it must contain the names of all persons killed or missing in action in the war; it must be in <u>harmony</u> with its location on the Mall.]

◆ ◆ ◆

More than one thousand designs were submitted for the competition. Eight judges had to decide which design best met the standards for winning: The memorial had to honor the memory of the soldiers who had died in the war. It had to blend in with the other monuments nearby. It had to be an important work of art. It also had to be practical to build and take care of.

The designs were displayed in an airplane hangar. They were labeled by number, instead of showing the designer's name, so that the judges could be objective. On May 1, 1981, the judges chose the winner and praised the winning design.

◆ ◆ ◆

This memorial, with its wall of names, becomes a place of quiet reflection, and a tribute to those who served their nation in difficult times. All who come here can find it a place of healing. This will be a quiet memorial, one that achieves an excellent relationship with both the Lincoln Memorial and Washington Monument, and relates the visitor to them. It is uniquely horizontal, entering the earth rather than piercing the sky.

♦ ♦ ♦

Americans were amazed when they learned that the winner of the contest was not a famous architect or sculptor. She was a 21-year-old college student named Maya Lin.

♦ ♦ ♦

Maya Lin, reporters soon discovered, was a Chinese-American girl who had been born and raised in the small midwestern city of Athens, Ohio. Her father, Henry Huan Lin, was a ceramicist of **considerable** reputation and dean of fine arts at Ohio University in Athens. Her mother, Julia C. Lin, was a poet and professor of Oriental and English literature.

♦ ♦ ♦

Maya Lin's parents were immigrants from China. Maya had always been interested in art, especially sculpture. At Yale University, she decided to major in architecture. She became interested in cemetery architecture, especially when she visited cemeteries in Europe, which were also used as parks.

In her senior year at Yale, one of Maya Lin's professors asked his students to enter

TAKE NOTES

Vocabulary Builder

Multiple-Meaning Words
The word *reflection* can mean "an image thrown back to the observer by a surface, such as a mirror." It can also mean "a state of deep thought." Which definition of *reflection* is used in the first sentence on this page?

_____
_____

Vocabulary Builder

Parts of Speech As a noun, the word *major* can refer to a military rank. As a verb, it means "study a specific subject at a college or a university." What does *major* mean in the paragraph that begins "Maya Lin's parents . . ."?

_____
_____

Everyday Words
considerable (kuhn SI der uh buhl) *adj.* large enough to have a noticeable effect

TAKE NOTES

Comprehension Builder

Which of Maya Lin's interests helped her design the Vietnam Veterans Memorial?

_____
_____
_____

Vocabulary Builder

Adjectives An adjective describes a noun or a pronoun. Circle three adjectives in the paragraph that begins "In her senior year . . ." Then underline the nouns the adjectives describe.

Fluency Builder

Take turns reading aloud the bracketed paragraph with a partner. Read the paragraph in a way that expresses its mood.

the Vietnam Veterans Memorial competition as a class assignment. Maya and two of her classmates traveled to Washington, D.C., to look at the site where the memorial would be built. While she was there, Maya was inspired. In her mind, she saw a vision of the memorial she wanted to design. Like the cemetery designs she had seen in Europe, her design fit in with the land around it and would maintain the site as a park.

◆ ◆ ◆

"When I looked at the site I just knew I wanted something horizontal that took you in, that made you feel safe within the park, yet at the same time reminding you of the dead. So I just imagined opening up the earth. . . ."

◆ ◆ ◆

Back at Yale, Maya made a clay model of her vision and then drew the design on paper. She mailed in her entry just in time to make the deadline. A month later, she got a call from Washington, D.C. She had won the competition. Her design would be used to build the Vietnam Veterans Memorial.

AFTER YOU READ

Thinking About the Selection

1. Fill in the chart with information about the life of Maya Ying Lin.

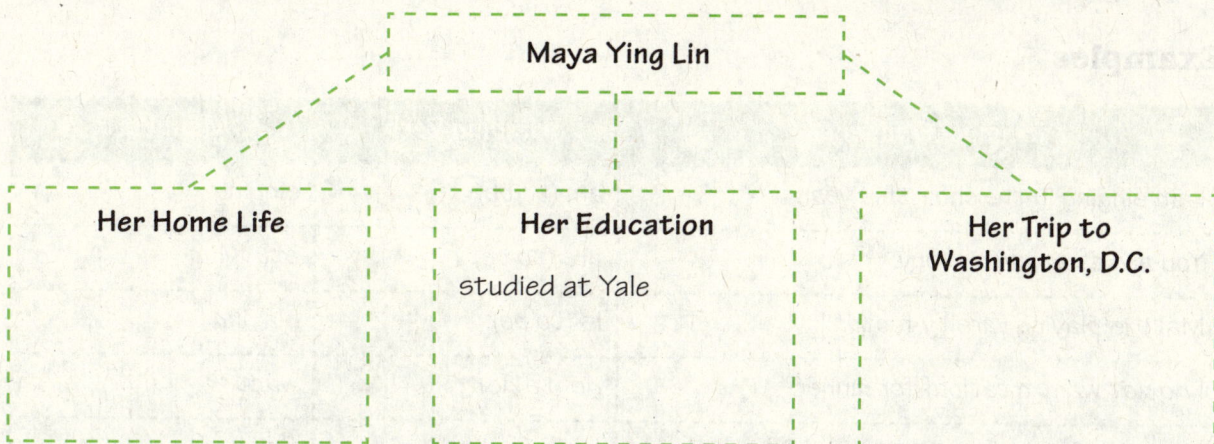

2. Everyone was surprised when Maya Ying Lin won the competition because _____
_____.

TALK ABOUT IT **In Your Opinion** Does Maya Ying Lin's memorial meet the design criteria? Why or why not? Discuss your opinion with a small group.

The memorial meets the design criteria because _____.

The memorial does not meet the design criteria because _____.

WRITE ABOUT IT **Design a Memorial** How would you design the Vietnam Memorial? What would be important to include in the design of the memorial? Write a paragraph, describing what your memorial would look like.

_____
_____
_____
_____

from Always to Remember ...

VOCABULARY SKILL REVIEW

Helping Verbs

A helping verb works with a main verb to show verb tense, pose a question, or make a negative statement. Three of the most common helping verbs are forms of the verbs *to be*, *to do*, and *to have*.

Examples

Sample Sentence	Helping Verb	Main Verb
I am singing in the choir this year.	am (to be)	singing
You are studying history.	are (to be)	studying
Matt is playing varsity football.	is (to be)	playing
I do not want meatloaf for dinner.	do (to do)	want
Have you finished your homework?	Have (to have)	finished

Now You Do It

Complete the chart by identifying the helping verb and the main verb for each sentence.

Sample Sentence	Helping Verb	Second Verb
Jena does not want oatmeal for breakfast.		
Willow and Maia are planning a party.		
We have studied hard this quarter.		
Jim is working at the grocery store.		
I am looking forward to vacation.		

TALK ABOUT IT **Introduce Yourself** With a partner, take turns asking and answering the following questions: What are you doing this week in school? What have you done in school this week? What else do you want to do? Make sure that your answers include helping verbs.

WRITE ABOUT IT **Write a Letter** Write a letter that answers the questions above. Write at least three sentences that contain helping verbs.

BEFORE YOU READ: FROM I KNOW WHY THE CAGED BIRD SINGS

Vocabulary

These words are highlighted in the selection. Listen to each word. Say it. Then, read the definition and the example sentence.

ceaseless (SEES lis) *adj.* Something that is **ceaseless** never stops.
   The birds' ceaseless chirping soon became annoying.

benign (bi NYN) *adj.* Something **benign** is kindly, favorable, and not harmful.
   His warm smile revealed a benign personality.

intolerant (in TAHL uhr uhnt) *adj.* Someone who is **intolerant** is not able or willing to accept the ideas or beliefs of others.
   Try not to be intolerant of others' opinions.

Vocabulary Practice

Read the first sentence in each group of three. Then, complete Sentence *a* by substituting another word or phrase that means the same as the underlined vocabulary word. Complete Sentence *b* with your own ideas and words.

1. Marie's ceaseless talking annoyed Tara.

   a. Marie's _____ talking annoyed Tara.

   b. Marie's ceaseless _____.

2. The benign dog greeted the visitor.

   a. The _____ dog greeted the visitor.

   b. The benign _____.

3. We should not be intolerant of other people's ideas.

   a. We should not be _____ of other people's ideas.

   b. We should not be intolerant _____.

Getting Ready to Read

During the 1940s, white and African American children living in the South went to separate schools. Many African American schools could not afford books and good teachers. African American students, like Maya Angelou, needed people who could inspire them. Tell a partner about someone who inspired you.

MAKING CONNECTIONS

from I Know Why the Caged Bird Sings
Maya Angelou

Summary In this story, the writer describes growing up in her grandmother's house in Stamps, Arkansas. She describes her friendship with a woman named Mrs. Flowers. Mrs. Flowers introduces her to poetry.

 Writing About the Big Question

How much information is enough? In *I Know Why the Caged Bird Sings,* a girl receives "lessons in living" that encourage her to gather wisdom from those around her. Complete these sentences:

The best way I have found to accumulate knowledge is _____
_____.

Note-taking Guide
Look at the chart below. Record events in the story that caused Marguerite to experience each emotion.

Pleased
She liked working in the store.

Sad and Depressed

Marguerite's Emotions

Happy

Proud

After You Read

Thinking About the Selection

1. Complete the chart below to contrast Marguerite's feelings and behavior before and after her visit with Mrs. Flowers. The first row has been completed for you.

Before	After
Before her visit, Marguerite believes that she is not good enough to visit someone like Mrs. Flowers.	After her visit, Marguerite realizes that she is liked just for being herself.
Before her visit, Marguerite	After her visit, Marguerite

2. When customers accuse Marguerite of cheating them, she feels _____ _____.

TALK ABOUT IT **What Does She Do?** What does Mrs. Flowers do when Marguerite visits her home? Discuss your answer with a partner.

When Marguerite visits, Mrs. Flowers _____.

WRITE ABOUT IT **Write a Thank-You Note** Write a note that Marguerite might have written to thank Mrs. Flowers for inspiring her. Be sure to list specific ways that Mrs. Flowers influenced Marguerite.

Dear Mrs. Flowers,

Thank you for _____
_____
_____
_____.

from *I Know Why the Caged Bird Sings* 175

VOCABULARY SKILL REVIEW

Word Families

Groups of words that share the same base word are called word families. A base word can stand alone or serve as the basis of new words. Often, new words are formed by adding affixes—such as prefixes, suffixes, verb endings and other words—to the base word.

Example

Base Word	Words Formed by Adding Prefixes, Suffixes, Verb Endings, and Other Words to the Base Word
school	preschool, schooling, schoolhouse, after-school, schooled, unschooled, schoolroom, schoolteacher, schoolboy, schoolgirl

Now You Do It

For each word below, identify whether a prefix, a suffix, a verb ending, or another word has been added to the base word to form the new word.

1. preschool _____
2. schooling _____
3. schoolhouse _____
4. after-school _____
5. schooled _____
6. unschooled _____
7. schoolroom _____
8. schoolteacher _____
9. schoolboy _____
10. schoolgirl _____

TALK ABOUT IT **Talk About School** Tell a partner what you usually do during a normal day at school. Use at least five words from this lesson in your conversation.

WRITE ABOUT IT **Write an Outline** Organize the word family with the base word *school* by writing an outline. Use the following headings to organize your outline: New words formed by adding prefixes, New words formed by adding suffixes, New words formed by adding verb endings, New words formed by adding both prefixes and verb endings, and New words formed by adding other words to the base word. List each word under its appropriate heading.

INFORMATIONAL TEXTS

Textbooks

About Textbooks

A **textbook** is a nonfiction book that presents information about one subject, such as math, history, or science. Different textbooks are alike in some ways.

- **Purpose:** Textbooks present information to students. The writer starts with a main idea and builds around it.
- **Structure:** Most textbooks have sections, chapters, or units. The table of contents lists the titles and page numbers of these parts.
- **Text Format:** Type size, color, and boldface type are used. They highlight key words or sections.

Reading Skill

To use a textbook effectively, you can **analyze the treatment, scope, and organization of ideas** presented in each unit or chapter. Treatment is the way a topic is presented, including the author's purpose for writing. In a textbook, the author's purpose is to inform or explain. The scope is the amount and type of information. A text with a narrow scope focuses on a single, limited topic, but a broad scope includes subtopics with much information. Organization is the way that ideas are arranged. One way to organize ideas is chronologically, or in the order in which they happen.

Treatment	Scope	Organization
• Is this a primary or secondary source? • Is the writer biased or neutral? • What is the writer's tone, or attitude toward the topic?	• Has the writer explored a single topic or a series of topics? • How in-depth is this exploration?	• How has the writer organized his or her information? • In what way does the organization of details enhance the writer's purpose?

© Pearson Education

Informational Texts 177

TAKE NOTES

Text Structure

Textbooks often include graphics, such as the map on this page, to provide additional information about the subject. What additional information does this map provide?

_____
_____
_____

Fluency Builder

Commas (,) tell the reader when to pause. Circle the commas in the second paragraph. Then, read aloud the paragraph with a partner, pausing briefly for each comma.

Vocabulary Builder

Adjectives An adjective is a word that describes a noun or pronoun. On the lines below, write six adjectives that appear in the third paragraph. Next to each adjective, write the noun that it describes.

_____
_____
_____
_____
_____
_____

178 Informational Texts

The War in Vietnam
War in Southeast Asia

Early Involvement in Vietnam

Vietnam is a narrow country that stretches about 1,000 miles along the South China Sea. Since the late 1800s, it had been ruled by France as a colony.

The United States became involved in Vietnam slowly, step by step. During the 1940s, Ho Chi Minh (HO CHEE MIHN), a Vietnamese nationalist and a Communist, had led the fight for independence. Ho's army finally defeated the French in 1954.

An international peace conference divided Vietnam into two countries. Ho Chi Minh led communist North Vietnam. Ngo Dinh Diem (NOH DIN dee EHM) was the noncommunist leader of South Vietnam. In the Cold War world, the Soviet Union supported North Vietnam. The United States backed Diem in the south.

Discontent Diem lost popular support during the 1950s. Many South Vietnamese thought that he favored wealthy landlords and was corrupt. He failed to help the nation's peasant majority and ruled with a heavy hand. As discontent grew,

© Pearson Education

many peasants joined the **Vietcong**— guerrillas who opposed Diem. **Guerrillas** (guh RIHL uhz) are fighters who make hit-and-run attacks on the enemy. They do not wear uniforms or fight in large battles. In time, the Vietcong became communist and were supported by North Vietnam. Vietcong influence quickly spread, especially in the villages.

American Aid Vietcong successes worried American leaders. If South Vietnam fell to communism, they believed, other countries in the region would follow—like a row of falling dominoes. This idea became known as the **domino theory.** The United States decided that it must keep South Vietnam from becoming the first domino.

During the 1950s and 1960s, Presidents Eisenhower and Kennedy sent financial aid and military advisers to South Vietnam. The advisers went to help train the South Vietnamese army, not to fight the Vietcong. Diem, however, continued to lose support. In November 1963, Diem was assassinated. A few weeks later, President John F. Kennedy was assassinated. Vice President Lyndon Baines Johnson became President.

The Fighting in Vietnam Expands

Lyndon Johnson was also determined to keep South Vietnam from falling to the communists. He increased aid to South Vietnam, sending more arms and advisers. Still, the Vietcong continued to make gains.

Gulf of Tonkin Resolution In August 1964, President Johnson announced that North Vietnamese torpedo boats had attacked an American ship patrolling the Gulf of Tonkin off the coast of North Vietnam. At Johnson's urging,

TAKE NOTES

Cultural Understanding
Capitalism is the economic system used in the United States. The government limits its involvement in the economy. Citizens can own businesses. They can also make and sell goods to earn a profit.

Text Structure
Text format is important in textbooks. It helps you find and understand information. On this page, type size and boldface are both used. Circle an example of each. Then, explain how they help you understand the information on this page.

Type size: _____
_____

Boldface: _____
_____

Vocabulary Builder
Multiple-Meaning Words
The word *falling* can mean "moving or dropping toward the ground." It can also mean "losing power." What does *falling* mean in the paragraph beginning "Lyndon Johnson was also determined . . ."?

_____
_____

TAKE NOTES

Comprehension Builder

What did President Johnson use the Gulf of Tonkin Resolution to do?

_____
_____
_____

Text Structure

How does the author organize information about the fighting in Vietnam? Explain.

_____
_____
_____

Congress passed the Gulf of Tonkin Resolution. It allowed the President "to take all necessary measures to repel any armed attack or to prevent further aggression." Johnson used the resolution to order the bombing of North Vietnam and Vietcong-held areas in the south.

With the Gulf of Tonkin Resolution, the role of Americans in Vietnam changed from military advisers to active fighters. The war in Vietnam escalated, or expanded. By 1968, President Johnson had sent more than 500,000 troops to fight in Vietnam.

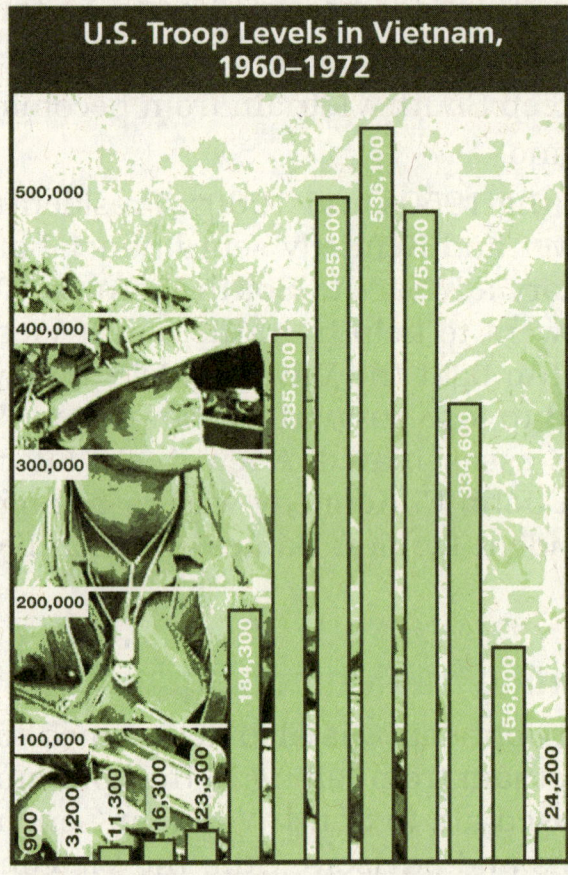

U.S. Troop Levels in Vietnam, 1960–1972

1960: 900
1961: 3,200
1962: 11,300
1963: 16,300
1964: 23,300
1965: 184,300
1966: 385,300
1967: 485,600
1968: 536,100
1969: 475,200
1970: 334,600
1971: 156,800
1972: 24,200

Source: U.S. Department of Defense

180 Informational Texts

AFTER YOU READ

Thinking About the Textbook

1. Explain the significance of the domino theory.
   _____

2. How did the Vietcong make fighting even more difficult for the Americans?
   _____

Reading Skill

3. What is the writer's purpose in writing about this subject?
   _____

4. Is the scope of this textbook narrow or broad? Explain.
   _____

WRITE ABOUT IT Timed Writing: Explanation (20 minutes)

Choose one of the following features. Explain how it could help you learn the information in this chapter. Use this chart to help you.

Feature	How It Could Help Me
Key Terms	
Taking Notes	
Outlining the Material	

Informational Texts

UNIT 3

BEFORE YOU READ: THE TROUBLE WITH TELEVISION

Vocabulary

These words are underlined in the selection. Listen to each word. Say it. Then, read the definition and the example sentence.

concentration (kahn suhn TRAY shuhn) *n.* Focusing all of one's thought on a particular activity is called **concentration.**
   The final exam took all of Jude's concentration.

constructive (kuhn STRUK tiv) *adj.* To be **constructive** means to serve or help to improve.
   Dad's constructive advice helped solve my problem.

diverts (duh VERTS) *v.* When something **diverts** us, it distracts us or refocuses our attention on something else.
   A movie diverts her from her worries.

Vocabulary Practice

Read the first sentence in each group of three. Then, complete Sentence *a* by substituting another word or phrase that means the same as the underlined vocabulary word. Complete Sentence *b* with your own ideas and words.

1. The ringing telephone ruined my concentration.

    a. The ringing telephone ruined my _____.

    b. _____ ruined my concentration.

2. Seth's constructive ideas improved the presentation.

    a. Seth's _____ ideas improved the presentation.

    b. Seth's constructive _____.

3. Television diverts your attention from homework.

    a. Television _____ your attention from homework.

    b. Television diverts your attention from _____.

Getting Ready to Read

According to research, the average American watched more than thirty hours of television a week in 2002. How much time do you spend watching television each week? Discuss with a small group some interesting activities that you might do during the time that you normally watch television.

MAKING CONNECTIONS

The Trouble With Television
Robert MacNeil

Summary Robert MacNeil has worked as a reporter for radio and television. He thinks that watching television keeps people from paying close attention to things. He thinks that television has a bad effect on people.

 Writing About the Big Question

How much information is enough? In "The Trouble With Television," Robert MacNeil expresses doubts about the quality of the information television offers. Complete this sentence:

The **exploration** of ideas on TV news shows is usually _____

_____.

Note-taking Guide
Use the chart to list the main reasons that MacNeil believes television is a bad influence.

MacNeil's Ideas About Television
1.
2.
3.
4.

The Trouble With Television **183**

TAKE NOTES

Cultural Understanding

By the age of 70, the average American will have spent between 7 and 10 years of his or her life watching television.

Vocabulary Builder

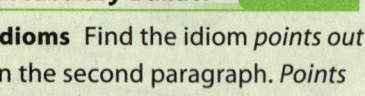

Idioms Find the idiom *points out* in the second paragraph. *Points out* means to "call attention to something." Complete the sentence, using *points out*.

When MacNeil thinks about the amount of time that Americans spend watching television, he

_____
_____.

Vocabulary Builder

Multiple-Meaning Words
The word *encourages* has more than one meaning. It can mean "provides with courage or hope." It can also mean "makes something more likely to happen." Which meaning does MacNeil use in the third paragraph?

_____
_____

The Trouble With Television
Robert MacNeil

It is difficult to escape the influence of television. If you fit the **statistical** averages, by the age of 20 you will have been **exposed** to at least 20,000 hours of television. You can add 10,000 hours for each decade you have lived after the age of 20. The only things Americans do more than watch television are work and sleep.

◆ ◆ ◆

MacNeil points out that time spent watching television could be put to better use. For example, he says that you could earn a college degree instead. You could read classic works of literature in their original languages. Or you could walk around the world and write a book about the experience.

◆ ◆ ◆

The trouble with television is that it discourages concentration. Almost anything interesting and rewarding in life requires some constructive, consistently applied effort. The dullest, the least gifted of us can achieve things that seem miraculous to those who never concentrate on anything. But television encourages us to apply no effort. It sells us instant **gratification**. It diverts us only to divert, to make the time pass without pain.

Everyday Words
statistical (stuh TIS ti kuhl) *adj.* having to do with numerical data
exposed (ik SPOHZD) *v.* shown
gratification (grat uh fuh KAY shuhn) *n.* the act of pleasing or satisfying

184 English Learner's Notebook

Capturing your attention—and holding it—is the prime motive of most television programming and **enhances** its role as a profitable advertising vehicle. Programmers live in constant fear of losing anyone's attention—anyone's. The surest way to avoid doing so is to keep everything brief, not to strain the attention of anyone but instead to provide constant stimulation through variety, **novelty,** action and movement. Quite simply, television operates on the appeal to the short attention span.

◆ ◆ ◆

MacNeil is worried about television's effect on the values of our society. He believes that Americans have come to want "fast ideas." He also believes that television news does not accurately portray events. It does not provide viewers with enough details.

◆ ◆ ◆

I believe that TV's appeal to the short attention span is not only inefficient communication but decivilizing as well. Consider the casual assumptions that television tends to cultivate: that complexity must be avoided, that visual stimulation is a substitute for thought, that verbal precision is an anachronism[1]. It may be old-fashioned, but I was taught that thought is words, arranged in grammatically precise ways.

◆ ◆ ◆

MacNeil says that television has caused a crisis of literacy in the United States. About

Everyday Words
enhances (in HANTS iz) *v.* adds to or improves the quality of something else
novelty (NAHV uhl tee) *n.* the quality of being new

1. **anachronism** (uh NAK ruh niz uhm) *n.* anything that seems to be out of its proper place in history.

TAKE NOTES

Fluency Builder
Read the bracketed paragraph silently. Notice the dashes. A dash (—) suggests a change of thought or emphasizes information. It tells the reader to pause and indicates a change in tone. Read aloud the bracketed paragraph, making sure to pause and change the tone of your voice for the text after each dash.

Vocabulary Builder
Prefixes The prefix *in-* means "not." The word *inefficient* means "not working well and wasting energy and time." According to MacNeil, how is television *inefficient*?

Television is an *inefficient*
_____
_____.

Comprehension Builder
Work with a partner to summarize what MacNeil believes about television's appeal to the short attention span.

_____
_____
_____
_____

TAKE NOTES

Fluency Builder

The bracketed paragraph contains many words with three or more syllables. Find each long word, and draw a line between each syllable. Then, pronounce the word. After you have marked all the long words, read the paragraph silently. Then, take turns with a partner reading the paragraph aloud.

Vocabulary Builder

Parts of Speech The word *form* can be used as a noun meaning "one of the many types in which something exists." It can also be used as a verb meaning "give something shape." How is *form* used in the underlined sentence?

_____

_____

30 million Americans cannot read and write well enough to answer a want ad or to understand instructions on a medicine bottle.

◆ ◆ ◆

[Everything about this nation—the structure of the society, its forms of family organization, its economy, its place in the world—has become more complex, not less. Yet its dominating communications instrument, its principal form of national linkage, is one that sells neat resolutions to human problems that usually have no neat resolutions. It is all symbolized in my mind by the hugely successful art form that television has made central to the culture, the thirty-second commercial: the tiny drama of the earnest housewife who finds happiness in choosing the right toothpaste.]

◆ ◆ ◆

In conclusion, MacNeil warns that television threatens our society's values. He believes that television negatively affects our language. He thinks it discourages our interest in complex issues. He calls on others to join him in resisting television's influence.

AFTER YOU READ

Thinking About the Selection

1. Fill in the graphic organizer by completing the sentences telling about MacNeil's ideas about television.

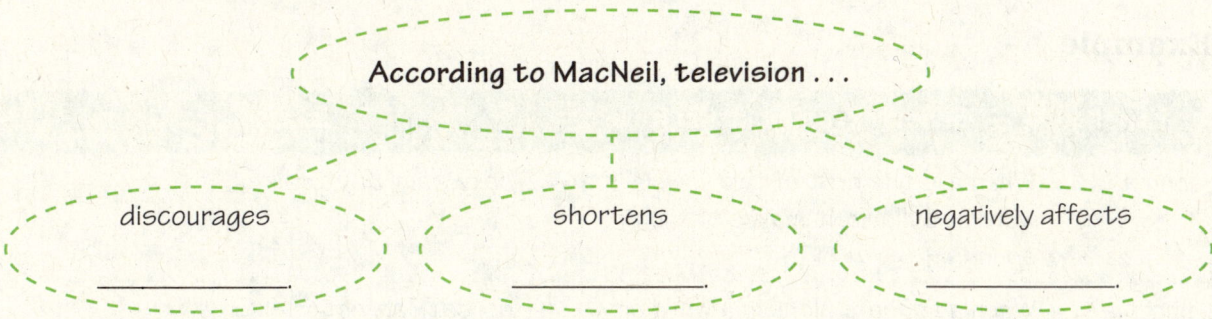

2. According to MacNeil, television shortens our attention span by _____
_____.

TALK ABOUT IT **Do You Agree or Disagree?** MacNeil believes that the main problem with television is that it reduces viewers' ability to concentrate on complex ideas. Do you agree with MacNeil? Discuss your answer with a partner.

I agree with MacNeil because _____.

I disagree with MacNeil because _____.

WRITE ABOUT IT **Too Much Television?** Has television affected your own ability to concentrate? Expand your ideas from the discussion above, and write about how the amount of television that you watch has affected you. Support your ideas with examples from your own experience.

In my experience, watching television has _____
_____
_____
_____.

VOCABULARY SKILL REVIEW

Long and Short A

The pronunciation of the vowel *a* depends on its position within a word. Sometimes it is pronounced with a long sound, which means it sounds like its name. At other times, it is pronounced with a short sound. General rules guide the pronunciation of the vowel *a*.

Example

Vowel	General Pronunciation Rule	Examples
long *a*	When *a* is the first of two vowels in a word or syllable, it makes the long sound.	cake, rain, day, praise
short *a*	When *a* appears alone in a word or syllable and is followed by a consonant, it makes the short sound.	at, cat, lab, actor

Now You Do It

Say each word quietly, or sound it out in your mind. In the space provided, write *long* if the vowel makes a long sound and *short* if it makes the short sound.

day _____   spray _____

tackle _____   trace _____

taxi _____   calf _____

say _____   cap _____

stain _____   pass _____

TALK ABOUT IT **Check It Out** With a partner, check your pronunciation of the words above. Say each word and explain why you pronounced the vowel with a long sound or a short sound.

WRITE ABOUT IT **Write a Poem** List rhyming words that have the short *a* sound—such as bat, flat, and mat—and list rhyming words that have the long *a* sound—such as bake, make, and rake. Use those words to write a silly, eight-line poem.

BEFORE YOU READ: ON WOMAN'S RIGHT TO SUFFRAGE

Vocabulary

These words are highlighted in the selection. Listen to each word. Say it. Then, read the definition and the example sentence.

mockery (MAHK uhr ee) *n.* **Mockery** is the act of making fun of others using false or insulting actions.

His disrespectful comments during the ceremony were a mockery.

violation (vy uh LAY shuhn) *n.* A **violation** is the breaking or ignoring of rules, laws, or rights.

The officer ticketed the driver for a traffic violation.

rebellion (ri BEL yuhn) *n.* A **rebellion** is a fight or open resistance to authority or control.

The peasants staged a rebellion to overthrow the wicked king.

Vocabulary Practice

Read the first sentence in each group of three. Then, complete Sentence *a* by substituting another word or phrase that means the same as the underlined vocabulary word. Complete Sentence *b* with your own ideas and words.

1. His mockery of the speech was disrespectful.

    a. His _____ of the speech was disrespectful.

    b. His mockery _____.

2. Jordan's violation was touching the soccer ball with his hand.

    a. Jordan's _____ was touching the soccer ball with his hand.

    b. Jordan's violation _____.

3. The king wanted to stop the rebellion over high taxes.

    a. The king wanted to stop the _____ over high taxes.

    b. The king wanted to stop the rebellion _____.

TALK ABOUT IT ## Getting Ready to Read

Suffrage is the right to vote. Before 1920, women in the United States did not have the right to vote in any elections. Why is it important for all people to have the right to vote? Discuss your thoughts with a partner.

MAKING CONNECTIONS

On Woman's Right to Suffrage
Susan B. Anthony

Summary Susan B. Anthony gives a speech to United States citizens in 1873. It is a time when women cannot vote. She says that the U.S. Constitution protects all people. She says that women should have the same rights as men.

 Writing About the Big Question

How much information is enough? In "On Woman's Right to Suffrage," Susan B. Anthony discusses the importance of many voices to a democracy. Complete this sentence:

Discrimination may have a negative effect on democracy because it prevents _____.

Note-taking Guide
Use the graphic organizer to record details that support Susan B. Anthony's argument.

The Constitution says "We the people," not "We, the white male citizens."

Women should have the right to vote.

AFTER YOU READ

Thinking About the Selection

1. What argument does Anthony make for why women should be allowed to vote? Write your answers in the chart below.

Susan B. Anthony's Argument
Anthony says that the dictionary defines *citizen* as _____.

↓

Because women are persons, Anthony argues that _____.

↓

Therefore, Anthony claims that laws that do not allow women to vote are _____.

2. Anthony was accused of the crime of _____.

TALK ABOUT IT **What Is a Democracy?** Why does Anthony say that she does not live in a true democracy? Discuss your ideas with a small group.

Anthony believes that she does not live in a true democracy because _____.

WRITE ABOUT IT **Write a News Article** Suppose that you had attended Anthony's speech. Write a short news article summarizing the speech and describing the event. Be sure to include a headline.

_____
_____
_____

VOCABULARY SKILL REVIEW

Suffixes

The suffix *-able* means "capable of," "worthy of," or "fit for." It is often added to a verb to make an adjective. Adding the suffix *-able* does not change the meaning of the base word. However, it changes the word's part of speech so that the new word can describe another idea.

Examples

Base word + suffix	Definition	Sample Sentence
agree + able = agreeable	capable of agreeing, pleasing	Marcela has an *agreeable* personality.
honor + able = honorable	worthy of honor	Robert is an *honorable* man.

Now You Do It

Add the suffix *-able* to each base word listed below. Then, write a sentence that contains the new word.

1. accept + able = _____

   _____

2. present + able = _____

   _____

3. adapt + able = _____

   _____

TALK ABOUT IT **Is It Agreeable?** With a partner, discuss a topic about which you both agree. Talk about why you both find the topic agreeable. Use the other words from this lesson in your conversation.

WRITE ABOUT IT **An Honorable Person** Think about a person you know who is honorable. Write a short biography that describes this person and explains why you believe he or she is honorable.

_____

_____

_____

UNIT 3

BEFORE YOU READ: FROM SHARING IN THE AMERICAN DREAM

Vocabulary

These words are underlined in the selection. Listen to each word. Say it. Then, read the definition and the example sentence.

compassionate (kuhm PASH uhn it) *adj.* To be **compassionate** means to be deeply sympathetic.
My doctor is always compassionate when I am in pain.

generous (JEN er uhs) *adj.* A **generous** person gives time or money to help others.
Because Aunt Laura is generous, she gave a large donation to the hospital building fund.

deferred (di FERD) *adj.* When something is described as **deferred**, it means it has been delayed or put off until a later time.
He took a deferred admission to college and traveled.

Vocabulary Practice

Read the first sentence in each group of three. Then, complete Sentence *a* by substituting another word or phrase that means the same as the underlined vocabulary word. Complete Sentence *b* with your own ideas and words.

1. Carla is a <u>compassionate</u> friend who is always willing to listen.

    a. Carla is a _____ friend who is always willing to listen.

    b. Carla is a compassionate _____.

2. He thanked the <u>generous</u> donors for their support.

    a. He thanked the _____ donors for their support.

    b. He thanked the generous _____.

3. All <u>deferred</u> assignments will be due next month.

    a. All _____ assignments will be due next month.

    b. All deferred _____.

Getting Ready to Read

In the United States, many people volunteer each year at schools, hospitals, nursing homes, and libraries. Why do you think people volunteer? Discuss your ideas with a partner.

MAKING CONNECTIONS

from Sharing in the American Dream
Colin Powell

Summary Former Secretary of State Colin Powell shares his beliefs about volunteer work. He encourages listeners to volunteer their time to help others in some way. He believes that this is an important part of keeping the United States strong.

 Writing About the Big Question

How much information is enough? In "Sharing in the American Dream," Colin Powell calls on all members of society to help one another achieve their dreams. Complete this sentence:

An effective way to challenge people to volunteer is _____

_____.

Note-taking Guide
Fill in the chart to record the main points of Powell's speech.

People Who Need Help	What They Need	Who Should Help
		each and every one of us

194 English Learner's Notebook

from Sharing in the American Dream
Colin Powell

This selection is taken from a speech that Colin Powell gave. He was speaking to a meeting of government leaders in Philadelphia. He begins his speech by referring to the leaders of the American Revolution, who met in Philadelphia more than 200 years before to sign the Declaration of Independence. He quotes from the Declaration to inspire his listeners.

◆ ◆ ◆

They pledged their lives, their fortune and their sacred honor to secure **inalienable** rights given by God for life, liberty and pursuit of happiness—pledged that they would provide them to all who would inhabit this new nation.

◆ ◆ ◆

Powell says that the signers of the Declaration are present at the meeting in spirit. They are proud of what Americans have achieved, but America still has not completely achieved the dream described in the Declaration.

◆ ◆ ◆

Despite more than two centuries of moral and material progress, despite all our efforts to achieve a more perfect union, there are still Americans who are not sharing in the American Dream.

◆ ◆ ◆

Powell quotes from the poem "A Dream Deferred," by Langston Hughes. The poem asks how people react when they are not able to achieve their dreams. It suggests that such people may turn to violence.

Everyday Words
inalienable (in AYL yuhn uh buhl) *adj.* not capable of being taken away; nontransferable

TAKE NOTES

Vocabulary Builder

Parts of Speech As a verb, the word *sign* means "write one's name." As a noun, it means "a board or notice that gives directions or warnings." What does *sign* mean in the first paragraph?

_____
_____

Vocabulary Builder

Pronouns A pronoun is a word that replaces a noun in a sentence. The following words are pronouns: *he, him, his, she, her, hers, they, them, their, theirs, it,* and *its.* On the lines below, write the pronouns in the second paragraph. Then, write the nouns the pronouns replace.

_____
_____
_____

Cultural Understanding

In 1931, James Truslow Adams was the first person to use the term *American Dream.* According to Adams, the American Dream refers to the belief that all people, regardless of birth or position in society, have the opportunity to live and improve their lives according to their abilities and achievements.

TAKE NOTES

Vocabulary Builder

Adjectives Read the bracketed paragraph. Then circle three adjectives in the paragraph. What noun do all three adjectives describe?

_____

Vocabulary Builder

Idioms The idiom *to reach out* means "to make a special effort to help." To whom does Powell ask his listeners *to reach out*?

Powell asks his listeners *to reach out* to _____
_____.

Fluency Builder

A comma (,) separates the items in a series of three or more items in a sentence. Read the paragraph that begins "He asks his listeners . . ." As you read, be sure to pause slightly after each comma.

Powell then asks his listeners to pledge that no one in America will be denied the promise of the American Dream. He says that in order for the dream to come true, fortunate Americans must reach out to help the less fortunate.

♦ ♦ ♦

We are a compassionate and caring people. We are a generous people. We will reach down, we will reach back, we will reach across to help our brothers and sisters who are in need.

♦ ♦ ♦

He urges his listeners to reach out to those who most need help—America's children.

♦ ♦ ♦

As you've heard, up to 15 million young Americans today are at risk . . .

♦ ♦ ♦

Powell says that helping children in need may seem like too big a job. Actually, though, it is something we all can do because we all know what children need. They need adults who care for them, safe homes and schools, health care, skills, and opportunities.

He asks his listeners to make a commitment to American children today. He says that government, corporations, nonprofit agencies, churches, and individuals can all work together to make sure that all children get what they need.

♦ ♦ ♦

You heard the governors and the mayors, and you'll hear more in a little minute that says the real answer is for each and every one of us, not just here in Philadelphia, but across this land—for each and every one of us to reach out and touch someone in need.

◆ ◆ ◆

Powell ends his speech by again referring to the spirit of the Declaration of Independence, which was signed in Philadelphia more than 200 years before.

◆ ◆ ◆

<u>All of us can spare 30 minutes a week or an hour a week.</u> All of us can give an extra dollar. . . . There is a spirit of Philadelphia that will leave Philadelphia tomorrow afternoon and spread across this whole nation—

◆ ◆ ◆

Powell says that all Americans must help spread the promise of the American Dream. It must be done in order to make the promises of the Declaration of Independence come true.

◆ ◆ ◆

Let us make sure that no child in America is left behind, no child in America has their dream <u>deferred</u> or denied.

TAKE NOTES

Vocabulary Builder

Parts of Speech The word *spare* can be used as a noun meaning "something extra." It can also be used as a verb meaning "contribute something." What does *spare* mean in the underlined sentence?

_____
_____

Comprehension Builder

Summarize the main points of Powell's speech.

_____
_____
_____
_____
_____
_____

from Sharing in the American Dream

AFTER YOU READ

Thinking About the Selection

1. What does Powell say the leaders of the American Revolution pledged? Write your answers in the chart below.

   ```
   The leaders of the      ┌──────────────┐
   American Revolution  ──►│              │
   pledged...              └──────────────┘
                           ┌──────────────┐
                        ──►│              │
                           └──────────────┘
   ```

2. Powell explains that although Americans have worked hard and made much progress, there are still people who _____.

TALK ABOUT IT **Promises of the Declaration** According to Powell, what does the Declaration of Independence promise all Americans? Discuss your ideas with a partner.

The Declaration of Independence promises all Americans _____.

WRITE ABOUT IT **Keeping Promises** Write a speech explaining how people in your community can make sure that the promises of the Declaration of Independence are kept for all citizens.

_____
_____
_____
_____
_____

VOCABULARY SKILL REVIEW

Multiple-Meaning Words

Many words have more than one meaning. Often, the only way to determine the particular meaning of a word is to understand a word's context, or the other words in the sentence or surrounding sentences that provide clues to the meaning of the word.

Examples

Word	Meaning
face	• (verb) accept that a problem exists and be willing to deal with it • (verb) be turned toward someone or something
shrink	• (verb) become smaller or make something smaller • (verb) avoid doing something difficult

Now You Do It

Complete the sentences with words from the chart. Make sure that the word fits the context of the sentence. Then, write the meaning of the word on the lines provided.

He could not _____ from his difficult responsibilities.

_____

She turned to _____ her friends.

_____

Andre had to _____ his fear of flying.

_____

He watched the balloon _____ as Trina let the air out of it.

_____

TALK ABOUT IT **Guessing Game** With a partner, take turns saying aloud sentences that use the words from this lesson in different ways. Guess the meaning of the word based on the way it is used in each sentence.

WRITE ABOUT IT **Write a Story** Use the multiple-meaning words from this lesson to write a funny short story. Use each word in as many ways as you can. Underline the words each time that you use them.

_____

_____

from Sharing in the American Dream

UNIT 3

BEFORE YOU READ: SCIENCE AND THE SENSE OF WONDER

Vocabulary

These words are highlighted in the selection. Listen to each word. Say it. Then, read the definition and the example sentence.

exultantly (eg ZUHL tuhnt lee) *adv.* When one acts **exultantly**, one acts triumphantly.

"We won!" he yelled exultantly.

awed (AWD) *v.* To feel a great sense of wonder is to be **awed**.

We were awed by the sheer size and beauty of the Grand Canyon.

conceivable (khun SEEV uh buhl) *adj.* Something that is **conceivable** is able to be imagined.

It is conceivable, but unlikely, that he walked all the way here.

Vocabulary Practice

Read the first sentence in each group of three. Then, complete Sentence *a* by substituting another word or phrase that means the same as the underlined vocabulary word. Complete Sentence *b* with your own ideas and words.

1. The winning team ran across the field exultantly after the game.

   a. The winning team ran across the field _____ after the game.

   b. The winning team ran across the field exultantly _____.

2. We were awed by the beautiful fireworks display.

   a. We were _____ by the beautiful fireworks display.

   b. We were awed _____.

3. It is conceivable that he could score the winning goal.

   a. It is _____ that he could score the winning goal.

   b. It is conceivable that _____.

 **Getting Ready to Read**

Isaac Asimov is a famous science-fiction writer. A story is called science fiction if it features science that is incredible or that does not obey scientific rules. These stories are often set in the future and in faraway places—sometimes on other planets. Discuss why a science-fiction writer might write an essay that encourages people to appreciate science.

MAKING CONNECTIONS

Science and the Sense of Wonder
Isaac Asimov

Summary Isaac Asimov says that he does not agree with a poem Walt Whitman wrote. Whitman says in his poem that people should forget about science. He says that people should enjoy the sky's beauty. Asimov says that people enjoy the sky more when they know science.

Writing About the Big Question

How much information is enough? In "Science and the Sense of Wonder," Asimov argues that scientific knowledge adds to our sense of wonder about the universe. Complete these sentences:

The more knowledge I accumulate about how natural systems work,

the (more/less) curious I feel. This is because _____

_____

Note-taking Guide

Use the chart to recall Asimov's reasons for why science makes watching the sky more interesting.

- Some of those bright spots in the sky are "worlds of red-hot liquid."

How science makes watching the night sky more interesting

Science and the Sense of Wonder **201**

AFTER YOU READ

Thinking About the Selection

1. Contrast Whitman's view of understanding the universe with Asimov's view. Complete the sentences in the boxes below.

Whitman's View	Asimov's View
To truly appreciate the beauty of the universe, one does not need to know about _____.	Learning about science adds to _____.
One can look at _____.	

2. Asimov explains how small the Milky Way is by _____.

TALK ABOUT IT **Is It Fair?** Asimov suggests that Whitman had little respect for scientific study. Do you think that Asimov makes a fair judgment? Why or why not? Discuss your ideas with a partner.

Asimov makes a fair judgment because _____.

Asimov does not make a fair judgment because _____.

WRITE ABOUT IT **What Have You Learned?** What have you learned from reading the selection? How will your new knowledge change the way you look at the night sky? Write your answers below.

I learned that _____
_____
_____

VOCABULARY SKILL REVIEW

Active and Passive Verbs

A verb is active when it describes what the subject is doing. A verb is passive when it describes what is happening to the subject.

Examples

Passive Verbs	Active Verbs
The student was helped by the teacher.	The teacher helped the student.
All the children were given prizes.	Someone gave all the children prizes.

Now You Do It

Rewrite each sentence below with an active verb.

Passive Verbs	Active Verbs
The story was read by Phillip.	
Tony's award was presented by the mayor.	
Two dozen cookies were sold by Marty.	
The gift was wrapped by Juanita.	

TALK ABOUT IT **What Happened?** With a partner, use sentences with passive verbs to describe what you did in class yesterday. As you say a sentence, your partner will write the subject and verb. Say at least three sentences each.

_____
_____
_____

WRITE ABOUT IT **Action!** Now, rewrite each sentence so that the verb is active.

_____
_____
_____

Science and the Sense of Wonder

Newspaper Editorials

About Newspaper Editorials

Newspaper editorials are written to express an opinion on a topic. The purpose of an editorial is to persuade readers to agree with the writer's point of view. Some editorials ask readers to take action on an issue. Editorial writers support their opinions with facts, examples, and statistics.

Reading Skill

To understand the writer's point of view and purpose for writing, readers must **analyze the proposition and support patterns** in the editorial. The writer states a problem and describes how it affects the reader. Then, the writer provides one or more solutions to the problem. The writer may use both facts and opinions to support the solution. Ask the following questions when reading a newspaper editorial:

- What problem does the writer present?
- Does the writer's solution to the problem make sense?
- Does the writer support the solution with facts, examples, and statistics?

Error in Logic	Example	Problem
Oversimplification	If you own a cellphone you should support the right to use it anywhere you want to.	Ignores other alternatives
False analogy	Outlawing cellphone use while driving is like outlawing eating while reading.	The comparison is irrelevant
Insufficient evidence	I do not know anyone who has had an accident because of a cellphone so I do not think they are a problem.	False conclusion
Jumping on the bandwagon	Everyone I know drives while talking on the cellphone, so it should be legal.	Assumes an opinion is correct because it is popular

The Mercury News

Langberg: Hands-free law won't solve the problem

FRIDAY, SEPTEMBER 1, 2006

By Mike Langberg

Driving while talking on a cell phone clearly increases your risk of getting into an accident, but here's a surprise: The problem is all in your head.

The mental distraction of conversing behind the wheel is so great that switching to a headset or other "hands-free" approach—instead of taking one hand off the wheel to hold the phone to your ear—does nothing to reduce the danger.

But politicians never let facts get in the way of making themselves look good.

The result is hands-free legislation that passed the California Assembly and Senate last week, and is likely to be signed into law this month by Gov. Arnold Schwarzenegger.

The California Wireless Telephone Automobile Safety Act of 2006, the bill's formal name, says: "A person shall not drive a motor vehicle while using a wireless telephone unless that telephone is specifically designed and configured to allow hands-free listening and talking, and is used in that manner while driving. Using a hand-held phone, you'll get an almost painless fine of $20 for the first offense. The penalty doesn't get much worse for additional violations, moving up to just $50.

Using a hand-held phone would only be allowed in emergency situations, such as calling 911.

The new rules wouldn't take effect until July 1, 2008.

So we're getting a nearly toothless law, two years down the line, that doesn't offer a real solution to a serious problem.

The first part of that problem is the awesome popularity of cell phones.

There are now 208 million cell phone subscribers in the United States, equal to 69 percent of the total population. Almost every adult American, in other words, now has a cell phone.

The National Highway Traffic Safety Administration says an average 6 percent of drivers on the road at any given moment are talking on a cell phone. The number goes up to 10 percent during daylight hours.

Driver distraction or inattention contributes to nearly 80 percent of accidents, according to a research study completed earlier this year by NHTSA and Virginia Tech.

Although overall death and injury rates continue to decline slowly over time, there's no question cell phones are a factor in many highway accidents. Last year, NHTSA reports, highway accidents killed 43,443 people last year and injured 2.7 million.

> The writer does not provide evidence to support these claims.

There's an obvious solution: Ban talking on a cell phone while driving.

But that's not going to happen, at least not anytime soon. The cell phone lobby is too powerful, and the public is too enamored with chatting behind the wheel.

Instead, we're getting hands-free laws that give politicians the appearance of taking action.

New York, New Jersey, Connecticut and the District of Columbia already have hands-free laws, and many other states are considering similar steps.

These laws are moving forward despite a persuasive and growing list of academic studies, involving both simulator testing and analysis of real-world crash data, showing hands-free phone calls are no less risky than holding a phone.

Think about it: If you're fully aware of what's happening on the road ahead of you, such as a car suddenly slamming on its brakes, your response time isn't going to vary much whether you've got one or two hands on the wheel.

But your response time will suffer if you're in the middle of an argument on the phone with your boss or spouse.

I'll raise my hand here and admit I'm part of the problem. I've come close to rear-ending other drivers on a few occasions because I was talking on my cell phone. And I don't believe my sluggish reaction would have changed if I'd been using a headset.

David L. Strayer, a psychology professor at the University of Utah, has been studying cell phone distraction for more than five years.

Last week, he told me there are at least six studies showing no safety benefit from hands-free talking.

"This . . . suggests that legislative initiatives that restrict handheld devices but permit hands-free devices are not likely to eliminate the problems associated with cell phones while driving." Strayer and two colleagues wrote in the summer 2006 issue of the journal *Human Factors*.

I asked Strayer if there's a safe way to participate in a phone call while driving.

"Not unless we somehow rewire our brains," he responded. There's no technological remedy, in other words, to the mental distraction created during a cell phone conversation.

At the same time, there are possible side effects—both good and bad—from hands free laws.

On the good side, some drivers might not want to go through the hassle of buying and using a headset or other hands-free gadget. They would give up talking while driving, collectively reducing auto accidents.

On the bad side, some drivers might get a false sense of security and decide it's OK to talk even more.

Here's my prediction: California's hands-free law, and similar laws elsewhere, will do nothing to change the number of accidents tied to drivers using cell phones.

Once everyone realizes these laws accomplish nothing, we'll have to decide whether cell phones require further restrictions or should be categorized with other dangerous behind-the-wheel distractions—everything from noisy children to complicated audio systems—that aren't restricted.

How much information is enough?
Does this editorial change the way you think about cell phone use while driving? Why or why not?

Speech

Features:
- text spoken aloud to an audience
- remarks that highlight the significance of an event
- language intended to engage listeners and encourage support for the speaker's ideas

Transcript of Governor Arnold Schwarzenegger Signing Legislation Requiring Drivers to Use Hands Free Devices

DATE: *Friday, September 15, 2006*
TIME: *11:15 a.m.*

EVENT: *Oakland Hilton, California Room, 1 Hegenberger Rd, Oakland, CA*

GOVERNOR SCHWARZENEGGER:

. . . Today we will be signing SB 1613. This is the hands-free cell phone bill that will save lives by making our roads safer. And I want to say thank you to Senator Simitian for his great, great work on this bill and for working with my office on this bill to perfect the bill. I want to thank him also for his great commitment to . . . California, and to make our roads safe. He has been really extraordinary, to protect the people of California and I want to say thank you for that.

The speaker opens his speech by stating his proposition.

The simple fact is that it is really dangerous when you talk on your cell phone and drive at the same time. Hand-held cell phones are responsible for 1,000 accidents every month, and we have seen that there are very dangerous situations sometimes. We want to avoid that, and this is why we have here this bill. This bill doesn't mean that you can't talk on a cell phone; it just means that you should not hold a hand-held cell phone, you should use a headset or use a speaker system.

Also, there is an exception here that if you have to make an emergency call, then you can use the hand-held phone. And also, what is important is that this law will go into effect on July 1 of 2008. There will be a $20 fine if you're caught the first time using a cell phone, and then $50 after that.

I think it is very important for people to know that even though the law begins in 2008, July of 2008, stop using your cell phones right now, because you're putting people at risk. You just look away for a second, or for a split second, from what's going on in front of you, and at that moment a child could be running out, and you could kill this child just because you were busy looking down and dialing on your cell phone. So pay attention to that, take this seriously. We want to really save lives here.

Thank you very much again, and now I would like to have Senator Simitian come out and say a few words, please.

SENATOR SIMITIAN:

Thank you all very much for being here today. And some of you know, but perhaps

Informational Texts

not all of you, that this is the sixth hands-free cell phone bill I've introduced during the past six years. The question I've been asked quite frequently of late is, "Why did you keep introducing the bill?" And the answer is really very simple. I introduced the bill because I believe it will save lives. It's just that simple. You've got a readily available technology that costs next to nothing and saves lives. Why on earth wouldn't we use it?

This bill isn't a perfect solution, it isn't a total solution, but it is a significant and important improvement over the current state of affairs, and it will save lives, and that was the goal from Day 1. . . .

> The speaker oversimplifies the issue of cost involved in using a hands-free cellphone device.

CHIEF BECHER:

. . . I'm proud to be here today for the signing of this bill. It represents a collaborative effort between the legislature, the Governor, [the phone company] and the many backers and traffic safety officials throughout the state, to make the roadways of California a safer place to drive.

Statewide, collisions caused by distracted drivers result in countless hours of roadway delay, congestion, injury and death. This legislation is another useful tool for law enforcement to curb the growing number of collisions caused either partially or wholly by distracted drivers.

Prior to this cell phone law going into effect, the CHP plans a major public education campaign to ensure the public is aware of the changes. Education is a major focus for the CHP, because public awareness of the issue and voluntary compliance wtih this new law can have a significant impact on crashes even before the new law goes into effect. The Governor is exactly right. Start now.

Our goal is to have all drivers in the state keep both hands on the wheel and have the attention and awareness so that they can navigate [their] driving environment. It is always incumbent on drivers to drive attentively. Many devices and activities taking place inside today's vehicles can cause that split second distraction that may result in an unnecessary traffic collision. Cell phones are among the more prominent of these distractions.

And finally, thanks to all in the creation and implementation of this bill. The California Highway Patrol supports this new legislation as part of our No. 1 goal, to prevent traffic collisions and to save lives. Thank you.

> **THE BIG ?** **How much information is enough?**
> Do the remarks of the speakers provide enough information for you to make an informed judgment about cellphone use while driving? Explain your response.

AFTER YOU READ

Thinking About the Newspaper Editorial

1. Find one sentence in Langberg's editorial that states his opinion about using cell phones while driving. Write that sentence on the line below.
   _____

2. In Governor Schwarzenegger's speech, what reason does the governor give for choosing to sign the hands-free cell phone bill?
   _____

Reading Skill

3. Langberg states that hands-free phones are not likely to eliminate the problems of using cell phones while driving. How does Langberg support his statement?
   _____

4. How does Governor Schwarzenegger support his decision to sign the hands-free cell phone bill?
   _____

WRITE ABOUT IT Timed Writing: Editorial Writing (40 minutes)

Use one of the editorials as a model to write an editorial. Research an issue in your school or community. State your opinion on the issue, propose a solution, and support your solution with facts and examples.

- What is the issue?
  _____

- What is your opinion on the issue?
  _____

- What solution do you propose?
  _____

- What facts support your solution?
  _____

Informational Texts

UNIT VOCABULARY REVIEW

Word Bank

accumulate	explanation	quality
challenge	exploration	quantity
decision	factor	reveal
development	global	statistics
discrimination	inequality	valuable

A. **Word Match** Complete the chart below by drawing a line from the word found in the word bank to the word or phrase that best describes it. The first one has been done for you.

accumulate	question
challenge	throughout the world
quantity	make known
quality	look closely
examine	highest standard
reveal	of great usefulness
inequality	amount
valuable	unequal
global	choice
decision	collect

(accumulate — collect)

B. **Word Web** Complete the graphic organizer by selecting words from the word bank on the previous page that represent challenges in our world today.

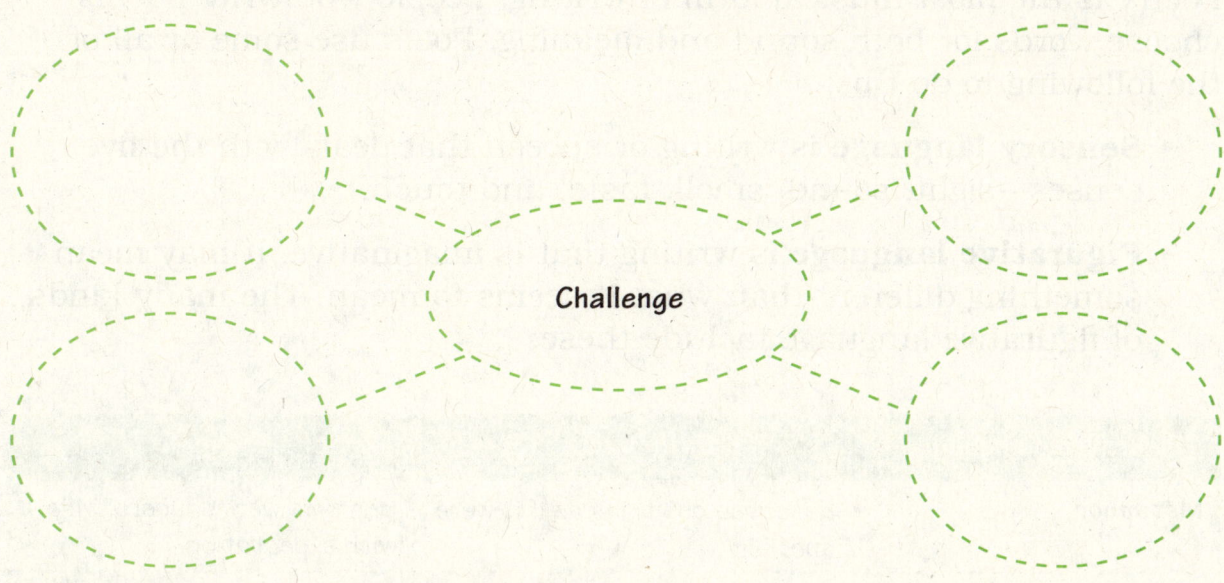

TALK ABOUT IT **Challenges Facing Teens** Everyone faces challenges—even teens. With a partner or small group, talk about challenges that teens face at school. List those challenges in the space below. Then, talk about ways students can meet those challenges.

_____

_____

WRITE ABOUT IT **What Can You Do?** Write a letter to the editor of your school newspaper. Pick one of the challenges discussed above, and explain to the editor how students in your school might deal with that challenge.

_____

_____

_____

_____

_____

Unit Vocabulary Review

Unit 4: Exploring Poetry

Describe Somebody • Almost a Summer Sky

Poetry is the most musical form of writing. People who write poems choose words for both sound and meaning. Poets use some or all of the following to do this:

- **Sensory language** is writing or speech that deals with the five senses—sight, sound, smell, taste, and touch.
- **Figurative language** is writing that is imaginative. It may mean something different than what it seems to mean. The many kinds of figurative language include these:

Figurative Language	Definition	Example
Metaphor	• describes one thing as if it were another	Her eyes were saucers, wide with expectation.
Simile	• uses *like* or *as* to compare two unlike things	The drums were as loud as a fireworks display.
Personification	• gives human qualities to something that is not human	The clarinets sang.

Sound devices add a musical quality to poetry. Some sound devices include these:

Sound Device	Definition	Example
Alliteration	• repetition of consonant sounds at the beginning of words	feathered friend
Repetition	• repeated use of a sound, word, or phrase	water, water everywhere
Assonance	• repetition of a vowel sound followed by different consonants in stressed syllables	fade/hey

EXPLORING POETRY

Other sound devices include these:

Sound Device	Definition	Example
Consonance	• repetition of a consonant sound at the end of stressed syllables with different vowel sounds	end/hand
Onomatopoeia	• use of words that imitate sounds	buzz, whack
Rhyme	• repetition of sounds at the ends of words	dear, cheer, here
Meter	• the pattern of unstressed and stressed syllables in a poem	A **horse**, a **horse**! My **king**dom **for** a **horse**!

The structure of a poem determines its form. Most poems are written in lines. These lines are grouped into stanzas. This list describes several forms of poetry.

- **Lyric** poetry describes the thoughts and feelings of one speaker. The **speaker** is the person who speaks in the poem. Lyric poetry usually seems musical.
- **Narrative** poetry tells a story in verse. It often includes some of the same things that are found in short stories.
- **Ballads** are songlike poems that tell a story. They often tell about adventure and romance.
- **Free verse** is poetry that has no set structure. It does not have to rhyme or have regular meter. Lines do not have to be a specific length. There may be no specific stanza pattern.
- **Haiku** is a three-line Japanese form. The first and third lines have five syllables each. The second line has seven syllables.
- **Rhyming couplets** are a pair of lines that rhyme. The lines usually have the same meter and length.
- **Limericks** are funny poems with five lines. They have a specific rhythm pattern and rhyme scheme.

Describe Somebody • Almost A Summer Sky

UNIT 4

BEFORE YOU READ: POETRY OF WOODSON

Vocabulary

These words are underlined in the poems. Listen to each word. Say it. Then, read the definition and the example sentence.

skinny (SKIN ee) *adj.* Someone or something that is **skinny** is thin.
The shirt looked huge on him because he is so skinny.

choir (KWY er) *n.* A group of people sing together in a **choir**.
We listened to the choir practice for the concert.

dabbing (DAB ing) *v.* A person who is **dabbing** something is lightly touching it several times to dry it.
Mary was dabbing her wet eyes with a tissue.

Vocabulary Practice

Read the first sentence in each group of three. Then, complete Sentence *a* by substituting another word or phrase that means the same as the underlined vocabulary word. Complete Sentence *b* with your own ideas and words.

1. The skinny dog crawled under the low fence.

   a. The _____ dog crawled under the low fence.

   b. The skinny dog _____.

2. Our school's choir performed at the hospital.

   a. Our school's _____ performed at the hospital.

   b. Our school's choir _____.

3. Carla was dabbing the child's mouth with a towel.

   a. Carla was _____ the child's mouth with a towel.

   b. Carla was dabbing _____.

Getting Ready to Read

Both "Describe Yourself" and "Almost a Summer Sky" take place in Brooklyn, New York. Brooklyn is one of New York City's five boroughs, or districts. Have you ever visited Brooklyn or another borough of New York City? If not, why would you like to visit or not visit New York City? Discuss your answer with a partner.

MAKING CONNECTIONS

Describe Somebody • Almost a Summer Sky
Jacqueline Woodson

Summaries In "Describe Somebody," a teacher asks her class to write a poem that describes someone. This poem describes Lonnie's thoughts as he thinks about the assignment. In "Almost a Summer Sky," Lonnie and his brother Rodney walk to the park. This poem shares Lonnie's thoughts as the two boys walk.

Note-taking Guide
Use this chart to record main ideas from the poems.

	Speaker	Characters	What the Speaker Learns or Realizes
Describe Somebody	Lonnie	Lonnie, Ms. Marcus, Eric, Miss Edna, Lamont	
Almost a Summer Sky			

Describe Somebody • Almost a Summer Sky 215

TAKE NOTES

Vocabulary Builder

Slang *Gonna* is slang, or an informal word used by a certain group of people. *Gonna* means "going to," or "will," which is the future tense.

The students in Ms. Marcus's class are *gonna*

_____

_____.

Vocabulary Builder

Slang Like *gonna*, *kinda* is a slang contraction of *kind of*, which means "somewhat." Using the term *kind of*, complete this sentence that describes Eric in line 18:

Eric is *kind of*

_____.

Fluency Builder

Notice that the narrator uses italics, or slanted type, to show the words said by another person. With a partner, take turns reading aloud the text on this page. Be sure to change your voice when you read to show that another person is speaking.

Describe Somebody
Jacqueline Woodson

Today in class Ms. Marcus said
Take out your poetry notebooks and describe somebody.
Think carefully, Ms. Marcus said.
You're gonna read it to the class.
5   I wrote, Ms. Marcus is tall and a little bit skinny.
Then I put my pen in my mouth and stared down
at the words.
Then I crossed them out and wrote
Ms. Marcus's hair is long and brown.
10 Shiny.
When she smiles it makes you feel all good inside.
I stopped writing and looked around the room.
Angel was staring out the window.
Eric and Lamont were having a pen fight.
15 They don't care about poetry.
Stupid words, Eric says.
Lots and lots of stupid words.
Eric is tall and a little bit mean.
Lamont's just regular.
20 Angel's kinda chubby. He's got light brown hair.

Sometimes we all hang out,
play a little ball or something. Angel's real good
at science stuff. Once he made a volcano
for science fair and the stuff that came out of it
25 looked like real lava. Lamont can
draw superheroes real good. Eric—nobody
at school really knows this but
he can sing. Once, Miss Edna[1] took me
to a different church than the one
30 we usually go to on Sunday.
I was surprised to see Eric up there
with a choir robe on. He gave me a mean look
like I'd better not
say nothing about him and his dark green robe with
35 gold around the neck.
After the preacher preached
Eric sang a song with nobody else in the choir singing.
Miss Edna started dabbing at her eyes
whispering *Yes, Lord.*
40 Eric's voice was like something
that didn't seem like it should belong
to Eric.
Seemed like it should be coming out of an angel.

Now I gotta write a whole new poem
45 'cause Eric would be real mad if I told the class
about his angel voice.

---

1. **Miss Edna** Lonnie's foster mother.

TAKE NOTES

Vocabulary Builder

Idioms *Hang out* means "relax with or be with other people." Complete this sentence:

The speaker likes to *hang out* with his friends by

_____

_____.

Vocabulary Builder

Parts of Speech As a verb, the word *look* means "turn your eyes toward something in order to see it." As a noun, it means "an expression that a person makes to show how he or she feels." What does *look* mean in line 32?

_____

_____

_____.

Comprehension Builder

Why must the speaker write a whole new poem? Underline the text that tells you.

TAKE NOTES

Vocabulary Builder

Multiple-Meaning Words As an adjective, *light* can mean "weighing very little." It can also mean "small amount." What does *light* mean in line 2?

_____

Fluency Builder

Pay attention to the punctuation when you read a poem. The punctuation tells the reader when to pause. If a line does not end with punctuation, the reader should not pause. Read aloud the first two stanzas of the poem smoothly and with expression.

Cultural Understanding

Upstate is a term used by New Yorkers. It refers to areas of New York State that are north of New York City.

Almost a Summer Sky
Jacqueline Woodson

It was the trees first, Rodney[1] tells me.
It's raining out. But the rain is light and warm.
And the sky's not all close to us like it gets sometimes. It's way up there with
5   some blue showing through.
Late spring sky, Ms. Marcus says. *Almost summer sky.*
And when she said that, I said
Hey Ms. Marcus, that's a good title for a poem, right?
10   *You have a poet's heart, Lonnie.*
That's what Ms. Marcus said to me.
I have a poet's heart.
That's good. A good thing to have.
And I'm the one who has it.

15   Now Rodney puts his arm around my shoulder
We keep walking. There's a park
eight blocks from Miss Edna's house
That's where we're going.
Me and Rodney to the park.
20   Rain coming down warm
Rodney with his arm around my shoulder
Makes me think of Todd and his pigeons
how big his smile gets when they fly.
The trees upstate ain't like other trees you seen, Lonnie
25   Rodney squints up at the sky, shakes his head
smiles.

No, upstate they got maple and catalpa and scotch pine,[2]
all kinds of trees just standing.
Hundred-year-old trees big as three men.

---

1. **Rodney** one of Miss Edna's sons.
2. **catalpa** (kuh TAL puh) *n.* tree with heart-shaped leaves; **scotch pine** tree with yellow wood, grown for timber.

30 *When you go home this weekend,*
       Ms. Marcus said.
   Write about a perfect moment.

   Yeah, Little Brother, Rodney says.
   You don't know about shade till you lived
       upstate.
   Everybody should do it—even if it's just for
       a little while.

35 *Way off, I can see the park—blue-gray sky*
   touching the tops of trees.

   I had to live there awhile, Rodney said.
   Just to be with all that green, you know?
   I nod, even though I don't.
40 *I can't even imagine moving away from*
       here,
   from Rodney's arm around my shoulder,
   from Miss Edna's Sunday cooking,
   from Lily[3] *in her pretty dresses and great*
   big smile when she sees me.

45 *Can't imagine moving away*

   From
   Home.

   You know what I love about trees, Rodney
       says.
   It's like . . . It's like their leaves are hands
       reaching
50 *out to you. Saying Come on over here,*
       Brother.
   Let me just . . . Let me just . . .
   Rodney looks down at me and grins.
   Let me just give you some shade for a while.

3. **Lily** Lonnie's sister, who lives in a different foster home.

TAKE NOTES

Vocabulary Builder

Idioms Find the phrase *just for a little while* in line 34. The idiom *a little while* means "a brief amount of time."

Rodney thinks that everybody should live upstate for *a little while* so they can

_____
_____.

Comprehension Builder

Describe Lonnie's feelings about the day and his walk.

_____
_____
_____

Vocabulary Builder

Simile A simile describes something by comparing it to something very different. A simile always contains *like* or *as*. Complete this sentence:

A tree's leaves are like

_____.

Almost a Summer Sky 219

AFTER YOU READ

Thinking About the Selection

1. In "Almost Summer Sky," what is Rodney's perfect moment? What is Lonnie's perfect moment? Complete the sentences in the chart below.

Rodney's perfect moment is . . .	Lonnie's perfect moment is . . .

2. In "Describe Somebody," Lonnie learns something about Eric that no one else knows. He learns that _____
_____.

TALK ABOUT IT **What Do You Think?** Do you agree that Lonnie has the heart of a poet? Discuss your opinion with a partner.

I think that Lonnie [**does** or **does not**] have the heart of a poet because _____.

WRITE ABOUT IT **Write a Poem** Lonnie is the speaker of the poem "Almost a Summer Sky." What do you think Rodney is thinking in the poem? Rewrite "Almost a Summer Sky" as Rodney might tell it.

It was the trees first, I tell Lonnie.

_____
_____
_____

VOCABULARY SKILL REVIEW

Parts of Speech

Some words can be used as different parts of speech. When the same word is used as different parts of speech, its meaning changes. You can figure out the meaning of the word by thinking about how it is used in a sentence and by looking at the other words around it.

Examples

charter	• (noun) a statement of the duties and purposes of an organization • (verb) pay a company for the use of its boat, plane, etc.
seal	• (noun) a large sea animal • (verb) close something tightly

Now You Do It

Draw a line from the sentence to the correct meaning of the word.

The **seal** balanced a ball on its nose!	close something tightly
Do you plan to **charter** a plane for the trip?	a statement of duties and purposes of an organization
A framed copy of our club's **charter** hangs on the wall.	a large sea animal
Be sure to **seal** that bag before you put it in the refrigerator.	pay a company for the use of its boat, plane, etc.

TALK ABOUT IT **What Have You Seen?** Choose a word from the lesson that reminds you of something you have seen in real life, on television, or in the movies. For example, you may have seen a seal at the zoo. Tell a partner about what you saw. Use the word two or three times in your conversation.

WRITE ABOUT IT **Write a Travel Story** Suppose that you are taking a trip on boat or a plane. Write a story about what happens. Use each word from the lesson in two different ways.

_____

_____

RESEARCH THE AUTHOR

Poetry Reading

Arrange a **poetry reading**. Follow these steps to prepare for your poetry reading.

- Read some of the author's works. Jacqueline Woodson's books include *Locomotion, Last Summer with Maizon,* and *Between Madison and Palmetto.* Be sure to read several of the poems included in *Locomotion.*

  What I learned from Woodson's writing:
  _____
  _____
  _____
  _____

- Search the Internet. Use words and phrases such as "Jacqueline Woodson article."

  What I learned about Jacqueline Woodson:
  _____
  _____
  _____
  _____

- Watch the video interview with Jacqueline Woodson. Review your source material.

  Additional information learned about the author:
  _____
  _____
  _____
  _____
  _____
  _____

Use your notes as you prepare for your poetry reading.

BEFORE YOU READ: POETRY OF FARJEON, DE LA MARE, AND JOHNSON

UNIT 4

Vocabulary

These words are underlined in the poems. Listen to each word. Say it. Then, read the definition and the example sentence.

flatterer (FLAT er er) *n.* A **flatterer** is one who insincerely praises in order to win approval.
  Louisa is a flatterer, so I do not take her compliments seriously.

scampering (SKAM per ing) *v.* If one is **scampering**, one is moving quickly.
  The scared rabbit went scampering away.

immensity (i MEN si tee) *n.* **Immensity** is great size, vastness.
  The immensity of the universe makes me feel small and insignificant.

Vocabulary Practice

Read the first sentence in each group of three. Then, complete Sentence *a* by substituting another word or phrase that means the same as the underlined vocabulary word. Complete Sentence *b* with your own ideas and words.

1. Because Carl is a flatterer, Teresa never believes his compliments.

   a. Because Carl is a _____, Teresa never believes his compliments.

   b. Because Carl is a flatterer, _____.

2. The children were scampering around the playground.

   a. The children were _____ around the playground.

   b. The children were scampering _____.

3. The boat's immensity surprised the passengers.

   a. The boat's _____ surprised the passengers.

   b. The boat's immensity _____.

 ## Getting Ready to Read

The Moon rotates around Earth. It is the brightest object in the sky next to the Sun. The Moon shines at night because the Sun's light reflects off the Moon's surface. What else do you know about the Moon? Discuss what you know with a small group.

Poetry Collection 1 **223**

MAKING CONNECTIONS

Poetry Collection 1

Summaries "Cat!" uses fun language and sounds to describe a frightened and angry cat. The speaker in "Silver" creates a silvery image of a moonlit night. "Your World" challenges the reader to push past life's limitations.

Writing About the Big Question

What is the secret to reaching someone with words? In "Poetry Collection 1," poets go beyond relying on the meaning of words to communicate. Complete this sentence:

I (notice/do not notice) the sensory effect of words like swoosh, smush, scrunch, crunch, munch, and splash. Some words I like for their sounds are _____ and _____ because _____.

Note-taking Guide
Use this chart to record the topic and actions in each poem.

Poem	Topic	Two Actions in the Poem
Cat!		
Silver	the moon	
Your World		

224 English Learner's Notebook

Cat!
Eleanor Farjeon

     Cat!
     Scat!
After her, after her,
Sleeky flatterer,
5   Spitfire chatterer,
Scatter her, scatter her
    Off her mat!
    Wuff!
    Wuff!
10   Treat her rough!
Git her, git her,
Whiskery spitter!
Catch her, catch her,
Green-eyed scratcher!
15   Slathery
    Slithery
    Hisser,
    Don't miss her!
Run till you're dithery,[1]
20   Hithery
    Thithery[2]
    Pftts! pftts!
    How she spits!
    Spitch! Spatch!
25   Can't she scratch!
Scritching the bark
Of the sycamore tree,
She's reached her ark
And's hissing at me

1. **dithery** (DITH er ee) *adj.* nervous and confused; in a dither.
2. **Hithery/Thithery** made-up words based on *hither* and *thither*, which mean "here" and "there."

TAKE NOTES

Cultural Understanding
This poem is based on animal sounds that most American children learn when they are young.

Vocabulary Builder

Parts of Speech The word *treat* has more than one meaning. As a verb, it can mean "behave toward someone in a certain way." As a noun, it can mean "something special that you give someone." What does *treat* mean in the line "Treat her rough!"?

_____

_____

Comprehension Builder

Onomatopoeia Sound devices allow poets to use the musical quality of words to express ideas. Onomatopoeia is a sound device in which poets use words to imitate sounds. Underline two words that imitate cat sounds. How do they help you imagine the poem's action?

_____

_____

_____

TAKE NOTES

Vocabulary Builder

Adverbs An adverb describes a verb, an adjective, or another adverb. Which two adverbs in line 1 describe the verb in line 2?

_____

_____

Fluency Builder

Read lines 7 and 8 silently. Then, write the lines in your own words, using sentence form. Doing so will help you find the subject of the lines, its description, and the action. After you understand the meaning of lines 7 and 8, reread the lines smoothly and with expression.

_____

_____

_____

_____

Comprehension Builder

What "walks the night"? Underline the text that tells you.

---

30   *Pftts! pftts!*
      Wuff! wuff!
          Scat,
          Cat!
          That's
35   *That!*

Silver
Walter de la Mare

Slowly, silently, now the moon
Walks the night in her silver shoon;[1]
This way, and that, she peers, and sees
Silver fruit upon silver trees;
5   One by one the casements[2] catch
Her beams beneath the silvery thatch;[3]
Couched in his **kennel,** like a log,
With paws of silver sleeps the dog;
From their shadowy coat the white breasts
      peep
10 Of doves in a silver-feathered sleep;
A harvest mouse goes scampering by,
With silver claws, and silver eye;
And moveless fish in the water gleam,
By silver reeds in a silver stream.

Everyday Words
kennel (KEN uhl) *n.* a place where dogs are kept

---

1. **shoon** (SHOON) *n.* old-fashioned word for "shoes."
2. **casements** (KAYS muhnts) *n.* windows that open out, as doors do.
3. **thatch** (THACH) *n.* roof made of straw or other plant material.

Your World
Georgia Douglas Johnson

Your world is as big as you make it.
I know, for I used to abide
In the narrowest nest in a corner,
My wings pressing close to my side.

5   But I sighted the distant horizon
Where the sky line encircled the sea
And I throbbed with a burning desire
To travel this <u>immensity</u>.

I battered the cordons[1] around me
10 And cradled my wings on the breeze
Then soared to the uttermost reaches
With **rapture,** with power, with ease!

TAKE NOTES

Fluency Builder

Rhyme is the repetition of sounds at the end of words. Read lines 2 and 4. *Abide* in line 2 rhymes with *side* in line 4. The ending *-ide* is repeated in both words. Circle the end rhymes in the remaining lines of the poem "Your World." With a partner, read the words that you circled and listen to the end rhymes.

Vocabulary Builder

Context Clues Context is the text around a particular word. Context clues give you more information about a word. Underline the words in the second stanza that help you figure out the meaning of *immensity*. What does *immensity* mean?

_____

Fluency Builder

Poets do not always stop sentences at the end of lines. Sentences end with periods, question marks, and exclamation marks. Read aloud the entire poem, pausing only when you see a punctuation mark.

Everyday Words
rapture (RAP cher) *n.* ecstasy

1. **cordons** (KAWR duhnz) *n.* lines or cords that restrict free movement.

AFTER YOU READ

Thinking About the Selection

1. Complete the sentences in the chart below to tell about the poem "Cat!"

| The cat in the poem runs off her _____ _____. | → | The cat is running because _____ _____. | → | The reader knows that the poem's speaker dislikes the cat because _____ _____. |

2. The speaker of "Silver" tells about _____
_____.

TALK ABOUT IT **Interpret the Poem** What message does the speaker of the poem "Your World" want the reader to understand? Discuss your ideas with a partner.

The speaker of "Your World" wants the reader to understand that
_____.

WRITE ABOUT IT **Do You Agree?** Think about your answer to the above question. Do you agree with the speaker's message? Write a brief paragraph explaining why you agree or disagree.

I [agree or disagree] with the speaker of "Your World" because
_____
_____
_____

VOCABULARY SKILL REVIEW

The Prefix *anti-*

A prefix is added to the beginning of a base word. Adding the prefix *anti-* changes the meaning of the base word to its opposite. It means "against" or "opposed to." Study the examples below.

Examples

Base Word	New Word	New Meaning
climax	anticlimax	something that seems disappointing because it happens after something that was much better
social	antisocial	unwilling to meet people and talk to them
freeze	antifreeze	a substance that is put in the water in car engines to stop it from freezing
aircraft	antiaircraft	able to be used against enemy aircraft

Now You Do It

Write a sentence for each word from this lesson.

anticlimax _____

antisocial _____

antifreeze _____

antiaircraft _____

TALK ABOUT IT **Antisocial Actions** How do you think an antisocial person behaves? With a partner, discuss how someone who is antisocial might behave at a party, on a bus, and in a department store.

WRITE ABOUT IT **Write a News Story** Write three newspaper headlines, one for each of these words: *antiaircraft, antifreeze,* and *anticlimax.* For each headline, write a short paragraph that briefly explains the news story. The stories may be serious or funny.

UNIT 4

BEFORE YOU READ: POETRY OF MERRIAM, GIOVANNI, AND TENNYSON

Vocabulary

These words are highlighted in the poems. Listen to each word. Say it. Then, read the definition and the example sentence.

resounding (ri ZOWND ing) *adj.* A **resounding** sound is a loud, echoing sound.
   His voice echoed, resounding in the empty hall.

strife (STRYF) *n.* **Strife** is conflict or the act of fighting.
   Strife between the two groups led to war.

spite (SPYT) *n.* **Spite** is a mean or nasty feeling toward another person.
   His angry, hateful words were spoken out of spite.

Vocabulary Practice

Read the first sentence in each group of three. Then, complete Sentence *a* by substituting another word or phrase that means the same as the underlined vocabulary word. Complete Sentence *b* with your own ideas and words.

1. The resounding thunder scared the younger children.

   a. The _____ thunder scared the younger children.

   b. The resounding thunder _____.

2. She did not want to cause strife at school.

   a. She did not want to cause _____ at school.

   b. She did not want to cause strife _____.

3. He did not have spite for the other team.

   a. He did not have _____ for the other team.

   b. He did not have spite _____.

Getting Ready to Read

A person's fingerprints are unique. No two people have the same fingerprints. They can be used to identify a person. The author of "Thumbprint" celebrates her individuality by comparing it to her thumbprint. Why do you think that some people highly value their individuality? Discuss your answer with a partner.

MAKING CONNECTIONS

Poetry Collection 2

Summaries The speaker in "Thumbprint" is glad that no one is exactly like her. The speaker in "The Drum" describes different people in terms of drums. The speaker in "Ring Out, Wild Bells" wants the bells to ring out the bad and ring in the good.

 Writing About the Big Question

What is the secret to reaching someone with words? The writers of the poems in "Poetry Collection 2" take advantage of the musical quality of poetry with readers. Complete this sentence:

Words set to a beat, whether poetry or song lyrics, can create a

memorable experience for a listener because _____

_____ .

Note-taking Guide
Use this chart to note details about the subject of each poem.

	Thumbprint	The Drum	Ring Out, Wild Bells
Subject of the poem	the speaker's thumbprint		
Words that describe the subject			

Poetry Collection 2   231

AFTER YOU READ

Thinking About the Selection

1. According to "The Drum," what kinds of drums exist? Write your answers in the graphic organizer.

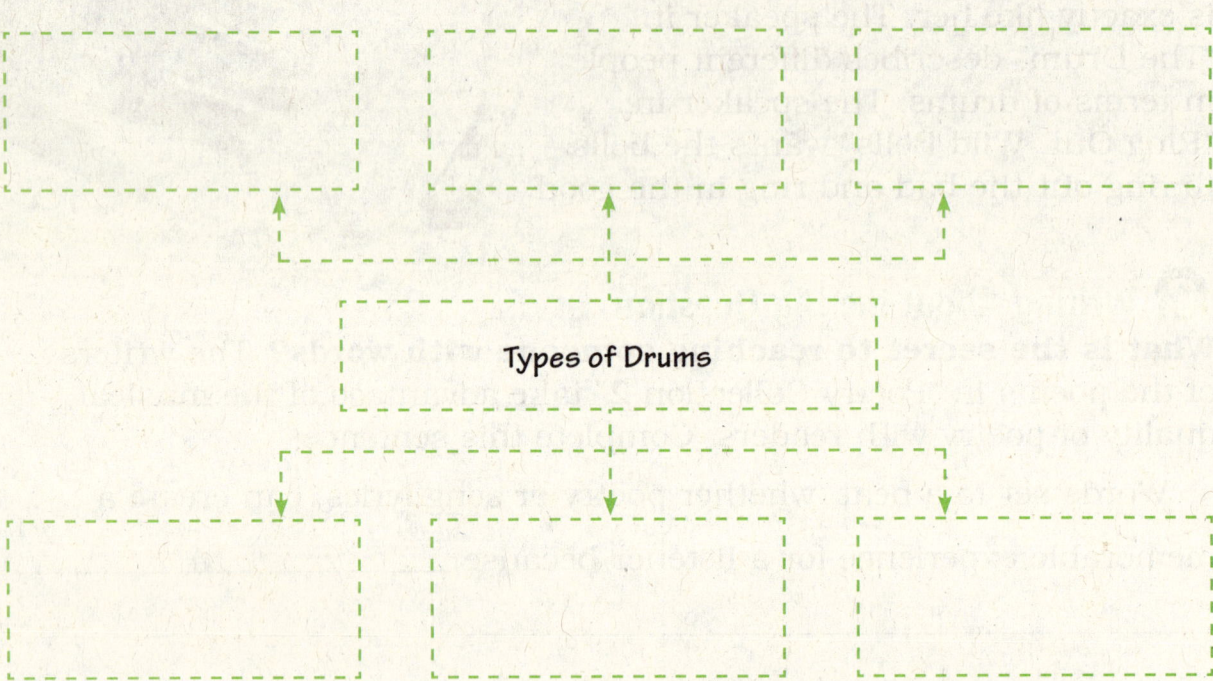

2. In "Thumbprint," the speaker's thumbprint is important to her because _____.

TALK ABOUT IT **Recall Details** With a partner, list four things the speaker of "Ring Out, Wild Bells" wants to "ring out" and "ring in."

The speaker wants to "ring out" _____
and "ring in" _____.

WRITE ABOUT IT **Letter to the Editor** Write a letter to the editor, describing the kind of future the speaker of "Ring Out, Wild Bells" sees.

_____
_____
_____

VOCABULARY SKILL REVIEW

Word Families
Word families are groups of words that share the same base word. Knowing the meaning of the base word helps determine the meanings of other words in the word family.

Example

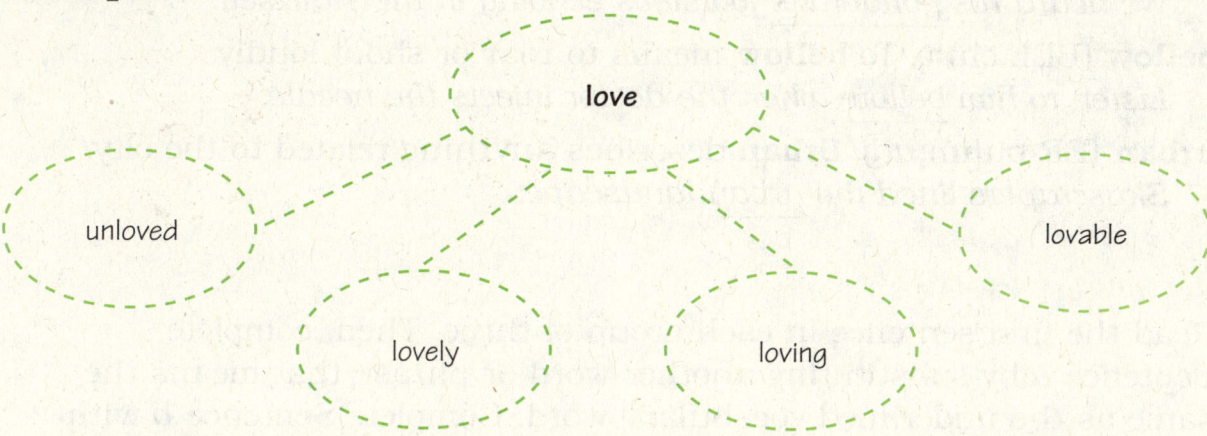

Now You Do It
Complete the sentences below using words from the diagram above. Use each word one time only. Make sure the sentences make sense with the word you selected. The first one has been done for you.

Don't you just <u>love</u> this color?

You are wearing a _____ dress.

He pays attention to his dog so it never feels _____.

This teddy bear is so _____ that I cannot keep from hugging it.

Tina is such a _____ person.

TALK ABOUT IT **Tell About a Person You Love** Tell a partner about a person you love. Use at least three words from the *love* word family.

WRITE ABOUT IT **Family Building** Write a letter to a good friend using words from the *love* word family. Include at lease three words from the word family in the letter.

Poetry Collection 2   233

UNIT 4
BEFORE YOU READ: POETRY OF GARCIA, HUGHES, AND HUBBELL

Vocabulary

These words are underlined in the poems. Listen to each word. Say it. Then, read the definition and the example sentence.

ponderous (PAHN duhr uhs) *adj.* Something that is **ponderous** is large, heavy, and massive.
  We heard his ponderous footsteps echoing in the stairwell.

bellow (BEL oh) *v.* To **bellow** means to roar or shout loudly.
  Listen to him bellow when the doctor injects the needle.

urban (ER buhn) *adj.* **Urban** describes anything related to the city.
  Skyscrapers lined the urban landscape.

Vocabulary Practice

Read the first sentence in each group of three. Then, complete Sentence *a* by substituting another word or phrase that means the same as the underlined vocabulary word. Complete Sentence *b* with your own ideas and words.

1. The <u>ponderous</u> box was difficult to carry upstairs.

   a. The _____ box was difficult to carry upstairs.

   b. The ponderous _____.

2. I heard Tommy <u>bellow</u> from the other room.

   a. I heard Tommy _____ from the other room.

   b. I heard Tommy bellow _____.

3. We live in an <u>urban</u> neighborhood.

   a. We live in a(n) _____ neighborhood.

   b. We live in an urban _____.

 **Getting Ready to Read**

During the Industrial Revolution of the 1700s and 1800s, many people moved from farming areas to find jobs in the cities. As more people moved to cities, the cities grew into the large areas we have today. Describe to a partner some of the things that you can see and hear in a city today.

MAKING CONNECTIONS

Poetry Collection 3

Summaries Concrete mixers and elephants are compared in "Concrete Mixers." The speaker of "The City Is So Big" feels frightened by the city at night. The speaker in "Harlem Night Song" invites a loved one to enjoy the beauty of the night sky over the city.

 Writing About the Big Question

What is the secret to reaching someone with words? In "Poetry Collection 3," three poets carefully craft their words to help us experience life in a big city. Complete this sentence:

Even if you have never been to a place, a talented poet can help you experience how it might feel to be there by _____

_____.

Note-taking Guide
Use this chart to help you record the imagery in each poem.

	Imagery
Concrete Mixers	elephant tenders, tough gray-skinned monsters, muck up to their wheel caps
The City Is So Big	
Harlem Night Song	

Poetry Collection 3 **235**

TAKE NOTES

Cultural Understanding

A concrete mixer is a machine that is usually attached to a large truck. The device has a large container in which sand, gravel, cement, and water are mixed to form concrete. The concrete is used to construct buildings, sidewalks, roads, and so on.

Vocabulary Builder

Pronouns Pronouns are words that take the place of nouns. Some pronouns include *it, they, him,* and *she*. The noun or pronoun to which a pronoun refers is called an *antecedent*. Underline the antecedent of *they* in line 9.

Vocabulary Builder

Similes Read lines 13, 14, and 15. Each *like* phrase is a simile. A simile is a comparison of two unlike things. Complete this sentence to make a simile of your own about concrete mixers:

The concrete mixers turn like

_____

_____ .

Concrete Mixers
Patricia Hubbell

The drivers are washing the concrete
    mixers;
Like elephant tenders they hose them
    down.
Tough gray-skinned monsters standing
    ponderous,
Elephant-bellied and elephant-nosed,
5 Standing in muck up to their wheel-caps,
Like rows of elephants, tail to trunk.
Their drivers perch on their backs like
    mahouts,[1]
Sending the sprays of water up.
They rid the trunk-like trough of concrete,
10 Direct the spray to the bulging sides,
Turn and start the monsters moving.
        Concrete mixers
        Move like elephants
        Bellow like elephants
15   Spray like elephants,
Concrete mixers are urban elephants,
Their trunks are raising a city.

---

1. **mahouts** (muh HOWTS) *n.* in India and the East Indies, elephant drivers or keepers.

The City Is So Big
Richard García

The city is so big
Its bridges quake with fear
I know, I have seen at night

The lights sliding from house to house
5 And trains pass with windows shining
Like a smile full of teeth

I have seen machines eating houses
And stairways walk all by themselves
And elevator doors opening and closing
10 And people disappear.

TAKE NOTES

Vocabulary Builder

The word *quake* in line 2 means "tremble." To remember this word, think of earthquakes. The earth trembles and shakes during an earthquake.

Comprehension Builder

How does the speaker describe a train's windows?
_____
_____
_____
_____

Fluency Builder

Only the last line of the poem ends with a punctuation mark. With a partner, take turns reading aloud the poem without pausing or stopping at the end of each line.

TAKE NOTES

Cultural Understanding

Harlem is a section of New York City whose name refers to a cultural movement in the 1920s known as the Harlem Renaissance. Many talented writers and musicians were part of the Harlem Renaissance.

Vocabulary Builder

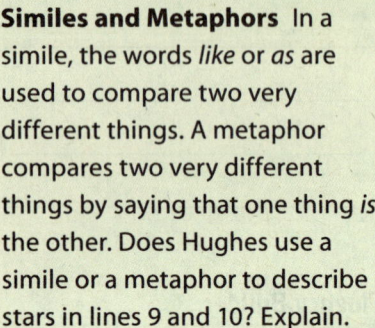

Similes and Metaphors In a simile, the words *like* or *as* are used to compare two very different things. A metaphor compares two very different things by saying that one thing *is* the other. Does Hughes use a simile or a metaphor to describe stars in lines 9 and 10? Explain.

_____

_____

Comprehension Builder

What word explains what the speaker wants the listener to join him in doing as they "roam the night together"? Circle the answer in the text.

Harlem Night Song
Langston Hughes

Come,
Let us **roam** the night together
Singing.

I love you.

5 Across
The Harlem roof-tops
Moon is shining.
Night sky is blue.
Stars are great drops
10 Of golden dew.

Down the street
A band is playing.

I love you.

Come,
15 Let us roam the night together
Singing.

Everyday Words
roam (rohm) *v.* go aimlessly; wander

AFTER YOU READ

Thinking About the Selection

1. In the chart below, list three unusual events that the speaker in "The City Is So Big" mentions. The first one has been listed for you.

	Unusual Events the Speaker Sees
1	bridges quaking with fear
2	
3	

2. The speaker of "Harlem Night Song" asks the listener to sing because _____
_____.

TALK ABOUT IT **Find Similarities** What common subject do all three of the poems in this selection share? Discuss your ideas with a partner.

All three poems in this collection discuss _____.

WRITE ABOUT IT **Make a Choice** Think about the common subject of the three poems. Which poem in this collection do you think best describes the common subject? Write a paragraph explaining your reasons.

I think that _____ best describes the common subject because _____
_____
_____
_____.

Poetry Collection 3

VOCABULARY SKILL REVIEW

Homophones

A homophone is a word that sounds the same as another word, but its meaning is different. Often its spelling is different. Homophones sound alike when they are spoken. They often are mistaken for one another. Context clues will help you determine the correct meaning.

Examples

Pronunciation	Word and Definition	Sentence
(RYT)	**right** (adjective) correct or true	You have the **right** answer.
	write (verb) to form words, letters, or numbers with a pen or pencil	I have to **write** a thank-you note to my grandmother.
(ROHD)	**road** (noun) a specially prepared hard surface for vehicles to travel on	Be careful crossing the **road**!
	rode (verb) the past tense of ride	We **rode** on the train.

Now You Do It

Write sentences using the words in the above chart. Make sure you use each word correctly in your sentence.

right _____

write _____

road _____

rode _____

TALK ABOUT IT **What Do You Mean?** With a small group, take turns saying aloud a sentence containing one of the homophones explained in this lesson. Guess the meaning of the homophone in each sentence.

WRITE ABOUT IT **Write a Poem** Write a poem using the homophones in this lesson. Be sure to use the correct meaning of each word in its context. With a partner, read your poem aloud.

BEFORE YOU READ: POETRY OF NERUDA, BISHOP, AND DICKINSON

UNIT 4

Vocabulary

These words are highlighted in the poems. Listen to each word. Say it. Then, read the definition and the example sentence.

uneasily (un EEZ i lee) *adv.* **Uneasily** means a manner that is restless and anxious.
   Awake, she tossed uneasily all night.

unresponsive (un ri SPAHN siv) *adj.* To be **unresponsive** means to remain unchanged when acted upon by something.
   Her illness was unresponsive to treatment.

debates (di BAYTS) *v.* When one **debates**, one considers the reasons for and against a course of action.
   Tim debates whether to go out or stay in.

Vocabulary Practice

Read the first sentence in each group of three. Then, complete Sentence *a* by substituting another word or phrase that means the same as the underlined vocabulary word. Complete Sentence *b* with your own ideas and words.

1. She slept uneasily during the thunderstorm.
   a. She slept _____ during the thunderstorm.
   b. She slept uneasily _____.

2. The audience was unresponsive to the entertainer's jokes.
   a. The audience was _____ to the entertainer's jokes.
   b. The audience was unresponsive _____.

3. Kara debates whether to jump into the pool.
   a. Kara _____ whether to jump into the pool.
   b. Kara debates _____.

 ## Getting Ready to Read

Weather is the temperature outside. The amount of sun, clouds, rain, snow, and wind affect the weather. With a small group, discuss how the following types of weather make you feel: a sunny day in a forest, a thunderstorm at a beach, and a cold winter day.

Poetry Collection 4   241

MAKING CONNECTIONS

Poetry Collection 4

Summaries The speaker of "Ode to Enchanted Light" enjoys the beauty of nature. A thunderstorm at the beach is described in "Little Exercise." The speaker of "The Sky Is Low, the Clouds Are Mean" humorously describes a dark winter day.

Writing About the Big Question

What is the secret to reaching someone with words? The poets in "Poetry Collection 4" share their ideas about nature. Complete this sentence:

Written works about nature that get the most positive feedback from me are ones that _____

_____.

Note-taking Guide
Use this chart to recall the main image in each poem.

Ode to Enchanted Light	Little Exercise	The Sky Is Low, the Clouds Are Mean
a forest with light shining through the trees		

AFTER YOU READ

Thinking About the Selection

1. What three images does the speaker in "Little Exercise" ask the reader to think of? Write your answers in the chart below.

   The speaker in "Little Exercise" asks the reader to think of . . .

_____	_____	_____

2. In "Ode to an Enchanted Light," Pablo Neruda describes the world as _____.

TALK ABOUT IT **Which Do You Prefer?** Which poem in this collection contains the most memorable images of nature? Discuss your ideas with a partner.

I think that _____ contains the most memorable images because _____.

WRITE ABOUT IT **Rewrite the Poem** Which poem do you think contains the least memorable images of nature? Rewrite the poem so that it contains images that are more memorable for you.

_____
_____
_____
_____

Poetry Collection 4   243

VOCABULARY SKILL REVIEW

Homographs

Homographs are spelled exactly the same but are pronounced differently and mean different things. How a homograph is pronounced depends on how the word is used in the sentence. Look at the chart below for some examples of homographs.

Examples

Pronunciation	Word and Definition	Sentence
(WOOND)	**wound** (noun) an injury	The *wound* is bleeding so you must place a bandage on it.
(WOWND)	**wound** (verb) the past tense of wind	The clock is *wound* too tightly to chime correctly.
(TAYR)	**tear** (verb) to pull apart by force or by accident	Be careful or you will *tear* your shirt!
(TEER)	**tear** (noun) a drop of water that falls from the eye	Is that a *tear* falling down your face?

Now You Do It

Draw a line from the sentence to the correct meaning of the word.

Did you **tear** the hem from your dress?	an injury
A **tear** dropped from the tip of his nose.	the past tense of wind
The toy broke because I **wound** it too hard.	pull apart by force or by accident
I fell and caused the **wound** on my knee.	a drop of water that falls from the eye

TALK ABOUT IT **How Is It Pronounced?** With a partner, say a sentence for each word in this lesson. After you say a sentence, have your partner explain the meaning of the word used in the sentence. Take turns saying sentences and giving the words' meanings.

WRITE ABOUT IT **Write Clues in a Dialogue** Write a dialogue using the words from this lesson. Include information that will give the reader clues to the correct meanings of the words.

English Learner's Notebook

INFORMATIONAL TEXTS

Recipes and Food Labels

About Recipes and Food Labels

Recipes are directions that explain how to make a type of food or drink. You will find recipes much easier to follow after you have learned the different parts of a recipe. These parts include

- a title that names the dish
- a list of ingredients
- directions that tell the steps to follow
- the number of servings the dish will make

Food labels give information about food products. Reading a food label can tell you

- the number of calories per serving
- the amount of fat, cholesterol, sodium, carbohydrates, protein, and nutrients in the product

Reading Skill

You can **compare and contrast features of consumer materials** to understand how to make a recipe or how to read nutritional information about a product. Some features identify ingredients, highlight important information, or help show what should be done. These features include headings, subheadings, numbers, signal words, illustrations, captions, and italicized and boldfaced type.

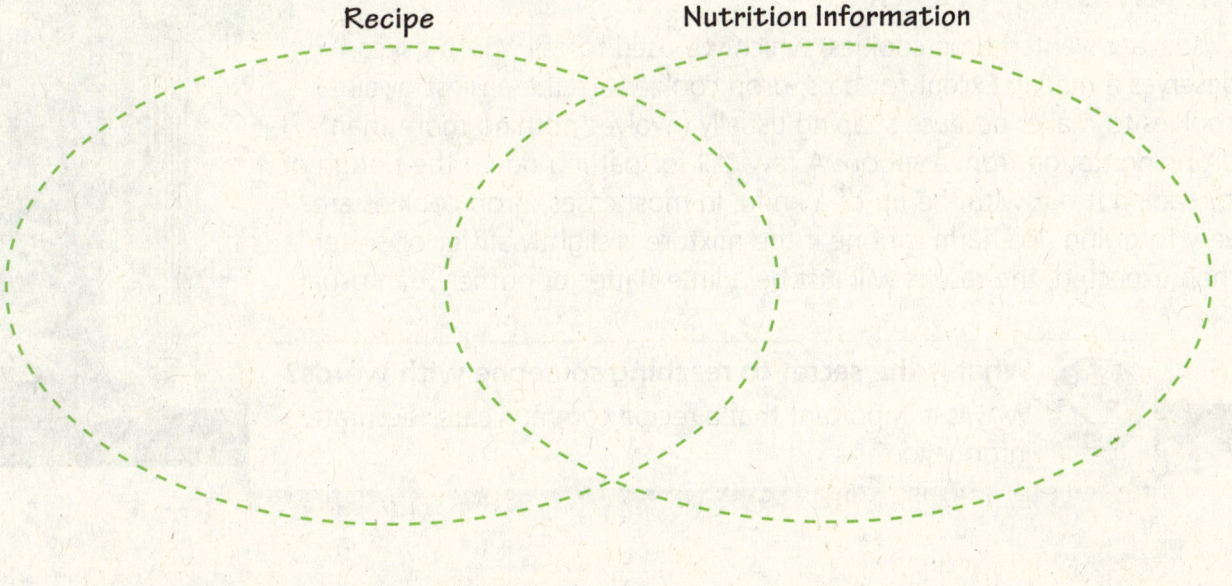

Informational Texts **245**

Thumbprint Cookies

½ cup brown sugar
1 cup butter
2–3 egg yolks
2 cups flour
egg whites
1½ cups chopped nuts
raspberry preserves

A list of ingredients tells readers what goes into the food they will be making.

To separate eggs, crack each egg in half. Over a bowl, pour the egg back and forth between the cracked halves. Let the egg white fall into the bowl, keeping the egg yolk intact in the shell. Cream together sugar, butter, and egg yolks. Beat flour into this mixture. Form balls and dip into slightly beaten egg whites. Roll balls in chopped nuts. Put on lightly greased cookie sheet and make a thumbprint on each ball. Bake at 350° for 8 minutes. Remove from oven and reset thumbprint. Bake 8 to 10 minutes longer. Fill print with raspberry preserves.

Preparation: 25 min.
Baking: 18 min

Yield: 30
Can freeze

Recipe

Features:
- a title that names the food being prepared
- a list of ingredients
- directions that explain how to prepare a certain kind of food
- text written for a general audience

Separating an egg

Using a teaspoon

ABOUT DROP COOKIES

Whoever invented drop cookies, which we used to call "drop cakes," deserves a medal. Except for bars, drop cookies are the easiest of all cookies to make, because shaping usually involves nothing more than dropping dough from a spoon. A few call for patting down the dough or spreading it out with the tip of a knife. In most cases, drop cookies are very forgiving: No harm is done if the mixture is slightly stiffer or softer than expected; the results will just be a little flatter or puffier than usual.

The recipe includes tips for preparing the food successfully.

 **THE BIG Q** What is the secret to reaching someone with words?
Why is it important that a recipe communicates accurate information?

246 Informational Texts

Product Information

Features:
- information provided for the benefit of consumers
- numerical data
- guidelines, warnings, or recommendations regarding the use of a product
- text written for a general audience

USE THE NUTRITION FACTS LABEL TO EAT HEALTHIER

U.S. Food and Drug Administration

Check the serving size and number of servings.
- The Nutrition Facts Label information is based on ONE serving, but many packages contain more. Look at the serving size and how many servings you are actually consuming. If you double the servings you eat, you double the calories and nutrients, including the Percent Daily Values.
- When you compare calories and nutrients between brands, check to see if the serving size is the same.

The label provides information about specific nutrients found in foods.

For protein, choose foods that are lower in fat.
- Most Americans get plenty of protein, but not always from the healthiest sources.
- When choosing a food for its protein content, such as meat, poultry, dry beans, milk and milk products, make choices that are lean, low-fat, or fat free.

Look for foods that are rich in these nutrients.
- Use the label not only to limit fat and sodium, but also to increase nutrients that promote good health and may protect you from disease.
- Some Americans don't get enough vitamins A and C, potassium, calcium, and iron, so choose the brand with the higher Percent Daily Values for these nutrients.
- Get the most nutrition for your calories—compare the calories to the nutrients you would be getting to make a healthier food choice.

Nutrition Facts

Serving Size 1 cup (228g)
Servings Per Container 2

Amount Per Serving

Calories 250   Calories from Fat 110

	% Daily Value*
Total Fat 12g	18%
Saturated Fat 3g	15%
Trans Fat 3g	
Cholesterol 30mg	10%
Sodium 470mg	20%
Potassium 700mg	20%
Total Carbohydrate 31g	10%
Dietary Fiber 0g	0%
Sugars 5g	
Protein 5g	
Vitamin A	4%
Vitamin C	2%
Calcium	20%
Iron	4%

* Percent Daily Values are based on a 2,000 calorie diet. Your Daily Values may be higher or lower depending on your calorie needs.

		Calories: 2,000	2,500
Total fat	Less than	65g	80g
Sat fat	Less than	20g	25g
Cholesterol	Less than	300mg	300mg
Sodium	Less than	2,400mg	2,400mg
Total Carbohydrate		300g	375g
Dietary Fiber		25g	30g

AFTER YOU READ

Thinking About the Recipe and the Food Label

1. Why do most recipes list all of the ingredients needed before explaining how to use the ingredients?
   _____
   _____

2. Why is it important to check a Nutritional Facts label for both the suggested serving size and the number of servings per container?
   _____
   _____

Reading Skill

3. What information do you learn from the illustrations in the thumbprint cookies recipe?
   _____
   _____

4. How might comparing and contrasting the nutritional facts on a package of cookies help you decide whether to buy the package?
   _____
   _____

Timed Writing: Explanation (15 minutes)

Write directions for a food you know how to make.

- What ingredients are needed for this recipe?
   _____

- What tools are needed?
   _____

- What steps do you take in following the recipe?
   _____

BEFORE YOU READ: POETRY OF HAYDEN, SHAKESPEARE, AND SÁNCHEZ

UNIT 4

Vocabulary

These words are underlined in the poems. Listen to each word. Say it. Then, read the definition and the example sentence.

ingratitude (in GRAT uh tood) *n.* **Ingratitude** means lack of appreciation, ungrateful.
   Your ingratitude makes me want to take back my gift.

legacy (LEG uh see) *n.* A **legacy** is something physical or spiritual handed down from an ancestor.
   Amy's legacy from her grandpa was her mischievous sense of humor.

supple (SUP puhl) *adj.* Something described as **supple** bends easily and is flexible.
   The baby's skin was soft and supple.

Vocabulary Practice

Read the first sentence in each group of three. Then, complete Sentence *a* by substituting another word or phrase that means the same as the underlined vocabulary word. Complete Sentence *b* with your own ideas and words.

1. I was surprised by Laura's ingratitude for the gift.
   a. I was surprised by Laura's _____ for the gift.
   b. I was surprised by Laura's ingratitude _____.

2. My grandmother left a legacy of love and generosity.
   a. My grandmother left a(n) _____ of love and generosity.
   b. My grandmother left a legacy _____.

3. Jackson napped on the soft, supple leather couch.
   a. Jackson napped on the soft, _____ leather couch.
   b. Jackson napped on the soft, supple _____.

Getting Ready to Read

William Shakespeare was born in 1564 in Stratford-on-Avon, a small town in England. He moved to London and worked as an actor and a writer. What else do you know about Shakespeare? Discuss what you know with a small group.

Poetry Collection 5   249

MAKING CONNECTIONS

Poetry Collection 5

Summaries In "Runagate Runagate," the speaker describes a frightening escape. "Blow, Blow, Thou Winter Wind" uses images from winter to describe a false friendship. In "Old Man," the speaker celebrates his grandfather.

Writing About the Big Question

What is the secret to reaching someone with words? The poems in "Poetry Collection 5" convey a wide range of emotions such as bitterness, betrayal, fear, courage, love, and loss. Complete this sentence:

I can find poems written in the past relevant as long as they

_____.

Note-taking Guide

Use this chart to list the emotions expressed in each poem.

	Emotion
Runagate Runagate	
Blow, Blow, Thou Winter Wind	
Old Man	

250 English Learner's Notebook

Runagate Runagate
Robert Hayden

The poem opens with images and thoughts of an escaping slave—a "runagate"—who is being pursued by hunters and dogs.

◆ ◆ ◆

> **I.**
> Runs falls rises stumbles on from darkness
>   into darkness
> and the darkness thicketed with shapes of
>   terror
> and the hunters pursuing and the hounds
>   pursuing

◆ ◆ ◆

The poem continues with more of the escaped slave's thoughts. He is determined to escape the auction block and the lash. The narrator refers to the "mythic North," where freedom is possible. Then the poem shifts to another point of view. We now hear from a slaveholder—the "subscriber"—who has placed an ad in a newspaper.

◆ ◆ ◆

> If you see my Pompey, 30 yrs of age,
> new breeches, plain stockings, negro
>   shoes:
> if you see my Anna, likely young
>   mulatto
> branded E on the right cheek, R on
>   the left,
> catch them if you can and notify
>   subscriber.

◆ ◆ ◆

The slaveholder goes on to say that the slaves will be hard to catch. He says that they will do anything to escape—even that they will turn into scorpions when anyone gets close. The point of view shifts back to that of the runaway slave. The narrator expresses

TAKE NOTES

Comprehension Builder
Describe what is happening in the first stanza of the poem.

_____
_____
_____
_____
_____

Vocabulary Builder
Nouns Find the nouns *auction block* and *lash* in the bracketed paragraph. An *auction block* is a platform from which things are sold to the person who is willing to pay the most money. A *lash* is a whip.

Vocabulary Builder
Abbreviations An abbreviation is a short form of a word or an expression. An abbreviation for the word *years* appears in the line that begins "if you see my Pompey, . . ." Circle the abbreviation.

TAKE NOTES

Vocabulary Builder

Idioms Find the phrase *make it* in the sentence that begins "Harriet Tubman . . ." *Make it* is an idiom that means "succeed." Complete the following sentence:

The people escaping slavery are afraid that they will not *make it* because _____

_____.

Vocabulary Builder

Informal Language *Folks* is an informal word meaning "people." To which group of people is Harriet Tubman referring in the bracketed passage?

_____
_____
_____

Cultural Understanding

The Underground Railroad was not a real railroad. It was a network of people who helped others escape slavery. Railroad terms were used to keep their actions secret. A person called a *conductor* led *passengers,* or escaping slaves, to *stations,* or houses where they could eat and sleep.

his determination to escape. The second section of the poem opens with a reference to Harriet Tubman. She risked her life many times to help slaves escape. Harriet Tubman shows her strength as the escaped slaves begin to doubt that they will make it.

♦ ♦ ♦

> we'll never make it. *Hush that now,*
> and she's turned upon us, leveled pistol
> glinting in the moonlight:
> Dead folks can't jaybird-talk, she says:
> you keep on going now or die, she says.

♦ ♦ ♦

The poem tells about the wanted posters for Harriet Tubman. A reward is offered for her, dead or alive. The poem then shifts back to the point of view of the escaped slave. He wonders whether divine help will be offered. Then, the narrator talks about the "train" that is carrying the escaped slaves to freedom. The reader is invited to come ride the train, too. The poem ends with the narrator expressing a strong determination to be free.

Blow, Blow, Thou Winter Wind
William Shakespeare

Blow, blow, thou winter wind.
Thou art not so unkind
   As man's ingratitude.
Thy tooth is not so keen,
5 Because thou art not seen,
   Although thy breath be rude.
Heigh-ho! Sing, heigh-ho! unto the green holly.
Most friendship is feigning, most loving mere folly.[1]
   Then, heigh-ho, the holly!
10   This life is most jolly.

Freeze, freeze, thou bitter sky,
That dost not bite so nigh
   As benefits forgot.
Though thou the waters warp,[2]
15 Thy sting is not so sharp
   As friend remembered not.
Heigh-ho! Sing, heigh-ho! unto the green holly.
Most friendship is feigning, most loving mere folly.
   Then, heigh-ho, the holly!
20   This life is most jolly.

1. **feigning … folly** Most friendship is fake, most loving is foolish.
2. **warp** v. freeze.

TAKE NOTES

Vocabulary Builder

Homographs The word *wind* has two pronunciations: WIND and WYND. Pronounced WIND, it means "air that moves with much force." Pronounced WYND, it means "turn or twist repeatedly." What does *wind* mean in the first line of the poem? Explain.

_____
_____
_____
_____

Comprehension Builder

Notice the words *thou, thy, art,* and *dost*. People no longer use these words in everyday language. People replace these words with *you, your, are,* and *does*. Select two lines that use these old words. Put the lines into your own words. Use everyday language.

_____
_____
_____

Fluency Builder

Remember that lines of poems may or may not be the ends of sentences. With a partner, read each stanza aloud, pausing for punctuation and reading lines as they form sentences.

TAKE NOTES

Vocabulary Builder

Base Words The word *remembrance* is a noun meaning "recalling and giving honor to someone who has died." The base word of *remembrance* is the verb *remember,* meaning "to have a picture or an idea in mind of people, events, or places from the past." The poet wrote "Old Man" in *remembrance* of

_____.

Fluency Builder

Circle each punctuation mark at the end of the lines of the second stanza. Then, take turns reading each line with a partner. Remember to pause at each comma as you read aloud. When you come to the ellipsis at the end of the stanza, remember to change your tone as your voice trails off.

Comprehension Builder

What does the speaker say that the old man's rivulets, or wrinkles, represent? Underline the text that tells you.

Old Man
Ricardo Sánchez

remembrance
(smiles/hurts sweetly)
October 8, 1972

old man
with brown skin
talking of past
    when being shepherd
5   in utah, nevada, colorado and
        new mexico
was life lived freely;

old man,
    grandfather,
10 wise with time
running rivulets on face,
deep, rich furrows,[1]
    each one a legacy,
deep, rich memories of life . . .

15 "you are indio,[2]
    among other things,"
he would tell me
    during nights spent
so long ago
20   amidst familial gatherings
in albuquerque . . .

1. **rivulets ... furrows** here, the wrinkles on the old man's face.
2. **indio** (IN dee oh) *n.* Indian; Native American.

old man, loved and respected,
he would speak sometimes
of pueblos,³
25   san juan, santa clara,
and even santo domingo,
and his family, he would say,
came from there:
some of our blood was here,
30   he would say,
before the coming of coronado,⁴
other of our blood
came with los españoles,⁵
and the mixture
35   was rich,
though often painful . . .
old man,
who knew earth
by its awesome aromas
40   and who felt
the heated sweetness
of chile verde⁶
by his supple touch,
gone into dust is your body
45   with its **stoic** look and resolution,
but your reality, old man, lives on
in a mindsoul touched by you . . .

Old Man . . .

TAKE NOTES

Vocabulary Builder

Multiple-Meaning Words The word *rich* can mean "wealthy," "entertaining," or "significant." Which definition does the speaker use line 35?

_____

Vocabulary Builder

Idioms *Gone into dust* means "dead and broken down." In line 44, what does the speaker mean when he says "gone into dust is your body"? Rewrite line 44 in your own words.

_____
_____
_____

Everyday Words
stoic (STOH ik) *adj.* calm in the face of suffering

3. **pueblos** (PWEB lohs) *n.* here, Native American towns in central and northern New Mexico.
4. **coronado** (kawr uh NAH doh) sixteenth-century Spanish explorer Francisco Vasquez de Coronado journeyed through what is today the American Southwest.
5. **los españoles** (los es pan YOH les) *n.* Spaniards.
6. **chile verde** (CHEE lay VER day) *n.* green pepper.

Poetry Collection 5

AFTER YOU READ

Thinking About the Selection

1. Rewrite the lines shown on the chart for each poem in your own words. The first one has been completed for you.

Poem	Lines	What They Mean
Runagate Runagate	1–2 ("Runs falls rises stumbles . . .")	We continually run, fall, and get up again, stumbling on in the darkness night after night. The darkness is filled with fearful images.
Blow, Blow, Thou Winter Wind	8 ("Most friendship is feigning . . .")	
Old Man	8–14 ("old man, grandfather . . .")	

2. The subject of the poem "Blow, Blow, Thou Winter Wind" is _____.

TALK ABOUT IT **A Warm, Fuzzy Feeling** Discuss with a small group the thoughts and feelings the speaker has about his grandfather in "Old Man." What overall impression does the poem create?

The speaker feels _____.

The overall feeling of the poem is _____.

WRITE ABOUT IT **What It Means To You** Which poem did you find most meaningful? Write a short paragraph to explain why it was meaningful.

I found _____ most meaningful because _____
_____
_____
_____.

VOCABULARY SKILL REVIEW

Idioms

An idiom is a word or phrase that has a special meaning different from the words' ordinary meaning. Look at the three examples below. The first sentence in each pair uses an idiom. The second sentence means the same thing, but it does not use the idiom.

Examples

- I passed the test *with flying colors!*
- I passed the test *very successfully.*

- I did not respond because I *drew a blank.*
- I did not respond because I *could not think of anything to say.*

- I better *crack the books* since final examinations are next week.
- I better *start studying* since final examinations are next week.

Now You Do It

Write the correct idiom to complete each sentence.

Let's meet to _____ before the test on Friday.

Esteban won the race _____.

When he asked me that question, I _____.

TALK ABOUT IT **Guess the Idiom** With a partner, discuss how you could describe each idiom on this page. Then, write a short clue that describes the idiom. Share your clues with another pair. Take turns guessing the idioms from the clues each pair wrote.

WRITE ABOUT IT **Descriptive Writing** Use the idioms in this lesson to write a description of a typical day at school. Be sure to use interesting language to show how the day at school relates to the idiom.

_____

_____

_____

_____

UNIT 4
BEFORE YOU READ: POETRY OF LAZARUS, LONGFELLOW, AND DUNBAR

Vocabulary
These words are highlighted in the poems. Listen to each word. Say it. Then, read the definition and the example sentence.

yearning (YERN ing) *adj.* When one is **yearning,** one is filled with a deep longing or desire for something.
They watched the clock, yearning for lunchtime.

somber (SAHM ber) *adj.* **Somber** means dark and gloomy.
It is hard to joke with someone who is in a somber mood.

peril (PEHR uhl) *n.* A **peril** is a condition that may cause danger, harm, death, or destruction.
Her reckless actions put her health and safety in peril.

Vocabulary Practice
Read the first sentence in each group of three. Then, complete Sentence *a* by substituting another word or phrase that means the same as the underlined vocabulary word. Complete Sentence *b* with your own ideas and words.

1. We looked out the window, yearning to play in the snow.

   a. We looked out the window, _____ to play in the snow.

   b. _____ yearning to play in the snow.

2. The cold, dark, and somber room frightened us.

   a. The cold, dark, and _____ room frightened us.

   b. The cold, dark, and somber room _____.

3. Climbing the mountain put Juan in peril.

   a. Climbing the mountain put Juan in _____.

   b. _____ put Juan in peril.

Getting Ready to Read
The Statue of Liberty is just over 305 feet tall and weighs about 150 tons. It is covered in a thin layer of copper. The statue looks light green because of the way that copper reacts with the weather. Have you ever visited the Statue of Liberty or seen it in pictures? Discuss your experience with a small group.

MAKING CONNECTIONS

Poetry Collection 6

Summaries In "The New Colossus," the speaker describes the Statue of Liberty. In "Paul Revere's Ride," the speaker tells the story of Paul Revere's ride. In "Harriet Beecher Stowe," the speaker praises Harriet Beecher Stowe, who helped people understand the fight against slavery.

 Writing About the Big Question

What is the secret to reaching someone with words? The poems in "Poetry Collection 6" recall important events and people in American history. Complete this sentence:

The description of an event from history needs to _____ _____ in order to have significance for me.

Note-taking Guide
Use this chart to recall the key parts of the poems.

	The New Colossus	Paul Revere's Ride	Harriet Beecher Stowe
Main Subject	The Statue of Liberty		
Main Idea		Paul Revere rode a horse all night to warn people that the British troops were coming.	
Why is the poem's subject important?			Her book helped bring about the end of slavery.

AFTER YOU READ

Thinking About the Selection

1. In "The New Colossus," whom does the United States welcome? Write your answers in the graphic organizer below.

   The United States welcomes . . .

   [ ] [ ] [ ] [ ] [ ]

2. If the British were attacking by sea, Revere's friend was supposed to _____.

TALK ABOUT IT **Always Remember** The poems "Paul Revere's Ride" and "Harriet Beecher Stowe" celebrate two important people in United States history. Why is it important to remember and celebrate historical figures? Discuss your ideas with a small group.

It is important to remember and celebrate historical figures because _____.

WRITE ABOUT IT **Write a Review** Which poem in this collection interests you the most? Write a review of the poem that tells why it interests you.

_____
_____
_____
_____

VOCABULARY SKILL REVIEW

Irregular Verbs

Most verbs form the past tense by adding *-ed* or *-d*. Irregular verbs do not follow this rule. Some examples of irregular verbs are shown in the chart below. Recall that a past participle is used with a helping verb such as *have*.

Examples

Verb	Past Tense	Past Participle
freeze	froze	frozen
give	gave	given
forget	forgot	forgotten

Now You Do It

Complete the sentences with the correct tense of the words from the above chart. The first one has been done for you.

I have <u>forgotten</u> the title of the movie.

It was very cold last night, and some of the plants _____.

She has _____ her favorite book to her cousin.

Yesterday you _____ to bring your books home to study.

My uncle _____ me a bicycle last year.

The pond has _____, so we can go ice-skating.

TALK ABOUT IT **Tell What Happened** With a partner, use at least two of the words in this lesson to tell about something that happened to you or something you did. Be sure to use past tenses in your story.

WRITE ABOUT IT **Write an Adventure** Write a short adventure story using the words from the lesson. Read your story to a small group.

UNIT 4
BEFORE YOU READ: POETRY OF UPDIKE, MOMADAY, AND WALKER

Vocabulary
These words are underlined in the poems. Listen to each word. Say it. Then, read the definition and the example sentence.

recede (ri SEED) *v.* To **recede** means to go or move back.
As the clouds began to recede, the sky brightened.

remote (ri MOHT) *adj.* To be **remote** means to be far off and distant or not closely related.
He was once friendly, but since his wife died he has grown remote.

extinguished (ik STING gwishd) *v.* When something is **extinguished**, it is put out, ended.
His dream of a football career was extinguished when he injured his knee.

Vocabulary Practice
Read the first sentence in each group of three. Then, complete Sentence *a* by substituting another word or phrase that means the same as the underlined vocabulary word. Complete Sentence *b* with your own ideas and words.

1. Carlos watched the sea recede from the beach.

    a. Carlos watched the sea _____ from the beach.

    b. Carlos watched the sea recede _____.

2. Julianne seemed remote as she spoke to Terri.

    a. Julianne seemed _____ as she spoke to Terri.

    b. Julianne seemed remote _____.

3. Chores extinguished my hope for a restful weekend.

    a. Chores _____ my hope for a restful weekend.

    b. Chores extinguished _____.

Getting Ready to Read
One goal of the civil rights movement was to provide the same quality of education to all students, regardless of race. What else do you know about the civil rights movement? What were its goals and who were its leaders? Discuss your knowledge with a small group.

MAKING CONNECTIONS

Poetry Collection 7

Summaries In "January," the speaker describes images connected with winter. "New World" shares different parts of the day in nature. In "For My Sister Molly Who in the Fifties," the speaker talks about her relationship with her sister.

The Magpie(detail), 1869, Claude Monet, Musee d'Orsay, Paris

 Writing About the Big Question

What is the secret to reaching someone with words? The poets in "Poetry Collection 7" carefully choose words to convey a speaker's ideas about specific people and places. Complete this sentence:

If someone who did not know me asked me to describe my hometown or my family, I would choose sensory images such as _____ and _____.

Note-taking Guide

Use this chart to record the main image or images in each poem.

January	New World	For My Sister Who...
snowy footsteps		

Poetry Collection 7   263

TAKE NOTES

Vocabulary Builder

Adjectives An adjective describes a noun or a pronoun. Which two adjectives describe the noun *footsteps* in line 5?

_____

_____

Vocabulary Builder

Onomatopoeia Onomatopoeia is the use of words that sound like what they mean, such as *roar*, *hiss*, or *buzz*. Circle an example of onomatopoeia in this poem.

Comprehension Builder

What things does the speaker associate with the month of January? Write two examples from the poem on the lines below.

_____

_____

_____

_____

January
John Updike

    The days are short,
        The sun a spark
    Hung thin between
        The dark and dark.

5   Fat snowy footsteps
        Track the floor,
    And parkas pile up
        Near the door.

    The river is
10   A frozen place
    Held still beneath
        The trees' black lace.

    The sky is low.
        The wind is gray.
15   The radiator
        Purrs all day.

New World
N. Scott Momaday

1.

    First Man,
    behold:
    the earth
    glitters
5 with leaves;
    the sky
    glistens
    with rain.
    Pollen
10 is borne
    on winds
    that low
    and lean
    upon
15 mountains.
    Cedars
    blacken
    the slopes—
    and pines.

2.

20 At dawn
    eagles
    hie and
    hover[1]
    above
25 the plain
    where light
    gathers
    in pools.
    Grasses

Everyday Words

glistens (GLI suhnz) *v.* shines; sparkles

1. **hie and hover** fly swiftly and then hang as if suspended in the air.

TAKE NOTES

Vocabulary Builder

Parts of Speech The word *leaves* can be a verb that means "goes away" or a noun that is the plural of *leaf*, "flat green part of a plant or tree." Which meaning does the poet use in line 5?

_____

_____

Fluency Builder

Preview the text on this page. Examine any unfamiliar words. Use the lines below to write the pronunciation and definition of each word. Then, reread this page aloud smoothly and with expression.

_____

_____

_____

Vocabulary Builder

Parts of Speech The word *light* is a noun, a verb, and an adjective. As a noun, *light* can mean "brightness from the sun or electricity." As a verb, *light* can mean "make something burn." As an adjective, it can mean "weighing very little." Which form does the speaker use in line 26?

_____

TAKE NOTES

Vocabulary Builder

Similes A simile compares two things that are not alike but are similar in some way. A simile always contains either *like* or *as*. The speaker uses a simile to describe shadows. Circle the sentence in which the simile appears. The speaker compares

_____ with

_____.

Comprehension Builder

Paraphrase lines 37 through 51.

_____

_____

_____

_____

Vocabulary Builder

Multiple-Meaning Words
The blackbirds are described as being "fixed." *Fixed* can mean "repaired," "arranged," "unchangeable," or "immovable." What does *fixed* mean in line 58? Explain.

_____

_____

_____

30 shimmer
and shine.
Shadows
withdraw
and lie
35 away
like smoke.

3.
At noon
turtles
enter
40 slowly
into
the warm
dark loam.[2]
Bees hold
45 the swarm.
Meadows
recede
through planes
of heat
50 and pure
distance.

4.
At dusk
the gray
foxes
55 stiffen
in cold;
blackbirds
are fixed
in the
60 branches.

---

2. **loam** (lohm) rich, dark soil.

Rivers
follow
the moon,
the long
65 white track
of the
full moon.

For My Sister Molly Who in the Fifties
Alice Walker

FOR MY SISTER MOLLY WHO IN THE
   FIFTIES
Once made a fairy rooster from
Mashed potatoes
Whose eyes I forget
5 But green onions were his tail
And his two legs were carrot sticks
A tomato slice his crown.
Who came home on vacation
When the sun was hot
10 and cooked
and cleaned
And minded least of all
The children's questions
A million or more
15 Pouring in on her
Who had been to school
And knew (and told us too) that certain
Words were no longer good
And taught me not to say us for we
20 No matter what "Sonny said" up the
road.

TAKE NOTES

Vocabulary Builder

Pronouns A pronoun replaces a noun. Circle the pronoun *his* in the first stanza of "For My Sister Molly Who in the Fifties." To which noun does *his* refer?

_____

_____

Vocabulary Builder

Parts of Speech As a noun, the word *slice* means "a piece of something." As a verb, it means "cut." What does *slice* mean in line 7?

_____

_____

Vocabulary Builder

Idioms Lines 13–15 state that Molly answered millions of children's questions *pouring in on her*. The idiom *pouring in* means "flooding" or "arriving quickly and in large amounts." Complete the following sentence:

The hot sun was *pouring in* through the window on Molly as she

_____.

Take Notes

Vocabulary Builder

Idioms *Carry a tune* is an idiom that means "able to sing well." Complete the following sentence:

Molly helped the speaker *carry a tune* by

_____

_____.

Fluency Builder

With a partner, read aloud lines 36 through 51. Be sure to read the stanza smoothly and with expression.

Vocabulary Builder

Parts of Speech As a verb, *bites* means "cuts or crushes something with teeth." As a noun, it means "injuries from holes in skin caused by insects or animals." Which meaning does *bites* have in line 48?

_____

_____

With a partner, discuss how you know the meaning of the word.

FOR MY SISTER MOLLY WHO IN THE
    FIFTIES
Knew Hamlet[1] well and read into the night
And coached me in my songs of Africa
25 A continent I never knew
But learned to love
Because "they" she said could carry
A tune
And spoke in accents never heard
30 In Eatonton.
Who read from Prose and Poetry
And loved to read "Sam McGee from
    Tennessee"[2]
On nights the fire was burning low
And Christmas wrapped in angel hair[3]
35 And I for one prayed for snow.

WHO IN THE FIFTIES
Knew all the written things that made
Us laugh and stories by
The hour   Waking up the story buds
40 Like fruit. Who walked among the flowers
And brought them inside the house
And smelled as good as they
And looked as bright.
Who made dresses, braided
45 Hair. Moved chairs about
Hung things from walls
Ordered baths
Frowned on wasp bites
And seemed to know the endings
50 Of all the tales
I had forgot.

---

1. **Hamlet** play by William Shakespeare.
2. **"Sam McGee from Tennessee"** reference to the title character in the Robert Service poem, "The Cremation of Sam McGee."
3. **angel hair** fine, white, filmy Christmas tree decoration.

WHO OFF INTO THE UNIVERSITY
Went exploring   To London and
To Rotterdam
55 Prague and to Liberia
Bringing back the news to us
Who knew none of it
But followed
crops and weather
60 funerals and
Methodist Homecoming;
easter speeches,
groaning church.

WHO FOUND ANOTHER WORLD
65 Another life   With gentlefolk
Far less trusting
And moved and moved and changed
Her name
And sounded precise
70 When she spoke   And frowned away
Our sloppishness.

WHO SAW US SILENT
Cursed with fear   A love burning
Inexpressible
75 And sent me money not for me
But for "College."
Who saw me grow through letters
The words misspelled   But not
The longing   Stretching
80 Growth
The tied and twisting
Tongue
Feet no longer bare
Skin no longer burnt against
85 The cotton.

TAKE NOTES

Vocabulary Builder

Affixes *Unbearable* has three word parts: the base word *bear*, the prefix *un-*, and the suffix *-able*. The prefix *un-* means "not," and the suffix *-able* means "capable of." Find two more words on this page that contain affixes and write them in the space below.

_____

_____

Comprehension Builder

Summarize the way that the speaker describes her family.

_____

_____

_____

_____

_____

WHO BECAME SOMEONE OVERHEAD
A light   A thousand watts
Bright and also blinding
And saw my brothers cloddish
90 And me destined to be
Wayward[4]
My mother remote   My father
A wearisome farmer
With heartbreaking
95 Nails.

FOR MY SISTER MOLLY WHO IN THE
    FIFTIES
Found much
Unbearable
Who walked where few had
100 Understood   And sensed our
Groping after light
And saw some extinguished
And no doubt mourned.

FOR MY SISTER MOLLY WHO IN THE
    FIFTIES
Left us.

---

4. **wayward** (WAY werd) *adj.* headstrong; disobedient.

AFTER YOU READ

Thinking About the Selection

1. What four things does the speaker in "For My Sister Molly Who in the Fifties" learn from Molly? Write your answers in the graphic organizer below.

2. The poem "New World" identifies the following times of day: _____.

TALK ABOUT IT **Images of Winter** With a small group, discuss three of the things that the speaker in "January" associates with winter. How does the speaker describe these things?

Three things that the speaker describes are _____.

WRITE ABOUT IT **Feelings About Winter** Write a short paragraph that explains how the speaker in "January" feels about winter. Use details from the poem to support your response.

_____
_____.

Poetry Collection 7   271

VOCABULARY SKILL REVIEW

The Suffix -ize

A suffix is a word part added to the end of a base word. The suffix *-ize* changes nouns and adjectives into verbs that mean "to make" or "become."

Examples

Base Word			New Word	New Meaning
modern	+ -ize	=	modernize	to make modern
final	+ -ize	=	finalize	to make final
formal	+ -ize	=	formalize	to make formal

Now You Do It

Write sentences using words from the above chart. Make sure you use the word correctly in the sentence.

Base Word	Suffix	Sentence
modern +		_____
final +	-ize	_____
formal +		_____

TALK ABOUT IT — **Ask Questions** With a partner, take turns asking and answering questions that contain the words from this lesson. For example, you might ask and answer this question: *How do you finalize an essay before you hand it to the teacher? Before I hand an essay to the teacher, I finalize it by _____.*

WRITE ABOUT IT — **Write a Poem** Write a poem that contains all three words from the lesson. Read your poem to a partner.

_____

_____

BEFORE YOU READ: POETRY OF LING, ROSE, AND CUMMINGS

Vocabulary

These words are highlighted in the poems. Listen to each word. Say it. Then, read the definition and the example sentence.

vertical (VER ti kuhl) *adj.* Something **vertical** is straight up and down, perpendicular to a horizontal line.
   A pine tree's trunk is tall and vertical.

burrow (BER roh) *n.* A **burrow** is a passage or hole dug in the ground by animals.
   The gopher dove into its burrow.

exquisite (ik SQWIZ it) *adj.* Something that is **exquisite** is very beautiful, the best quality.
   The exquisite vase was hand-painted by the artist.

Vocabulary Practice

Read the first sentence in each group of three. Then, complete Sentence *a* by substituting another word or phrase that means the same as the underlined vocabulary word. Complete Sentence *b* with your own ideas and words.

1. The <u>vertical</u> cliffs rose high above the road.

   a. The _____ cliffs rose high above the road.

   b. The vertical cliffs _____.

2. The fox hid in its <u>burrow</u> in the side of the hill.

   a. The fox hid in its _____ in the side of the hill.

   b. The fox hid in its burrow _____.

3. We really enjoyed Terrell's <u>exquisite</u> painting.

   a. We really enjoyed Terrell's _____ painting.

   b. We really enjoyed Terrell's exquisite _____.

 ## Getting Ready to Read

Sometimes people do not need to communicate by speaking. A person's body language and body movements can communicate ideas. Have you ever tried to communicate with someone without speaking? Discuss your experience with a small group.

MAKING CONNECTIONS

Poetry Collection 8

Summaries In "Grandma Ling," the speaker travels to Taiwan to meet her grandmother. She and her grandmother do not speak the same language. They still feel close to each other. In "Drum Song," the lines flow like the beat of a drum. The speaker tells how a turtle, a woodpecker, a snowhare, and a woman move through the world to their own beat. The speaker in "your little voice/Over the wires came leaping" talks to a special person on the telephone. Her voice makes him dizzy. He thinks of flowers. He feels as though he is dancing.

 ## Writing About the Big Question

What is the secret to reaching someone with words? The poems in "Poetry Collection 8" explore how words make connections between people and the world. Complete this sentence:

I had a connection to other people when I _____

_____ .

Note-taking Guide
Use this chart to help you note the events of each poem.

Grandma Ling	Drum Song	your little voice/Over the wires came leaping
The speaker visits her grandmother in Taiwan.		

AFTER YOU READ

Thinking About the Selection

1. What is each animal in "Drum Song" doing? Complete the sentences in the graphic organizer.

The turtle is …	The woodpecker is …	The snowhare is …
_____ _____ _____	_____ _____ _____	_____ _____ _____

2. In "your little voice / Over the wires came leaping" the voice on the telephone makes the speaker feel _____.

TALK ABOUT IT **Words Painting Pictures** Discuss with a partner what you imagined when you read each poem. Use the sentence frame to help you begin your discussion.

As I read _____,
I imagined _____.

WRITE ABOUT IT **Most Vivid** Which poem has the most vivid imagery? Write a paragraph explaining your reasons.

_____
_____
_____
_____
_____

Poetry Collection 8

VOCABULARY SKILL REVIEW

Word Families
Word families are groups of words that share the same base word.

Example

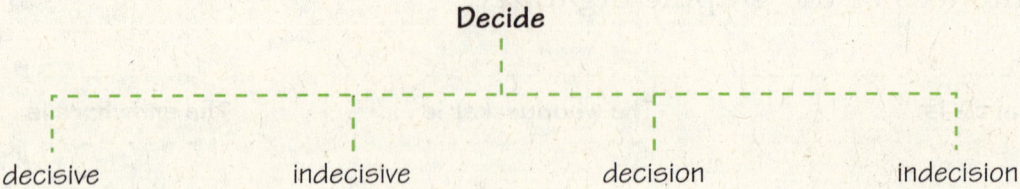

Now You Do It
Complete the sentences below using words from the word family *decide*. Use each word one time only. Make sure the sentences make sense with the word you selected.

The coach's _____ is causing a delay in the start of practice sessions.

My _____ is final!

Her _____ announcement revealed her confidence.

We were late to the movie because you were so _____.

TALK ABOUT IT **Decide Quickly** With a partner, talk about the qualities that make a person decisive. List the qualities, and talk about a person whom you find decisive.

WRITE ABOUT IT **Write a Paragraph** Write a paragraph describing a decision you had to make. Include at least three words from the lesson.

_____
_____
_____
_____
_____

INFORMATIONAL TEXTS

Manuals

About Manuals

A **manual** is a set of directions. It tells how to use a tool or product. Most manuals have these parts:
- a drawing or picture of the product with the parts and features labeled
- step-by-step directions for putting the item together and using it
- safety information
- a guide that tells how to fix common problems
- customer service information, such as telephone numbers, addresses, and Web site addresses

Reading Skill

You use a manual to perform a task. In order to use a manual effectively, you must **analyze the technical directions.** Study the drawings, diagrams, headings, lists, and labels to help you follow the directions. Bold type and capital letters often signal specific sections and important information.

Checklist for Following Technical Directions

❑ Read all the directions completely before starting to follow them.

❑ Look for clues such as bold type or capital letters that point out specific sections or important information.

❑ Use diagrams to locate and name the parts of the product.

❑ Follow each step in the exact order given.

❑ Do not skip any steps.

Informational Texts 277

Using Your Answering Machine

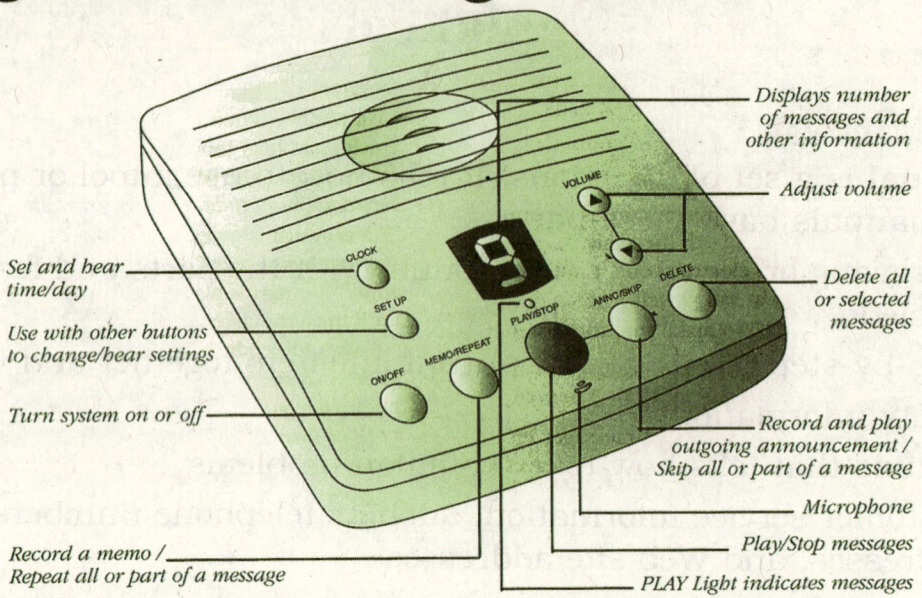

Set and hear time/day

Use with other buttons to change/hear settings

Turn system on or off

Record a memo / Repeat all or part of a message

Displays number of messages and other information

Adjust volume

Delete all or selected messages

Record and play outgoing announcement / Skip all or part of a message

Microphone

Play/Stop messages

PLAY Light indicates messages

Setting the Clock
You'll need to set the clock so that it can announce the day and time that each message is received. Press [PLAY/STOP] to exit Setting the Clock at any time.

1. Press and hold [CLOCK] until the Message Window displays [CLOCK], and the default day is announced.
2. To change the day setting, hold down [MEMO/REPEAT] or [ANNC/SKIP] until the correct day is announced. Then release the button.
3. Press and release [CLOCK]. The current hour setting is announced.
4. To change the hour setting, hold down [MEMO/REPEAT] or [ANNC/SKIP] until the correct hour is announced. Then release the button.
5. Press and release [CLOCK]. The current minutes setting is announced.
6. To change the minutes setting, hold down [MEMO/REPEAT] or [ANNC/SKIP] until the correct minutes setting is announced. Then release the button.
7. Press and release [CLOCK]. The new day and time are announced.

To check the clock, press and release [CLOCK].

NOTE: In the event of a power failure, see the instructions on the bottom of the unit to reset the clock.

Recording Your Announcement
Before using this answering system, you should record the announcement (up to one minute long) that callers will hear when the system answers a call. If you choose not to record an announcement, the system answers with a prerecorded announcement: *"Hello. Please leave a message after the tone."*

1. Press and hold [ANNC/SKIP]. The system beeps. Speak toward the microphone normally, from about nine inches away. While you are recording, the Message Window displays —.
2. To stop recording, release [ANNC/SKIP]. The system automatically plays back your announcement.

To review your announcement, press and release [ANNC/SKIP].

Turning the System On/Off
Use [ON/OFF] to turn the system on and off. When the system is off, the Message Window is blank.

Volume Control
Use volume buttons (▲ and ▼) to adjust the volume of the system's speaker. Press the top button (▲) to increase volume. Press the bottom button (▼) to decrease volume. The system beeps three times when you reach the maximum or minimum volume setting.

2

Announcement Monitor

You can choose whether to hear the announcement when your system answers a call, or have it silent (off) on your end (your caller will still hear an announcement).

1. Press and hold SET UP. After the Ring Select setting is announced, continue to press and release SET UP until the system announces "*Monitor is on (or off)*."
2. Press and release ANNC/SKIP or MEMO/REPEAT until the system announces your selection.
3. Press and release PLAY/STOP or SET UP to exit.

Listening to Your Messages

As the system plays back messages, the Message Window displays the number of the message playing. Before playing each message, the system announces the day and time the message was received. After playing the last message, the system announces "*End of messages*."

Play all messages — Press and release PLAY/STOP. If you have no messages, the system announces "*No messages*."

Play new messages only — Hold down PLAY/STOP for about two seconds, until the system begins playing. If you have no new messages, the system announces "*No new messages*."

Repeat entire message — Press and release MEMO/REPEAT.

Repeat part of message — Hold down MEMO/REPEAT until you hear a beep, then release to resume playing. The more beeps you hear, the farther back in the message you will be when you release the button.

Repeat previous message — Press MEMO/REPEAT twice, continue this process to hear other previous messages.

Skip to next message — Press and release ANNC/SKIP.

Skip part of a message — Hold down ANNC/SKIP until you hear a beep, then release to resume playing. The more beeps you hear, the farther into the message you will be when you release the button.

Stop message playback — Press and release PLAY/STOP.

Saving Messages

The system automatically saves your messages if you do not delete them. The system can save about 12 minutes of messages, including your announcement, for a total of up to 59 messages. When memory is full, you must delete some or all messages before new messages can be recorded.

Deleting Messages

Delete all messages — Hold down DELETE. The system announces "*Messages deleted*" and permanently deletes messages. The Message Window displays **0**. If you haven't listened to all of the messages, the system beeps five times, and does not delete messages.

Delete selected messages — Press and release DELETE while the message you want to delete is being played. The system beeps once, and continues with the next message. If you want to check a message before you delete it, you can press MEMO/REPEAT to replay the message before deleting it.

When the system reaches the end of the last message, the messages not deleted are renumbered, and the Message Window displays the total number of messages remaining in memory.

Recording a Memo

You can record a memo to be stored as an incoming message. The memo can be up to three minutes long, and will be played back with other messages.

1. Press and hold MEMO/REPEAT. After the beep, speak toward the microphone.
2. To stop recording, release MEMO/REPEAT.
3. To play the memo, press PLAY/STOP.

When Memory is Full

The system can record approximately 12 minutes of messages, including your announcement, for a total of up to 59 messages. When memory is full, or 59 messages have been recorded, the Message Window flashes **F**. Delete messages to make room for new ones.

When memory is full, the system answers calls after 10 rings, and sounds two beeps instead of your announcement.

4

AFTER YOU READ

Thinking About the Manual

1. You may use some of the answering machine features more than others. Which features do you think are most important? Explain.
_____
_____

2. Look at the diagram. How does it make the text easier to follow?
_____
_____

TALK ABOUT IT Reading Skill

3. Many words in the answering machine manual are boxed and set in italic type. What does this formatting tell about these words?
_____
_____

4. How are the steps in the process for "Setting the Clock" identified?
_____
_____

WRITE ABOUT IT Timed Writing: Analyze Technical Directions (20 minutes)

Reread the section of the manual headed "Setting the Clock." Explain how text features (headings, numbering, boxed terms, and italic type) help the reader understand the text. Use these questions to help organize your writing.

1. Why are parts of the text numbered? _____

2. Why are some words set inside a box? _____

3. What information is set in italic type? _____

UNIT VOCABULARY REVIEW

Word Bank

benefit	feedback	misunderstand
connection	individuality	relevant
cultural	inform	sensory
experience	meaningful	significance
express	media	valid

A. **Sentence Completion** Complete each sentence by telling what something is and then what it is not. Follow the language in each sentence so that your words make sense. The first one has been completed for you.

IS		NOT
A benefit is something that helps	but	it is not something that harms.
1. A connection is	but	it is not
2. An experience is	but	it is not
3. Feedback is	but	it is not
4. Individuality is	but	it is not
5. To misunderstand something may lead to	but	it should not lead to
6. Information that is relevant does	but	it does not
7. Something that is valid is	but	it is not
8. To inform is	but	it is not
9. Something meaningful is	but	it is not

B. **Word Sort** Place each word from the word bank in the appropriate column below. If the word names a person, place, or thing, list it in the Noun column. If the word states an action, place it in the Verb column. If the word describes a noun, place it in the Adjective column. If the word can be more than one part of speech, write it in all of the columns that apply.

Noun	Verb	Adjective

TALK ABOUT IT **The Effect of Words** Do the words people use influence the way that others feel or behave? Discuss your ideas with a small group. Use the sentence frame to begin the discussion.

The words people use [do *or* do not] affect the way that others feel and behave because _____

_____.

WRITE ABOUT IT **What Can You Do?** Write a speech that warns listeners to be more careful about the words they use when speaking. Use at least four words from the word bank.

_____

_____

_____

_____

EXPLORING DRAMA

from Anne Frank & Me

Drama is written to be performed, or acted out. Dramas, or plays, can include elements of fiction such as plot, conflict, and setting. They also use some elements that occur only in dramas, or plays. These special elements include those listed in the chart below.

Element	Definition	Example
Playwright	• author of a play	William Shakespeare
Script	• written form of a play	Romeo and Juliet
Acts	• units of the action in a play	Act III
Scenes	• parts of an act	Act III, scene ii
Characterization	• the playwright's technique of creating believable characters	A character hangs his head to show that he is ashamed.
Dialogue	• words that characters say • words that characters speak appear next to their names • much of what you learn about the play is revealed through dialogue	JIM: When did you recognize me? LAURA: Oh, right away.
Monologue	• a long, uninterrupted speech that is spoken by a single character	HAMLET: To be, or not to be . . .
Stage Directions	• bracketed information that tells the cast, crew, and readers of the play about sound effects, actions, and sets • this information can also describe a character's gestures or emotions	[whispering]
Set	• scenery on stage that suggests the time and place of the action	a kitchen, a park
Props	• small, portable items that make actions look realistic	plates, a book

EXPLORING DRAMA

There are different types of drama. Several types are listed below.

Comedy is a drama that has a happy ending. Comedies often have normal characters in funny situations. Comedies can be written to amuse their audiences. They can also point out what is wrong in a society.

Tragedy is often contrasted with comedy. Events in a tragedy lead to the downfall of the main character. This character can be an average person. More often the main character is an important person. He or she could be a king or queen or another type of heroic figure.

Drama is often used to describe plays that talk about serious things. Some dramas are not acted on a stage. These types of drama are listed below.

- **Screenplays** are scripts for films. They include instructions for the person using the camera. A screenplay usually has many more scene changes than a stage play.

- **Teleplays** are scripts for television. They often contain the same elements that screenplays have.

- **Radio plays** are scripts for radio broadcasts. They include sound effects. A radio play does not have a set.

BEFORE YOU READ: FROM ANNE FRANK AND ME

Vocabulary

These words are underlined in the play. Listen to each word. Say it. Then, read the definition and the example sentence.

confided (cuhn FYD uhd) *v.* If you **confided** in someone, you revealed or told that person a secret.
  The dentist confided that she did not like to brush her teeth.

distraction (di STRAK shuhn) *n.* A **distraction** is an interruption that takes a person's attention from something that is happening.
  Reading provided a distraction from her daily chores.

certainly (SER ten lee) *adv.* For something to happen **certainly**, it must occur definitely and without a doubt.
  He certainly believed that she was telling the truth.

Vocabulary Practice

Read the first sentence in each group of three. Then, complete Sentence *a* by substituting another word or phrase that means the same as the underlined vocabulary word. Complete Sentence *b* with your own ideas and words.

1. Stella confided her fears to her brother.

    a. Stella _____ her fears to her brother.

    b. Stella confided _____.

2. Not much causes distraction at the library.

    a. Not much causes _____ at the library.

    b. Not much causes distraction _____.

3. She certainly thought that she would win the race.

    a. She _____ thought that she would win the race.

    b. She certainly _____.

TALK ABOUT IT — Getting Ready to Read

Anne Frank & Me is a play. Authors intend that plays will be performed by actors and seen by audiences. Sometimes plays are filmed as movies. How are plays different from movies? Discuss your ideas with a partner.

MAKING CONNECTIONS

from Anne Frank & Me
Cherie Bennett

Summary An American teenager named Nicole travels back in time to Paris in 1942. Her family is arrested for being Jewish. They are put on a train going to a prison camp. Nicole recognizes Anne Frank on the train. She tells Anne details about Anne's life. Both girls are shocked by what Nicole knows.

Note-taking Guide
Use this diagram to compare and contrast the main characters.

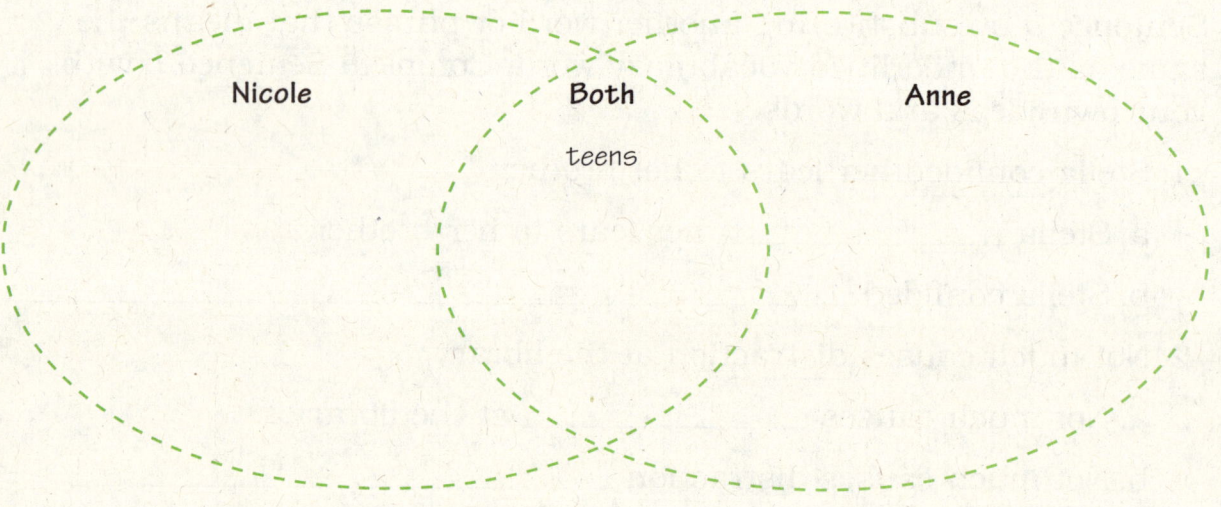

from Anne Frank & Me
Cherie Bennett

During this monologue, which takes place in a cattle car, Nazis push people into the car. The pre-recorded voice of Nicole explains that the car is in Westerbork, Holland, the date is September 3, 1944, and she expects the war to be over soon.

Nicole approaches a girl who is sitting in front of the toilet bucket with her back to the audience. Nicole explains that she needs to use the bucket and the girl offers to shield Nicole with her coat. Nicole tells the girl that she boarded the train just outside Paris and has been traveling for 17 days.

Nicole explains that, although she is from Paris and the other girl is from Amsterdam, Nicole somehow knows the girl.

♦ ♦ ♦

NICOLE. I do know you. Your name is . . . Anne Frank.[1]

ANNE. *(shocked)* That's right! Who are you?

NICOLE. Nicole Bernhardt. I know so much about you...you were in hiding for a long time, in a place you called . . . the Secret Annex[2]—

♦ ♦ ♦

Nicole continues describing her memories of Anne. Anne has been in hiding in the Secret Annex with her parents, her older sister Margot, and the Van Daans, whose son, Peter, is Anne's boyfriend. Anne is shocked that Nicole knows this information, some of which she has <u>confided</u> only to her diary.

♦ ♦ ♦

---

1. **Anne Frank** a young German Jewish girl who wrote a diary about her family's hiding in The Netherlands during the Holocaust. The Holocaust was the mass killing of European Jews and others by the Nazis during World War II.
2. **Secret Annex** name given to the space in an Amsterdam office building, where in 1942, thirteen-year-old Anne Frank and her family went into hiding.

TAKE NOTES

Vocabulary Builder

Prefixes Circle the word *pre-recorded* in the first paragraph. The prefix *pre-* means "before." *Recorded* means "made a copy of sounds." What does *pre-recorded* mean?

_____

_____

Vocabulary Builder

Parts of Speech As a noun, *coat* means "a piece of clothing with long sleeves that you wear to stay warm." As a verb, it means "cover a surface with a thin layer of something." Which meaning of *coat* does the author use in the sentence that begins "Nicole approaches a girl"? Explain.

_____

_____

Fluency Builder

Commas (,) indicate a brief pause in the text. They also separate words or items in a list. Read the bracketed paragraph silently. Circle every comma. Then, read the paragraph aloud, pausing at each comma.

TAKE NOTES

Vocabulary Builder

Idioms The phrase *playing a joke* means "doing something that makes another person look silly." Use the idiom to complete the following sentence:

Anne believes that Peter or her father _____ on her.

Comprehension Builder

What does Anne believe that Nicole is?

_____
_____

Vocabulary Builder

Contractions A contraction is a short form of two words that is missing a letter. The letter is replaced with an apostrophe ('). Circle the contractions on this page. Write the words that each contraction replaces.

_____
_____

NICOLE. You kept a **diary.** I read it.

ANNE. But . . . I left my diary in the Annex when the Gestapo[3] came. You couldn't have read it.

NICOLE. But I did.

♦ ♦ ♦

Anne believes that this very strange conversation the two girls are having may be a practical joke that Peter or Anne's father came up with as a <u>distraction</u>. Nicole denies that she is playing a joke on Anne.

♦ ♦ ♦

NICOLE. Do you believe in time travel?

ANNE. I'm to believe that you're from the future? Really, I'm much more **intelligent** that I look.

NICOLE. I don't know how I know all this. I just do.

ANNE. Maybe you're an angel.

NICOLE. That would <u>certainly</u> be news to me.

Everyday Words

diary (DY uh ree) *n.* book in which a person writes important or interesting things that happen in his or her life

intelligent (in TEL uh juhnt) *adj.* having a high level of ability to learn, understand, and think about things

---

3. **Gestapo** German security police under the Nazis.

AFTER YOU READ

Thinking About the Selection

1. What does Nicole say that she knows about Anne? Write your answers in the chart below.

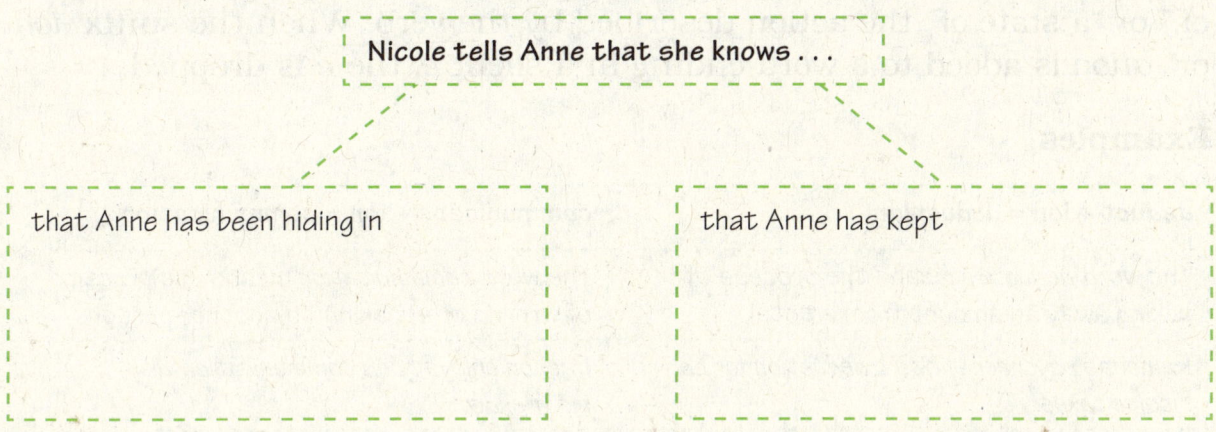

2. Anne believes that the conversation that she is having with Nicole is _____.

TALK ABOUT IT **How Does She Feel?** How does Anne feel when Nicole tells her details about Anne's personal life? Discuss your ideas with a partner.

When Nicole tells Anne personal details about Anne's life, Anne feels _____.

WRITE ABOUT IT **Rewrite the Scene** Write a new scene that describes what could have happened if Anne and Nicole had been friends before they met in the cattle car. What might they have said to each other? How might they have treated each other?

Nicole approaches a girl who is sitting with her back to her and realizes that _____
_____
_____
_____.

from Anne Frank & Me

VOCABULARY SKILL REVIEW

Suffixes

A suffix is added to the end of a base word. A suffix changes the meaning of the base word. Sometimes it changes the word's part of speech. The suffixes *-ion* and *-ation* are often added to a verb to form a noun. The noun usually means "an example of," "the practice of," "a way of," or "a state of" the action described by the verb. When the suffix *-ion* or *-ation* is added to a word ending in a silent *e*, the *e* is dropped.

Examples

deduct + ion = deduction	communicate + ion = communication
The word *deduction* means the process of taking away an amount from a total.	The word *communication* means the practice of writing or speaking to another person.
Ramona's paycheck shows a deduction for her income taxes.	Dashon enjoys good communication with his friends.

Now You Do It

Add the suffix *-ion* to the base words in the first column. Add the suffix *-ation* to the base words in the second column. Write the correct word on the blank next to the base word. Spellings may change when you add a suffix.

subtract _____   generalize _____

separate _____   represent _____

fascinate _____   globalize _____

pollute _____   inform _____

TALK ABOUT IT **School Subject *-ions* and *-ations*** In school you will probably learn many words that end with the suffixes *-ion* and *-ation*. Match the words in the activity above to subjects that you learn in school. Discuss your ideas with a partner.

WRITE ABOUT IT **What's Your Fascination?** *Fascination* is the state of being greatly interested. Write a paragraph describing a fascination that you have. Use at least three other words from this lesson.

RESEARCH THE AUTHOR

Bulletin Board Display

Create a **bulletin board display**. Following these tips will help prepare you to create a bulletin board display.

- Read some of the author's works. Cherie Bennett's books include *Zink, Life in the Fat Lane, Searching for David's Heart,* and *A Heart Divided.*

    What I learned from Bennett's writing:
    _____
    _____
    _____
    _____

- Search the Internet. Use words and phrases such as "Cherie Bennett."

    What I learned about Cherie Bennett:
    _____
    _____
    _____
    _____

- Watch the video interview with Cherie Bennett. Add what you learn from the video to what you have already learned about the author.

    Additional information learned about the author:
    _____
    _____
    _____
    _____

Use your notes to create your bulletin board display.

from *Anne Frank & Me*

UNIT 5

BEFORE YOU READ: THE GOVERNESS

Vocabulary

These words are underlined in the play. Listen to each word. Say it. Then, read the definition and the example sentence.

inferior (in FIR ee er) *adj.* **Inferior** means lower in status or rank than someone else.
   The king and queen thought that the peasants were inferior.

deduct (di DUKT) *v.* To **deduct** means to subtract an amount.
   Our teacher will deduct from our scores if we turn in homework late.

objects (uhb JEKTS) *v.* **Objects** means protests or opposes an idea.
   She objects to seeing the scary movie.

Vocabulary Practice

Read the first sentence in each group of three. Then, complete Sentence *a* by substituting another word or phrase that means the same as the underlined vocabulary word. Complete Sentence *b* with your own ideas and words.

1. The inferior team played poorly and lost the game.

   a. The _____ team played poorly and lost the game.

   b. The inferior _____.

2. Mom will deduct from my allowance if I do not do my chores.

   a. Mom will _____ from my allowance if I do not do my chores.

   b. Mom will deduct _____.

3. He objects to the candidates for class president.

   a. He _____ the candidates for class president.

   b. He objects _____.

Getting Ready to Read

In the nineteenth century, upper-class families hired governesses to teach their children. Usually, a governess was an unmarried woman who could not find other work. How would your education differ if you learned from a governess? Discuss your ideas with a partner.

292 English Learner's Notebook

MAKING CONNECTIONS

The Governess
Neil Simon

Summary A wealthy mistress plays a joke on her shy employee, Julia. The mistress subtracts money from Julia's pay. Julia is left with much less money than she is owed. The mistress hopes that Julia will become angry and stand up for herself.

Writing About the Big Question

Is it our differences or our similarities that matter most? The characters in *The Governess* come from different levels of society, which affects the way they treat each other. Complete this sentence:

An employer might discriminate against an employee, or treat her

unfairly because _____

_____.

Note-taking Guide
Use this chart to record the actions of the mistress and the way the governess responds to these actions.

Mistress's Action	Governess's Response

The Governess 293

TAKE NOTES

Cultural Understanding

This play is set in the nineteenth century. During that time, wealthy American and Russian families hired governesses to care for their children. Governesses were expected to supervise and educate the children and teach them good manners.

Vocabulary Builder

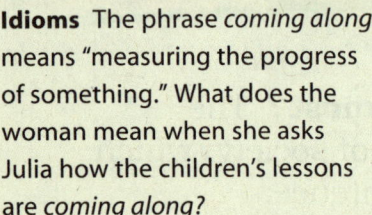

Idioms The phrase *coming along* means "measuring the progress of something." What does the woman mean when she asks Julia how the children's lessons are *coming along?*

_____

_____

_____

Vocabulary Builder

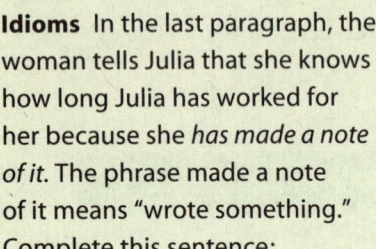

Idioms In the last paragraph, the woman tells Julia that she knows how long Julia has worked for her because she *has made a note of it.* The phrase made a note of it means "wrote something." Complete this sentence:

The mistress *made a note of it*

that _____

_____

_____.

The Governess
Neil Simon

The play opens as a woman calls out to Julia, the young governess who has been hired to teach the woman's children. When Julia enters, she curtsies and keeps her head down. The woman keeps telling Julia to keep her head up, but Julia finds this difficult. The woman asks Julia how the children's lessons in French and mathematics are coming along. Julia assures her that the children are doing well. The woman tells Julia again to keep her head up. She says that if Julia thinks of herself as inferior, people will treat her that way. Then the woman announces that she wants to pay Julia for the past two months of work.

◆ ◆ ◆

MISTRESS. Let's see now, we agreed on thirty **rubles** a month, did we not?

JULIA. *(Surprised)* Forty, ma'am.

MISTRESS. No, no, thirty. I made a note of it. *(Points to the book)* I always pay my **governess** thirty . . . Who told you forty?

◆ ◆ ◆

The woman insists that the rate of pay is thirty rubles a month. Julia accepts this. They then discuss how long Julia has been there. The woman says it has been two months exactly, but Julia says it has been two months and five days. The woman says she has made a note of it, and Julia accepts this. Then the woman wants to subtract nine Sundays, saying that they had agreed earlier on this.

Everyday Words

rubles (ROO buhlz) *n.* Russian currency; similar to U.S. dollars

governess (GUV uhr nes) *n.* a female teacher who lives with a family and teaches its children at home

© Pearson Education

294 English Learner's Notebook

Although Julia does not remember this, she says she does. The woman then subtracts three holidays: Christmas, New Year's, and Julia's birthday. Even though Julia worked on her birthday, she agrees to what the woman says.

◆ ◆ ◆

MISTRESS. Now then, four days little Kolya was sick, and there were no lessons.

JULIA. But I gave lessons to Vanya.

MISTRESS. True. But I **engaged** you to teach two children, not one. Shall I pay you in full for doing only half the work?

JULIA. No, ma'am.

MISTRESS. So we'll deduct it . . . Now, three days you had a toothache and my husband gave you permission not to work after lunch. Correct?

JULIA. After four. I worked until four.

MISTRESS. *(Looks in the book)* I have here: "Did not work after lunch." We have lunch at one and are finished at two, not at four, correct?

JULIA. Yes, ma'am. But I—

MISTRESS. That's another seven rubles . . . Seven and twelve is nineteen . . . Subtract . . . that leaves . . . forty-one rubles . . . Correct?

JULIA. Yes, ma'am. Thank you, ma'am.

◆ ◆ ◆

Now the woman wants to subtract more money to cover a teacup and saucer that Julia broke, even though Julia broke only the saucer. She also wants to deduct money because her son climbed a tree and tore his jacket, even though Julia had told him not to climb the tree. Julia also gets charged for the son's shoes that had been stolen by the

Everyday Words
engaged (en GAJD) *v.* employed

TAKE NOTES

Comprehension Builder
Why does the Mistress say that she should not have to pay Julia for the days that Kolya was sick?
_____
_____
_____

Vocabulary Builder
Slang Julia addresses the Mistress as "ma'am." *Ma'am* is pronounced MAM (rhymes with ham). It is a shortened version of the word *madam*. Addressing a woman as "ma'am" is a sign of respect. Complete the following setence:

Julia calls the mistress *ma'am*

because _____
_____
_____.

Fluency Builder
Read the line spoken by the Mistress that begins "That's another seven . . ." Circle the punctuation marks. With a partner, take turns reading the line aloud. Remember to pause at each ellipsis (. . .), and raise the tone of your voice when you come to a question mark (?). Think about the Mistress's personality, and try to express it as you read aloud.

The Governess

TAKE NOTES

Fluency Builder

With a partner, read aloud the dialogue between the mistress and Julia. Take turns reading aloud the lines for each character. Read each character's dialogue with expression to show the way each character feels.

Comprehension Builder

Summarize what the Mistress did to cheat Julia.

_____
_____
_____
_____

Vocabulary Builder

Adjectives Read the bracketed passage. Underline five adjectives in the passage. Remember that an adjective may follow the noun it describes. Then, circle the noun that each adjective describes.

---

maid. The reason for this is that the woman says Julia is paid to "watch everything." More deductions are made for money the woman claims she gave to Julia earlier. Julia <u>objects</u> weakly, saying she never got any money. Finally, the woman pays Julia, saying she is giving her eleven rubles. When Julia counts only ten, the woman says she must have dropped one on the floor. Julia accepts this, thanks the woman for the money, and starts to leave. She is called back by the woman.

◆ ◆ ◆

MISTRESS. Why did you thank me?

JULIA. For the money, ma'am.

MISTRESS. For the money? . . . But don't you realize what I've done? I've cheated you . . . *Robbed* you! I have no such notes in my book. I made up whatever came into my mind. Instead of the eighty rubles which I owe you, I gave you only ten. I have actually stolen from you and you still thank me . . . Why?

JULIA. In the other places that I've worked, they didn't give me anything at all.

MISTRESS. Then they cheated you even worse than I did . . . I was playing a little joke on you. A cruel lesson just to teach you. You're much too trusting, and in this world that's very dangerous . . . I'm going to give you the entire eighty rubles. *(Hands her an envelope)* It's all ready for you. The rest is in this envelope. Here, take it.

JULIA. As you wish, ma'am.

◆ ◆ ◆

Julia turns to leave, but the woman calls her back again. The woman asks her why she does not speak up for herself. She asks if it is possible to be "such a simpleton." Julia tells her yes, that it is possible. Julie curtsies and leaves. The woman looks after her, completely baffled.

AFTER YOU READ

Thinking About the Selection

1. What reasons does the Mistress give for paying Julia less money? Complete the sentences in the chart below.

	The Mistress's Reasons for Paying Julia Less Money
1	The Mistress says that she agreed to pay Julia _____.
2	The Mistress subtracts money for the following days: _____.
3	The Mistress deducted half of Julia's pay for four days because _____.
4	The Mistress deducted money for the three days that _____.
5	The Mistress subtracted money because she says that Julia broke _____.

2. At the end of the play, the Mistress reveals that _____.

TALK ABOUT IT **What Do You Think?** Do you think that the Mistress's lesson was kind or cruel? Discuss your reasons with a partner.

The Mistress's lesson was [**kind** or **cruel**] because _____.

WRITE ABOUT IT **Will She Learn?** Do you think that Julia will behave differently the next time someone tries to cheat her? Explain your ideas in a paragraph.

The next time someone tries to cheat Julia, she will _____.

The Governess 297

VOCABULARY SKILL REVIEW

Multiple-Meaning Words

Some words have more than one meaning. The chart below lists some multiple-meaning words. Often, the different meanings are different parts of speech.

Examples

alarm	• (noun) a bell, noise, or light that warns people of danger • (noun) a feeling of fear that a dangerous event might occur
bank	• (noun) a business that keeps and lends money • (noun) land along the side of a lake or river
field	• (noun) an area of land that people use • (noun) a subject that people study

Now You Do It

Draw a line from the sentence to the correct meaning of the word in the chart below. The first one has been done for you.

Sentence	Meaning
The sound of the fire **alarm** caused everyone to leave the building.	a feeling of fear that a dangerous event might occur
I enjoy walking along the **bank** and looking at the river flow.	a bell, noise, or light that warns people of danger
I stopped at the **bank** to cash a check.	an area of land that people use
Jamal is an expert in the **field** of United States history.	land along the side of a lake or river
Flying in an airplane always causes Tasha to feel **alarm**.	a business that keeps and lends money
We enjoy going to the **field** to play baseball.	a subject that people study

TALK ABOUT IT **Two in One!** With a partner, say aloud a single sentence that contains both meanings of each word from this lesson. For example, *The fire alarm caused everyone to feel alarm.*

WRITE ABOUT IT **Write a Silly Story** Write a silly story that contains the words from this lesson. Remember that each of these words has more than one meaning. Be sure to use the correct meaning of each word.

INFORMATIONAL TEXTS

Public Documents

About Public Documents

Public documents are government records or documents. They could also deal with citizens' rights and responsibilities according to the law. Some examples of public documents are:

- laws
- legal notices
- government publications
- notes taken at public meetings

Reading Skill

You may need to read a public document in order to find the answer to a question, make a decision, or solve a problem. You can **compare and contrast features and elements** in a document to help you understand the information it presents. Features and elements may include headings, boldface type, numbering, and bullets.

Information	+	Information	=	Generalization
The U. S. Department of Labor permits youth ages 14–15 to work fewer hours on school days than on non-school days.		The contract for the work-study program includes academic requirements.		Employers and the U.S. Department of Labor do not want young people's jobs to interfere with their schoolwork.

Informational Texts

Wage and Hour Division
Basic Information

U.S. Department of Labor
Employment Standards Administration

The U.S. Department of Labor's Wage and Hour Division (WHD) administers and enforces laws that establish minimally acceptable standards for wages and working conditions in this country, regardless of immigration status.

Youth Employment

The FLSA also regulates the employment of youth.

Jobs Youth Can Do:

- 13 or younger: baby-sit, deliver newspapers, or work as an actor or performer
- Ages 14–15: office work, grocery store, retail store, restaurant, movie theater, or amusement park
- Age 16–17: Any job not declared hazardous
- Age 18: No restrictions

Hours Youth Ages 14 and 15 Can Work:

- After 7 A.M. and until 7 P.M.
- (Hours are extended to 9 P.M. June 1–Labor Day)
- Up to 3 hours on a school day
- Up to 18 hours in a school week
- Up to 8 hours on a non-school day
- Up to 40 hours in a non-school week

Note: Different rules apply to youth employed in agriculture. States also regulate the hours that youth under age 18 may work. To find State rules, log on to **www.youthrules.dol.gov**

AFTER YOU READ

Thinking About the Public Document

1. Young people cannot work in some jobs. In others, they can work only a few hours each day. Why do you think young people have these limits?
   _____

2. The Department of Labor allows students, ages 14 and 15, to work as many as 40 hours during a non-school week. The same students are permitted to work no more than 18 hours during a school week. What conclusion can you draw based on these rules?
   _____

TALK ABOUT IT **Reading Skill**

3. Review the section headed "Hours Youth Ages 14 and 15 Can Work." What feature makes this specific information easy to read and understand?
   _____
   _____

4. How does the format of the note at the bottom of the page differ from the format of the other information? Why is the note formatted differently?
   _____
   _____

WRITE ABOUT IT **Timed Writing: Explanation (15 minutes)**

Think about laws for wages and working conditions. Explain why these laws are important. Include problems that people could have if these laws were not in place.
_____
_____
_____

UNIT 5

BEFORE YOU READ: THE DIARY OF ANNE FRANK, ACT 1

Vocabulary

These words are underlined in the play. Listen to each word. Say it. Then, read the definition and the example sentence.

emigrated (EM uh grayt uhd) *v.* A person who has **emigrated** from his or her home country moved from it to live in another country.
  My family emigrated from Europe in 1920.

mimics (MIM iks) *v.* Someone who **mimics** another person copies the way that person acts.
  Terrence mimics Aisha as she tells the story.

rebellious (ri BEL yuhs) *adj.* Someone who is **rebellious** is disobedient and may show disrespect for those in authority.
  He felt rebellious when he stayed awake after eleven.

Vocabulary Practice

Read the first sentence in each group of three. Then, complete Sentence *a* by substituting another word or phrase that means the same as the underlined vocabulary word. Complete Sentence *b* with your own ideas and words.

1. The man emigrated from his home country to find a job.

    a. The man _____ from his home country to find a job.

    b. The man emigrated _____.

2. She mimics Alberto as he practices his speech.

    a. She _____ Alberto as he practices his speech.

    b. She mimics _____.

3. She was never rebellious as a student.

    a. She was never _____ as a student.

    b. She was never rebellious _____.

 ### Getting Ready to Read

Many teachers and counselors suggest that students keep a journal. They say that writing in a journal can help improve a person's writing and problem-solving abilities. If you had a journal, would you hide it? Would you share it with others? Discuss your ideas with a partner.

302 English Learner's Notebook

MAKING CONNECTIONS

The Diary of Anne Frank, Act I
Frances Goodrich and Albert Hackett

Summary World War II is over. Anne Frank's father returns to Amsterdam to say goodbye to a friend, Miep Gies. Gies gives him his daughter's diary. Mr. Frank opens the diary and begins reading. Anne's voice joins his and takes over. The story goes back to 1942. Anne's family and another family are moving into the space above their friends' business. There they will live and hide from the Nazis for two years.

 Writing About the Big Question

Is it our differences or our similarities that matter most? In *The Diary of Anne Frank, Act I,* five adults and three teenagers struggle with their differences but face a common danger. Complete this sentence:

Danger tends to (unify/divide) people because _____
_____.

Note-taking Guide
Fill in this chart with important details from each scene in Act I.

Scene 1	After World War II, Mr. Frank returns to the attic in which his family had hidden from the Nazis. Miep shows him Anne's diary. He begins to think back to those terrible days.
Scene 2	
Scene 3	

The Diary of Anne Frank, Act I 303

TAKE NOTES

Vocabulary Builder

Prepositions A preposition comes before a noun, a pronoun, or a gerund. It often shows the place where something happens. For example, Nazis sent Jews *to prison camps*. *To* is a preposition showing place. Another common preposition showing place is *in*. Read the last two sentences in the bracketed paragraph. Underline the preposition *in*. Circle each place that the preposition shows.

Comprehension Builder

Where does this play take place?

_____

_____

Vocabulary Builder

Compound Words The noun *notebook* is made up of two words, *note* and *book*. A *note* is something you write to remember information. A *book* contains sheets of paper that you can read or write on. What does *notebook* mean?

_____

_____

The Diary of Anne Frank
Frances Goodrich and Albert Hackett

Act I, Scene 1

The Diary of Anne Frank is a play based on a diary kept during World War II by Anne Frank. The Nazis were hunting down Jews and sending them to prison camps during the war. The Franks and the Van Daans—both Jewish families—spent two years in hiding from the Nazis. In the small, cramped rooms where they are hiding, the families try to cope with their constant fear and lack of privacy. Thirteen-year-old Anne records her innermost thoughts and feelings in her diary.

The play opens in November 1945, several months after the end of World War II. Mr. Frank has returned to the upstairs rooms above his old factory—the place where his family and the Van Daans hid during the war. Miep, a loyal employee, watched over the family during those years. She is helping Mr. Frank to sort through some old papers.

◆ ◆ ◆

MIEP. *(Hurrying to a cupboard)* Mr. Frank, did you see? There are some of your papers here. *(She brings a bundle of papers to him.)* We found them in a heap of rubbish on the floor after . . . after you left.

MR. FRANK. Burn them. *(He opens his rucksack to put the glove in it.)*

MIEP. But, Mr. Frank, there are letters, notes . . .

MR. FRANK. Burn them. All of them.

MIEP. Burn this? *(She hands him a paper-bound notebook.)*

MR. FRANK. *(quietly)* Anne's diary. *(He opens the diary and begins to read.)* "Monday, the sixth of July, nineteen forty-two." *(To* MIEP)

Nineteen forty-two. Is it possible, Miep? . . . Only three years ago. *(As he continues his reading, he sits down on the couch.)* "Dear Diary, since you and I are going to be great friends, I will start by telling you about myself. My name is Anne Frank. I am thirteen years old. I was born in Germany the twelfth of June, nineteen twenty-nine. As my family is Jewish, we emigrated to Holland when Hitler came to power."

(As MR. FRANK reads on, another voice joins his, as if coming from the air. It is ANNE'S VOICE.)

MR. FRANK and ANNE. "My father started a business, importing spice and herbs. Things went well for us until nineteen forty. Then the war came, and the Dutch capitulation,[1] followed by the arrival of the Germans. Then things got very bad for the Jews. . . . (The Nazis) forced Father out of his business. We had to wear yellow stars.[2] I had to turn in my bike. I couldn't go to a Dutch school anymore. I couldn't go to the movies, or ride in an automobile, or even on a streetcar, and a million other things. . . .

◆ ◆ ◆

Act I, Scene 2

In Scene 2, the action flashes back to July 1942. The Franks and Van Daans are moving into hiding in their cramped upstairs rooms. Mr. Frank explains to everyone that when the employees are working in the factory below, everyone must remain very quiet. People cannot run water in the sink or use the toilet. They must speak only in whispers. They must walk without shoes.

1. **capitulation** (kuh pich uh LAY shuhn) *n.* surrender.
2. **yellow stars** Stars of David, which are six-pointed stars that are symbols of Judaism. The Nazis ordered all Jews to wear them sewn to their clothing so that Jews could be easily identified.

TAKE NOTES

Cultural Understanding
Anne begins her diary on July 6, 1942. World War II began with Hitler's invasion of Poland on September 1, 1939. America did not enter the war until Japan attacked Pearl Harbor on December 7, 1941.

Fluency Builder
With a partner, read aloud the bracketed passage. Read with expression and emotion as you consider how Anne might have felt when she wrote this passage in her diary.

Vocabulary Builder
Pronouns A pronoun replaces a noun so that the noun is not repeated. Read the last three sentences in the final paragraph, starting with the sentence beginning "People cannot use." What noun in the first sentence does the pronoun *They* replace in the final two sentences? Write the answer on the line below.

_____

TAKE NOTES

Vocabulary Builder

Idioms *Taking it off* means "removing it." What does Peter mean when he says that he is *taking it off*?

_____

_____

_____

Fluency Builder

An ellipsis consists of three evenly spaced dots or periods (. . .). It can be used to show long pauses or thoughts that are not finished. Circle the ellipses in the bracketed passage. Then, read aloud the passage, pausing at each ellipsis.

Comprehension Builder

What is Peter going to do with his Star of David after he takes it off? Explain his reasons.

_____

_____

_____

As the families are getting settled, Anne, thirteen, starts to talk to Peter, sixteen. She notices that he is taking off his yellow star. She asks him why he is doing that.

♦ ♦ ♦

ANNE. What are you doing?

PETER. Taking it off.

ANNE. But you can't do that. They'll arrest you if you go out without your star.

(He tosses his knife on the table.)

PETER. Who's going out?

ANNE. Why, of course, You're right! Of course we don't need them any more. *(She picks up his knife and starts to take her star off.)* I wonder what our friends will think when we don't show up today?

PETER. I didn't have any dates with anyone.

ANNE. Oh, I did. I had a date with Jopie to go and play ping-pong at her house. Do you know Jopie de Waal?

PETER. No.

ANNE. Jopie's my best friend. I wonder what she'll think when she telephones and there's no answer? . . . Probably she'll go over to the house . . . I wonder what she'll think . . . we left everything as if we'd suddenly been called away . . . breakfast dishes in the sink . . . beds not made . . . *(As she pulls off her star, the cloth underneath shows clearly the color and form of the star.)* Look! It's still there!

(PETER goes over to the stove with his star.)

What are you going to do with yours?

PETER. Burn it.

ANNE. *(She starts to throw hers in, and cannot.)* It's funny, I can't throw mine away. I don't know why.

PETER. You can't throw . . . ? Something they branded you with . . . ? That they made you wear so they could spit on you?

ANNE. I know. I know. But after all, it is the Star of David, isn't it?

◆ ◆ ◆

Mr. Frank gives Anne a diary that she can write in. She is very excited. She has always wanted to keep a diary, and now she has the chance. She starts to run down to the office to get a pencil to write with, but Mr. Frank pulls her back.

◆ ◆ ◆

MR. FRANK. Anne! No! *(He goes after her, catching her by the arm and pulling her back.)*

ANNE. *(Startled)* But there's no one in the building now.

MR. FRANK. It doesn't matter. I don't want you ever to go beyond that door.

ANNE. *(Sobered)* Never . . . ? Not even at nighttime, when everyone is gone? Or on Sundays? Can't I go down to listen to the radio?

MR. FRANK. Never. I am sorry, Anneke.[3] It isn't safe. No, you must never go beyond that door.

(For the first time Anne realizes what "going into hiding" means.)

◆ ◆ ◆

Mr. Frank tries to comfort Anne by telling her that they will be able to read all sorts of wonderful books on all sorts of subjects: history, poetry, mythology. And she will never have to practice the piano. As the scene ends, Anne comments, in her diary, about the families' situation.

◆ ◆ ◆

3. **Anneke** (AN uh kuh) nickname for Anne.

TAKE NOTES

Vocabulary Builder

Idioms *Goes after* is an idiom that means "tries to catch." Complete the following sentence:

Mr. Frank *goes after* Anne because _____
_____.

Vocabulary Builder

Contractions On the lines below, write five contractions that appear in the bracketed dialogue. Then, write the two words that make up each contraction.

_____
_____
_____
_____
_____

TAKE NOTES

Comprehension Builder

A simile compares two unlike things using the words *like* or *as*. Read the underlined sentences, and identify the simile. What is Anne being compared to in this simile? Why does this upset her?

_____
_____
_____

Fluency Builder

With a small group, take turns reading the bracketed dialogue between Anne, Mr. Frank, and Mrs. Van Daan. Use the stage directions and punctuation to help you understand how to change the tone of your voice as you read.

Vocabulary Builder

Parts of Speech The word *watch* can be used as a noun or a verb. As a noun, it means "a small clock worn on the wrist." As a verb, it can mean "look at something." Read Anne's dialogue line that begins "Can I." What does *watch* mean?

_____
_____

ANNE'S VOICE. . . . Friday, the twenty-first of August, nineteen forty-two. Today I'm going to tell you our general news. Mother is unbearable. She insists on treating me like a baby, which I **loathe**. Otherwise things are going better. . . .

Act I, Scene 3

Two months have passed. All is quiet for the time being. As the scene opens, the workers are still downstairs in the factory, so everyone is very quiet in the upstairs rooms where the families are hiding. Peter and Anne are busy with their schoolwork. After the last worker leaves the downstairs factory, Mr. Frank gives the signal that the families can start to move around and use the bathroom.

♦ ♦ ♦

ANNE. (*Her pent-up energy explodes.*) WHEE!

MR. FRANK. (*Startled, amused*) Anne!

MRS. VAN DAAN. I'm first for the w.c.[4] . . .

MR. FRANK. Six o'clock. School's over.

♦ ♦ ♦

Anne teases Peter by hiding his shoes. They fall to the floor in playful wrestling. Anne asks him to dance, but he says he must go off to feed his cat, Mouschi, which he keeps in his room.

♦ ♦ ♦

ANNE. Can I watch?

PETER. He doesn't like people around while he eats.

ANNE. Peter, please.

Everyday Words

loathe (lohth) *v.* to dislike something or someone greatly

---

4. w.c. water closet; bathroom.

PETER. No! *(He goes into his room.* ANNE *slams his door after him.)*

MRS. FRANK. Anne, dear, I think you shouldn't play like that with Peter. It's not **dignified.**

ANNE. Who cares if it's dignified? . . .

MRS. FRANK. *(To* ANNE*)* You complain that I don't treat you like a grownup. But when I do, you resent it.

ANNE. I only want some fun . . . someone to laugh and clown with . . . After you've sat still all day and hardly moved, you've got to have some fun. I don't know what's the matter with that boy.

MR. FRANK. He isn't used to girls. Give him a little time.

ANNE. Time? Isn't two months time? I could cry. *(Catching hold of* MARGOT*)* Come one, Margot . . . dance with me. Come on, please.

MARGOT. I have to help with supper.

ANNE: You know we're going to forget how to dance . . . When we get out we won't remember a thing. . . .

◆ ◆ ◆

They hear a car screeching to a stop on the street. All of them freeze with fear. When the car moves away, they relax again. Anne appears. She is dressed in some of Peter's clothes, and he teases her back. He calls her Mrs. Quack! Quack! because of her constant talking.

Mrs. Frank feels Anne's forehead. She wonders if Anne is sick. Mrs. Frank asks to see her tongue. Anne objects but then obeys.

Everyday Words
dignified (DIG ni fyd) *v.* deserving esteem or respect

TAKE NOTES

Vocabulary Builder

Adverbs An adverb describes a verb, an adjective, or another adverb. Adverbs explain how things are done. They often end with the letters *-ly*. Read the bracketed dialogue. Circle two adverbs in the passage. Which verb does each adverb describe?

_____
_____

Vocabulary Builder

Idioms The phrase *freeze with fear* means "stop moving because you are afraid." Complete the following sentence:

Peter and the Frank family *freeze with fear* _____
_____
_____

Vocabulary Builder

Prefixes The word *forehead* refers to the upper area of the human face. It is a combination of the prefix *fore-*, which means "front," and the noun *head,* which can mean "the top part of the body." What does *forehead* mean?

_____
_____

The Diary of Anne Frank, Act I

TAKE NOTES

Vocabulary Builder

Idioms The idiom *cooped up* means "stuck in an particular area." Use the idiom to complete the following sentence:

Mr. Frank thinks that Anne is tired of being _____ in the apartment.

Fluency Builder

The underlined text is a sentence fragment. It is not a complete sentence. Sometimes writers use fragments in dialogue to show how people really speak. Read aloud the bracketed text a few times. Continue to practice reading aloud until you say the text as if you were speaking to a friend.

Vocabulary Builder

Compound Words Circle two compound words in the last paragraph. What does each word mean?

_____
_____
_____
_____

Mr. Frank thinks Anne is not sick. He thinks she is just tired of being cooped up in the apartment. They find out that they will have beans again for dinner. They all say that they are sick of the beans.

After a brief discussion of Anne's progress with her schoolwork, they turn to a more personal subject.

◆ ◆ ◆

ANNE. Mrs. Van Daan, did you have a lot of boyfriends before you were married?

MRS. FRANK. Anne, that's a personal question. It's not courteous to ask personal questions.

MRS. VAN DAAN. Oh I don't mind. *(To* ANNE*)* Our house was always swarming with boys. When I was a girl we had . . .

MR. VAN DAAN. Oh, no. Not again!

MRS. VAN DAAN. *(Good-humored)* Shut up! *(Without a pause, to* ANNE, MR. VAN DAAN *mimics* MRS. VAN DAAN*, speaking the first few words in unison with her.)*

[One summer we had a big house in Hilversum. The boys came buzzing round like bees around a jam pot. And when I was sixteen! . . . We were wearing our skirts very short those days, and I had good-looking legs. . . .]

MR. VAN DAAN. Look at you, talking that way in front of her! Don't you know she puts it all down in that diary?

◆ ◆ ◆

The talk then turns to Peter's uneven progress with his schoolwork. Mr. Frank generously offers to tutor Peter as well as his own daughters. Anne spreads out on the floor to try to hear the radio downstairs. Mr. Van Daan complains that Anne's behavior is not ladylike. Mrs. Van Daan claims he is so bad-tempered from smoking cigarettes.

◆ ◆ ◆

MRS. VAN DAAN. You're smoking up all our money. You know that, don't you?

MR. VAN DAAN. Will you shut up? (. . . MR. VAN DAAN *turns to see* ANNE *staring up at him.*) And what are you staring at?

ANNE. I never heard grownups quarrel before. I thought only children quarreled.

MR. VAN DAAN. This isn't a quarrel! It's a discussion. And I never heard children so rude before.

ANNE *(Rising,* **indignantly***)* I, rude!

MR. VAN DAAN. Yes!

MRS. FRANK. *(Quickly)* Anne, will you get me my knitting. . . .

◆ ◆ ◆

Anne continues to argue with Mr. Van Daan. He accuses her of doing nothing but talking all the time. He asks her why she is not nice and quiet like her sister, Margot. He says that men prefer quiet girls who love to cook and sew and follow their husband's orders. But Anne tells him that kind of life is not for her.

◆ ◆ ◆

ANNE. I'd cut my throat first! I'd open my veins! I'm going to be remarkable! I'm going to Paris . . .

MR. VAN DAAN. *(Scoffingly)* Paris!

ANNE. . . . to study music and art.

MR. VAN DAAN. Yeah! Yeah!

◆ ◆ ◆

Anne then makes a sweeping gesture. She knocks her glass of milk on Mrs. Van

Everyday Words
indignantly (in DIG nuhnt lee) *adv.* in a manner that expresses anger over something unjust or unfair
scoffingly (SCOFF ing lee) *adv.* in a mocking manner

TAKE NOTES

Vocabulary Builder
Idioms Read Mr. Van Daan's dialogue that begins "Will you shut up?" The phrase *shut up* means "be quiet." It is usually spoken in a rude manner or when someone is irritated. Complete the following sentence:

Mr. Van Daan tells Mrs. Van Dann to *shut up* because _____
_____
_____
_____.

Vocabulary Builder
Regular Plurals To make regular nouns plural, add the letter *s* to the end of a singular noun. Read the bracketed dialogue. *Veins* is a regular plural noun. Underline two more regular plural nouns on this page.

Comprehension Builder
What does Anne want to do when she becomes older? Do you think that she will do these things? Explain.

_____
_____
_____
_____
_____
_____

TAKE NOTES

Vocabulary Builder

Idioms *Walk all over someone* is an idiom that means "treat someone unkindly." Complete the following sentence:

Anne refuses to allow _____ and _____ to *walk all over* her.

Fluency Builder

Exclamation marks are used to show excitement and a lot of feeling. Read the bracketed dialogue. Circle the exclamation marks in the dialogue. With a partner, read aloud the sentences that end with exclamation marks. Practice raising your voice to show emotion and feeling.

Vocabulary Builder

Homophones Read the underlined sentences. The words *new* and *knew* are homophones. *New* means "recently brought." *Knew* means "was sure about." Use *new* and *knew* to complete this sentence:

"Mr. Frank _____ that Mr. Van Dann would agree with his decision to allow the _____ arrival, Mr. Dussel, to hide with their families."

Daan's precious fur coat. Even though Anne apologizes, Mrs. Van Daan remains very angry. Mrs. Frank tells Anne that she needs to be more calm and respectful toward the adults. She says that Anne shouldn't answer back so much. But Anne says that she will not let people walk all over her.

◆ ◆ ◆

MRS. FRANK. I'm not afraid that anyone is going to walk all over you, Anne. I'm afraid for other people, that you'll walk on them. I don't know what happens to you, Anne. You are wild, self-willed. If I had ever talked to my mother as you talk to me . . .

ANNE. Things have changed. People aren't like that anymore. "Yes, Mother." "No, Mother." "Anything you say, Mother." I've got to fight things out for myself! Make something of myself!

MRS. FRANK. It isn't necessary to fight to do it. Margot doesn't fight, and isn't she . . . ?

ANNE. *(Violently rebellious)* Margot! Margot! Margot! That's all I hear from everyone . . . how wonderful Margot is . . . "Why aren't you like Margot?"

◆ ◆ ◆

Mr. Kraler, along with Miep, is helping to hide the families. He arrives with supplies. Mr. Kraler announces that he has brought a man named Dussel, a Jewish dentist who also needs a hiding place. Mr. Frank tells Mr. Kraler to bring him up. Mr. Frank then tells Mr. Van Daan about the new arrival.

◆ ◆ ◆

MR. FRANK. Forgive me. I spoke without consulting you. But I knew you'd feel as I do.

MR. VAN DAAN. There's no reason for you to consult anyone. This is your place. You have a right to do exactly as you please. The only thing I feel . . . there's so little food as it is . . . and to take in another person . . .

(PETER *turns away, ashamed of his father.*) . . .

♦ ♦ ♦

After they agree that Mr. Dussel will share a room with Anne, Mrs. Van Daan finds out about Dussel.

♦ ♦ ♦

MRS. VAN DAAN. What's happening? What's going on?

MR. VAN DAAN. Someone's moving in with us.

MRS. VAN DAAN. In here? You're joking.

MARGOT. It's only for a night or two . . . until Mr. Kraler finds another place.

MR. VAN DAAN. Yeah! Yeah!

♦ ♦ ♦

Dussel tells the families that things have gotten much worse for the Jews of Amsterdam. They are being rounded up everywhere. Even Anne's best friend, Jopie, has been taken to a concentration camp. Anne is very upset to hear this.

Dussel is a very stiff and proper man. He doesn't seem like a good roommate for a spirited girl like Anne. Sure enough, several weeks later, Anne writes about their disagreements in her diary.

♦ ♦ ♦

ANNE'S VOICE. . . . Mr. Dussel and I had another battle yesterday. Yes, Mr. Dussel! According to him, nothing, I repeat . . . nothing, is right about me . . . my appearance, my character, my manners. While he was going on at me I thought . . . sometime I'll give you such a smack that you'll fly right up to the ceiling! Why is it that every grownup thinks he knows the way to bring up children? . . .

TAKE NOTES

Comprehension Builder

Predict whether Anne and Mr. Dussel will get along. Explain your answer.

_____
_____
_____

Cultural Understanding

During World War II, the Nazis held Jews in concentration camps. A concentration camp is a prison where people are kept in very bad conditions during a war. As a result of living under the terrible conditions in the Nazi concentration camps, many Jews died during the war.

Vocabulary Builder

Idioms The phrase *bring up children* means "teach and instruct children." Who does Anne accuse of pretending to know how to *bring up children*? Underline the text that tells you.

AFTER YOU READ

Thinking About the Selection

1. What five words or phrases would you use to describe Anne Frank? Fill in the web with words you think are appropriate.

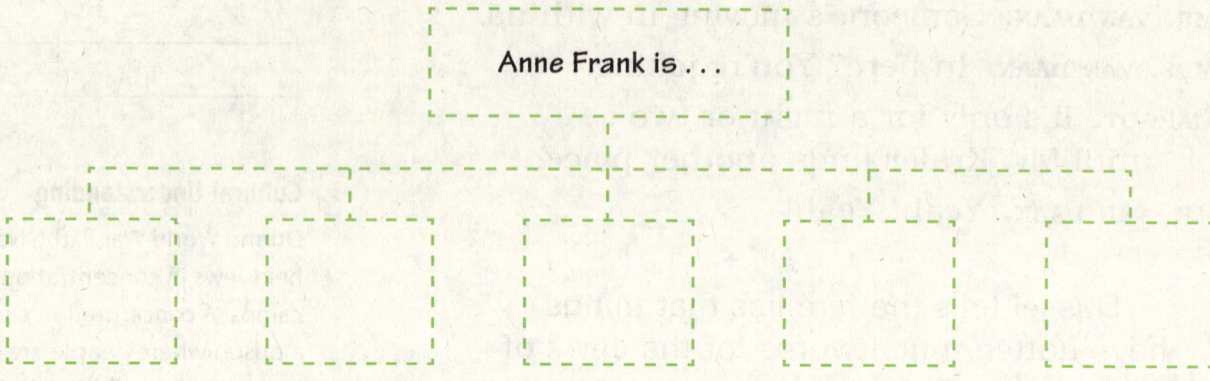

2. Anne and Mr. Dussel battle because he tells her that _____
   _____
   _____.

TALK ABOUT IT **Strict Rules** The Franks, the Van Daans, and Mr. Dussel must obey strict rules so that no one will find their hiding place. Discuss with a partner some of the rules that the families must obey.

The families must _____.

WRITE ABOUT IT **Most Difficult Rules** Think about the rules you discussed with your partner. Which rules would be most difficult for you to obey? Write a paragraph to explain your reasons.

It would be most difficult to _____
_____
_____
_____
_____.

VOCABULARY SKILL REVIEW

Compound Words

A compound word combines two or more words. The new word often combines the meanings of the separate words. The spellings of the words that form a compound word usually do not change.

Examples

- *every* + *one* = **everyone** (all people)
- *class* + *room* = **classroom** (a place where a class meets)
- *day* + *time* = **daytime** (the hours during the day)
- *air* + *plane* = **airplane** (a vehicle that flies in the sky)
- *text* + *books* = **textbooks** (books that contain information about subjects)
- *sun* + *light* = **sunlight** (light that comes from the Sun)

Now You Do It

Use the example words to complete the sentences below.

1. _____ in the _____ listened to the teacher.

2. The _____ flew its passengers over the Atlantic Ocean.

3. In the _____, I like to watch the _____ reflecting off of clouds in the sky.

4. We read our science _____ for homework.

TALK ABOUT IT **Tell About Yourself** Use words from this lesson to tell at least three things about yourself to a partner. For example, you might say the following three sentences: *When I am not in the classroom, I enjoy playing soccer. I enjoy playing games in the daytime. I also like to fly in airplanes.*

WRITE ABOUT IT **Compound the Problem** Use at least three compound words from this lesson to write a paragraph about what you do during a normal day.

_____

_____

_____

UNIT 5

BEFORE YOU READ: THE DIARY OF ANNE FRANK, ACT II

Vocabulary

These words are highlighted in the play. Listen to each word. Say it. Then, read the definition and the example sentence.

apprehension (ap ree HEN shuhn) *n.* An **apprehension** is a worry or a fearful feeling about what will happen next.
Sam squeezed into the dark cave, despite his apprehension.

forlorn (fawr LAWRN) *adj.* Someone who is **forlorn** is sad and lonely.
The child was forlorn when he was the last to be picked up at school.

intuition (in too I shuhn) *v.* **Intuition** is instinct, or the ability to know something immediately, without reasoning.
Pat's intuition told her that something was wrong.

Vocabulary Practice

Read the first sentence in each group of three. Then, complete Sentence *a* by substituting another word or phrase that means the same as the underlined vocabulary word. Complete Sentence *b* with your own ideas and words.

1. Despite her apprehension, Siena gave an excellent speech.

    a. Despite her _____, Siena gave an excellent speech.

    b. Despite her apprehension, Siena _____.

2. Mimi was forlorn after her dog ran away.

    a. Mimi was _____ after her dog ran away.

    b. Mimi was forlorn _____.

3. His intuition told him to kick the ball to his teammate.

    a. His _____ told him to kick the ball to his teammate.

    b. His intuition _____.

Getting Ready to Read

In 1955, ten years after Anne Frank's death, *The Diary of Anne Frank* was performed in New York City. Later, the play was made into a movie. How do you think the movie differed from the play? How do you think the two were similar? Discuss your ideas with a partner.

316 English Learner's Notebook

MAKING CONNECTIONS

The Diary of Anne Frank, Act II
Frances Goodrich and Albert Hackett

Summary The Franks, the Van Daans, and Mr. Dussel have been hiding for a year and a half. The eight of them have managed to live together, but they do not always get along. Food is scarce, and they are constantly afraid. Anne and Peter have become close friends. Soon, they learn that the Allies have invaded Europe, and they become excited.

Writing About the Big Question

Is it our differences or our similarities that matter most? As the war drags on, conditions worsen in the "Secret Annex" and differences among the residents lead to conflict. Complete this sentence:

Superficial differences between people can become magnified when

_____.

Note-taking Guide
Use this chart to list four important events in Act II.

Act II: Important Event 1	Carl asks Mr. Kraler about the Franks and then asks for more money.
Act II: Important Event 2	
Act II: Important Event 3	
Act II: Important Event 4	

AFTER YOU READ

Thinking About the Selection

1. Identify the cause and effect of each action listed in the graphic organizer.

Cause	Action	Effect
	Mrs. Frank changes her mind about wanting the Van Daans to leave.	
	The Gestapo comes to the annex to arrest the families.	

2. On New Year's Day, Mr. Kraler tells the families the bad news that _____.

TALK ABOUT IT **Discuss Your Ideas** What do you like best about Anne Frank? Would you be her friend? Discuss your ideas with a partner.

I think that Anne Frank is _____. I [**would** or **would not**] like to be her friend because _____.

WRITE ABOUT IT **Write a Diary Entry** Suppose that you are friends with Anne Frank before World War II begins. Write a diary entry in which you describe a day that you spend with her. What would the two of you do? Where might you spend your time together?

_____

_____

VOCABULARY SKILL REVIEW

The Perfect Tenses

A perfect tense describes an action that has been completed in the past, continues to be completed in the present, or will be completed in the future. To form a perfect tense, use the past participle of the main verb and a helping verb. The helping verb changes tense.

Examples

Verb Tense	Helping Verb	Past Participle
Present Perfect: an action in the past that continues into the present *I have walked every morning for three years.*	have or has	walked
Past Perfect: an action in the past that happened before a specific time in the past *Tom had walked to school before his family moved.*	had	walked
Future Perfect: an action in the future before a specific time in the future *Tamika will have walked five miles when the race ends.*	will have	walked

Now You Do It

Complete each sentence by writing the verb in parentheses in the perfect tense shown in brackets.

1. By the time Manual takes his test, he (study) _____ for three weeks. [future perfect]

2. Carlos (play) _____ the quarterback position before. [present perfect]

3. Sonya (finish) _____ her homework before her friend arrived. [past perfect]

TALK ABOUT IT **When Will You Use It?** With a partner, talk about when you are most likely to use the perfect tenses. Will you use them in history class or science class? Will you use them in talking about something special you did today or something you do every day?

WRITE ABOUT IT **Changing the Past to Perfect** Write five sentences in the present perfect tense. Then, trade papers with a partner and change the verb tenses to past perfect.

The Diary of Anne Frank, Act II

INFORMATIONAL TEXTS

Online Information

About Web Sites

A Web site is a certain place on the Internet. Sponsors create and update Web sites. Sponsors can be groups, companies, or individuals. Think about whether the information on a Web site is likely to be true. Look at the Web site's sponsor to assess credibility. Most Web sites have these parts:

- The **Web address:** where you can find the site on the Internet.
- A **Web page:** one screen within the Web site.
- **Navigation bars** and **links:** tools to help you go to other Web pages.

Reading Skill

A Web site must be designed for unity and coherence so that it is useful and easy to read. It has unity when all of its parts flow smoothly together and provide a complete source of information. A Web site has coherence when its individual parts and features relate to and support one another. Look at the chart below. It tells you how to **analyze the unity and coherence** of a Web site.

Checklist for Evaluating a Text

☐ Do details all relate to the main idea?

☐ Do sentences, paragraphs, and graphic elements flow in a logical sequence?

☐ Is information clear, consistent, and logical?

☐ Does the author provide reliable facts, statistics, or quotations to support main points?

Florida Holocaust Museum

EDUCATION   EVENTS   EXHIBITIONS   GET INVOLVED   PRESS ROOM   VISITOR INFORMATION

VISITOR INFORMATION

About the Museum

Mission

The Florida Holocaust Museum honors the memory of millions of innocent men, women, and children who suffered or died in the Holocaust. The Museum is dedicated to teaching members of all races and cultures to recognize the inherent worth and dignity of human life in order to prevent future genocides.

Founders Walter and Edie Loebenberg

History

One of the largest Holocaust museums in the country, the Florida Holocaust Museum is the result of St. Petersburg businessman and philanthropist, Walter P. Loebenberg's remarkable journey and vision. He escaped Nazi Germany in 1939 and served in the United States Army during WWII. Together, with a group of local businessmen and community leaders, the concept of a living memorial to those who suffered and perished was conceived. Among the participating individuals were Survivors of the Holocaust and individuals who lost relatives, as well as those who had no personal investment, other than wanting to ensure that such atrocities could never again happen to any group of people.

To this end, the group enlisted the support of others in the community and were able to involve internationally renowned Holocaust scholars. Thomas Keneally, author of *Schindler's List*, joined the Board of Advisors and Elie Weisel was named Honorary Chairman of this Holocaust Center.

Web Site

Features:
- description of the organization
- contact information
- links to other pages
- illustrations or graphics
- general or specific audience

The home page provides an organized, logical list of topics covered by the Web site.

The topic of the text is introduced under the first heading and carried throughout the text.

In 1992, the Museum rented a space it could afford but would soon outgrow, on the grounds of the Jewish Community Center of Pinellas County in Madeira Beach, Florida, tucked away from the mainstream of Tampa Bay life. Starting with only one staff member and a small group of dedicated volunteers, it quickly surpassed all expectations.

Within the first month, over 24,000 visitors came to see *Anne Frank in the World*, the Center's inaugural exhibit. The Tampa Bay showing of this exhibition—which traces a young Jewish girl's journey from a complacent childhood in pre-World War II Holland, through her early teens hiding from the Nazis, to her death at Bergen-Belsen—poignantly touched all visitors.

During the next five years, the new Holocaust Center greeted more than 125,000 visitors to view internationally acclaimed exhibits. Thousands more participated in lectures, seminars and commemorative events at the Center, which now reached directly into schools in an eight county area surrounding Tampa Bay with study guides, teacher training programs, and presentations by Center staff and Holocaust Survivors.

The Center expanded to encompass a growing print and audio-visual library, a photographic archive, a repository for historic artifacts, and a research facility for educators and scholars—all of this crowded into a 4,000 square foot facility that was not designed for museum or educational purposes.

A painting from the exhibition *The Holocaust Through Czech Children's Eyes*

Is it our differences or similarities that matter most? Does an organization such as the Florida Holocaust Museum place more emphasis on recognizing our differences, or on recognizing our similarities? Explain your answer.

AFTER YOU READ

Thinking About Online Information

1. How is using a Web site different from looking up information in a magazine or book?
   _____
   _____

2. What part of the museum Web site would be most useful to people who want to visit the museum?
   _____

Reading Skill

3. Which page of the Florida Holocaust Museum Web site unifies all of the parts of the site?
   _____

4. Scan the Florida Holocaust Museum site. What tabs and links do you find on the navigation bar? Explain how each of these works with the others to produce a coherent web browsing experience.
   _____

Timed Writing: Evaluation (15 minutes)

Think about the museum Web site from this lesson. Then, answer the following questions.

- Does the home page unify the site?
   _____

- Is the information included on the Web site coherent?
   _____

- Does the site meet its goal?
   _____
   _____

Informational Texts 323

UNIT VOCABULARY REVIEW

Word Bank

assumption	divide	separate
class	generalization	superficial
common	identify	sympathy
discriminate	judge	tolerance
distinguish	represent	unify

A. **Sentence Completion** Complete the chart by drawing a line between a sentence starter and its completion. Follow the language of each sentence so that all sentences make sense.

When you have something in **common** with someone,	to bring people together.
If you **separate** two things,	you understand what that person is feeling.
An **assumption** is something that a person believes	to recognize.
Superficial is a synonym for	without proof.
If a you feel **sympathy** for someone,	you divide the items.
To **unify** means	disapproval.
If you **judge** someone,	true in all situations.
To **identify** means	the other person is treated unfairly.
To **distinguish** between two things means to	tell them apart.
A **generalization** may not be	you form an opinion about that person.
When a person **discriminates** against someone else,	shallow.
Tolerance is an antonym for	you share similarities with that person.

B. **Word Sorting** Organize the words from the word bank on the previous page. If the word names a person, place, or thing, put the word in the Noun column. If the word shows an action, put it in the Verb column. If the word describes a person or an object, put it in the Adjective column. A word can be placed in more than one column.

Noun	Verb	Adjective

TALK ABOUT IT

What Makes People Special? Do you think that people are special because of their similarities or because of their differences? Discuss your ideas with a partner. Use the following sentence frame.

People's [**differences** *or* **similarities**] make them special because _____.

WRITE ABOUT IT

Design an Advertisement Design an advertisement for a cultural fair at your school. In your advertisement, list activities that people can do, foods that will be provided, demonstrations that will take place, and so on. Your advertisement should show how the cultures represented at the fair are similar and different.

_____

_____

_____

UNIT 6
EXPLORING THEMES IN AMERICAN STORIES

Water Names

The **oral tradition** is stories that were once told out loud. These stories were passed down from older people to younger people. Stories in the oral tradition have these elements:

- **Theme:** a central message about life. Some themes are **universal**. Universal themes appear in many cultures and many time periods.
- **Heroes** and **heroines:** men and women who do great and often impossible things.

Storytellers tell their stories aloud. They need to hold their listeners' attention. Look at the chart for some ways that storytellers make stories more interesting and entertaining for their audiences.

Technique	Definition	Example
Hyperbole	exaggeration or overstatement, often to make people laugh	That basketball player was as tall as the Empire State Building.
Personification	human qualities or characteristics given to animals or things	The clouds shed tears.
Idioms	expressions in a language or culture that do not mean exactly what they say	"a chip off the old block" "as easy as pie"

American folk literature is a living tradition. This means that it is always changing. Many of the subjects and heroes from American folk literature can be found in the movies, sports heroes, or even politics of today.

EXPLORING THEMES IN AMERICAN STORIES

There are different types of stories in the oral tradition.

- **Myths:** stories about the actions of gods, goddesses, and heroes. Some myths tell how things came to be. Every culture has its own **mythology**. A mythology is a collection of myths.

- **Fables:** short stories that usually have a moral. A moral is a lesson. The characters in fables are often animals that act like humans.

- **Tall tales:** stories that use exaggeration to make them funny. This kind of exaggeration is called **hyperbole**. Heroes of tall tales often do impossible things. Tale tales are one kind of **legend**. A legend is a story that is based on fact but that becomes less true with each telling.

- **Epics:** long poems about great heroes. These heroes go on dangerous journeys called **quests**. The quests are an important part of the history of a culture or nation.

UNIT 6

BEFORE YOU READ: WATER NAMES

Vocabulary

These words are underlined in the story. Listen to each word. Say it. Then, read the definition and the example sentence.

scarcely (SKERS lee) *adv.* When something **scarcely** happens, it barely, or does not quite, happen.
I scarcely passed the history test.

torrential (tuh REN shuhl) *adj.* A **torrential** rain contains large amounts of water that moves quickly in a particular direction.
The torrential rain made it difficult to see through the window.

emerged (i MERJD) *v.* When something has appeared after being hidden, it has **emerged**.
The Sun emerged over the horizon.

Vocabulary Practice

Read the first sentence in each group of three. Then, complete Sentence *a* by substituting another word or phrase that means the same as the underlined vocabulary word. Complete Sentence *b* with your own ideas and words.

1. The girl <u>scarcely</u> left her room.

   a. The girl _____ left her room.

   b. The girl scarcely _____.

2. The <u>torrential</u> rain flooded the basement.

   a. The _____ rain flooded the basement.

   b. The torrential rain _____.

3. The cars and trucks <u>emerged</u> from the tunnel.

   a. The cars and trucks _____ from the tunnel.

   b. The cars and trucks emerged _____.

 **Getting Ready to Read**

The Yangtze River is China and Asia's longest river. Almost one-third of China's population lives near the Yangtze River. It is an important source of water. What important role does water play in your daily life? Discuss your ideas with a partner.

328 English Learner's Notebook

MAKING CONNECTIONS

Water Names
Lan Samantha Chang

Summary Three girls sit on a back porch on the prairie. Their grandmother Waipuo reminds them of how important China's longest river was in the lives of their ancestors. She tells them a story in Chinese about a girl who falls in love with a water ghost.

Note-taking Guide
Use this chart to record details about the story within the story.

In the present

Who:

three girls and their grandmother

Where:

What happens:

1,200 years ago

Who:

Wen Zhiqing and his daughter

Where:

What happens:

TAKE NOTES

Vocabulary Builder

Adverbs Underline the adverb *immediately* in the first paragraph. Adverbs describe verbs, adjectives, or other adverbs. *Immediately* describes when the sisters stopped arguing. Adverbs often end in *-ly*. Circle one more adverb in this paragraph. Which verb does the adverb describe?

_____

Cultural Understanding

The number of people who were born in China but now live in America has increased over time. In 1960, fewer than 100,000 people in America were born in China. In 2000, more than 1.5 million people living in America were born in China.

Vocabulary Builder

Adjectives An adjective describes a noun or a pronoun. *Beautiful* is an adjective that means "someone or something that is very attractive to look at." Use the adjective *beautiful* to complete the sentence:

Wen Zhiqing's had a _____

_____ who loved to

_____ .

Water Names
Lan Samantha Chang

During summer evenings, the sisters would sit on the back porch. They would fight and argue with one another. Their grandmother scolded the girls for fighting. The sisters would stop their arguing immediately. Some nights their grandmother sat quietly in her chair. Other times, she would tell stories about China.

◆ ◆ ◆

"In these prairie crickets I often hear the sound of rippling waters, of the Yangtze River," she said. "Granddaughters, you are descended on both sides from people of the water country, near the mouth of the great Chang Jiang, as it is called, where the river is so grand and broad that even on clear days you can scarcely see the other side."

◆ ◆ ◆

The grandmother tells the girls that they are related to great men and women. The family has lived through floods and bad times. It runs together like rain. It has the spirit of the river. But even people of the river must be careful of water.

When the grandmother was young, her own grandmother told her a story. Twelve hundred years ago, Wen Zhiqing lived near the Yangtze River. He trained birds to catch fish for him. The birds would sit on the side of the boat. Then they would dive into the water.

Wen Zhiqing had a beautiful daughter. She loved the river. She also loved to go out in the boat to fish. She did not worry about the dangers of the river.

◆ ◆ ◆

"One clear spring evening, as she watched the last bird dive off into the blackening waters, she said, 'If only this catch would bring back something more than another fish!'

"She leaned over the side of the boat and looked at the water. The stars and moon reflected back at her. And it is said that the spirits living underneath the water looked up at her as well. And the spirit of a young man who had drowned in the river many years before saw her lovely face."

♦ ♦ ♦

The bird was gone for a long time. It came back with a very large fish. Inside the fish Wen found a pearl ring.

Wen's daughter was happy that her wish came true. In the evenings she stared at the water. Sometimes she thought she saw a young man looking back. She longed for the young man. She became sad and afraid. She knew that she would leave her family soon.

Her father told her that she was seeing only the moon's reflection in the water. The daughter told him that there was a kingdom in the river. The prince wanted to marry her. The ring was a gift to her father. Wen did not believe his daughter. He told her to stay away from the water.

For a year, nothing happened. Then a terrible flood came in the spring. The flood destroyed almost everything.

♦ ♦ ♦

"In the middle of the torrential rain, the family noticed that the daughter was missing. She had taken advantage of the confusion to hurry to the

TAKE NOTES

Fluency Builder

A preposition is used before a noun or pronoun to show place, time, or direction. Some prepositions that show place are *at, over, in, under, off,* and *on*. Circle the prepositions in the bracketed paragraph. Then, read aloud the paragraph smoothly and with expression.

Comprehension Builder

What did Wen find in the stomach of the fish she caught?

_____
_____

Vocabulary Builder

Word Families The word *reflect* means "to throw back light or an image." *Reflect* is part of a word family, a group of words that share the same base word. Underline two words on this page in the same word family as *reflect*.

TAKE NOTES

Vocabulary Builder

Idioms The phrase *lost her mind* means "had become insane." Complete the following sentence:

Some people think that Wen *lost her mind* because _____
_____.

Vocabulary Builder

Negatives There are different ways to express a negative in English. For example: I *do not want* any more food. I *want no more* food. Circle the sentence that expresses the idea in this sentence in a different way: "The grandmother did not answer any more questions."

Comprehension Builder

A simile compares two unlike things by using *like* or *as*. Circle the simile the author uses to describe the ground.

---

river to visit her beloved. The family searched for days but they never found her."

♦ ♦ ♦

The grandmother stopped talking. One of the sisters asked what happened to the girl.

♦ ♦ ♦

"Who knows?" Waipuo said. "They say she was seduced by a water ghost. Or perhaps she lost her mind to desiring."

♦ ♦ ♦

The grandmother answered no more questions. She rose from her chair. Soon the light went on in her bedroom.

The sisters stayed on the porch. They did not talk. They were thinking about Wen Zhiqing's daughter. They wondered what she looked like. They wondered how old she was. They wondered why no one remembered her name.

♦ ♦ ♦

While we weren't watching, the stars had emerged. Their brilliant pinpoints mapped the heavens. They glittered over us, over Waipuo in her room, the house, and the small city we lived in, the great waves of grass that ran for miles around us, the ground beneath as dry and hard as bone.

After You Read

Thinking About the Selection

1. What unusual things happen to Wen's daughter? Complete the sentences in the graphic organizer below.

Unusual Things That Happen to Wen's Daughter
Wen's daughter found a _____.
When looking into the river, Wen's daughter sometimes _____.
Wen's daughter believed that there was a _____.

2. The people thought that Wen's daughter disappeared because she had been seduced by a ghost or had _____.

TALK ABOUT IT **Heroic Characters** Many legends feature heroic characters who are powerful and impressive or who perform impossible tasks. Do you think Wen's daughter is heroic? Share your opinions with others in small groups.

I think that Wen's daughter is heroic because she _____.

I think that Wen's daughter is not heroic because she _____.

WRITE ABOUT IT **What About You?** Write more about your own opinion. You may think that Wen's daughter was heroic in some ways and not heroic in others. If so, write about both. Use this sentence frame to begin writing:

I think Wen's daughter was _____

_____

_____

_____.

VOCABULARY SKILL REVIEW

Suffixes

A suffix is a word part added to the end of a base word. A suffix often changes the word's meaning and its part of speech. The suffix *-ful* means "having the quality of something." The suffix makes a noun an adjective.

Examples stress + ful = stressful   care + ful = careful
beauty + ful = beautiful

The suffix *-ly* usually makes an adjective an adverb. An adverb is a word that describes a verb, an adjective, or another adverb. It can tell how or when something is done.

Examples immediate + ly = immediately   quiet + ly = quietly
scarce + ly = scarcely

Now You Do It

Add the suffix *-ful* to each base word in the first column and the suffix *-ly* to each base word in the second column. Write the correct word on the blank beside each base word. Spelling may change when you add a suffix.

success _____   quick   _____

grace   _____   angry   _____

wonder   _____   soft   _____

skill   _____   unfortunate _____

TALK ABOUT IT **Pairing Up** With a partner, pair a word in the first column with a word in the second column. Use these two words to make a sentence. For example, *The graceful dancer quickly left the stage.* Say aloud each sentence you make.

WRITE ABOUT IT **Suffix Scenes** With a group, write and present a short scene that includes all of the words from this lesson.

_____

_____

RESEARCH THE AUTHOR

Storytelling Hour

Plan a **storytelling hour** during which you will retell a variety of Chinese folk tales. Follow these steps to gather information for your storytelling hour.

- Go to the library and search the online catalog for collections of Chinese folklore. Record the titles and short summaries of stories that you think will interest the class.

  What I found: _____
  _____
  _____

- Search the Internet. Search for "Chinese folklore" or "Chinese folk tales." Record short summaries of the stories that you find.

  What I found: _____
  _____
  _____

- Watch the video interview with Lan Samantha Chang. Review your source material. Use this information to record additional information for your storytelling hour.

  Additional information: _____
  _____
  _____
  _____
  _____
  _____
  _____
  _____

Use your notes to prepare your storytelling hour.

UNIT 6
BEFORE YOU READ: COYOTE STEALS THE SUN AND MOON

Vocabulary
These words are underlined in the story. Listen to each word. Say it. Then, read the definition and the example sentence.

sacred (SAY kred) *adj.* Something **sacred** is something holy or having to do with religion.
   The temple was a sacred place for ancient Greeks.

shrivel (SHRIV uhl) *v.* To **shrivel** is to dry up, shrink, and wrinkle.
   The hot Sun will shrivel the grass until it is dry and brown.

curiosity (kyoo ree OS it ee) *n.* **Curiosity** is the strong desire to get information.
   Out of curiosity, she peeked behind the curtain.

Vocabulary Practice
Read the first sentence in each group of three. Then, complete Sentence *a* by substituting another word or phrase that means the same as the underlined vocabulary word. Complete Sentence *b* with your own ideas and words.

1. The burial ground was a sacred place for their ancient relatives.

   a. The burial ground was a _____ place for their ancient relatives.

   b. The burial ground was a sacred _____.

2. The fruit will shrivel in the Sun.

   a. The fruit will _____ in the Sun.

   b. The fruit will shrivel _____.

3. Out of curiosity, the dog sniffed the tree trunk.

   a. Out of _____, the dog sniffed the tree trunk.

   b. Out of curiosity, _____.

TALK ABOUT IT — Getting Ready to Read

"Coyote Steals the Sun and Moon" is a Zuñi myth. The Zuñi are a group of Native Americans. Coyote is a popular character in Zuñi myths. What other stories use animal characters? What human qualities did the animals have? Discuss your examples with a partner.

MAKING CONNECTIONS

Coyote Steals the Sun and Moon
Zuñi Myth, Retold by Richard Erdoes and Alfonso Ortiz

Summary This myth tells about how the sun and the moon got into the sky. Coyote and Eagle team up to steal the sun and moon to light up their dark world. Coyote's curious nature causes them to lose both. The sun and moon escape into the sky.

Writing About the Big Question

Are yesterday's heroes important today? "Coyote Steals the Sun and Moon" explains a specific event in nature and features Coyote, a popular character in mythology. Complete this sentence:

Myths and their heroes have **endured** through the ages because they

_____.

Note-taking Guide

Use this chart to write the explanations this myth gives for questions about nature.

Questions About Nature	Explanations
• How did the sun and the moon get into the sky? • Why do we have seasons of fall and winter?	

Coyote Steals the Sun and Moon   337

TAKE NOTES

Vocabulary Builder

Idioms In the first paragraph, Coyote decides to *team up with* Eagle to get more food. The phrase *team up with* means "work with something or someone to accomplish a goal." Complete this sentence:

If Coyote did not *team up with* Eagle, he might _____
_____.

Vocabulary Builder

Parts of Speech As a noun, *light* can mean "energy given by the Sun or a lamp that allows one to see." As an adjective, it can mean "not heavy." What does *light* mean in the bracketed paragraph?

_____
_____

Vocabulary Builder

Antonyms An antonym is a word that means the opposite of another word. For example, an antonym for the word *small* is *big*. Read the paragraph that begins "Coyote sees two boxes." What is another antonym for *small*?

_____

Coyote Steals the Sun and Moon
Zuñi Myth, Retold by Richard Erdoes and Alfonso Ortiz

The main characters of this story are two animals: Coyote, an eager but bad hunter, and Eagle, a very good hunter. Eagle catches many rabbits, but Coyote only catches little bugs because he has trouble seeing in the dark. So Coyote decides to team up with Eagle to get more food. Eagle agrees.

So the two hunters begin to look for the light. They set out to find the sun and the moon.

♦ ♦ ♦

At last they came to a pueblo,[1] where the Kachinas[2] happened to be dancing. The people invited Eagle and Coyote to sit down and have something to eat while they watch the sacred dances. Seeing the power of the Kachinas, Eagle said, "I believe these are the people who have light."

♦ ♦ ♦

Coyote sees two boxes, one large and one small. The Kachinas open these boxes whenever they want light. The big box gives off more light than the small box.

♦ ♦ ♦

Coyote nudged Eagle. "Friend, did you see that? They have all the light we need in the big box. Let's steal it."

---

1. **pueblo** (PWEB loh) *n.* Native American village in the southwestern United States.
2. **Kachinas** (kuh CHEE nuhz) *n.* masked dancers who imitate gods or the spirits of their ancestors.

"You always want to steal and rob. I say we should just borrow it."

"They won't lend it to us."

"You may be right," said Eagle. "Let's wait till they finish dancing and then steal it."

♦ ♦ ♦

After the Kachinas go to sleep, Eagle scoops up the large box and flies off. Coyote runs along as fast as he can, but he can't keep up. Coyote begs Eagle to let him carry the box a little way. But Eagle refuses.

♦ ♦ ♦

"No, no," said Eagle, "you never do anything right."

He flew on, and Coyote ran after him. After a while Coyote shouted again: "Friend, you're my chief, and it's not right for you to carry the box; people will call me lazy. Let me have it."

"No, no, you always mess everything up." And Eagle flew on and Coyote ran along.

♦ ♦ ♦

Coyote keeps begging to carry the box. Finally, Eagle agrees to let him carry the box for a while. But first he makes Coyote promise not to open it. Coyote gives his promise not to open the box. But as Eagle flies ahead, Coyote gets more and more curious. He hides behind a hill and sneaks a look inside the box. Coyote finds that Eagle has put both the sun and the moon in a single box.

When Coyote opens the box, the moon flies high into the sky. All the plants shrivel up and turn brown. The leaves fall off the trees. Winter comes. Then the sun flies out into the sky. All the fruits of the earth shrivel up and turn cold.

♦ ♦ ♦

TAKE NOTES

Fluency Builder

With a partner, read aloud the bracketed dialogue between Eagle and Coyote. Take turns reading the dialogue for each character. As you read, think about how each character feels. Read the dialogue smoothly and with expression.

Vocabulary Builder

Idioms The idiom *mess everything up* means "make mistakes."

Eagle does not give Coyote the box because he is afraid that

_____

_____.

Comprehension Builder

What does Eagle make Coyote promise before allowing him to carry the box?

_____

_____

_____

TAKE NOTES

Vocabulary Builder

Contractions A contraction is a short form of a word or words. In a contraction, an apostrophe (') takes the place of missing letters. For example, *it's* is a contraction of *it is*. Circle five contractions in the last two paragraphs.

Comprehension Builder

Summarize the reason why winter occurs every year.

_____
_____
_____

Eagle turned and flew back to see what had delayed Coyote. "You fool! Look what you've done!" he said. "You let the sun and moon escape, and now it's cold." Indeed, it began to snow, and Coyote shivered. "Now your teeth are chattering," Eagle said, "and it's your fault that cold has come into the world."

It's true. If it weren't for Coyote's <u>curiosity</u> and mischief making, we wouldn't have <u>winter</u>; we could enjoy summer all the time.

340 English Learner's Notebook

AFTER YOU READ

Thinking About the Selection

1. The chart below splits this story into four parts. Next to each part, list the most important events that occur. This will help you summarize the story. **The Hunt** has been summarized for you.

Part	Event
The Hunt	Eagle catches many rabbits. Coyote catches only bugs.
At the Kachina's Dance	
Running Away	
Coyote's Mistake	

2. Eagle makes Coyote promise not to _____.

TALK ABOUT IT **Good Quality?** Coyote is a very curious character. Do you think Coyote's curiosity is a good or a bad quality? Share your opinions with a partner.

I think Coyote's curiosity is a good quality because _____.

I think Coyote's curiosity is a bad quality because _____.

WRITE ABOUT IT **What About You?** Write about a time when curiosity either got you into trouble or led you to discover something important. Perhaps it did both.

My curiosity got me into trouble by _____
_____.

My curiosity led me to discover _____
_____.

Coyote Steals the Sun and Moon

VOCABULARY SKILL REVIEW

Multiple-Meaning Words

Some words have more than one meaning. Many words have several meanings. The meaning of the word depends on how it is used in a sentence. A reader can look for clues in the sentence and the paragraph in which the word appears to help determine its meaning.

Examples

call	• (verb) telephone someone • (verb) describe someone or something in a certain way
sign	• (noun) paper, metal and so on that is in a public place and gives information • (noun) event, fact, and so on that shows that something exists, is happening, or will happen

Now You Do It

Each sentence below contains one of the words in the chart above. Read each sentence, and write the definition of the boldfaced word on the line below it. Use the chart to help you.

1. I had to **call** Pedro to ask him a question about today's homework.
   _____

2. Studying a week before the test is a **sign** of a good student.
   _____

3. English speakers **call** that bird a robin.
   _____

4. The **sign** says to turn left at the water fountain.
   _____

TALK ABOUT IT **Guessing Game** With a partner, take turns saying aloud sentences that use each meaning of the words from this lesson. Guess the meaning of the word, given the way it is used in each sentence.

WRITE ABOUT IT **Write a Short Story** Write a short story in which you use each meaning of the words from this lesson at least once.

_____
_____

BEFORE YOU READ: WHY THE WAVES HAVE WHITECAPS

UNIT 6

Vocabulary

These words are highlighted in the story. Listen to each word. Say it. Then, read the definition and the example sentence.

bragged (BRAGD) *v.* If one **bragged** about oneself, one talked too proudly about what one has done.
   The student bragged about his good grades.

thirst (THERST) *n.* **Thirst** is the feeling of wanting or needing to drink water or another liquid.
   I had a thirst for water.

worried (WER eed) *adj.* A person is **worried** when he or she is concerned about a problem or about something bad that might happen.
   Dolly was worried about her performance in the play.

Vocabulary Practice

Read the first sentence in each group of three. Then, complete Sentence *a* by substituting another word or phrase that means the same as the underlined vocabulary word. Complete Sentence *b* with your own ideas and words.

1. The team <u>bragged</u> about being undefeated.

   a. The team _____ about being undefeated.

   b. The team bragged about _____.

2. The runner had a <u>thirst</u> for water after the race.

   a. The runner had a _____ for water after the race.

   b. The runner had a thirst _____.

3. Danny was <u>worried</u> when we did not arrive on time.

   a. Danny was _____ when we did not arrive on time.

   b. Danny was worried _____.

 ### Getting Ready to Read

In this story, the wind and the water are personified, or given human characteristics. Have you ever observed something in nature that reminded you of a person? What "human" characteristics did the natural element have? Discuss your experience with a partner.

MAKING CONNECTIONS

Why the Waves Have Whitecaps
Zora Neale Hurston

Summary The story is an African American folk tale. Mrs. Wind brags about her children. Mrs. Water grows tired of it and drowns the children. Mrs. Wind looks for her children but sees only white feathers on the water. That is why there are whitecaps. Storms at sea are the wind and water fighting over children.

 Writing About the Big Question

Are yesterday's heroes important today? "Why the Waves Have Whitecaps" is a story in which characters act in ways that are humorous, but unheroic. Complete this sentence:

I think that story characters who (do/do not) behave admirably

have more relevance today because _____

_____.

Note-taking Guide
Record the sequence of events of "Why the Waves Have Whitecaps" in this chart.

Mrs. Wind and Mrs. Water sit and talk. → ☐ → ☐

↓

☐ → Whitecaps are feathers coming up when Mrs. Wind calls for her children. → The storms at sea are the wind and water fighting over the children.

344 English Learner's Notebook

AFTER YOU READ

Thinking About the Selection

1. In this story, both women brag about their children. What does each claim about her children? Write your answers in the chart below.

Mrs. Wind	Mrs. Water

2. Mrs. Water drowns Mrs. Wind's children because _____.

TALK ABOUT IT **Feeling Jealous** People often do silly or hurtful things when they are jealous. Why do you think Mrs. Water might be jealous of Mrs. Wind? Share your opinions with others in a small group.

Mrs. Water might be jealous of Mrs. Wind because _____.

WRITE ABOUT IT **Alternate Ending** How would the story change if Mrs. Water had not drowned Mrs. Wind's children? Write a brief alternate ending to the story that still explains the whitecaps on the waves.

_____
_____
_____
_____

VOCABULARY SKILL REVIEW

Homographs

Homographs are words that are spelled the same but are pronounced differently and have different meanings. Here are some common homographs:

Examples **bass** (BAS) *n.* a fish
bass (BAYS) *n.* a type of musical instrument
bow (BOH) *n.* a type of knot
bow (BOW) *v.* bend forward
live (LIV) *v.* have or make a home
live (LYV) *adj.* not dead or artificial

Now You Do It

Draw a line from the sentence in the left column to the correct meaning of the boldfaced word in the right column.

The loud **bass** hurt David's ears.	a fish
In Japan, it is polite to **bow** to other people.	not dead or artificial
It was the largest **bass** Tomika had ever caught.	a type of musical instrument
He tied his shoelaces in a **bow**.	have or make a home
They **live** in the city.	a type of knot
The snake always eats **live** rats.	bend forward

TALK ABOUT IT **Clever Clues** With a partner, discuss how you could describe each homograph on this page. Then, write a short clue that describes each pair. Share your clues with another pair. Take turns guessing the homographs from the clues.

WRITE ABOUT IT **Write Silly Sentences** For each pair of homographs on this page, write a silly sentence. For example, you could write the following sentence for *bass*: *I once heard a story about a bass that could play the bass.*

BEFORE YOU READ: CHICORIA • FROM THE PEOPLE, YES

UNIT 6

Vocabulary

These words are highlighted in the selections. Listen to each word. Say it. Then, read the definition and the example sentence.

cordially (KORD juh lee) *adv.* To act **cordially** means to act politely, warmly, and friendly.
The host welcomed his guests cordially.

haughty (HAW tee) *adj.* One who is **haughty** shows too much pride, is scornful, and acts superior to others.
The haughty prince was rude.

cyclone (SY klohn) *n.* A **cyclone** is a violent storm with rotating winds, or a tornado.
The cyclone ripped the roofs from houses.

Vocabulary Practice

Read the first sentence in each group of three. Then, complete Sentence *a* by substituting another word or phrase that means the same as the underlined vocabulary word. Complete Sentence *b* with your own ideas and words.

1. The host <u>cordially</u> invited her guests to her home.
   a. The host _____ invited her guests to her home
   b. The host cordially _____.

2. The waiter's <u>haughty</u> attitude ruined our meal.
   a. The waiter's _____ attitude ruined our meal.
   b. The waiter's haughty _____.

3. The <u>cyclone</u> blew the roof off the warehouse.
   a. The _____ blew the roof off the warehouse.
   b. The cyclone _____.

 ### Getting Ready to Read

Every culture has its own stories and folk tales. These cultures use folk tales to share their values and beliefs. List three folk tales that you know. Discuss the ways that the folk tales on your list are similar to and different from the folk tales on a partner's list.

Chicoria • from The People, Yes

MAKING CONNECTIONS

Chicoria • from The People, Yes

Summaries In "Chicoria," a rancher invites a poet to dinner. The poet is asked to share poetry, but not to eat. The poet uses a folk tale to point out the rancher's rude behavior. In the selection from *The People, Yes*, the speaker talks about his love for America. He describes the adventures of famous characters from American folklore, such as Paul Bunyan and John Henry.

Writing About the Big Question

Are yesterday's heroes important today? In both "Chicoria" and the excerpt from *The People, Yes*, the values and beliefs of a culture are passed on by showing what qualities and abilities that culture finds **admirable** in its heroes. Complete these sentences:

In today's stories, qualities such as _____ and _____ may be considered **outdated** for a heroic character. On the other hand, qualities such as **bravery**, honesty, and _____ are still relevant.

Note-taking Guide

Use this graphic organizer to record how "Chicoria" and the selection from *The People, Yes* have some of the same folk story traits.

Chicoria	Chicoria	Chicoria
It is rude not to invite all guests to eat.		
Message	**Exaggeration**	**Humor**
from The People, Yes	from The People, Yes	from The People, Yes
People exaggerate.		

348 English Learner's Notebook

AFTER YOU READ

Thinking About the Selections

1. How does the wealthy ranch owner change throughout "Chicoria"? Complete the sentences in the chart.

At the beginning of the story...	At the end of the story...
the ranch owner behaves _____ _____ _____	the ranch owner realizes that _____ _____ _____

2. In the selection from *The People, Yes,* Sandburg says that Pecos Bill _____ _____.

TALK ABOUT IT **You Choose** Which of these selections did you enjoy more? Discuss what you enjoyed about the selection with a partner.

I enjoyed _____ more because _____.

WRITE ABOUT IT **Write Your Own** Think about why you enjoyed the selection that you talked about with your partner. Write your own folk tale that contains the qualities you enjoyed. For example, if you liked "Chicoria" because Chicoria was clever, write a folk tale with a clever character. Share your folk tale with the class.

_____
_____
_____
_____
_____

VOCABULARY SKILL REVIEW

Irregular Verbs
The past tense describes actions that took place in the past. Most English verbs form the past tense by adding -ed or -d. Some verbs, called irregular verbs, do not follow this rule.

Examples

Present-Tense Form	Past-Tense Form
find	found
begin	began
choose	chose
win	won

Now You Do It
Write a sentence that contains the past-tense verb form for each irregular verb. Use a different pronoun (I, you, he, she, we, they) in each sentence.

find _____

begin _____

choose _____

win _____

TALK ABOUT IT **What Happened Last Week?** With a partner, talk about something you did last week. Use at least three past-tense verbs from the chart above in your discussion.

WRITE ABOUT IT **Write a Story** People often use past-tense verbs when telling a story. Write a short story about something that happened to you in the past. Use at least three verbs from this lesson.

_____

_____

BEFORE YOU READ: BRER POSSUM'S DILEMMA • JOHN HENRY

UNIT 6

Vocabulary

These words are underlined in the stories. Listen to each word. Say it. Then, read the definition and the example sentence.

lifted (LIFT uhd) *v.* If something is **lifted,** it is raised or moved higher.
   I lifted my backpack onto my shoulders.

refused (ri FYOOZD) *v.* If a person **refused** to do something, he or she would not do it.
   My mom refused to drive me to the mall.

flagged (FLAGD) *v.* **Flagged** means gave a signal to stop.
   The stranded travelers flagged a passing car to ask for help.

Vocabulary Practice

Read the first sentence in each group of three. Then, complete Sentence *a* by substituting another word or phrase that means the same as the underlined vocabulary word. Complete Sentence *b* with your own ideas and words.

1. She lifted the box onto the shelf.
   a. She _____ the box onto the shelf.
   b. She lifted _____.

2. Terese refused to go to the movie.
   a. Terese _____ to go to the movie.
   b. Terese refused _____.

3. We flagged the tow-truck driver.
   a. We _____ the tow-truck driver.
   b. We flagged _____.

 **Getting Ready to Read**

"Brer Possum's Dilemma" is a story told in the oral tradition. A story in the oral tradition is meant to be told aloud. What stories do you know that are meant to be told aloud? Discuss examples in a small group.

MAKING CONNECTIONS

Brer Possum's Dilemma • John Henry

Summary In "Brer Possum's Dilemma," Brer Snake asks Brer Possum for help. "John Henry" is a ballad, or song, that tells the story of an African American hero who races a steam drill.

Writing About the Big Question

Are yesterday's heroes important today? The human-like animal characters in "Brer Possum's Dilemma" and the larger-than-life folk hero in "John Henry" are typical one-dimensional folk tale characters. Complete this sentence:

Although the **accomplishments** of folk heroes are exaggerated, these stories have value because _____

_____.

Note-taking Guide

Folk tales often pass along important life lessons. Use this chart to record the lessons in each folk tale.

Folk Tale	What Lesson It Taught
Brer Possum's Dilemma	
John Henry	Nothing is impossible when you set your mind to it.

352 English Learner's Notebook

Brer Possum's Dilemma
Jackie Torrence

Back in the days when the animals could talk, there lived ol' Brer[1] Possum. He was a fine feller. Why, he never liked to see no critters[2] in trouble. He was always helpin' out, a-doin' somethin' for others.

◆ ◆ ◆

[While walking one day, Brer Possum saw a big hole in the road. He looked in. He saw Brer Snake in the bottom of the hole. Brer Snake had a brick on his back. Brer Possum decided to leave. He knew that Brer Snake might bite him. He began to walk away.

Brer Snake called out for help. Brer Possum went back. Brer Snake asked Brer Possum to help get the brick off his back.]

◆ ◆ ◆

Brer Possum thought.
"Now listen here, Brer Snake. I knows you. You's mean and evil and lowdown, and if'n I was to git down in that hole and git to liftin' that brick offa your back, you wouldn't do nothin' but bite me."

Ol' Brer Snake just hissed.
"Maybe not. Maybe not. Maaaaaaaybe not."

◆ ◆ ◆

Brer Possum saw a dead branch hanging from a tree. He climbed up the tree and broke off the branch. He poked the brick off Brer Snake's back. Then he ran away.

Brer Snake called for help again. Brer Possum went back to the hole. Brer Snake said that he could not get out of the hole. He asked Brer Possum to help. Brer Possum again said that he was afraid that Brer Snake

---

1. **Brer** (BRER) dialect for "brother," used before a name.
2. **critters** (KRIT erz) dialect for "creatures"; animals.

TAKE NOTES

Vocabulary Builder
Action Verbs Read the bracketed paragraph. Then, circle six action verbs in the paragraph.

Fluency Builder
Sometimes a writer spells a word differently so that it mimics a sound. Circle the words *Maybe, Maybe,* and *Maaaaaaaybe.* Read the line aloud. As you read, mimic the hissing of a snake when you say *Maaaaaaaybe?*

Comprehension Builder
Predict whether Brer Snake will harm Brer Possum after Brer Possum helps him. Give reasons for your prediction.

_____
_____
_____
_____
_____

TAKE NOTES

Vocabulary Builder

Compound Adjectives A compound adjective is formed when two or more adjectives describe the same noun. The words in a compound adjective may be separated by a hyphen (-). Read the paragraph that begins "Brer Snake called." Circle the compound adjective in the paragraph.

Fluency Builder

A dialect is the language spoken by people in a certain region that is different from the way it is spoken in other areas. Reading a story written in an unfamiliar dialect can be difficult. With a partner, read aloud the bracketed passage. First, read the passage slowly, making sure that you understand what the words mean. Then, increase your speed until you can read the passage smoothly.

Vocabulary Builder

Parts of Speech The word *trouble* can be a verb or a noun. As a noun, it means "problems that make something difficult." In the story, the noun *trouble* refers to Brer Snake. As a verb, *trouble* means "to annoy or bother." Read the underlined sentence. Put the letter *V* where *trouble* is a verb, and the letter *N* where it is a noun.

---

would bite him. Brer Snake said that he might not bite him. Brer Possum pushed the dead branch under Brer Snake. He lifted Brer Snake out of the hole and tossed him into the tall grass. Then Brer Possum ran away.

Brer Snake called for help once more. Good-hearted Brer Possum once again went back to the hole. Brer Snake said that he was cold. He asked Brer Possum to put him in Brer Possum's pocket.

Brer Possum refused. If he put Brer Snake in his pocket, Brer Snake would bite him. Brer Snake said that he might not bite him. Brer Possum began to feel sorry for him.

◆ ◆ ◆

"All right," said Brer Possum. "You must be cold. So jist this once I'm a-goin' to put you in my pocket."

◆ ◆ ◆

Brer Snake was quiet and still. Brer Possum forgot about him. Suddenly, Brer Snake crawled out of the pocket. He hissed at Brer Possum.

◆ ◆ ◆

"I'm a-goin' to bite you."

But Brer Possum said, "Now wait a minute. Why are you a-goin' to bite me? I done took that brick offa your back, I got you outa that hole, and I put you in my pocket to git you warm. Why are you a-goin' to bite me?"

Brer Snake hissed.

"You knowed I was a snake before you put me in you pocket."

And when you're mindin' your own business and you spot trouble, don't never trouble trouble 'til trouble troubles you.

John Henry
Traditional

John Henry was a lil baby,
Sittin' on his mama's knee,
Said: 'The Big Bend Tunnel on the
   C. & O. road[1]
Gonna cause the death of me,
5 Lawd, Lawd, gonna cause the death of me.'

Cap'n says to John Henry,
'Gonna bring me a steam drill 'round,
Gonna take that steam drill out on the job,
Gonna whop that steel on down,
10 Lawd, Lawd, gonna whop that steel
   on down.'

John Henry tol' his cap'n,
Lightnin' was in his eye:
'Cap'n, bet yo' las, red cent on me,
Fo' I'll beat it to the bottom or I'll die,
15 Lawd, Lawd, I'll beat it to the bottom or
   I'll die.'

Sun shine hot an' burnin',
Wer'n't no breeze a-tall,
Sweat ran down like water down a hill,
That day John Henry let his hammer fall,
20 Lawd, Lawd, that day John Henry let his
   hammer fall.

John Henry went to the tunnel,
An' they put him in the lead to drive,
The rock so tall an' John Henry so small,
That he lied down his hammer an' he cried,
25 Lawd, Lawd, that he lied down his hammer
   an' he cried.

1. **C. & O. road** Chesapeake and Ohio Railroad. The C&O's Big Bend railroad tunnel was built in the 1870s through a mountain in West Virginia.

TAKE NOTES

Vocabulary Builder

Idioms The phrase *red cent* is an American idiom that means "a very small amount of money." What would *your last red cent* mean? Rewrite the underlined phrase on the lines below in your own words.

_____
_____
_____
_____

Vocabulary Builder

Parts of Speech As a verb, *fall* means "drop toward the ground." As a noun, it refers to the season between summer and winter. How is *fall* used in line 19?

_____
_____
_____

Fluency Builder

Circle the punctuation in the last stanza on the page. Then, underline unfamiliar words such as *an'* and *Lawd,* and practice saying these words aloud. Take turns with a partner reading the stanza aloud. Remember to pause briefly when you come to a comma, and to pause longer when you reach a period.

TAKE NOTES

Cultural Understanding
One theme of this poem is human against a machine. Over the past 100 years in America, many machines have replaced people. For example, people do not dig large holes; they run the machines that do the work.

Vocabulary Builder

Idioms The phrase *took sick* means "became ill." Complete the following sentence:

When John Henry *took sick*,

Polly Ann _____

_____

_____.

Vocabulary Builder

Parts of Speech As a helping verb, *better* means "should." As an adjective, it means "more or to a higher degree." What does *better* mean in line 47?

_____

John Henry started on the right hand,
The steam drill started on the lef'—
'Before I'd let this steam drill beat
   me down,
I'd hammer my fool self to death,
30 Lawd, Lawd, I'd hammer my fool self
   to death.'

John Henry had a lil woman,
Her name were Polly Ann,
John Henry took sick an' had to go to bed,
Polly Ann drove steel like a man,
35 Lawd, Lawd, Polly Ann drove steel like
   a man.

John Henry said to his shaker,[2]
Shaker, why don' you sing?
I'm throwin' twelve poun's from my hips
   on down,
Jes' listen to the col' steel ring,
40 Lawd, Lawd, jes' listen to the col' steel ring.'

Oh, the captain said to John Henry,
'I b'lieve this mountain's sinkin' in.'
John Henry said to his captain, oh my!
'Ain' nothin' but my hammer suckin' win',
45 Lawd, Lawd, ain' nothin' but my hammer
   suckin' win'.'

John Henry tol' his shaker,
'Shaker, you better pray,
For, if I miss this six-foot steel,
Tomorrow'll be yo' buryin' day,
50 Lawd, Lawd, tomorrow'll be yo' buryin' day.'

---

2. **shaker** (SHAY kuhr) *n.* person who sets the spikes and places the drills for a steel-driver to hammer.

John Henry tol' his captain,
'Look yonder what I see—
Yo' drill's done broke an' yo' hole's
    done choke,
An' you cain' drive steel like me,
55 Lawd, Lawd, an' you cain' drive steel
    like me.'

The man that invented the steam drill,
Thought he was mighty fine.
John Henry drove his fifteen feet,
An' the steam drill only made nine,
60 Lawd, Lawd, an' the steam drill only
    made nine.

The hammer that John Henry swung,
It weighed over nine pound;
He broke a rib in his lef'-han' side,
An' his intrels³ fell on the groun',
65 Lawd, Lawd, an' his intrels fell on
    the groun'.

All the womens in the Wes',
When they heared of John Henry's death,
Stood in the rain, flagged the eas'-boun
    'train,
Goin' where John Henry fell dead,
70 Lawd, Lawd, goin' where John Henry
    fell dead.

John Henry's lil mother,
She was all dressed in red,
She jumped in bed, covered up her head,
Said she didn' know her son was dead,
75 Lawd, Lawd, didn' know her son was dead.

---

3. **intrels** (IN trelz) *n.* dialect for entrails—internal organs.

TAKE NOTES

Fluency Builder

Read the bracketed passage aloud with a partner. Be sure to read the passage smoothly and with expression.

Vocabulary Builder

Dialect In order to show how some words are pronounced in this dialect, an apostrophe (') replaces the final letter of a word. Read the underlined passage. Then, rewrite the words with apostrophes from the passage as complete words.

_____
_____
_____

Comprehension Builder

Summarize how John Henry dies.

_____
_____
_____

TAKE NOTES

Dey took John Henry to the graveyard,
An' they buried him in the san',
An' every locomotive come roarin' by,
Says, 'There lays a steel-drivin' man,
80 Lawd, Lawd, there lays a steel-drivin' man.'

Vocabulary Builder

Prepositional Phrases
Prepositions come before nouns or noun phrases. They often introduce a place where something happens. *In* is a preposition showing place. Read line 77 and underline the preposition *in*. Then, circle the place that the preposition shows.

Vocabulary Builder

Idioms Find the phrase *come roarin' by* in line 78. This idiom means "drive loudly past something or someone." In the poem, what machine *comes roarin'* by John Henry's grave?

_____

358 English Learner's Notebook

AFTER YOU READ

Thinking About the Selection

1. Complete this timeline by listing the main events in "John Henry."

   | Baby John Henry foresees his death. | | | | | | | John Henry is buried. |

2. Brer Possum puts Brer Snake in his pocket because _____
_____.

TALK ABOUT IT **What Do You Think?** What makes John Henry a hero? Discuss your ideas with a partner.

John Henry is a hero because _____.

WRITE ABOUT IT **Writing Obituaries** What kind of person was John Henry? How do you know? Write an obituary that describes John Henry and his life. Use the following sentence frame to begin your obituary:

John Henry was a man who _____
_____
_____
_____
_____
_____.

John Henry   359

VOCABULARY SKILL REVIEW

Word Families

Words families are groups of words that share a common base word. A base word is the word to which prefixes and suffixes are added.

Example
Base word: Health
Health means "the state of being without illness."

Words That Share the Base Word	Part of Speech	Meaning
healthy	adjective	physically strong
unhealthy	adjective	likely to make a person ill
healthful	adjective	likely to make a person feel physically strong

Now You Do It

Fill in the blank with the correct word from the chart above.

1. It is important to eat _____ food.

2. Juan is _____ because he eats plenty of vegetables.

3. Pollution has caused the air in the city to be _____.

TALK ABOUT IT **What Is Healthy?** With a partner, talk about activities that people do that are healthful. List these activities, and talk about which activities you enjoy doing.

WRITE ABOUT IT **Write a Paragraph** Write a paragraph describing the benefits of being healthy. Include at least two words from the lesson.

_____
_____
_____
_____
_____

INFORMATIONAL TEXTS

Reviews

About Reviews

A **book review** gives a feeling or opinion about a book. You can find book reviews in different places, such as newspapers, magazines, television, or online.

Some book review writers know a great deal about a book's topic or author. Most book reviews have these parts:

- basic information such as author, price, and publisher
- a summary of the book
- opinions about the book's good and bad points
- an opinion about whether the book is worth reading

Reading Skill

Text features organize and highlight information in a written work. When you read, you can **use text features to analyze information,** which will help you understand the text. For example, looking at headings and subheadings will help you identify main ideas. Study the graphic organizer below to learn more about using text features to analyze information.

Structural Features of Book Reviews

- **heading:** large, bold text that identifies the book being reviewed
- **byline:** a line that shows who wrote the review
- **introduction:** an opening section that briefly describes the book being reviewed or provides information that is useful for context
- **conclusion:** a closing section that sums up the book's contents and the reviewer's opinion of it

TAKE NOTES

Text Structure

A book review includes basic information about a book. You can use this information to find the book. Circle the title, editor, publisher, and publication date for *A Life in Letters*. Why would these pieces of information be useful to a reader?

_____
_____

Vocabulary Builder

Multiple-Meaning Words The verb *penned* has more than one meaning. *Penned* can mean "wrote a note or a letter with a pen." It can also mean "prevented a person or an animal from leaving an enclosed area." What does *penned* mean in the first paragraph?

_____
_____

Cultural Understanding

The United States Postal Service began in 1775 when Benjamin Franklin was appointed the first Postmaster General. Postage stamps were introduced in 1847. Packages began traveling through the mail in 1913.

A Life in Letters

**Book Review
by Zakia Carter**

Zora Neale Hurston:
A Life in Letters.

Edited by Carla Kaplan
Doubleday; October 2002;
896 pages

Within days of having *Zora Neale Hurston: A Life in Letters* in my possession, I was inspired to devote the total of my lunch hour to selecting beautiful blank cards and stationery, a fine ink pen and a book of stamps. By the end of the day, I had penned six letters, the old-fashioned way, to friends and relatives—something I haven't done since summer camp. In our haste to save time, we check our inboxes with an eagerness that was once reserved for that moment before pushing a tiny silver key into a mailbox door. E-mail has replaced paper and pen, so much so that the U.S. Postal Service is losing business. But the truth of the matter is, folks will neither salvage nor cherish e-mail as they might a handwritten letter.

And so *A Life in Letters* is a gift. It includes more than 500 letters and postcards written by Zora Neale Hurston over four decades. The 800-plus-page collection reveals more about this brilliant and complex woman than perhaps the entire body of her published works combined, including her notoriously unrevealing autobiography, *Dust Tracks on the Road*. Amazingly, the urgency and immediacy (typos and all) we associate with e-mail can also be found in Zora's letters. She writes to a veritable who's who in American history and society, including Langston Hughes, Carl Van Vechten, Charlotte Osgood Mason, Franz Boas, Dorothy West and W.E.B. Du Bois among others, sometimes more than once or twice a day. In these, her most intimate writings, Zora comes to life.

While we are familiar with Zora the novelist, essayist, playwright and anthropologist, *A Life in Letters* introduces us to Zora the filmmaker; Zora the Barnard College undergrad and Columbia University student; Zora the two-time Guggenheim fellow; Zora the chicken specialist; Zora the thrice-married wife; and Zora the political pundit. Zora's letters are at times flip, ironic, heartbreaking and humorous. They are insightful, biting and candid as journal entries. One can only wish for responses to Zora's words, but the work is not incomplete without them.

A treasure trove of information, in addition to the annotated letters, a chronology of Zora's life, a glossary of the people, events, and institutions to which she refers in her letters, and a thorough bibliographical listing are generously included by editor Carla Kaplan. Each decade of writing is introduced by an essay on the social, political, and personal points of significance in Zora's life. Kaplan's is a fine, well edited and utterly revealing work of scholarship into the life of one of the greatest and often most misunderstood American writers. In many ways, *A Life in Letters* is, in fact, a long love letter for Zora. It is a reminder to salvage and cherish what should not be forgotten and an admonishment to write what you love on paper.

—**Zakia Carter is an editor at Africana.com.**

TAKE NOTES

Vocabulary Builder

Uncommon Terms Find the word *pundit* in the first full paragraph on this page. *Pundit* means "someone who knows a lot about a particular subject." About what subject does the author believe Zora knows a lot?

_____

Vocabulary Builder

Idioms Read the first sentence of the bracketed paragraph. The phrase *a treasure trove of information* means "a large collection of important facts and details." What parts of *A Life in Letters* make up the *treasure trove of information*?

_____
_____
_____

Comprehension Builder

Summarize the main points of this book review.

_____
_____
_____
_____
_____

AFTER YOU READ

Thinking About the Book Review

1. The reviewer says that there is some information in *A Life in Letters* that is not in Hurston's other books. What kind of information would not be found in other books?

   _____

   _____

2. A **book review** gives an opinion about a book. Some readers know Hurston only as a novelist and storywriter. What is in the review that might surprise these readers?

   _____

   _____

TALK ABOUT IT Reading Skill

3. What information does the heading of this review provide?

   _____

   _____

4. How does the author organize the first complete paragraph on page 363?

   _____

   _____

WRITE ABOUT IT Timed Writing: Summary (20 minutes)

Summarize the **review**. Include the author's main points and opinions. Use this chart to get started.

What does Carter think about *A Life in Letters*?	
What does Carter think readers will gain from reading *A Life in Letters*?	

BEFORE YOU READ: FROM OUT OF THE DUST

Vocabulary

These words are underlined in the selections. Listen to each word. Say it. Then, read the definition and the example sentence.

drought (DROWT) *n.* A **drought** is a long period of dry weather with little or no rain.
The plants shriveled and died during the drought.

streamed (STREEMD) *v.* Something that **streamed** has flowed or moved quickly in one direction.
A long line of cars streamed past my window.

sag (SAG) *v.* **Sag** means droop, sink, or bend below the usual position.
The boards sag from the weight of the boxes.

Vocabulary Practice

Read the first sentence in each group of three. Then, complete Sentence *a* by substituting another word or phrase that means the same as the underlined vocabulary word. Complete Sentence *b* with your own ideas and words.

1. The drought caused many farmers to lose their crops.

   a. The _____ caused many farmers to lose their crops.

   b. The drought _____.

2. Water streamed from the faucet.

   a. Water _____ from the faucet.

   b. Water streamed _____.

3. The tabletops sag from the many plates of food.

   a. The tabletops _____ from the many plates of food.

   b. The tabletops sag _____.

TALK ABOUT IT — Getting Ready to Read

The Dust Bowl refers to areas in Colorado, Kansas, Texas, Oklahoma, and New Mexico that experienced drought in the 1930s. Dust storms destroyed crops and killed livestock. Discuss with a partner what else you know about these kinds of storms.

MAKING CONNECTIONS

from Out of the Dust
Karen Hesse

Summary "Out of the Dust" includes three poems. The speaker in "Debts" describes the faith her father has that it will rain again. "Fields of Flashing Light" describes a dust storm on the prairie. In "Migrants," people leave their dried-up farms behind.

Writing About the Big Question
Are yesterday's heroes important today?
In *Out of the Dust,* Hesse explores the responses of ordinary people to the destructive effects of a long drought and an economic depression. Complete these sentences:

Courage can come from unexpected places. One person that others might not consider heroic, but I do, is _____

because _____.

Note-taking Guide
Use this chart to list the ways that dust and drought affect the people in each of the three poems.

Effects of Dust and Drought		
Debts	Fields of Flashing Light	Migrants

366 English Learner's Notebook

Debts

Daddy is thinking
of taking a loan from Mr. Roosevelt and his men,[1] . . .

◆ ◆ ◆

Daddy will use the money to plant new wheat. His winter crop has dried up and died. He will not have to repay the money until he harvests the crop. He is sure that it will soon rain and the wheat will grow.

Ma worries that it might not rain. Daddy disagrees. Ma tells Daddy that there has not been enough rain in the last three years.

Daddy is angry. He goes to the barn. He does not want to argue with Ma. The speaker asks Ma why Daddy is sure that it will rain. Ma says that it rains just enough to give people hope.

◆ ◆ ◆

But even if it didn't
your daddy would have to believe.
It's coming on spring,
and he's a farmer."

March 1934

TAKE NOTES

Vocabulary Builder

Parts of Speech As a noun, *loan* means "an amount of money borrowed from a bank." As a verb, it means "let someone borrow something." Which meaning does the speaker use in the text? Underline the text that tells you.

_____

Vocabulary Builder

Prefixes The prefix *dis-* means "not." The word *agrees* means "has the same opinon." What does the word *disagrees* mean?

_____

Comprehension Builder

What reason does Ma give to explain Daddy's strong belief that it will rain?

_____
_____
_____

---

1. **. . . a loan from Mr. Roosevelt and his men.** In 1933, President Franklin D. Roosevelt began a series of government programs, called the New Deal, to help Americans suffering from the effects of the Great Depression. Among these programs were government loans to help Dust Bowl farmers.

TAKE NOTES

Vocabulary Builder

Multiple-Meaning Words
Some words have more than one meaning. The word *fry* can mean a way of cooking food, or it can mean to be destroyed by too much heat. Reread the underlined sentence. Which way is the word *fry* used?

_____

Vocabulary Builder

Prepositions A preposition is a word used before a noun or pronoun to show place, time, or direction. Some prepositions are *at, over, in, under, into,* and *on.* Circle the prepositions in the bracketed passage.

Comprehension Builder

What does the speaker do to keep the dust out of the house? Underline the lines that tell you.

Fields of Flashing Light

The wind woke the speaker from sleep. The speaker went outside to watch the lightning. Then the speaker heard the dust coming. It destroyed the fields of winter wheat.

◆ ◆ ◆

I watched the plants,
surviving after so much drought and so much wind,
I watched them fry, . . .

◆ ◆ ◆

The dust began to blow at the house. The speaker ran back inside the house. When the dust blew against the windows, Daddy woke up. He quickly went out into the storm.

◆ ◆ ◆

his overalls half-hooked over his union suit.
"Daddy!" I called. "You can't stop dust."

◆ ◆ ◆

Ma asked the speaker to cover the beds. The speaker pushed rugs against the doors and wet the rags around the windows. Ma made coffee and biscuits. She waited for Daddy to return.

After four in the morning, Ma sat down. She covered her face. Daddy was gone for many hours. It started to snow. At first, they were glad to see the snow. But the wind blew the snow away. All that was left was dust. Daddy returned. He sat down and blew his nose.

◆ ◆ ◆

Mud streamed out.
He coughed and spit out
mud.
If he had cried,
his tears would have been mud too,
but he didn't cry.
And neither did Ma.

March 1934

Migrants

The neighbors say that they will return when it rains again. They fill their cars with everything they own. The springs on their cars sag with heavy loads. They ask the speaker's family to remember them.

♦ ♦ ♦

And so they go,
Fleeing the blowing dust, . . .

♦ ♦ ♦

The neighbors say that they will come back. Some of them will travel to Texas or to Arkansas. They hope to rent a farm and start over. Still, they promise to come back when it rains. They take everything they own. Some of them are going to California. They might stay there if life is better.

♦ ♦ ♦

Don't forget us, they say.
But there are so many leaving,
how can I remember them all?

April 1935

TAKE NOTES

Vocabulary Builder

Singular and Plural Nouns A singular noun means one of something. A plural noun means more than one. Most nouns add *s* or *es* to form a plural. Underline four plural nouns in the first paragraph. Circle *s* or *es* at the end of each noun.

Cultural Understanding

The farmers in this poem are moving to California. California did not suffer as much from drought and dust during the 1930s as other states did. Many people fled the Dust Bowl in the 1930s hoping to find work and a better life in California. The Dust Bowl was a section of the United States that experienced a drought during the 1930s.

Fluency Builder

Read the bracketed passage aloud. Practice reading the lines with expression and feeling. Remember to pause at commas and to raise the tone of your voice at the question mark.

AFTER YOU READ

Thinking About the Selection

1. What effect did the dust storms have on the people and places in the poems? Write your answers in the graphic organizer below.

   The dust storms . . .

2. In "Fields of Flashing Light," the family's wheat crop _____
_____.

TALK ABOUT IT **Leaving Home** In "Migrants," why do the family's neighbors move? Discuss your thoughts with a partner.

The family's neighbors move because _____.

WRITE ABOUT IT **Write a Poem** Write a poem describing how the family feels after its neighbors have left. What might the family do now?

_____
_____
_____
_____
_____

VOCABULARY SKILL REVIEW

Prefixes

A prefix is a group of letters that is added to the beginning of a word to form a new word with a new meaning. Adding the prefix *dis-* to a word makes the new word mean the opposite of the original word.

Examples

Respect means "admire a person for his or her knowledge and skills."	*Disrespect* means "show dislike for someone."
Prove means "show that something is true."	*Disprove* means "show that something is not true."
Honest means "truthful."	*Dishonest* means "not truthful."

Now You Do It

Write a sentence for each word shown below.

disrespect: _____

prove: _____

dishonest: _____

TALK ABOUT IT **Discuss the Meanings** Add the prefix *dis-* to the words *comfort*, *order*, and *obey*. With a partner, discuss the meaning of each word before and after you add the prefix. Use a dictionary to help you.

WRITE ABOUT IT **Letter to the Editor** Write a letter to the editor of your school newspaper that describes an issue with which you *agree* or *disagree*. In your letter, use the word *disagree* as well as other words on this page.

_____

_____

_____

_____

UNIT 6

BEFORE YOU READ: ELLIS ISLAND

Vocabulary

These words are highlighted in the selection. Listen to each word. Say it. Then, read the definition and the example sentence.

meadows (MED ohz) *n.* **Meadows** are areas of grassy land, or grasslands.
  In fall, the green grassy meadows become gold fields of hay.

native (NAY tiv) *adj.* **Native** means related to the place of one's birth.
  He traveled far from his native land.

invaded (in VAYD id) *v.* When a place is **invaded,** it is attacked and entered by a group that wants to conquer.
  In the film, aliens from another galaxy invaded Earth.

Vocabulary Practice

Read the first sentence in each group of three. Then, complete Sentence *a* by substituting another word or phrase that means the same as the underlined vocabulary word. Complete Sentence *b* with your own ideas and words.

1. We crossed several meadows and forests on our hike.

   a. We crossed several _____ and forests on our hike.

   b. We crossed several meadows _____.

2. These flowers are native to this part of the state.

   a. These flowers are _____ to this part of the state.

   b. These flowers are native _____.

3. Ants invaded the picnic basket to get to the food.

   a. Ants _____ the picnic basket to get to the food.

   b. Ants invaded _____.

 ### Getting Ready to Read

Between 1892 and 1924, about seventeen million European immigrants entered the United States through Ellis Island in New York Harbor. How do you think European immigrants felt when they arrived at Ellis Island? Discuss your ideas with a small group.

MAKING CONNECTIONS

Ellis Island
Joseph Bruchac

Summary The poet imagines his Slovak grandparents as they arrive in the United States. Their first stop in the land of their dreams was Ellis Island in New York. He then writes of his Native American grandparents. He points out that they had always lived in America. Their way of life was destroyed when the Europeans came.

 Writing About the Big Question

Are yesterday's heroes important today? In "Ellis Island," Joseph Bruchac writes of the conflicting feelings the famous immigrant processing station awakens in him. Complete this sentence:

Many people view the accomplishments of their immigrant ancestors

with pride because _____

_____.

Note-taking Guide
Some of the phrases in the poem are hard to understand. They use words that paint pictures and stand for other things. Use this graphic organizer to record some of the hidden messages.

the red brick of Ellis Island	the island of the tall woman	green as dreams and meadows	nine decades the answerer of dreams
The building at Ellis Island is made of red bricks.			

AFTER YOU READ

Thinking About the Selection

1. Who are the relatives that the speaker of "Ellis Island" mentions? Write your answers in the graphic organizer below.

The speaker's relatives include . . .

2. The "tall woman, green / as dreams of forests and meadows" is _____.

TALK ABOUT IT **Two Different Ideas About Land** What do the speaker's relatives think about land ownership? In a small group, discuss how these ideas are different.

The speaker's _____ relatives want to _____ _____.

The speaker's _____ relatives did not believe that _____.

WRITE ABOUT IT **The Influence of Family** Write a paragraph describing how the speaker's relatives influence the way he feels about Ellis Island.

_____
_____
_____
_____

VOCABULARY SKILL REVIEW

Idioms

An idiom is a word or phrase with a special meaning that is different from the ordinary meaning of the words.

Examples

Idiom	Explanation
fit for a king	of highest quality
flip out	become angry
get one's just deserts	get a deserved punishment
quick on the uptake	able to understand things quickly
tables have turned	situation has changed

Now You Do It

Write a sentence that uses each idiom in the chart above.

1. fit for a king _____
2. flip out _____
3. get one's just deserts _____
4. quick on the uptake _____
5. tables have turned _____

TALK ABOUT IT **Guess the Idiom** With a partner, discuss how you could describe each idiom on this page. Then, write a clue that describes the idiom. Share your clues with another pair. Take turns guessing the idioms from the clues each pair wrote.

WRITE ABOUT IT **Write a Detective Story** Write a short detective story that contains at least three idioms from the lesson. Read your story to a partner.

_____
_____
_____

UNIT 6

BEFORE YOU READ: CHOICE: A TRIBUTE TO MARTIN LUTHER KING, JR.

Vocabulary

These words are underlined in the selection. Listen to each word. Say it. Then, read the definition and the example sentence.

brutal (BROO tuhl) *adj.* Something **brutal** is cruel and often violent.
   The brutal guards abused the prisoners.

sensibility (sen suh BIL uh tee) *n.* One's **sensibility** is one's capacity for intellectual and artistic feelings.
   It was part of her sensibility to face danger without fear.

disinherit (dis in HER it) *v.* To **disinherit** means to deprive someone of his or her rights as a citizen.
   The activist shouted, "We must change laws that disinherit our people!"

Vocabulary Practice

Read the first sentence in each group of three. Then, complete Sentence *a* by substituting another word or phrase that means the same as the underlined vocabulary word. Complete Sentence *b* with your own ideas and words.

1. Kira's brutal remarks hurt her friend's feelings.

   a. Kira's _____ remarks hurt her friend's feelings.

   b. Kira's brutal _____.

2. The artist's sensibility was shown in the colors he chose.

   a. The artist's _____ were shown in the colors he chose.

   b. The artist's sensibility _____.

3. We should not disinherit people of the right to free speech.

   a. We should not _____ people of the right to free speech.

   b. We should not disinherit _____.

Getting Ready to Read

Between 1916 and 1970, millions of African Americans left the southern states to find jobs in northern states. After the civil rights movement, many African Americans returned to the southern states. In a small group, discuss what you know about the civil rights movement.

376 English Learner's Notebook

MAKING CONNECTIONS

Choice: A Tribute to Martin Luther King, Jr.
Alice Walker

Summary The author describes Dr. King's successes with the civil rights movement. She explains how Dr. King inspired African Americans to appreciate their heritage.

 Writing About the Big Question

Are yesterday's heroes important today? In "Choice," Alice Walker recalls the tremendous influence of Martin Luther King, Jr. on herself and her community. Complete this sentence:

A figure from the past, besides King, who continues to influence

people today is _____ because

_____.

Note-taking Guide
Use this diagram to recall the reasons that Alice Walker looks up to Martin Luther King, Jr.

- He was not afraid to be arrested for his beliefs.

Why Alice Walker looks up to Martin Luther King, Jr.

Choice: A Tribute to Martin Luther King, Jr. **377**

TAKE NOTES

Vocabulary Builder

Parts of Speech As a verb, *address* means "try to find a way to solve a problem." As a noun, it means "a formal speech." What does *address* mean in the first paragraph?

_____

_____

Vocabulary Builder

Idioms The phrase *worked the land* is an idiom that means "planted and harvested crops." Complete this sentence:

The speaker's family *worked the land* during _____

_____.

Fluency Builder

Commas, semicolons, and periods show relationships between groups of words. Read the bracketed passage on this page. Circle the commas, periods, and semicolons. Then, reread the passage, pausing appropriately for each punctuation mark.

Choice: A Tribute to Martin Luther King, Jr.
Alice Walker

This address was made in 1973 at a Jackson, Mississippi, restaurant that had refused to serve people of color until forced to do so by the civil rights movement a few years before.

♦ ♦ ♦

Walker begins by telling the story of her great-great-great-grandmother, a slave who walked with two babies from Virginia to Eatonton, Georgia, and describing the family cemetery in which generations of ancestors are buried.

♦ ♦ ♦

Yet the history of my family, like that of all black Southerners, is a history of **dispossession.** We loved the land and worked the land, but we never owned it; . . .

♦ ♦ ♦

Walker and others of the 1960s generation were compelled to leave the South to avoid having happy memories replaced by bitter recollections of brutal treatment.

♦ ♦ ♦

[It is a part of the black Southern sensibility that we treasure memories; for such a long time, that is all of our homeland those of us who at one time or another were forced away from it have been allowed to have.]

♦ ♦ ♦

In 1960, Walker first saw Dr. Martin Luther King, Jr. on television being arrested

---

Everyday Words

dispossession (dis puh ZESH uhn) *n.* state of having had one's property or land taken

378 English Learner's Notebook

for demonstrating in support of Hamilton Holmes and Charlayne Hunter,[1] who were attempting to enter the University of Georgia. Dr. King's calmness and bravery impressed her; his example changed her life.

♦ ♦ ♦

At the moment I saw his resistance I knew I would never be able to live in this country without resisting everything that sought to disinherit me, and I would never be forced away from the land of my birth without a fight.

He was The One, The Hero, The One Fearless Person for whom we had waited.

♦ ♦ ♦

Walker reminds listeners of the public acts of Dr. King: his speeches, his philosophy, his books, his preaching, his honors, and his deep concern for all displaced people. She also notes that people of color would not be permitted to eat in the restaurant in which she is speaking but for Dr. King's struggles. Walker also thanks Dr. King for an equally important, yet perhaps less obvious, gift.

♦ ♦ ♦

He gave us back our heritage. He gave us back our homeland; the bones and dust of our ancestors, who may now sleep within our caring *and* our hearing. . . .

He gave us **continuity** of place, without which community is ephemeral.[2] He gave us home.

TAKE NOTES

Vocabulary Builder

Word Families Word families are groups of words that share the same base word. A base word is the word to which a prefix or suffix is added to make a new word. *Resist* is the base word for other words such as *resistible* and *resistant*. *Resist* means "withstand, oppose, stand firm against." Underline two words in the bracketed passage that also have *resist* as a base word.

Comprehension Builder

What does Walker say Dr. King gave African Americans?

_____
_____
_____
_____

Everyday Words

continuity (kahn tuh NOO uh tee) *n.* state of continuing, without problems, interruptions, or changes

---

1. **Hamilton Holmes and Charlayne Hunter** students who made history in January 1961 by becoming the first two African Americans to attend the University of Georgia.
2. **ephemeral** (i FEM uhr uhl) *adj.* short-lived; fleeting.

AFTER YOU READ

Thinking About the Selection

1. What does Walker realize when she sees Dr. King on television being arrested? Write your answers in the chart below.

> Walker realizes that . . .

2. Walker says that although African Americans loved and worked on the land, _____.

TALK ABOUT IT **What Does She Mean?** Walker says that Dr. King gave African Americans "continuity of place" and "home." What does she mean? Discuss your ideas in a small group.

Walker means that _____
_____.

WRITE ABOUT IT **Write a Speech** What message does Walker's speech have for people today? Write a speech that explains Walker's message and how we can apply it today.

The message from Walker's speech is that _____
_____
_____
_____.

VOCABULARY SKILL REVIEW

Word Families

Words that share the same base word make up a word family. Knowing the meaning of a base word can help determine the meaning of unfamiliar or difficult words in the same word family.

Base word: Differ

Differ means "to be unlike someone or something else."

Words That Share the Base Word	Part of Speech	Meaning
different	adjective	unlike someone or something else
difference	noun	a way in which two or more things are not the same
differentiate	verb	recognize the way that two or more things are not the same

Now You Do It

Use the words in the chart above to complete the sentences.

1. I feel no _____ between the weather we had this week and the weather we had last week.

2. The red apple is _____ from the green apple.

3. Sandra could not _____ between the two colors.

TALK ABOUT IT **Build a Story** In a small group, take turns saying sentences that contain words from this lesson. The first person should use a word from the family in a sentence. The next person continues the story by using another word from the family in a sentence, and so on.

WRITE ABOUT IT **Write a Poem** Write a poem that celebrates the importance of being different. Include at least two words from the lesson.

_____

_____

Choice: A Tribute to Martin Luther King, Jr.

UNIT 6

BEFORE YOU READ: AN EPISODE OF WAR

Vocabulary

These words are highlighted in the selection. Listen to each word. Say it. Then, read the definition and the example sentence.

winced (WINST) *v.* **Winced** means cringed or drew back slightly because of pain.
   The boy winced when the doctor touched his injured arm.

hostile (HAH stuhl) *adj.* **Hostile** means related to the enemy, angry, and unfriendly.
   The soldiers were engaged in a fierce battle with hostile forces.

tumultuous (tu MUL choo us) *adj.* Something that is **tumultuous** is wild and chaotic.
   The wind whipped the waves on the tumultuous sea.

Vocabulary Practice

Read the first sentence in each group of three. Then, complete Sentence *a* by substituting another word or phrase that means the same as the underlined vocabulary word. Complete Sentence *b* with your own ideas and words.

1. Danielle winced when the doctor touched her injured foot.

   a. Danielle _____ when the doctor touched her injured foot.

   b. Danielle winced _____.

2. The rivals became hostile during the game.

   a. The rivals became _____ during the game.

   b. The rivals became hostile _____.

3. The tumultuous sea caused the boat to rock.

   a. The _____ sea caused the boat to rock.

   b. The tumultuous _____.

Getting Ready to Read

The Civil War was fought from 1861 to 1865 between the United States federal government and Southern states that wanted to separate from the Union. What else do you know about the Civil War? Discuss your thoughts in small groups.

382 English Learner's Notebook

MAKING CONNECTIONS

An Episode of War
Stephen Crane

Summary A Civil War lieutenant is shot by a stray bullet. The other soldiers are worried for him. The doctors and medical staff act as if he is a bother. The lieutenant is ashamed that he was not shot in battle. His arm is removed. The lieutenant tells his family that missing an arm does not really matter.

 Writing About the Big Question

Are yesterday's heroes important today? "An Episode of War" explores various reactions to the wounding of a soldier, including those of the soldier himself. Complete this sentence:

The concept of heroism (is/is not) outdated in our times because

_____.

Note-taking Guide
Use this chart to record the attitudes of the different characters in "An Episode of War."

Characters	Attitudes	Reasons for Attitudes
Lieutenant		
Other soldiers	awed and sympathetic	
Surgeon		
Lieutenant's family		

AFTER YOU READ

Thinking About the Selection

1. Use this chart to record the main events of "An Episode of War." The first event has been recorded for you.

   > The lieutenant is shot in the arm.

   ↓

   > _____

   ↓

   > _____

   ↓

   > _____

2. Before he is shot, the lieutenant is _____.

TALK ABOUT IT **What Do You Think?** The lieutenant refuses to follow the doctor into the schoolhouse where his arm would be amputated. Why is the lieutenant afraid of losing his arm? Discuss your thoughts with a partner.

The lieutenant is afraid to lose his arm because _____.

WRITE ABOUT IT **Write a Journal Entry** Write a journal entry in which the lieutenant describes his feelings about his injury and losing his arm. How do you think he feels when he returns home to his family?

_____
_____
_____
_____

VOCABULARY SKILL REVIEW

Antonyms
Two words that mean the opposite of each other are called antonyms.

Examples
Fast means "moving quickly." Antonyms for *fast* include *slow, sluggish, leisurely,* and *unhurried.*

Slow means "not moving quickly." Antonyms for *slow* include *fast, swift, rapid, speedy,* and *quick.*

Now You Do It
Write a sentence that uses each pair of antonyms listed below.

1. slow/fast _____
2. sluggish/swift _____
3. leisurely/rapid _____
4. unhurried/speedy _____

TALK ABOUT IT **Living Fast or Slow?** With a partner, use the antonyms on this page to talk about the benefits of fast communication and transportation. Then, discuss why some people might want to slow down the way they live.

WRITE ABOUT IT **Write a Poem** Write a four-line poem that describes a word from this lesson. In the first three lines, use antonyms to tell what the word is not. Then, use the word in the last line. For example, *It is not fast, / It is not speedy, / It does not have a rapid movement / Because it is slow.* Share your poem with the class.

_____
_____
_____
_____
_____

Transcripts

About Transcripts

Transcripts are written records of speech. They use the exact words of the speakers. Transcripts provide a complete record of what was said at an event. They do not include opinions or rewording. People use transcripts to record:

- radio or television shows
- trials or government hearings
- interviews or oral histories
- debates or speeches

Reading Skill

Analyze the treatment, scope, and organization of ideas to help you understand information in a transcript. The treatment reveals the purpose of the piece of writing. The purpose of a transcript is to record what was said during an event. The scope of the transcript includes the entire record of what was said by all participants at an event. The scope can be broad and cover lots of topics. It can also be narrow and cover a specific subject. The organization of a transcript follows the questions and comments of the participants in the order in which they were spoken.

Checklist for Evaluating Treatment, Scope, and Organization

- ❑ Has the author addressed the topic in a way that is neutral or biased?
- ❑ Does the author cover different sides of an issue or only one?
- ❑ Does the author present ideas in a logical sequence?
- ❑ Are details organized in a way that enhances the author's points?

Build Understanding

Knowing these words will help you read this transcript.

paralyzed veterans (PAR uh lyzd VET uhr uhnz) *n.* people who have been in the military and now have arms and/or legs that cannot move

paraplegics (par uh PLEE jiks) *n.* people who have both legs paralyzed

spinal cord injuries (SPY nuhl KORD IN juh reez) *n.* damage to the nerves that run from the brain down the back

MORNING EDITION, NATIONAL PUBLIC RADIO

November 11, 2003

PROFILE: World War II veterans who founded the Paralyzed Veterans of America.

BOB EDWARDS, host: This is MORNING EDITION from NPR News. I'm Bob Edwards.

In February of 1947, a small group of World War II veterans gathered at Hines VA Hospital near Chicago. The fact that they were there at all was considered extraordinary. The men were paralyzed, living at a time when paraplegia was still an unfamiliar word and most people with spinal cord injuries were told they would die within a few years. But these wounded veterans had other ideas, so they came from hospital wards across the country to start a national organization to represent veterans with spinal cord injuries. Today on Veterans Day, NPR's Joseph Shapiro tells their story.

JOSEPH SHAPIRO reporting: The logo of the Paralyzed Veterans of America looks a bit like the American flag, except that it's got 16 stars, one for each of the men who started the PVA when they gathered at that first convention nearly 57 years ago. Today only one of those 16 paralyzed veterans is still alive. His name is Ken Seaquist. He lives in a gated community in Florida. . . . It's there that Seaquist sits in his wheelchair and flips through some yellowed newspaper clippings . . .

MR. KEN SEAQUIST: Oh, here it is. OK.

SHAPIRO: . . . until he finds a photo. . . . The picture shows that convention. It was held in a veterans hospital just outside Chicago. A large room is filled with scores of young men in wheelchairs. Others are in their pajamas and hospital beds, propped up on white pillows.

TAKE NOTES

Text Structure

You can use the text structure to understand transcripts. Look at the heading on this transcript. Circle the date the program aired and the name of the program. What was the program about on this day?

_____

_____

Comprehension Builder

Reading transcripts can be confusing. Different people are involved, but you cannot see any of them. So, you have to keep them straight by looking at their names. You also have to remember how each person is involved in the discussion. Explain how each person below is involved in this radio show.

Bob Edwards: _____

Joe Shapiro: _____

Ken Seaquist: _____

TAKE NOTES

Text Structure

The names of the speakers stand out in the formatting of the text. Circle the names of the three people who are talking on this page.

Note that a person's full name is given the first time the person talks. After the first time, names are written in shorter ways. Underline the names of a person who is talking for the first time on this page.

Vocabulary Builder

Prefixes Recall that a prefix is a word part added to the beginning of a base word. Find the word *antibiotics* in this transcript. The prefix *anti-* means "against." The base word *biotic* relates to bacteria, or very small living things that can cause diseases. What do you think the word *antibiotics* means?

_____

_____

Cultural Understanding

The president that Shapiro refers to is President Franklin D. Roosevelt. He was president of the United States from 1933–1945. He is the only president to serve four terms in office.

MR. SEAQUIST: There's Bill Dake. He came with us and then Mark Orr. Three of us came in the car from Memphis. Mark had one good leg, his right leg, and he was the driver of the car.

SHAPIRO: Ken Seaquist was a tall, lanky 20-year-old in an Army mountain ski division when he was wounded in Italy. He was flown back to the United States to a veterans hospital in Memphis. He came back to a society that was not ready for paraplegics.

MR. SEAQUIST: Before the war, people in our condition were in the closet. They never went out hardly. They didn't take them out.

SHAPIRO: Few people had ever survived for more than a few years with a spinal cord injury. Infections were common and deadly. But that was about to change. David Gerber is a historian at the University at Buffalo. He's written about disabled veterans.

MR. DAVID GERBER (UNIVERSITY AT BUFFALO): With the development of antibiotics, which came into general use in World War II, there were many healthy spinal cord-injured veterans who were able to survive and begin to aspire to have a normalized life.

SHAPIRO: Gerber says neither the wounded veterans, nor the world around them at that time knew what to make of men who were seen as having gone from manly warriors to dependent invalids.

MR. GERBER: The society is emphatically not ready for them, and nor is the medical profession. To this extent, it was often the paralyzed veterans themselves who were pioneers in the development of a new way of life for themselves.

SHAPIRO: Seaquist and the others set out to overcome the fear and pity of others. After Seaquist was injured, he never heard from his girlfriend. His mother's hair turned white in a matter of months. People stared when he went out in public. It was a time when a president with polio felt he had to hide the fact that he used a wheelchair. Beyond attitudes, there was a physical world that had to change. When Seaquist arrived at the Memphis hospital, he could not get off the ward. There were steps in the way.

MR. SEAQUIST: They had no idea of what they had to do for wheelchairs. So when we got there, they had to put in all these long ramps and this is what we were talking about. The ramping and just to get around the hospital and get out ourselves, you know; not having somebody help us all the time. We were an independent bunch.

SHAPIRO: There were about 2,500 soldiers with spinal cord injuries, most of them living in military hospitals around the country. Pat Grissom lived at Birmingham Hospital in California. He would become one of the first presidents of the PVA, but he was unable to travel from California to Chicago for that first convention. Grissom, too, had come back from war with little hope for his future.

MR. PAT GRISSOM: I just suppose that we were going to live the rest of our lives either in the hospital or go to an old soldiers home. We were just going to be there taking medicine and if you got sick, they would try to take care of you and you'd have your meals provided and your future was the hospital or the old soldiers home.

SHAPIRO: At Birmingham Hospital, Grissom met a doctor who was about to become a pioneer in the new field of spinal cord medicine. Dr. Ernst Bors did a lot to improve the physical care of paraplegics. He also pushed the men at Birmingham to set goals for their lives, to go back to school, get jobs and marry. Bors and the veterans at Birmingham Hospital were the subject of a Hollywood film, *The Men*. The realistic and sympathetic portrayal helped the American public better understand paralyzed veterans. In the film, the kindly doctor in a lab coat is based on Bors. He urges on a wounded soldier in a white T-shirt, played by a young Marlon Brando.

TAKE NOTES

Fluency Builder

When people speak, they may not use grammatically correct language. Read the sentence spoken by Mr. Seaquist that begins "The ramping and." Rewrite the entire sentence using grammatically correct language. You may need to incorporate ideas from other sentences in the paragraph.

_____
_____
_____

Now, read the entire paragraph aloud.

Vocabulary Builder

Proper Nouns A proper noun names a specific person, place, or thing. Proper nouns begin with capital letters. Read the paragraph beginning "SHAPIRO: There were about." Circle the proper nouns in this paragraph.

Comprehension Builder

How did injured soldiers' lives change due to the influence of Dr. Ernst Bors? Summarize the changes on the lines below.

_____
_____
_____
_____

TAKE NOTES

Text Structure

Read the bracketed passage. How is this passage different from the rest of the **transcript**?

_____
_____
_____
_____

Cultural Understanding

Long ago, all cars had manual transmissions. The driver had to change gears frequently while driving, in the same way that you might change gears on a bicycle while riding uphill. The automatic transmission changed gears when necessary without any action by the driver. *Oldsmobile* is a manufacturer of cars.

(Soundbite of The Men)

[**MR. MARLON BRANDO:** Well, what am I going to do? Where am I going to go?

Unidentified Actor: Into the world.

MR. MARLON BRANDO: I can't go out there anymore.

Unidentified Actor: You still can't accept it, can you?

MR. MARLON BRANDO: No. What did I do? Why'd it have to be me?

Unidentified Actor: Is there an answer? I haven't got it. Somebody always gets hurt in the war.]

Marlon Brando in *The Men*

SHAPIRO: For Grissom and the other paralyzed veterans, there was something else that helped them go out into the world, a new technology. The introduction of automatic transmission meant that a car could be modified with hand controls for the gas and brakes. Pat Grissom.

MR. GRISSOM: Oldsmobile came up with the hydromatic drive and they put on hand controls and they sent people out to start giving driving lessons to us and we started having visions of saving up enough money to get a car and then things were looking better all the time.

SHAPIRO: Ken Seaquist says driving opened up all kinds of possibilities, from going out to a restaurant with a bunch of friends to romance.

MR. SEAQUIST: In Memphis, we had—our favorite place was called the Silver Slipper and they welcomed us with open arms and we had maybe 10, 12 wheelchairs going with our dates. Generally it

Car modified with hand controls

was our nurses that we dated, 'cause, you know, we couldn't get out anywhere. We took the girls with us, you know. Eventually I married one of them.

SHAPIRO: Seaquist and his wife quickly had two daughters. And with a young family, he had to find work. He went to school and became a landscape architect. Ken Seaquist stopped seeing himself as an invalid and became a man with a future. So in 1947, he and the other founders of the PVA met in Chicago to put together a collective voice to express their dreams and what they needed to accomplish them. They came up with a slogan to get others to join, 'Awaken, gentlemen, lest we decay.' Ken Seaquist explains what it meant.

MR. SEAQUIST: If they forget us, we're going to decay. We're going to be left in the closet. We've got to get out there and speak out, getting things done so we can roll around this country and have access to the whole country.

SHAPIRO: The PVA quickly won some important legislative victories in Washington: money for paralyzed veterans to modify automobiles and houses, money for medical care. Later they would help push for laws that would make buildings and streets accessible to wheelchair users. The PVA has continued to advocate for veterans with spinal cord injuries through every war since World War II.

Joseph Shapiro, NPR News.

TAKE NOTES

Fluency Builder
With a partner, take turns reading aloud the first speech by Shapiro on this page. Read his words as though you were a radio announcer.

Comprehension Builder
Why did Mr. Seaquist and others found the PVA? Underline the sentences that tell the answer.

Vocabulary Builder
Multiple-Meaning Words The verb *push* can mean "move a person or thing by pressing with your hands." It can also mean "try to persuade someone to accept or do something." What meaning does the verb have in the bracketed passage?

_____
_____

AFTER YOU READ

Thinking About the Transcript

1. Why were veterans of World War II more likely to survive their injuries?
   _____
   _____

2. Why did the veterans form the Paralyzed Veterans of America?
   _____
   _____
   _____

TALK ABOUT IT Reading Skill

3. How does the organization of the transcript help you identify the comments by the veterans?
   _____
   _____
   _____

4. Describe the scope of the information presented in this transcript. Is the scope broad or narrow? Explain.
   _____
   _____
   _____

WRITE ABOUT IT Timed Writing: Explanation (20 minutes)

Paralyzed veterans face many stereotypes. Write a paragraph explaining why stereotyping can be hurtful.

- Identify examples of stereotypes from the transcript.
   _____
   _____
   _____

- Use these examples to explain why stereotyping can hurt people.
   _____
   _____
   _____

UNIT VOCABULARY REVIEW

Word Bank

accomplishments	cultural	influence
admirably	emphasize	outdated
aspects	endure	overcome
bravery	exaggerate	suffering
courage	imitate	symbolize

A. **Sentence Completion** Complete each sentence by telling what something is and then what it is not. Follow the language in each sentence so that your words make sense. The first one has been completed for you.

IS		NOT
Accomplishments are impressive	but	they are not ordinary
1. Bravery is	but	it is not
2. One can show courage by	but	one does not show it by
3. In order to emphasize something, one must	but	one must not
4. Influence is	but	it is not
5. If something is outdated it is	but	it is not
6. In order to overcome something, one should be	but	one should not be
7. Suffering is	but	it is not

B. **Word Sorting** Organize the words from the word bank on the previous page. If the word tells about an action, place it in the Verb column. If the word describes a thing, place it in the Adjective column. If the word is a person or thing, place it in the Noun column. Some words may fit in more than one column.

Noun	Verb	Adjective	Adverb

TALK ABOUT IT **Admirable Individuals** With a partner, talk about someone whom you admire. How has that person had a positive effect on your life? Use words from the word bank to help you complete these sentence starters while you talk.

Positive **aspects** of this person's personality include _____.

The person's influence has helped me _____.

Because of this person, I have been able to **endure** _____.

WRITE ABOUT IT **Success Story** Write a short story about a character who has to overcome an obstacle. Describe how the character resolves the problem. Include words from the word bank in your story.

_____
_____
_____
_____

PART 2: SUMMARY TRANSLATIONS

Selection Summaries in Eight Languages

Part 2 contains summaries of all selections in Prentice Hall Literature. Summaries are in:

- English
- Spanish
- Haitian Creole
- Filipino
- Hmong
- Chinese
- Vietnamese
- Korean

Use the summaries in Part 2 to preview or review the selections.

UNIT 1: SUMMARY TRANSLATIONS

from The Baker Heater League
Patricia C. McKissack and Fredrick McKissack

Summary This nonfiction selection explains how railroad workers called *porters* shared tales with one another. The porters would gather around a potbellied stove, called a Baker heater, to tell their stories. Legends such as those of Casey Jones and John Henry grew out of these stories.

de "La liga de la estufa de carbón"
Patricia C. McKissack y Fredrick McKissack

Resumen Esta selección de no ficción explica cómo los trabajadores ferroviarios, conocidos como "porteros", comparten historias. Los porteros se reúnen alrededor de una estufa barrigona, o estufa de carbón, para contar sus historias. Leyendas como las de Casey Jones y John Henry nacieron a partir de estas historias.

yon ekstrè nan Gwoup otou chofaj Baker a
Patricia C. McKissack, ak Fredrick McKissack

Rezime Seleksyon non-fiksyon sa a eksplike fason travayè chemennfè yo ki te rele *pòtè* te pataje istwa youn avèk lòt. Pòtè yo ta va rasanble otou yon fou won, ki te rele chofaj Baker, pou rakonte istwa yo. Kèk lejann tankou Casey Jones ak John Henry te vin twò gran pou istwa sa yo.

Mula sa Ang Liga ng "Baker Heater"
Patricia C. McKissack at Fredrick McKissack

Buod Ipinaliliwanag nitong kasulatang ito, na batay sa tunay na buhay, kung paano nagkukuwentuhan ang *mga portero*, ang tawag sa mga manggagawa sa riles ng tren. Ang mga portero ay nagpupulong-pulong sa paligid ng isang pugon na tinatawag na "Baker heater", upang magkuwentuhan. Ang mga alamat tulad ng tungkol kay Casey Jones at John Henry ay nagmulá sa mga kuwentuhang ito.

SUMMARY TRANSLATIONS

los ntawm Pab Pawg Hu Ua Baker Heater League

Patricia C. McKissack, thiab Fredrick McKissack, Jr.

Lub Ntsiab Zaj sau txog ib yam uas muaj tseeb no qhia txog tias cov neeg kho kev tsheb nqaj hlau hu ua *porters* piav dabneeg mloog uake. Cov porters los sib sau uake ncig lub cub tawg kheej kheej, hu ua Baker, thiab piav lawv cov dabneeg. Zaj dabneeg muaj ib txheej dhau ib txheej ib yam li zaj hais txog Casey Jones thiab John Henry yog los ntawm cov dabneeg no los.

改編自《貝克暖爐同好》(The Baker Heater League)

Patricia C. McKissack 與 Fredrick McKissack

摘要 這篇非小說的文選描寫被稱之為雜務工的鐵路工作人員彼此分享市井傳說的情形。這些雜務工會聚集在一個被膩稱為貝克暖爐的大肚爐灶旁訴說自己的故事。諸如凱西・瓊斯以及約翰・亨利等人的傳說即從這些故事中衍生而來。

trích từ Hiệp Hội Máy Sưởi Hiệu Baker

Patricia C. McKissack và Fredrick McKissack

Tóm Tắt Truyện có thật này giải thích làm thế nào những người phục vụ trong ngành đường sắt được gọi là "porters" truyền tai nhau các câu truyện dân gian. Những người phục vụ trong ngành đường sắt tập trung quanh một lò đốt củi có tên là lò sưởi Baker để kể nhau nghe các câu truyện của họ. Những huyền thoại về Casey Jones và John Henry đã ra đời từ những câu truyện này.

베이커 히터 리그 중에서 (The Baker Heater League)

Patricia C. McKissack 및 Fredrick McKissack

요약 "짐꾼"이라고 불리는 철도 노동자들은 베이커 히터라는 이름의 불룩한 모양의 스토브 주위에 둘러앉아 서로가 알고 있는 재미있는 이야기를 하나씩 들려준다. 캐시 존스의 전설이나 존 헨리의 전설도 바로 여기서 들려준 이야기들 중 하나이다.

SUMMARY TRANSLATIONS

The 11:59
Patricia C. McKissack

Summary Lester Simmons, a retired porter, hangs out every night at the porter house, telling stories to the other railroad employees. One night, he tells the young porters about the mysterious 11:59 Death Train. Lester's story becomes real. He tries to escape the train.

Las 11:59
Patricia C. McKissack

Resumen Lester Simmons, un portero retirado, frecuenta todas las noches la casa de los porteros y narra historias a los demás empleados ferroviarios. Una noche les cuenta a los jóvenes porteros sobre el misterioso tren de la muerte de las 11:59. La historia de Lester se convierte en realidad. Él trata de escaparse del tren.

11 è 59 la
Patricia C. McKissack

Rezime Lester Simmons, yon pòtè ki pran retrèt, vizite kay pòtè a chak swa, kote l rakonte istwa bay lòt anplwaye chemennfè yo. Yon jou swa, li rakonte jèn pòtè yo yon istwa konsènan Tren Lanmò misterye 11 è 59 la. Istwa Lester a vin yon reyalite. Li eseye sove sot nan tren an.

Ang 11:59
Patricia C. McKissack

Buod Si Lester Simmons, isang retiradong portero, ay tumatambay sa bahay ng mga portero gabi-gabi para magkuwento sa ibang mga empleyado sa tren. Isang gabi, nagkuwento siya sa mga batang portero tungkol sa misteryosong 11:59 Tren ng Kamatayan. Nagka-totoó ang kuwento ni Lester. Sinubukan niyang takasan ang tren.

SUMMARY TRANSLATIONS

Lub Uas Los Thaum 11:59
Patricia C. McKissack

Lub Ntsiab Lester Simmons, ib tug neeg ua haujlwm kho kev tsheb nqaj hlau, mus ua si txhua hmo tom lub tsev rau cov neeg kho kev tsheb nqaj hlau nyob, thiab piav dabneeg rau lwm cov neeg ua haujlwm mloog. Muaj ib hmos, nws piav rau cov tub ntxhais hluas kho kev tsheb nqaj hlau txog zaj hu ua 11:59 Tsheb Nqaj Hlau Kev Tuag. Lester zaj dabneeg tshwm sim los muaj tseeb. Nws sim khiav kom dhau lub tsheb nqaj hlau.

《11點59分》(The 11:59)
Patricia C. McKissack

摘要 雷斯特・西蒙斯是一位退休的雜務工，他每晚都會在雜務工室逗留，對其他鐵路員工講述故事。一天晚上，他對這群年輕的雜務工說了個有關神秘的 11:59 死亡火車的事。雷斯特的故事竟在現實中發生。他必須設法逃離這輛火車。

Chuyến Tàu Lúc 11:59
Patricia C. McKissack

Tóm Tắt Lester Simmons, một nhân viên đường sắt đã nghỉ hưu, thường quanh quẩn ở phòng trực nhà ga hàng đêm và kể chuyện cho các nhân viên đường sắt khác. Một đêm nọ, ông ta kể cho những nhân viên trẻ nghe về Chuyến Tàu Tử Thần bí hiểm rời ga lúc 11:59. Câu truyện của Lester trở thành sự thật. Ông ấy cố gắng thoát khỏi con tàu.

11:59발 열차 (The 11:59)
Patricia C. McKissack

요약 레스터 시몬은 은퇴한 짐꾼으로 밤이면 짐꾼들이 머무는 숙소에 들러 철도 노동자들에게 이야기 들려주는 것을 낙으로 삼고 있다. 어느 날 밤, 레스터는 11시 59분에 출발하는 미스터리 한 죽음의 열차에 대해 이야기를 한다. 그런데 그 이야기가 현실화 되고 레스터는 그 죽음의 열차에서 빠져 나오려 애쓴다.

UNIT 1: SUMMARY TRANSLATIONS

Raymond's Run
Toni Cade Bambara

Summary Squeaky is the fastest runner in her class. She cares for her "not quite right" brother Raymond. She protects him from teasing and from getting hurt. During the annual May Day races, Squeaky learns lessons about herself, a runner named Gretchen, and Raymond.

Raymond's Run (translation)
Toni Cade Bambara

Resumen Squeaky es la corredora más rápida de su clase. Y cuida de su hermano Raymond, que tiene algunos problemas mentales. Lo protege para que no se burlen de él ni se lastime. Durante las carreras anuales del 1º de mayo, Squeaky aprende lecciones sobre ella misma, una corredora llamada Gretchen y sobre Raymond.

Kous Raymond an
Toni Cade Bambara

Rezime Squeaky se kourè ki pi rapid nan klas li a. Li pran swen frè li Raymond ki "pa tèlman anfòm". Li pwoteje l pou lòt moun pa takinen l oswa fè l mal. Pandan kous anyèl fèt Premye Me a, Squeaky aprann kèk leson konsènan limenm, yon kourè ki rele Gretchen ak Raymond.

Ang Takbo ni Raymond
Toni Cade Bambara

Buod Si Squeaky ang pinakamatulin tumakbó sa kanyang klase. Mahal niya si Raymond, ang kanyang kapatid na lalaking "medyo may problema". Kanyang pinagtatanggol ito laban sa panunuksó, at para hindi ito masaktan. Noong taúnang karera ng takbuhan ng "May Day", may mga liksiyon na natutunan si Squeaky tungkol sa kanyang sarili, tungkol sa isang mananakbo na nagngangalang Gretchen, at tungkol kay Raymond.

SUMMARY TRANSLATIONS

Raymond Khiav
Toni Cade Bambara

Lub Ntsiab Squeaky yog tus khiav taus ceev tshaj plaws nyob rau hauv nws chav kawm ntawv. Nws hlub tshua txog nws tus nus Raymond uas "tsis zoo li suav daws." Nws tiv thaiv kom Raymond txhob raug luag thuam thiab txhob raug mob. Thaum txog hnub May Day uas lawv sib tw khiav txhua xyoo, Squeaky kawm tau tej yam txog nws tus kheej, txog ib tug neeg sib tw khiav hu ua Gretchen, thiab txog Raymond.

《雷蒙的路跑》(Raymond's Run)
Toni Cade Bambara

摘要 史桂姬是她班上跑得最快的人。她很照顧自己那位「不怎麼對勁」的弟弟雷蒙。她總是保護著他，以免他遭到戲弄及受傷害。在一年一度的五月天路跑賽期間，史桂姬學到了有關自己、一位名為葛瑞琴的跑者、及雷蒙的教訓。

Cuộc Chạy Của Raymond
Toni Cade Bambara

Tóm Tắt Squeaky là người chạy nhanh nhất lớp. Cô bé chăm sóc cho cậu em Raymond "không bình thường" của mình. Cô bé bảo vệ không để cậu em bị trêu chọc hay tổn thương. Qua các cuộc chạy thi hàng năm nhân ngày Quốc Tế Lao Động, Squeaky học được các bài học về bản thân mình, về một người chạy có tên là Gretchen, và về Raymond.

레이몬드의 질주 (Raymond's Run)
Toni Cade Bambara

요약 스퀴키라는 별명의 소녀는 자기 반에서 제일 빨리 달린다. 소녀는 "좀 정상이 아닌" 남동생 레이몬드를 돌본다. 레이몬드가 놀림을 받거나 다치지 않도록 지켜준다. 해마다 열리는 메이데이 기념 달리기 대회에 참가하면서 스퀴키는 동생 레이몬드와 그레친이란 이름으로 달리기를 하는 자신의 모습에 대해 교훈을 얻는다.

UNIT 1
SUMMARY TRANSLATIONS

A Retrieved Reformation
O. Henry

Summary Jimmy Valentine leaves prison and plans to go back to robbing safes. But he falls in love and decides to become honest. He changes his name and opens a store. A detective shows up to arrest Jimmy for recent robberies. However, Jimmy's actions show that he has changed.

Yon refòmasyon retwouve
O. Henry

Rezime Jimmy Valentine soti nan prizon epi li gen entansyon retounen al vòlè kèk kòfrefò. Men li vin tonbe anmoure epi li deside pou l vin yon moun onèt. Li chanje non li epi li ouvri yon magazen. Yon detektif parèt pou l arete Jimmy pou kèk vòl ki te fèt. Sepandan, aksyon Jimmy yo montre li te chanje.

Isang Muling-Nakamtang Pagbabago
O. Henry

Buod Nakalabas si Jimmy Valentine sa bilangguan, at siya'y nagplano na bumalik sa pagnanakaw sa mga kaha de yero. Ngunit siya ay umibig, at dahil dito ay nagpasiya siyang maging marangal. Pinalitan niya ang kanyang pangalan at nagbukas siya ng isang tindahan. May isang detektib na dumating upang dakipin si Jimmy para sa mga pagnanakaw na naganap kailan lamang, subalit ipinakita ng mga aksiyon ni Jimmy na siya'y nagbago na.

Una reforma recuperada
O. Henry

Resumen Jimmy Valentine deja la prisión y planea volver a robar cajas fuertes. Pero se enamora y decide convertirse en un hombre honesto. Se cambia de nombre y abre una tienda. Y aparece un detective para arrestar a Jimmy por algunos robos recientes. Sin embargo, las acciones de Jimmy demuestran que ha cambiado.

SUMMARY TRANSLATIONS

Hloov Rov Los Lawm
O. Henry

Lub Ntsiab Jimmy Valentine tawm hauv nkuaj los thiab npaj yuav rov qab mus ua ib tug neeg nyiag khoom. Tiamsis nws cia li qaug rau kev hlub thiab txiav txim siab los ua neeg ncaj ncees. Nws hloov nws lub npe thiab qhib ib lub khw muag khoom. Muaj ib tug tub ceev xwm cia li tuaj ntes Jimmy rau ib co xwm txheej nyiag khoom uas nyuam qhuav tshwm sim. Txawm li ntawd los, Jimmy txoj kev coj qhia tau rau lawv paub tias nws yog ib tug neeg hloov lawm tiag.

《重新做人》(A Retrieved Reformation)
O. Henry

摘要 吉姆・瓦倫泰出了獄，他計劃再去洗劫保險箱。但他戀愛了，並決定老實做人。他改名換性，並開了間店。一位警探出現並以吉姆涉及最近的搶案為由逮捕了他。但吉姆的行為證明了他確實改邪歸正了。

Một Cuộc Đổi Đời
O. Henry

Tóm Tắt Jimmy Valentine rời nhà tù với ý định quay trở lại con đường cũ, đi cướp các két sắt. Nhưng hắn đem lòng yêu một người và quyết định trở thành người dân lành. Anh ta đổi tên và mở một tiệm hàng. Một thám tử xuất hiện để bắt Jimmy vì những vụ cướp gần đây. Tuy nhiên, những hành động của Jimmy cho thấy anh ta đã thay đổi.

개심 (A Retrieved Reformation)
O. Henry

요약 지미 발렌타인은 형무소를 나오자마자 다시 금고를 털려고 마음을 먹는다. 그러나 사랑하는 사람이 생기게 되자 정직한 삶을 살기로 마음먹는다. 그래서 이름도 바꾸고 가게도 하나 열게 된다. 어느 날 최근 있었던 도난 사건의 범인으로 지미를 체포하려고 형사가 가게에 나타난다. 그러나 결국 지미가 보여준 행동으로 그가 이제는 예전의 금고털이범 지미가 아님을 증명하게 된다.

UNIT 1

SUMMARY TRANSLATIONS

Gentleman of Río en Medio
Juan A. A. Sedillo

Summary Don Anselmo is honest and proud. He sells his land to new American owners. They later have trouble with the village children. The new owners work with Don Anselmo to solve the problem with the children.

Caballero de Río en Medio
Juan A. A. Sedillo

Resumen Don Anselmo es un hombre honesto y orgulloso. Les vende sus tierras a unos nuevos propietarios estadounidenses. Luego, los propietarios tienen algunos problemas con los niños del pueblo. Los nuevos propietarios colaboran con Don Anselmo para solucionar el problema con los niños.

Mesye Rio en Medio a
Juan A. A. Sedillo

Rezime Don Anselmo se yon moun ki onèt epi ki fyè. Li vann nouvo pwopriyetè ameriken tè li a. Pita yo te vin gen pwoblèm ak timoun yo nan vilaj la. Nouvo pwopriyetè yo travay avèk Don Anselmo pou l rezoud pwoblèm lan ak timoun yo.

Mga Maginoong Lalaki ng Río en Medio
Juan A. A. Sedillo

Buod Si Don Anselmo ay marangal at malugod. Ibinenta niya ang kanyang lupa sa mga bagong may-aring Amerikano. Pagkatapos noon ay nagka-problema sila sa mga bata sa nayon. Ang mga bagong may-ari at si Don Anselmo ay nagtulong-tulong upang lutasin ang problema tungkol sa mga bata.

Cov Txiv Neeg Ntawm Lub Zos Rio en Medio
Juan A. A. Sedillo

Lub Ntsiab Don Anselmo yog ib tug neeg siab ncaj thiab saib nws tus kheej muaj nqis heev. Nws muag nws thaj av rau cov tswv Meskas tuaj tshiab. Tsis ntev ntawv, lawv muaj teeb meem nrog cov menyuam nyob hauv zos. Cov tswv av tshiab sib tham nrog Don Anselmo kom daws tau cov teeb meem nrog cov menyuam.

《麥迪歐河的紳士》 (Gentleman of Río en Medio)
Juan A. A. Sedillo

摘要 唐・安賽爾摩既誠實又自負。他將土地賣給了新的美國業主。他們之後與當地村落的小孩產生糾紛。新業主於是與唐・安賽爾摩一道努力來解決與這些孩子們之間的問題。

Các Quý Ông của Río en Medio
Juan A. A. Sedillo

Tóm Tắt Don Anselmo là người thật thà và tự hào. Ông bán đất của mình cho các ông chủ mới người Mỹ. Sau này họ gặp rắc rối với bọn trẻ trong làng. Những ông chủ mới hợp tác với Don Anselmo để giải quyết vấn đề với bọn trẻ.

리오 엔 메디오의 신사 (Gentleman of Río en Medio)
Juan A. A. Sedillo

요약 돈 안젤모는 정직하면서도 자존심이 강한 사람이다. 그는 자신의 토지를 미국인에게 판다. 나중에 새로운 땅 주인과 동네 아이들 사이에 말썽이 일어난다. 새로운 땅 주인은 돈 안젤모의 도움을 받아 말썽을 해결해 나간다.

SUMMARY TRANSLATIONS

Cub Pilot on the Mississippi
Mark Twain

Summary Mark Twain describes his experience as a cub pilot working on a Mississippi steamboat. He tries to please his boss, but nothing works. The conflict between them grows. Twain cannot control his anger.

Pilotillo en el Mississippi
Mark Twain

Resumen Mark Twain describe su experiencia cuando trabajaba como pilotillo en un barco de vapor en Mississippi. Y trata de complacer a su jefe pero nada le resulta. Crecen los conflictos entre ellos. Twain no puede dominar su enojo.

Pilòt debitan sou Misisipi a
Mark Twain

Rezime Mark Twain dekri eksperyans li kòm yon pilòt debitan k ap travay nan yon bato a vapè sou Misisipi a. Li eseye fè bòs li a plezi, men anyen pa mache. Konfli ki genyen ant yo menm vin ogmante. Twain paka kontwole kòlè l.

Baguhang Piloto sa Mississippi
Mark Twain

Buod Inilalarawan ni Mark Twain ang kanyang karanasan bilang isang baguhang piloto na nagtatrabaho sa isang "steamboat", o bapor na pinatatakbo ng usok, sa Mississippi. Anuman ang gawin niya ay hindi pa rin nasisiyahan ang kanyang amo. Ang pagkakasalungat nilang dalawa ay lumalalâ. Hindi mapigilan ni Twain ang kanyang galit.

UNIT 1

SUMMARY TRANSLATIONS

Tub Ntaus Pob Cub Tsav Dav Hlau Ntawm Dej Mississippi

Mark Twain

Lub Ntsiab Mark Twain sau txog nws txoj kev tau ua ib tug tub ntaus pob tsav dab hlau uas ua haujlwm rau saum ib lub nkoj nyob rau tus dej Mississippi. Nws sib zog ua kom nws tus thawj tswj haujlwm nyiam nws, tiamsis ua licas los tsim pab li. Txoj kev tsis sib haum ntawm nkawd loj zuj zus. Twain tswj tsis tau nws txoj kev chim li lawm.

《密西西比河上的新手領航員》(Cub Pilot on the Mississippi)

Mark Twain

摘要 作者馬克・吐溫描述自己在一艘密西西比河上的汽船擔任新手領航員的經歷。他試著想取悅老闆，但卻徒勞無功。他們之間的衝突日益增多。吐溫無法控制自己的怒火。

Hoa Tiêu Non Tay Trên Sông Mississippi

Mark Twain

Tóm Tắt Mark Twain miêu tả lại lần ông làm một hoa tiêu còn non tay cho một chiếc tàu chạy bằng hơi nước trên sông Mississippi. Ông cố gắng làm hài lòng ông chủ nhưng không thành công. Mâu thuẫn giữa họ ngày càng sâu sắc. Twain không thể kìm chế cơn giận dữ.

미시시피의 수습 조타수 (Cub Pilot on the Mississippi)

Mark Twain

요약 마크 트웨인이 미시시피강을 운항하는 증기선에서 수습 조타수로 일했던 당시의 경험을 이야기한다 마크는 상사와 재미있게 지내고자 노력하지만 오히려 둘 사이에 갈등만 깊어진다. 마크는 끓어 오르는 화를 참을 수 없게 된다.

SUMMARY TRANSLATIONS

From An American Childhood
Annie Dillard

Summary The author shares an experience that scared her as a young child. She thinks there is a "presence" that will harm her if it reaches her. She figures out what it is. She realizes that her inside world is connected to the outside world.

desde Una infancia estadounidense
Annie Dillard

Resumen La autora comparte una experiencia que la aterraba cuando era pequeña. Ella cree que hay una "presencia" que le hará daño si se le aproxima. Y descubre de qué se trata. Comprende que su mundo interior está conectado con el mundo exterior.

Ekstrè nan Yon anfans ameriken
Annie Dillard

Rezime Otè a pataje yon eksperyans ki te fè l pè lè l te yon jèn timoun. Li panse genyen yon "prezans" ki pral fè l ditò si l rive jwenn li. Li reyalize ki sa li ye. Li reyalize monn enteryè li a konekte ak monn eksteryè li a.

Mula sa Isang Kabataang Amerikano
Annie Dillard

Buod Ibinahagi ng manunulát ang isang karanasan na kinatakutan niya noong siya ay maliit na bata. Inaakala niya na "mayroong naroroon" na mananakit sa kanya kung siya ay maabutan nito. Nalaman niya kung ano ito. Kanyang natuklasan na ang mundo sa loob ng kanyang isipan ay konektado pala sa mundo sa labas.

UNIT 1

SUMMARY TRANSLATIONS

Los ntawm Ib Lub Neej Thaum Yau Nyob Tebchaws Meskas

Annie Dillard

Lub Ntsiab Tus sau zaj no qhia txog ib yam uas tshwm sim thaum nws tseem yau uas ua rau nws ntshai heev li. Nws xav tias muaj ib yam "dabtsi" uas yuav ua phem rau nws yog thaum los txog ntawm nws. Nws tshawb nrhiav tau tias yog dabtsi. Nws paub tau tias nws lub neej sab hauv los yeej txua nrog lub neej sab nraud thiab.

改編自《一個美國人的童年》(An American Childhood)

Annie Dillard

摘要 作者透露了一段她兒時令她極為害怕的經驗。她認定有某種「鬼怪」的存在，而且這種物體如果找到她，將會傷害她。她推斷出了這種物體的真面目。她也瞭解到自己的內心世界與外在世界是相連的。

Trích từ Tuổi Ấu Thơ Của Một Người Mỹ

Annie Dillard

Tóm Tắt Tác giả kể lại một chuyện đã làm cô sợ hãi khi còn nhỏ. Cô bé cho rằng có một "hồn ma" sẽ làm hại cô nếu nó chạm được cô. Cô khám phá ra đó là cái gì. Cô nhận ra rằng thế giới nội tâm của cô kết nối với thế giới bên ngoài.

한 미국인의 어린 시절 중에서 (An American Childhood)

Annie Dillard

요약 작가는 어린 시절 자신을 무섭게 했던 한 경험에 대해 이야기한다. 작가는 손을 뻗기만 하면 "존재"하는 그 무언가가 자신을 해칠 것이라고 생각했다. 나중에 그것이 무엇인지를 깨닫게 되고, 자신의 내부 세계가 외부 세계로 연결돼 있다는 것을 알게 된다.

SUMMARY TRANSLATIONS

The Adventure of the Speckled Band
Sir Arthur Conan Doyle

Summary Sherlock Holmes, a great detective, meets Miss Helen Stoner. She needs his help. Miss Stoner wants to know who killed her sister. She also fears for her own life. Holmes follows the clues to find the murderer.

La aventura de la banda de lunares
Sir Arthur Conan Doyle

Resumen Sherlock Holmes, un gran detective, conoce a la señorita Helen Stoner. Ella necesita su ayuda. La señorita Stoner quiere saber quién mató a su hermana. También teme por su propia vida. Holmes sigue las pistas para encontrar al asesino.

Avanti bann tachte a
Sir Arthur Conan Doyle

Rezime Sherlock Holmes, yon gran detektif, rankontre ak mis Helen Stoner. Li bezwen èd detektif la. Mis Stoner vle konnen kiyès ki touye sè l la. Epitou li pè pou pwòp vi pa l. Holmes suiv kèk endis pou ede l jwenn kriminèl la.

Ang Insidente ng Tali na Batik-batik
Sir Arthur Conan Doyle

Buod Nakilala ni Sherlock Holmes, isang tanyag na detektib, si Bb. Helen Stoner. Kinakailangan ni Bb. Stoner ang tulong niya. Nais malaman ni Bb. Stoner kung sino ang pumatay sa kanyang kapatid na babae. Siya rin ay natatakot at baka mapatay rin siya. Sinundan ni Holmes ang mga palatandaan upang malaman kung sino nga ang pumatay.

Tus Speckled Band Txoj Kev Ua Si
Sir Arthur Conan Doyle

Lub Ntsiab Sherlock Holmes, uas yog ib tug neeg txawj daws teeb meem heev, ntsib Miss Helen Stoner. Miss Helen Stoner xav tau nws txoj kev pab. Miss Stoner xav paub tias leej twg tua nws tus viv ncaus lawm. Nws ntshai tias tsam ho yuav tua nws tus kheej thiab. Holmes tshawb nrhiav raws tej yam uas pab nws nrhiav tau tus tua neeg ntawd.

《斑點帶子案件》(The Adventure of the Speckled Band)
Sir Arthur Conan Doyle

摘要 夏洛克・福爾摩斯是一位偉大的偵探，他與海倫・史托納女士會面。她需要他的協助。史托納女士希望知道誰殺了她的姊姊。她也擔心自己的生命安全。福爾摩斯追查線索找到了真兇。

Cuộc Phiêu Lưu của Dải Đốm
Ngài Arthur Conan Doyle

Tóm Tắt Sherlock Holmes, một thám tử xuất sắc, gặp Cô Helen Stoner. Cô cần sự giúp đỡ của ông. Cô Stoner muốn biết ai đã giết em gái cô. Cô cũng thấy lo sợ cho tính mạng của mình. Holmes lần theo các dấu vết và tìm thấy kẻ giết người.

얼룩 끈 (The Adventure of the Speckled Band)
Sir Arthur Conan Doyle

요약 명탐정 셜록 홈즈는 도움을 청하러 온 헬렌 스토너 양을 만난다. 그녀는 누가 언니를 죽였는지 밝혀 달라며, 자기 자신도 죽을지 모른다는 공포감에 떨고 있었다. 홈즈는 사건의 단서를 하나하나 찾아가며 범인을 밝히게 된다.

UNIT 1: SUMMARY TRANSLATIONS

from Travels With Charley
Excerpts 1 & 2
John Steinbeck

Summary John Steinbeck sets out across the United States to see the country and meet people. His dog, Charley, travels with him. This episode in his journey tells about his experiences in the Badlands of North Dakota.

de Viajes con Charley
Extractos 1 y 2
John Steinbeck

Resumen John Steinbeck viaja por todo los Estados Unidos para conocer el país y a nuevas personas. Charley, su perro, viaja con él. Este episodio del viaje trata sobre sus experiencias en la zona desértica de Dakota del Norte.

yon ekstrè nan Vwayaj ak Charley
Ekstrè 1 ak 2
John Steinbeck

Rezime John Steinbeck kòmanse yon vwayaj atravè Etazini pou l wè peyi a epi rankontre lòt moun. Chyen li an, Charley, vwayaje avèk li. Epizòd sa a nan vwayaj li a rakonte eksperyans li te fè nan Badlands (tè sèk) nan Dakota Dinò.

mula sa Mga Paglalakbay Kasama si Charley
Mga Maikling Bahagi 1 at 2
John Steinbeck

Buod Si John Steinbeck ay naglalakbay sa buong Amerika para makita niya ang bansa at para makakilala niya ang mga tao. Ang kanyang aso na si Charley ay kasama niyang naglakbay. Ang kabanatang ito sa kanyang paglalakbay ay tungkol sa kanyang mga karanasan sa "Badlands" sa North Dakota.

SUMMARY TRANSLATIONS

los ntawm zaj Ncig Tebchaws Nrog Charley
Nqe 1 & 2
John Steinbeck

Lub Ntsiab John Steinbeck tawm mus ncig lub Tebchaws Meskas mus saib xyuas lub tebchaws thiab ntsib neeg. Nws tus aub, Charley, mus nrog nws. Zaj no hauv nws txoj kev ncig qhia txog nws txoj kev ncig txog hauv thaj chaw Badlands uas nyob North Dakota.

選自《與查理同遊》(*from* Travels With Charley)
摘錄 1 和 2
John Steinbeck

摘要 作者出發橫越美國,他想瞭解這個國家,並認識各地居民。他的小狗查理與他同行。這段在他的旅程中發生的插曲描寫他在北達科他州班德蘭斯市的經歷。

trích từ Chuyến Du Hành Cùng Charley
Ñoaïn trích 1 & 2
John Steinbeck

Tóm Tắt John Steinbeck khởi hành đi dọc nước Mỹ để ngắm nhìn quê hương và gặp gỡ con người mọi nơi. Chú chó Charley của ông cũng đi với ông. Đoạn này trong cuộc hành trình của ông kể về những chuyện xảy ra với ông ở Vùng Badlands thuộc tiểu bang Bắc Dakota.

찰리와 함께 여행을 중에서 (*from* Travels With Charley)
발췌문 1 및 2
John Steinbeck

요약 존 스타인벡은 애견 찰리와 함께 미국 여행을 한다. 그는 여러 곳을 다니며 다양한 사람들을 만난다. 이 에피소드는 노스 다코타의 배드랜드에서 겪었던 경험을 그리고 있다.

UNIT 1: SUMMARY TRANSLATIONS

The American Dream
Martin Luther King, Jr.

Summary In this speech, Martin Luther King, Jr. describes his dream for America. He says that America does not make it possible for everyone to share in the dream. He discusses ways that Americans can help make his dream a reality.

El sueño americano
Martin Luther King, Jr.

Resumen En este discurso Martin Luther King, Jr. describe lo que sueña para los Estados Unidos. Él declara que no es posible que todos los estadounidenses compartan este sueño. Y habla de las maneras en que los estadounidenses pueden hacerlo realidad.

Rèv ameriken an
Martin Luther King, Jr.

Rezime Nan diskou li a, Martin Luther King, Jr. dekri rèv li pou Amerik. Li di konsa Amerik pa rann li posib pou tout moun pataje rèv sa a. Li diskite sou fason ameriken yo ka ede pou fè rèv li a vin yon reyalite.

Ang Pangarap para sa Amerika
Martin Luther King, Jr.

Buod Sa kanyang talumpating ito, inilalarawan ni Martin Luther King, Jr. ang kanyang pangarap para sa Amerika. Ayon sa kanya, hindi posibleng makamtan ng lahat ng tao sa Amerika ang kanyang pangarap sapagkat 'di ito pinahihintulutan ng Amerika. Kanyang tinalakay ang mga paraan kung paano makakatulong ang mga Amerikano upang maisakatuparan ang kanyang pangarap.

SUMMARY TRANSLATIONS

Txoj Kev Npau Suav Nyob Tebchaws Meskas

Martin Luther King, Jr.

Lub Ntsiab Hauv sob lus sau no, Martin Luther King, Jr. piav txog nws txoj kev npau suav kom tshwm sim rau lub Tebchaws Meskas. Nws hais tias Tebchaws Meskas tsis coj kom ncaj ncees rau suavdaws sib faib kom txhua leej ho tau ib feem ntawm txoj kev npau suav. Nws tham txog tej kev uas cov neeg Meskas yuav ua tau kom txhawb tau nws txoj kev npau suav no kom muaj tseeb.

《美國夢》(The American Dream)

Martin Luther King, Jr.

摘要 作者馬丁・路德・金在這篇演說中描述自己對美國的夢想。他說美國尚未達到使每個人都能實現夢想的理想目標。他論述了美國人能協助使他的夢想成真的方法。

Giấc Mơ Về Nước Mỹ

Martin Luther King, Jr.

Tóm Tắt Trong bài diễn văn này, Martin Luther King, Jr. miêu tả giấc mơ của ông về nước Mỹ. Ông nói rằng nước Mỹ không tạo điều kiện cho tất cả mọi người thực hiện giấc mơ đó. Ông bàn thảo những điều người Mỹ có thể làm để giúp biến giấc mơ của ông thành hiện thực.

아메리칸 드림 (The American Dream)

Martin Luther King, Jr.

요약 마틴 루터 킹 주니어 목사가 미국에 바라는 자신의 꿈이라는 제목으로 연설한 내용이다. 연설에서 그는 모든 이들과 그 꿈을 함께하는 것을 미국 사회가 불가능하게 만들고 있다고 한다. 그래서 어떻게 하면 미국인이 다같이 이 꿈을 실현시킬 수 있는지 그 방법을 의논해 보자고 한다.

UNIT 2

SUMMARY TRANSLATIONS

An Hour With Abuelo
Judith Ortiz Cofer

Summary Arturo is sent to a nursing home to spend an hour with his grandfather. Arturo is not excited about the visit. Arturo finds his grandfather writing his life story. Arturo listens to his grandfather's story. He loses all track of time.

Una hora con el abuelo
Judith Ortiz Cofer

Resumen Arturo es enviado a un hogar de ancianos para que pase una hora con su abuelo. Arturo no está muy contento con la visita. Pero encuentra a su abuelo escribiendo la historia de su vida. Y escucha la historia de su abuelo. Arturo pierde la noción del tiempo.

Inèdtan ak Abuelo
Judith Ortiz Cofer

Rezime Yo voye Arturo nan yon mezon retrèt pou l pase inèdtan ak granpè l. Arturo pa tèlman kontan pou l al wè granpè a. Arturo jwenn granpè l k ap ekri istwa lavi l. Arturo koute istwa granpè l la. Li vin bliye zafè kontwole lè.

Isang Oras na Kapiling si Lolo
Judith Ortiz Cofer

Buod Si Arturo ay ipinadala sa isang "nursing home" para magpalipas ng isang oras kapiling ang kanyang lolo. Si Arturo ay 'di nasasabik sa pagbisita. Nakita ni Arturo na isinusulat ng kanyang lolo ang kanyang kasaysayan ng buhay. Si Arturo ay nakinig sa kuwento ng kanyang lolo. Hindi niya namalayan ang pagdaan ng oras.

SUMMARY TRANSLATIONS

UNIT 2

Nyob Ib Teev Nrog Yawg
Judith Ortiz Cofer

Lub Ntsiab Arturo raug xa mus rau tom lub tsev laus kom nrog nws yawg nyob ib teev. Arturo tsis zoo siab txog qhov no li. Arturo kawm tau tias nws tus yawg tab tom sau zaj dabneeg ntawm tus yawg lub neej. Arturo mloog nws yawg zaj dabneeg. Nws cia li tsis nco qab txog sijhawm li lawm.

《與爺爺共渡的一小時》(An Hour With Abuelo)
Judith Ortiz Cofer

摘要 阿爾杜羅被送去一間療養院與他的爺爺相處一小時。阿爾杜羅對此行興味索然。阿爾杜羅發現爺爺正在寫自己的人生故事。阿爾杜羅於是聆聽爺爺的故事。他因此忘了時間。

Một Giờ Cùng Abuelo
Judith Ortiz Cofer

Tóm Tắt Arturo được cử đến nhà dưỡng lão để chơi với ông mình trong một tiếng đồng hồ. Arturo không hào hứng với cuộc viếng thăm này. Arturo thấy ông đang viết lại câu chuyện về đời mình. Arturo lắng nghe câu chuyện của ông và không còn để ý đến thời gian nữa.

아브엘로 할아버지와 보낸 한 시간 (An Hour With Abuelo)
Judith Ortiz Cofer

요약 아르트로는 양로원에 계신 할아버지를 찾아가 한 시간 정도 같이 보내기로 되어 있다. 아르트로는 할아버지와 시간을 보내러 양로원에 가는 것이 별로 달갑지 않다. 할아버지께서는 자신이 이제껏 살아온 인생을 글로 쓰고 계셨다. 아르트로는 시간 가는 줄 모르고 할아버지의 이야기를 듣게 된다.

UNIT 2: SUMMARY TRANSLATIONS

Who Can Replace a Man?
Brian Aldiss

Summary A group of machines does not receive orders as usual. The machines are programmed with different levels of intelligence. The smarter machines find out that all men have died. They try to figure out what to do.

¿Quién puede reemplazar a un hombre?
Brian Aldiss

Resumen Un grupo de máquinas no recibe las órdenes como de costumbre. Las máquinas están programadas con diferentes niveles de inteligencia. Las máquinas más inteligentes descubren que todos los hombres han muerto. Y tratan de resolver qué deben hacer.

Kiyès ki ka ranplase yon moun ?
Brian Aldiss

Rezime Yon gwoup machin pa resevwa kòmann yo kòm dabitid. Yo pwograme machin yo avèk nivo entèlijans ki diferan. Machin ki pi entèlijan yo aprann tout moun yo te mouri. Yo eseye chèche konnen ki sa pou yo fè.

Sino ang Maaring Pumalit sa Tao?
Brian Aldiss

Buod Ang grupo ng mga makina ay hindi tumanggap ng mga utos tulad ng karaniwang nangyayari. Ang mga makina ay naka-programa na may iba't-ibang antas ng katalinuhan. Nalaman ng mga mas matatalinong makina na lahat ng tao ay namatay na pala. Sinubukan nilang pag-isipan kung ano ang kanilang gagawin.

Leej Twg Thial Li Yuav Los Pauv Tau Ib Tug Txiv Neej?
Brian Aldiss

Lub Ntsiab Ib co cav uas tsim los ua haujlwm tsis ua raws li hais ib yam qub lawm. Cov cav no yog siv ntau qib kev txawj ntse coj los tsim tau. Cov cav uas ntse tshaj tau paub hais tias tagnrho cov neeg twb tau tuaj tas lawm. Lawv nrhiav tswv yim seb yuav ua li cas.

《誰能取代一個人?》(Who Can Replace a Man?)
Brian Aldiss

摘要 一組機器並未像平常一般的接收到指令。這些機器被輸入不同智慧等級的程式。較聰明的機器發現所有的人類都已死亡。它們於是必須設法推斷該做甚麼。

Ai Có Thể Thay Thế Con Người?
Brian Aldiss

Tóm Tắt Một nhóm máy móc lâu lắm không nhận lệnh từ người chủ. Những máy móc này được lập trình với các cấp độ thông minh khác nhau. Những máy móc thông minh hơn phát hiện ra rằng tất cả con người đều đã chết. Chúng cố phán đoán xem cần phải làm gì.

누가 인간을 대신할 수 있을까? (Who Can Replace a Man?)
Brian Aldiss

요약 한 무리의 기계들이 이제는 더 이상 평소처럼 명령을 따르지 않는다. 이들에게는 지금까지와는 비교할 수 없을 정도의 높은 수준의 지능이 프로그램화 되어 있다. 똑똑해진 기계들이 인간은 누구나 결국은 죽는다는 사실을 알아차린다. 기계들은 무엇을 해야 할지 생각해 내려 한다.

SUMMARY TRANSLATIONS

Tears of Autumn
Yoshiko Uchida

Summary Hana Omiya is from a traditional Japanese family. Her uncle is looking for a wife for a Japanese man in California. Hana has few chances for a better life. She goes to America to marry the man. When she arrives, she is nervous and disappointed. Then, she remembers why she came. She looks forward to her new life.

Lágrimas de otoño
Yoshiko Uchida

Resumen Hana Omiya pertenece a una familia japonesa tradicional. Su tío está buscando una esposa para un hombre japonés que vive en California. Y Hana tiene pocas posibilidades de lograr una mejor vida. Viaja a los Estados Unidos para casarse con el hombre. Cuando llega, está nerviosa y desilusionada. Y luego recuerda el motivo de su viaje. Hana espera que comience su nueva vida.

Dlo nan je otòn
Yoshiko Uchida

Rezime Hana Omiya soti nan yon fanmi japonè tradisyonèl. Tonton l ap chèche yon madanm pou yon mesye japonè ki abite an Kalifòni. Hana pa gen anpil chans pou yon lavi ki miyò. Li ale ann Amerik pou l marye ak mesye a. Lè l rive, li nève epi li desi. Ansuit, li sonje rezon ki fè l te vini. L ap atann nouvo vi li pral genyen an.

Mga Luha ng Panahong Taglagas
Yoshiko Uchida

Buod Si Hana Omiya ay galing sa isang tradisyonal na pamilyang Hapones. Ang kanyang tiyo ay naghahanap ng asawa para sa isang lalaking Hapón sa California. Kaunti lamang ang mga pagkakataon ni Hana na magkaroon ng mas mabuting buhay. Pumunta siya sa Amerika para pakasalan ang lalaki. Pagdating niya, siya ay ninenerbiyos at nakaramdam ng pagkabigo. Pagkatapos ay naalala niya kung bakit siya pumunta roon. May pag-asa na siya ngayon sa kanyang bagong buhay.

UNIT 2

SUMMARY TRANSLATIONS

Cov Kua Muag Caij Ntuj Tsaug
Yoshiko Uchida

Lub Ntsiab Hana Omiya los ntawm tsev neeg Yivpoom uas coj kev cai qub. Nws tus txiv ntxawm tab tom nrhiav ib tug pojniam los txis rau ib tug txiv neej Yivpoom nyob hauv California. Hana tsis muaj pestsawg zaus uas yuav muaj kev mus tau ib lub neej zoo. Nws mus rau Tebchaws Meskas mus yuav tus txiv neej ntawd. Thaum nws mus txog, nws txhawj thiab tas kev cia siab. Ces nws nco qab txog yog vim li cas nws thiaj li txiav txim tuaj. Nws pib muaj kev zoo siab tos txais lub neej yav tom ntej.

《秋天的眼淚》(Tears of Autumn)
Yoshiko Uchida

摘要 大宮花來自一個傳統的日本家庭。她的叔叔正在為一位住在加州的日本男人找妻子。大宮花能過更好生活的機會很渺茫。她於是出發前往美國想嫁給這個男人。當她抵達時，她既緊張又失望。接著，她想起自己前來美國的原因。她於是對於自己的新生活充滿希望。

Nước Mắt Mùa Thu
Yoshiko Uchida

Tóm Tắt Hana Omiya xuất thân từ một gia đình truyền thống Nhật Bản. Bác cô đang tìm vợ cho một người đàn ông Nhật Bản sống ở California. Hana không có mấy cơ hội để có được cuộc sống khá hơn. Cô tới Mỹ để kết hôn với người đàn ông đó. Khi tới nơi, cô hồi hộp và rồi thất vọng. Sau đó, cô nhớ ra tại sao mình tới đây. Cô trông mong vào cuộc sống mới của mình.

가을의 눈물 (Tears of Autumn)
Yoshiko Uchida

요약 하나 오미야는 전통적인 일본 가정에서 태어나고 자라난 여성이다. 삼촌이 미국 캘리포니아에 사는 어느 일본 남자의 신부가 될 여성을 찾고 있다는 소식에 하나는 보다 나은 인생을 위해 미국으로 건너가 그 남자와 결혼하기로 결심한다. 하지만 미국에 도착해 보니, 걱정도 앞서고 실망도 하게 된다. 그러나 자신이 왜 미국 행을 선택했는지 다시 한번 생각하며 이제부터 펼쳐질 새로운 삶을 즐거운 마음으로 기다리기로 한다.

SUMMARY TRANSLATIONS

Hamadi
Naomi Shihab Nye

Summary Susan is a Palestinian American high school student living in Texas. She enjoys spending time with Hamadi. He is like a grandparent to her. She likes the wisdom and kindness he shares.

Hamadi
Naomi Shihab Nye

Resumen Susan es una estudiante palestino-americana de una escuela secundaria y vive en Texas. Ella disfruta de la compañía de Hamadi. Él es como un abuelo para ella. A Susan le agrada su sabiduría y amabilidad.

Hamadi
Naomi Shihab Nye

Rezime Susan se yon elèv lise palestinyen ameriken ki abite nan Teksas. Li renmen pase tan avèk Hamadi. Hamadi se tankou yon granpè li ye pou li. Li renmen sajès ak bonte li genyen.

Hamadi
Naomi Shihab Nye

Buod Si Susan ay isang Palestinang Amerikanang estudyante ng mataas na paaralan na nakatirá sa Texas. Ikinagagalak niyang magpalipas ng oras kasama si Hamadi. Ito ay para na ring lolo niya. Gusto niya ang karunungan at kabaitan na ipinamamahagi nito.

Hamadi
Naomi Shihab Nye

Lub Ntsiab Susan yog ib tug neeg Palestinian Meskas kawm ntawv theem ob nyob rau hauv Texas. Nws nyiam siv sijhawm nyob nrog Hamadi. Hamadi zoo tam li ib leej yawg rau nws. Nws nyiam cov kev txawj ntse thiab kev siab zoo uas Hamadi muaj.

《哈瑪迪》 (Hamadi)
Naomi Shihab Nye

摘要 蘇珊是一位住在德州的巴勒斯坦裔美國高中生。她很喜歡與哈瑪迪在一起。對她而言，他就像祖父母一般。她喜歡他流露的智慧與慈祥。

Hamadi
Naomi Shihab Nye

Tóm Tắt Susan là một học sinh cấp ba người Mỹ gốc Palestin sống ở Texas. Cô rất thích giành thời gian ở cùng Hamadi. Trong mắt cô, ông giống như một người ông. Cô ngưỡng mộ sự thông thái và tử tế mà ông chia sẻ cùng cô.

하마디 (Hamadi)
Naomi Shihab Nye

요약 수잔은 팔레스타인계 미국인으로서 텍사스에 살고 있는 고등학생이다. 할아버지뻘 되는 하마디와 친해 자주 시간을 같이 보낸다. 하마디의 친절함과 지혜로움을 존경한다.

UNIT 2: SUMMARY TRANSLATIONS

The Tell-Tale Heart
Edgar Allan Poe

Summary The narrator describes how he murders an old man. He murders the man after careful planning. He is confident in his hiding place for the man's body parts. The arrival of the police and the sound of a beating heart haunt the narrator.

El corazón delator
Edgar Allan Poe

Resumen El narrador describe cómo asesina a un anciano. Lo asesina después de organizar un cuidadoso plan. Está seguro de que en su escondite podrá guardar las partes del cadáver. La llegada de la policía y el constante latido de un corazón persiguen al narrador.

Kè rapòtè a
Edgar Allan Poe

Rezime Naratè a dekri ki jan li asasinen yon ti granmoun. Li asasinen mesye a aprè l fin byen planifye zak la. Li gen konfyans nan kote li sere pati kò mesye l fin asasinen an. Naratè a vin santi l toumante lè lapolis vini ak lè l tande son yon kè k ap bat.

Ang Nagsiwalat na Puso
Edgar Allan Poe

Buod Inilalarawan ng nagsasalaysay kung paano niya pinatáy ang isang matandang lalaki. Kanyang pinatáy ito pagkatapos ng maingat na pagpaplano. Malakas ang kanyang loob na 'di-mahahanap ang lugar kung saan niya itinago ang mga iba't-ibang bahagi ng bangkay. Ang nagsasalaysay ay parang minumulto, at 'di-mapanatag ang loob niya sa pagdatíng ng pulis at sa tunog ng pusong tumitibok.

Lub Siab Uas Qhia
Edgar Allan Poe

Lub Ntsiab Tus piav zaj no qhia txog tias nws tau tua ib tug yawg laus laus li cas. Nws tau tua tom qab kev npaj zoo zoo lawm. Nws siab loj txog thaj chaw uas nws tau muab tus yawg laus ntawd lub cev txhoov coj mus faus. Thaum cov tub ceev xwm tuaj txog thiab thaum nws hnov lub siab dhia dhia ua rau nws ntshai tag.

《洩密的心》 (The Tell-Tale Heart)
Edgar Allan Poe

摘要 故事主人翁描述自己謀殺一位老人的過程。他在精心策畫後殺了這個人。他對自己藏匿此人屍體的地方極有信心。警察的到來以及心臟怦怦跳動的聲音卻讓主人翁深感困擾。

Trái Tim Thú Tội
Edgar Allan Poe

Tóm Tắt Người thuật truyện miêu tả hắn ta đã giết một ông già như thế nào. Hắn giết ông ta sau khi tính toán kỹ lưỡng. Hắn tự tin rằng không ai tìm được nơi giấu các bộ phận cơ thể của nạn nhân. Sự xuất hiện của cảnh sát và tiếng trái tim đập ám ảnh hắn.

고자질하는 심장 (The Tell-Tale Heart)
Edgar Allan Poe

요약 화자는 자신이 어떻게 노인을 살해했는지 묘사한다. 치밀한 계획을 세우고 살인을 하여 토막 낸 사체를 완벽히 숨겨 놓는다. 하지만 경찰의 방문과 두근거리는 심장 박동의 귀울림에 화자는 점점 괴로움에 시달리게 된다.

SUMMARY TRANSLATIONS

Charles
Shirley Jackson

Summary Laurie is rude to his parents after his first day of kindergarten. He tells his parents about a boy named Charles. Each day, Laurie has a new story about Charles. Laurie's mother is surprised when she learns the truth about Charles.

Charles
Shirley Jackson

Resumen Laurie se comporta de manera grosera con sus padres después de su primer día en el jardín de infantes. Les cuenta a sus padres acerca de un niño llamado Charles. Cada día, Laurie tiene una nueva historia sobre Charles. La madre de Laurie se sorprende cuando conoce la verdad sobre Charles.

Charles
Shirley Jackson

Rezime Laurie pa poli avèk paran l aprè premye jou li fè nan klas jadendanfan. Li rakonte paran l gen yon ti gason nan klas li a ki rele Charles. Chak jou, Laurie gen yon nouvo istwa pou rakonte sou Charles. Manman Laurie etone lè l aprann laverite sou kiyès Charles ye.

Charles
Shirley Jackson

Buod Si Laurie ay walang-galang sa kanyang mga magulang pagkatapos ng kanyang unang araw sa kindergarten. Nagkuwento siya sa kanyang mga magulang tungkol sa isang batang lalaking nagngangalang Charles. Araw-araw, si Laurie ay may bagong kuwento tungkol kay Charles. Ang nanay ni Laurie ay nagulat nang malaman niya ang katotohanan tungkol kay Charles.

UNIT 2
SUMMARY TRANSLATIONS

Charles
Shirley Jackson

Lub Ntsiab Laurie coj tau tus tsis paub cai li rau nws niam thiab txiv tom qab nws thawj hnub mus kawm ntawv qib K. Nws qhia nws niam thiab txiv txog ib tug menyuam tub hu ua Charles. Txhua hnub, Laurie muaj ib zaj dabneeg txog Charles. Laurie niam ceeb thaum uas nws paub tau qhov tseeb txog Charles.

《查爾斯》(Charles)
Shirley Jackson

摘要 羅利在第一天上幼稚園回家後對自己的父母很沒禮貌。他告訴父母有關一位名叫查爾斯的小男孩的事。每天羅利都會說一則有關查爾斯的新鮮事。當羅利的母親得知有關查爾斯的實情時，她頗為意外。

Charles
Shirley Jackson

Tóm Tắt Laurie tỏ ra thiếu lễ độ với ba mẹ mình sau ngày đầu tiên đi học mẫu giáo. Cậu kể cho ba mẹ mình nghe về một cậu bé có tên là Charles. Mỗi ngày, Laurie lại có một câu chuyện mới về Charles. Mẹ của Laurie thật ngạc nhiên khi bà khám phá ra sự thật về Charles.

찰스 (Charles)
Shirley Jackson

요약 로리는 유치원에 처음 갔다 온 날부터 부모님께 버릇없이 군다. 그리고는 찰스라는 이름의 한 소년에 대해 이야기한다. 매일 매일 찰스에 대한 새로운 이야기를 집에 와서 하게 된다. 로리의 어머니는 찰스에 대한 진상을 알고는 놀라게 된다.

SUMMARY TRANSLATIONS

Flowers for Algernon
Daniel Keyes

Summary Charlie is a factory worker who is chosen to be the subject of a new brain surgery. His skills are watched and compared with those of Algernon, a mouse. Charlie's skills grow. He becomes smarter than his doctors. However, Charlie's life is not perfect.

Flores para Algernon
Daniel Keyes

Resumen Charlie es un trabajador de fábrica que ha sido elegido para ser sujeto de una nueva operación de cerebro. Sus habilidades son observadas y comparadas con las de Algernon, un ratón. Las habilidades de Charlie comienzan a desarrollarse. Y se vuelve más inteligente que los médicos. Sin embargo, la vida de Charlie no es perfecta.

Flè pou Algernon
Daniel Keyes

Rezime Charlie se yon travayè nan faktori yo chwazi kòm yon sijè pou yon nouvo operasyon nan sèvo. Yo obsève epi konpare abilte l avèk Algernon, ki se yon sourit. Abilte Charlie vin ogmante. Li vin pi entèlijan pase doktè l yo. Sepandan, lavi Charlie pa pafè.

Mga Bulaklak para kay Algernon
Daniel Keyes

Buod Si Charlie ay isang manggagawa sa pabrika na napiling taong pag-aaralan ng isang bagong operasyon sa utak. Ang kanyang mga katalinuhan ay pinagmamasdan at inihahambing sa katalinuhan ng isang daga ng nagngangalang Algernon. Mas nagiging matalino si Charlie. Siya'y naging mas matalino kaysa sa kanyang mga doktor. Subalit hindi lubos na mahusay ang buhay ni Charlie.

UNIT 2
SUMMARY TRANSLATIONS

Ib Co Paj Rau Algernon
Daniel Keyes

Lub Ntsiab Charlie yog ib tug neeg ua haujlwm hauv ib lub chaw ua haujlwm uas raug xaiv los ua ib tug neeg ntawm qhov kev kho paj hlwb tshiab. Lawv saib nws cov kev kawm tau tshiab thiab muab piv nrog Algernon, uas yog ib tug nas. Charlie cov txuj ci siab zuj zus tuaj. Nws cia li txawj tshaj nws cov kws kho mob lawm. Tiamsis, Charlie lub neej zoo tsis tag.

《送給阿爾吉諾的花》(Flowers for Algernon)
Daniel Keyes

摘要 查理是一位工廠工人，他被選為一項新的腦部手術的實驗對象。他的技能受到監控，並被拿來與一隻叫艾爾吉諾的小老鼠比較。查理的技能的確進步了。他變得比他的醫生還聰明。然而，查理的人生並沒有變得完美。

Hoa Viếng Algernon
Daniel Keyes

Tóm Tắt Charlie là một công nhân nhà máy được chọn làm đối tượng của một cuộc phẫu thuật não mới. Kỹ năng của anh được theo dõi và so sánh với một con chuột có tên là Algernon. Kỹ năng của Charlie ngày càng trở nên điêu luyện hơn. Anh trở nên thông minh hơn cả những bác sĩ của mình nhưng cuộc đời của Charlie lại không hoàn hảo.

앨져넌에게 바치는 꽃다발 (Flowers for Algernon)
Daniel Keyes

요약 찰리는 공장 노동자로서 새로운 뇌 수술 실험 대상자로 선정된다. 찰리가 가지고 있는 손재주 솜씨는 면밀히 관찰되고 실험용 쥐 앨져넌의 솜씨와도 비교된다. 찰리의 손재주는 점점 발전하고 어느새 의사들을 능가하게 된다. 하지만 찰리의 인생이 완벽해진 것은 아니다.

SUMMARY TRANSLATIONS

Thank You, M'am
Langston Hughes

Summary A teenage boy tries to steal a woman's purse. The woman catches the boy and brings him to her home. She teaches him a lesson about kindness and trust.

Gracias, señora
Langston Hughes

Resumen Un adolescente trata de robarle la cartera a una mujer. La mujer agarra al adolescente y se lo lleva a su casa. Y le da una lección de amabilidad y confianza.

Mèsi, madam
Langston Hughes

Rezime Yon ti gason adolesan eseye vòlè bous yon madam. Madam lan kenbe ti gason an epi l mennen l lakay li. Li aprann li yon leson sou bonte ak konfyans.

Salamat, M'am
Langston Hughes

Buod Sinubukang nakawin ng isang lalaking tinedyer ang bag ng isang babae. Nahuli ng babae ang binatilyo at dinala niya ito sa kanyang bahay. Tinuruan niya ito ng liksiyon tungkol sa kagandahang-loob at pagtitiwala.

Ua Koj Tsaug
Langston Hughes

Lub Ntsiab Ib tug menyuam tub sim nyiag ib tug pojniam lub hnab kab paus. Tus pojniam caum tau tus menyuam tub thiab coj nws los tsev. Nws qhuab qhia tus menyuam tub txog kev siab zoo thiab kev ntseeg.

《謝謝妳，夫人》(Thank You, M'am)
Langston Hughes

摘要 一位青少年企圖偷一位女士的錢包。這位女士逮到了小男孩，並將他帶去她家。她為他上了有關仁慈與信任的一課。

Cám Ơn Quý Bà
Langston Hughes

Tóm Tắt Một cậu thiếu niên cố gắng lấy cắp ví tiền của một người phụ nữ. Bà ta bắt được cậu và đưa cậu về nhà mình. Bà dạy cho cậu một bài học về sự tử tế và lòng tin.

고마워요, 아줌마 (Thank You, M'am)
Langston Hughes

요약 한 십대 소년이 한 여인의 지갑을 훔치려다 붙잡히게 된다. 그 여인은 그 소년을 자기 집으로 데려가 친절함과 믿음에 대해 가르쳐 준다.

UNIT 2

SUMMARY TRANSLATIONS

The Story-Teller
Saki (H.H. Munro)

Summary A stranger on a train tells a story that entertains three children. The story's ending makes the children's aunt very angry. It goes against all of her lectures about proper behavior.

El cuentista
Saki (H.H. Munro)

Resumen Un extraño cuenta una historia en un tren que divierte a tres niños. El final de la historia hace que el tío de los niños se enfade. Contradice todos sus sermones sobre buenos modales.

Rakontè istwa a
Saki (H.H. Munro)

Rezime Yon etranje nan yon tren rakonte yon istwa ki amize twa timoun. Fen istwa a fè matant timoun yo fache anpil. Fen istwa a ale nan sans kontrè ak tout konsèy matant lan te ba yo konsènan konpòtman ki apwopriye.

Ang Tagapagsalaysay
Saki (H.H. Munro)

Buod Isang taong 'di-kilala na nasa tren ang nagkukuwento sa tatlong bata at sila'y nalibang nito. Lubos na nagalit ang tiya ng mga bata sa katapusan ng kuwento. Ito ay labag sa lahat ng kanyang mga turo ukol sa kagandahang-asal.

Tus Kws Piav Dabneeg
Saki (H.H. Munro)

Lub Ntsiab Ib tug neeg uas nyob saum lub tsheb nqaj hlau qhia ib zaj dabneeg uas lom zem rau peb tug menyuam mloog. Zaj dabneeg txoj kev xaus ua rau cov menyuam ntawd tus phauj chim siab heev. Qhov xaus ntawd tsis raws li tej kev cai uas tus phauj tau qhuab qhia txog kev coj zoo.

《說書人》(The Story-Teller)
Saki (H.H. Munro)

摘要 火車上的一位陌生人說了個故事逗三個小孩開心。這則故事的結局卻使小孩的姑姑極為憤怒。因為故事內容違反了她對合宜行為的所有教誨。

Người Kể Truyện
Saki (H.H. Munro)

Tóm Tắt Một người lạ trên một chuyến tàu kể truyện mua vui cho ba đứa trẻ. Kết thúc của câu truyện khiến cho dì bọn trẻ rất tức giận. Nó đi ngược lại với tất cả những bài giảng của bà về cách hành xử đúng mực.

이야기하는 사람 (The Story-Teller)
Saki (H.H. Munro)

요약 기차 안에서 한 낯선 사람이 세 명의 아이들에게 이야기를 들려준다. 그런데 이야기의 결말이 아이들의 이모를 화나게 만든다. 왜냐하면 그것은 이제까지 아이들에게 입이 닳도록 가르친 올바른 행동과 상반되는 것이기 때문이다.

SUMMARY TRANSLATIONS

Making Tracks on Mars: A Journal Based on a Blog
Andrew Mishkin

Summary Andrew Mishkin talks about the landing of the rover, *Spirit*, on Mars. The rover explores the planet. It experiences some problems. Mishkin describes his excitement and worry. He also talks about another Mars rover, *Opportunity*. He describes the pictures it takes of Mars.

Dejando huellas en Marte: Una publicación basada en un blog
Andrew Mishkin

Resumen Andrew Mishkin habla del aterrizaje del explorador *Spirit* en Marte. El explorador investiga el planeta. Y se encuentra con algunos problemas. Mishkin describe su entusiasmo y preocupación. También habla de otro explorador de Marte, *Opportunity*. Y describe las fotografías que toma en Marte.

Fè tras sou planèt Mas : Yon jounal ki baze sou yon blòg
Andrew Mishkin

Rezime Andrew Mishkin pale konsènan aterisaj wodè a, *Spirit*, sou planèt Mas. Wodè a eksplore planèt la. Li rankontre kèk pwoblèm. Mishkin dekri eksitasyon li ak enkyetid li. Epitou li pale konsènan yon lòt wodè sou Mas, ki rele *Opportunity*. Li dekri foto wodè a pran sou Mas.

Ang Paggawá ng Imprenta sa Mars: Isang Talaan Batay sa Isang "Blog"
Andrew Mishkin

Buod Pinag-uusapan ni Andrew Mishkin ang landing sa Mars ng "rover" na nagngangalang *Spirit*. Ginalugad ng "rover ang iba't-ibang bahagi ng planeta. Nagkaroon ito ng ilang mga problema. Inilalarawan ni Mishkin ang kanyang pananabik at pag-aalala. Pinag-uusapan din niya ang isa pang "rover" sa Mars, ang *Opportunity*. Inilalarawan niya ang mga retrato na kinuha nito sa Mars.

UNIT 3
SUMMARY TRANSLATIONS

Tsuj Hneev Taw Rau Saum Mars: Ib Phau Ntawv Sau Los Ntawm Ib Co Ntawv Sib Tham

Andrew Mishkin

Lub Ntsiab Andrew Mishkin tham txog thaum lub cav hu ua, *Spirit*, mus tsaw tau rau saum Mars. Lub cav mus ncig tshawb txog lub ntiaj teb txawv no. Nws ntsib tej co teeb meem. Mishkin piav txog nws cov kev zoo siab thiab txhawj xeeb. Nws ho tham txog lwm lub cav hu ua *Opportunity* uas mus rau saum Mars thiab. Nws tham txog cov duab uas lub cav thaij tau Mars.

《在火星上留下蹤跡：一則部落格上的日誌》(Making Tracks on Mars: A Journal Based on a Blog)

Andrew Mishkin

摘要 作者描寫精靈號探測車在火星上降落的經過。這輛探測車探索了這個星球。期間也經歷了一些問題。作者描寫自己的興奮之情與憂慮。他還描寫了另一輛火星探測車 — 契機號。他描述了探測車在火星上拍攝到的照片。

Tìm Đường Trên Sao Hỏa: Một Nhật Ký Dựa Trên Blog

Andrew Mishkin

Tóm Tắt Andrew Mishkin kể về việc hạ cánh lên Sao Hỏa của một máy thăm dò có tên là Linh Hồn (*Spirit*). Máy thăm dò khám phá hành tinh này. Nó trải qua vài rắc rối. Mishkin miêu tả sự phấn khích và lo lắng của mình. Anh ta cũng nói về một máy thăm dò khác trên Sao Hỏa có tên là Cơ Hội (*Opportunity*) và miêu tả các bức hình nó chụp được về Sao Hỏa.

화성에 길 만들기: 블로그를 바탕으로 쓴 화성 탐험 일지 (Making Tracks on Mars: A Journal Based on a Blog)

Andrew Mishkin

요약 화성 탐사선 "스피리트" 호가 화성에 착륙하는 순간을 시작으로, 탐사선이 화성을 탐사하는 과정과 탐사 시 부딪히는 여러 문제점 등을 기술하고 있다. 그리고 작가가 느꼈던 흥분과 걱정에 대해서도 이야기한다. 또 다른 탐사선 "어퍼튜니티" 호에 대해서도 언급하며, 어퍼튜니티 호가 전송한 화성의 사진들도 설명한다.

SUMMARY TRANSLATIONS

Baseball
Lionel G. García

Summary The author shares a memory from his childhood in this story. He describes the new rules of baseball that he and his childhood friends invented. García presents a snapshot into the world of a young Catholic boy through this story.

Béisbol
Lionel G. García

Resumen En esta historia el autor comparte un recuerdo de su infancia. Describe las nuevas reglas del béisbol que inventaron él y sus amigos de la infancia. A lo largo de la historia, García presenta una imagen del mundo de un joven católico.

Bezbòl
Lionel G. García

Rezime Otè a pataje yon souvni dafans li nan istwa sa a. Li dekri nouvo règ bezbòl li menm ak zanmi danfans li yo te envante. García prezante yon imaj enstantane nan monn yon jèn ti gason Katolik atravè istwa sa a.

Baseball
Lionel G. García

Buod Sa kuwentong ito, ibinabahagi ng awtor ang isang alaala mula sa kanyang kabataan. Inilalarawan niya ang mga bagong alituntunin ng baseball na inimbento niya at ng kanyang mga kaibigan. Sa kanyang pagkukuwento, si Garcia ay nagbibigay ng larawan ng daigdig ng isang batang lalaking Katoliko.

Ntau Pob
Lionel G. García

Lub Ntsiab Tus sau no qhia txog nws lub neej thaum tseem yog menyuam yaus hauv zaj dabneeg no. Nws sau txog cov cai tshiab nyob rau kev Ntau Pob uas nws thiab nws cov phooj ywg menyuam yaus tau tsim. García sau tau kom tus nyeem ntawv pom tau ib muag ntawm ib tug menyuam tub lub neej uas tsev neeg yog pawg ntseeg Catholic.

《棒球》 (Baseball)
Lionel G. García

摘要 作者在這則故事中透露一段自己兒時的回憶。他描寫自己和兒時玩伴所發明的新的棒球規則。作者透過這則故事讓我們一窺一位天主教小男孩的世界。

Bóng Chày
Lionel G. García

Tóm Tắt Tác giả chia sẻ một ký ức thời thơ ấu trong câu truyện này. Ông miêu tả những luật chơi mới cho môn bóng chày mà ông và các bạn thủa nhỏ nghĩ ra. García thể hiện thế giới của một cậu bé theo đạo Thiên Chúa Giáo xuyên suốt câu truyện.

야구 (Baseball)
Lionel G. García

요약 작가는 자신의 유년 시절의 추억을 회상한다. 친구들과 함께 새로운 야구 규칙을 만들어내는 등 한 가톨릭 계 집안 출신 소년의 일상 생활 단면을 보여 주고 있다.

UNIT 3
SUMMARY TRANSLATIONS

Harriet Tubman: Guide to Freedom
Ann Petry

Summary Harriet Tubman led a group of enslaved persons from Maryland to freedom in Canada. The trip was cold and difficult. Tubman worked hard to keep them going. She said that people would help them along the way.

Harriet Tubman: Guía hacia la libertad
Ann Petry

Resumen Harriet Tubman guió a un grupo de personas esclavas desde Maryland para que alcancen su libertad en Canadá. El viaje fue frío y difícil. Tubman trabajó arduamente para que siguieran la marcha. Ella decía que encontrarían personas a lo largo del camino que los ayudarían.

Harriet Tubman : Gid pou lalibète
Ann Petry

Rezime Harriet Tubman te alatèt yon gwoup moun ki te an esklavaj sot Marilann pou lalibète o Kanada. Vwayaj la te frèt epi difisil. Tubman te travay di pou ede yo kontinye. Li te di konsa gen moun ki ta va ede yo sou wout la.

Harriet Tubman: Isang Patnubay sa Kalayaan
Ann Petry

Buod Pinatnubayan ni Harriet Tubman ang isang grupo ng mga inalipin na tao mula sa Maryland patungo sa kalayaan nila sa Canada. Ang biyahe ay malamig at mahirap. Nagpursigi si Tubman upang ipagpatuloy nila ang pagbiyahe. Sinabi niya na tutulungan sila ng mga tao habang sila'y nagbibiyahe.

SUMMARY TRANSLATIONS

Harriet Tubman: Ib Tug Coj Kev Mus Txog Kev Ywj Pheej

Ann Petry

Lub Ntsiab Harriet Tubman coj kev rau ib pawg neeg uas raug yuam ua qhev nyob Maryland mus txog txoj kev ywj pheej hauv Canada. Lawv txoj kev mus mas no thiab nyuaj heev. Tubman rau siab ntso pab kom lawv muaj siab mus kom txog. Nws hais tias txoj kev lawv raws ntawd yeej yuav muaj neeg pab lawv.

《荷莉葉・吐伯曼：自由的指引》 (Harriet Tubman: Guide to Freedom)

Ann Petry

摘要 荷莉葉領導一個由被奴役的人組成的團體從馬利蘭州出發前往加拿大追求自由。這趟旅程既寒冷又艱辛。吐伯曼努力使這群人繼續前進。她描述了一路上幫助他們的人。

Harriet Tubman: Người Dẫn Đường Đến Sự Tự Do

Ann Petry

Tóm Tắt Harriet Tubman dẫn đầu một nhóm nô lệ đến từ Maryland tìm được tự do ở Canađa. Chuyến đi thực sự khó khăn và giá lạnh. Tubman đã cố gắng hết mình để giữ họ luôn tiến bước. Bà nói rằng mọi người sẽ giúp họ dọc cuộc hành trình.

해리어트 터브만: 자유를 향한 안내자 (Harriet Tubman: Guide to Freedom)

Ann Petry

요약 해리어트는 노예가 된 사람들을 이끌고 자유를 찾아 메릴랜드에서 캐나다로 가는 긴 여정에 오른다. 험난하고 추운 여정이었다. 해리어트는 사람들에게 끝까지 서로를 도우며 여정을 계속할 수 있도록 독려한다.

UNIT 3
SUMMARY TRANSLATIONS

from Always to Remember: The Vision of Maya Ying Lin
Brent Ashabranner

Summary In the early 1980s, more than 2,500 people entered a competition to design a memorial. The men and women who lost their lives in the Vietnam War would be honored by the memorial. This essay describes the competition. It also describes the college student who wins.

de Para recordar siempre: la visión de Maya Ying Lin
Brent Ashabranner

Resumen A principios de los '80, más de 2,500 personas se inscribieron en un concurso para diseñar un monumento conmemorativo. A través de este monumento se recordaría a los hombres y mujeres que perdieron la vida en la guerra de Vietnam. Este ensayo describe el concurso. También describe a los estudiantes universitarios que ganan el concurso.

yon ekstrè nan Toujou sonje : Vizyon Maya Ying Lin
Brent Ashabranner

Rezime Nan kòmansman ane 1980 yo, plis pase 2 500 moun te rantre nan yon konkou pou desine yon memoryal. Memoryal la ta va onore gason ak fi ki te pèdi lavi yo nan lagè Vyetnam lan. Disètasyon sa a dekri konkou a. Epitou li dekri elèv inivèsite ki te genyen konkou a.

from Always to Remember: The Vision of Maya Ying Lin
Brent Ashabranner

Buod Noong mga unang taón ng dekadang 1980, higit sa 2,500 na tao ang lumahok sa isang paligsahan ng pagdidisenyo ng isang memoryál. Ang mga lalaki at babae na namatay sa Digmaan sa Vietnam ay bibigyang-karangalan nitong memoryál. Inilalarawan ng sanaysay na ito ang paligsahan. Inilalarawan din nito ang estudyanteng nagwagi.

SUMMARY TRANSLATIONS

los ntawm Nco Qab Ntsoov Ib Sim: Maya Ying Lin Tus Duab

Brent Ashabranner

Lub Ntsiab Thaum cov xyoo 1980 pib, muaj tshaj 2,500 leej neeg nkag rau kev sib tw tsim ib yam los ua chaw nco txog cov neeg. Cov txiv neej thiab pojniam uas tau koom kev tsov rog nyob Nyab Laj Teb yuav tau txais kev hwm txog los ntawm qhov no. Zaj sau no yog hais txog txoj kev sib tw. Nws ho sau txog tus tub ntxhais kawm ntawv qib siab uas tau yeej thiab.

改編自《永遠記得：林櫻的遠見》 (*from* Always to Remember: The Vision of Maya Ying Lin)

Brent Ashabranner

摘要 1980 年代初，有超過 2,500 人參加一項設計紀念碑的競賽。這座紀念碑將表揚在越戰中喪生的男女。本文即描述這場競賽。其中也描述了贏得比賽的大學生。

trích từ Đời Đời Nhớ Ơn: Tầm Nhìn của Maya Ying Lin

Brent Ashabranner

Tóm Tắt Vào đầu những năm 1980, hơn 2,500 người tham gia cuộc thi thiết kế một đài tưởng niệm để tưởng nhớ những người phụ nữ và nam giới bị thiệt mạng trong cuộc chiến tranh Việt Nam. Bài viết này miêu tả lại cuộc so tài và người sinh viên đại học thắng cuộc.

항상 기억해야 하는 것: 마야 인 린의 통찰력 중에서 (*from* Always to Remember: The Vision of Maya Ying Lin)

Brent Ashabranner

요약 1980년대 초 2,500명이 넘는 사람들이 추모비 디자인 공모에 응모한다. 이 추모비는 베트남 전쟁에서 목숨을 잃은 사람들을 기리기 위해 세워진다. 이 에세이는 응모 과정과 응모에 당선된 어느 한 대학생에 대해 이야기하고 있다.

UNIT 3
SUMMARY TRANSLATIONS

from I Know Why the Caged Bird Sings
Maya Angelou

Summary In this story, the writer describes growing up in her grandmother's house in Stamps, Arkansas. She describes her friendship with a woman named Mrs. Flowers. Mrs. Flowers introduces her to poetry.

de Ahora sé por qué cantan las aves enjauladas
Maya Angelou

Resumen En esta historia, la escritora describe su niñez en la casa de su abuela en Stamps, Arkansas. Describe su amistad con una mujer a quien llaman señora Flowers. La señora Flowers la introduce en el mundo de la poesía.

yon ekstrè nan Mwen konnen poukisa zwazo nan kaj la ap chante
Maya Angelou

Rezime Nan istwa sa a, ekriven an dekri lè l t ap grandi kay granmè l nan vil Stamps, Akennsa. Li dekri amitye li avèk yon dam ki rele madan Flowers. Madan Flowers entwodui l nan pwezi.

mula sa Alam Ko Kung Bakit Umaawit ang Nakakulong na Ibon
Maya Angelou

Buod Sa kuwentong ito, inilalarawan ng manunulat ang kanyang paglakí sa bahay ng kanyang lola sa Stamps, Arkansas. Inilalarawan rin niya ang kanyang pagka-kaibigan sa isang aleng nagngangalang Gng. Flowers. Ipinakilala siya ni Gng. Flowers sa daigdig ng panunulá.

los ntawm zaj Kuv Paub Tias Vim Li Cas Tus Noog Raug Kaw Hauv Tawb Thiaj Li Quaj
Maya Angelou

Lub Ntsiab Hauv zaj dabneeg no, tus sau piav txog kev loj hlob hauv nws pog lub tsev hauv Stamps, Arkansas. Nws piav txog nws kev phooj ywg nrog ib tug pojniam hu ua Mrs. Flowers. Mrs. Flowers qhia txog kev sau pajhuam rau nws.

改編自《我知道為甚麼籠中鳥會唱歌》(from I Know Why the Caged Bird Sings)
Maya Angelou

摘要 作者在故事中描述自己在位於阿肯色州史丹姆斯鎮的奶奶家成長的過程。她描寫自己與一位名叫佛勞爾斯夫人的友誼。佛勞爾斯夫人帶她進入詩詞的世界。

trích từ Tôi Biết Tại Sao Chú Chim Trong Lồng Cất Tiếng Hót
Maya Angelou

Tóm Tắt Trong truyện này, nhà văn miêu tả sự trưởng thành của mình khi sống trong căn nhà của bà mình ở Stamps, Arkansas. Tác giả kể về tình bạn của mình với một người phụ nữ tên là bà Flowers, người đã đưa nhà văn đến với thơ ca.

새장 속의 새들이 지저귀는 이유를 나는 알고 있다 중에서 (from I Know Why the Caged Bird Sings)
Maya Angelou

요약 작가가 아칸소 주 스탬프스에 있는 할머니 댁에서 자라온 시절의 이야기를 들려준다. 작가는 플라워즈라는 이름의 한 여인과 우정을 쌓게 되고 플라워즈는 작가에게 시를 가르쳐 준다.

SUMMARY TRANSLATIONS

The Trouble With Television
Robert MacNeil

Summary Robert MacNeil has worked as a reporter for radio and television. He thinks that watching television keeps people from paying close attention to things. He thinks that television has a bad effect on people.

El problema de la televisión
Robert MacNeil

Resumen Robert MacNeil ha trabajado como periodista para la radio y la televisión. Él piensa que ver televisión hace que las personas dejen de prestar atención a otras cosas. Él cree que la televisión produce un efecto negativo en las personas.

Pwoblèm ki genyen ak televizyon
Robert MacNeil

Rezime Robert MacNeil te travay kòm yon jounalis pou radyo ak televizyon. Li panse lè moun ap gade televizyon sa anpeche yo pote atansyon sou lòt bagay. Li panse televizyon genyen yon efè negatif sou moun.

Ang Problema sa Telebisyon
Robert MacNeil

Buod Si Robert MacNeil ay nagtratrabaho bilang isang tagapagbalita sa radyo at telebisyon. Sa wari niya, hindi na maingat na napapansin ng mga tao ang mga bagay-bagay dahil sa panonood ng telebisyon. Sa palagay niya, ang telebisyon ay may masamáng epekto sa mga tao.

Qhov Teeb Meem Nrog Lub TV
Robert MacNeil

Lub Ntsiab Robert MacNeil tau ua haujlwm tshaj xov xwm rau ib lub chaw xov tooj cua thiab chaw TV. Nws xav tias kev saib TV ua rau neeg tsis mob siab saib txog lwm yam. Nws xav tias TV yog ib yam tsis zoo rau neeg.

《電視的麻煩》(The Trouble With Television)
Robert MacNeil

摘要 作者曾經在電台及電視台當記者。他認為看電視使人們不再仔細觀察事物。他認為電視對人造成不良影響。

Ảnh Hưởng Xấu Của Ti Vi
Robert MacNeil

Tóm Tắt Robert MacNeil làm phóng viên phát thanh và truyền hình. Anh nghĩ rằng xem ti vi khiến cho người ta không tập trung chú ý đến điều gì. Theo anh, ti vi có ảnh hưởng xấu đối với mọi người.

텔레비전이 갖는 문제점 (The Trouble With Television)
Robert MacNeil

요약 작가는 라디오와 텔레비전 방송국의 기자로 활동하고 있다. 텔레비전을 너무 많이 보게 되면서 사람들은 다른 것에 주의를 기울이지 않게 되었다. 텔레비전이 사람들에게 안 좋은 영향을 끼치게 되었다고 작가는 생각한다.

UNIT 3: SUMMARY TRANSLATIONS

On Woman's Right to Suffrage
Susan B. Anthony

Summary Susan B. Anthony gives a speech to United States citizens in 1873. It is a time when women can not vote. She says that the U.S. Constitution protects all people. She says that women should have the same rights as men.

Sobre el derecho de las mujeres al voto
Susan B. Anthony

Resumen Susan B. Anthony pronuncia un discurso para los ciudadanos de los Estados Unidos en 1873. En esta época las mujeres no pueden votar. Ella declara que la Constitución de los Estados Unidos protege a todas las personas. También dice que las mujeres deben tener los mismos derechos que los hombres.

Sou dwa fi genyen pou vote
Susan B. Anthony

Rezime Susan B. Anthony fè yon diskou de sitwayen amerikèn yo nan ane 1873. Se yon epòk lè fi pa t gen dwa pou yo vote. Li di konsa Konstitisyon Etazini an pwoteje tout kalite moun. Li di konsa fi dwe gen menm dwa gason genyen.

Ukol sa Karapatan ng Babaeng Bumoto
Susan B. Anthony

Buod Si Susan B. Anthony ay nagbigay ng isang talumpati sa mga mamamayan ng Estados Unidos noong 1873. Noong panahong iyong, ang mga babae ay 'di-maaring bumoto. Sinasabi niya na ang Konstitusyon ng Estados Unidos ay nagbibigay-proteksyon sa lahat ng tao. Sabi niya na ang mga karapatan ng mga babae ay dapat kapantay ng mga karapatan ng mga lalaki.

SUMMARY TRANSLATIONS

Hais Txog Pojniam Txoj Kev Ncaj Ncees Dim Kev Txom Nyem

Susan B. Anthony

Lub Ntsiab Susan B. Anthony hais ib zag lus rau cov pejxeem nyob Tebchaws Meskas rau xyoo 1873. Nov yog ib lub sijhawm uas pojniam tseem tsis tau muaj cai koom xaiv tsa nom tswv. Nws hais tias nyob rau hauv Tebchaws Meskas daim ntawv tswj cov cai hu ua Constitution muaj kev tiv thaiv txhua leej neeg. Nws hais tias pojniam los yuav tsum muaj tib co cai uas txiv neej muaj thiab.

《婦女的選舉權》 (On Woman's Right to Suffrage)

Susan B. Anthony

摘要 作者於 1873 年對美國民眾發表了一篇演說。當時婦女沒有投票權。她認為美國憲法保障所有人的權益。她還認為婦女應該擁有與男人同等的權利。

Về Cuộc Đấu Tranh Giành Quyền Bầu Cử Cho Phụ Nữ

Susan B. Anthony

Tóm Tắt Susan B. Anthony đọc diễn văn trước công chúng Mỹ năm 1873. Hồi đó, phụ nữ không được quyền bầu cử. Bà nói hiến pháp Mỹ bảo vệ mọi người, và rằng phụ nữ cũng nên có được mọi quyền như nam giới.

여성의 선거권에 대해 (On Woman's Right to Suffrage)

Susan B. Anthony

요약 수잔 B. 앤소니가 1873년에 미국인을 대상으로 한 연설로서 당시 여성에게는 투표권이 없었다. 미국 헌법은 모든 국민을 차별 없이 보호하며 여성도 남성과 똑같은 권리를 누려야 한다고 주장한다.

UNIT 3: SUMMARY TRANSLATIONS

from Sharing in the American Dream

Colin Powell

Summary Former Secretary of State Colin Powell shares his beliefs about volunteer work. He encourages listeners to volunteer their time to help others in some way. He believes that this is an important part of keeping the United States strong.

de Compartamos el sueño americano

Colin Powell

Resumen Colin Powell, ex Secretario de Estado, comparte sus pensamientos sobre el trabajo voluntario. Y alienta a los oyentes a que ofrezcan su tiempo para ayudar a otras personas de alguna manera. Él piensa que esto es muy importante para mantener fuerte a los Estados Unidos.

yon ekstrè nan Pataje rèv ameriken an

Colin Powell

Rezime Ansyen sekretè deta Colin Powell pataje kwayans li genyen konsènan travay volontè. Li ankouraje oditè yo pou yo pote yo volontè pou ede lòt moun nan kèk fason. Li kwè sa se yon pati enpòtan pou Etazini ka rete yon peyi djanm.

mula sa Ang Pamamahagi ng Pangarap ng Amerika

Colin Powell

Buod Ipinamamahagi ng dating Kalihim ng Estado na si Colin Powell ang kanyang mga paniwala tungkol sa pagtratrabaho nang boluntaryo. Inaanyayahan niya ang kanyang mga tagapakinig na magboluntaryo ng kanilang panahon para makatulong sa kanilang kapwa sa kahit anong paraan. Siya'y naniniwala na ito ay mahalaga sa pagpa-panatili ng lakas ng Estados Unidos.

SUMMARY TRANSLATIONS

UNIT 3

los ntawm Ntseeg Txog Tebchaws Meskas Txoj Kev Npau Suav

Colin Powell

Lub Ntsiab Tus qub Tub Khiav Dejnum Tswj Haujlwm Tebchaws Meskas Colin Powell tham txog nws cov kev ntseeg nrog ib co neeg uas pab ua haujlwm pub dawb. Nws txhawb kom sawvdaws pub lawv ib lub sijhawm los ua haujlwm pub dawb pab lwm tu thiab. Nws ntseeg tau tias nov yog ib yam tseem ceeb heev uas yuav tswj tau kom Tebchaws Meskas khov kho.

改編自《分享美國之夢》(*from* Sharing in the American Dream)

Colin Powell

摘要 前國務卿科林・鮑威爾分享自己對志願工作的理念。他鼓勵聽眾主動撥出時間以某種方式自願去幫助其他人。他相信這是保持美國強大非常重要的一項因素。

trích từ Cùng Có Chung Giấc Mơ Về Nước Mỹ

Colin Powell

Tóm Tắt Cựu Bộ Trưởng Ngoại Giao Colin Powell chia sẻ quan điểm của ông về công việc tự nguyện. Ông khuyến khích người nghe tự nguyện dùng thời gian của mình để giúp đỡ người khác bằng cách này hay cách kia. Ông tin tưởng rằng đây là một phương cách quan trọng để giữ cho Hợp Chủng Quốc Hoa Kỳ luôn vững mạnh.

함께 아메리칸 드림을 일구어 나 갑시다 중에서 (*from* Sharing in the American Dream)

Colin Powell

요약 국무 장관을 역임했던 콜린 파웰이 자원 봉사에 관한 자신의 생각을 이야기 한다. 그는 사람들에게 시간이 날 때마다 어떤 방법이라도 좋으니 누군가를 도와주기를 주문한다. 그렇게 하는 것이 미국을 강하게 만드는 데 일조하는 것이라고 주장한다.

UNIT 3: SUMMARY TRANSLATIONS

Science and the Sense of Wonder
Isaac Asimov

Summary Isaac Asimov says that he does not agree with a poem Walt Whitman wrote. Whitman says in his poem that people should forget about science. He says that people should enjoy the sky's beauty. Asimov says that people enjoy the sky more when they know science.

La ciencia y el sentido de la admiración
Isaac Asimov

Resumen Isaac Asimov dice que no está de acuerdo con un poema escrito por Walt Whitman. En su poema Whitman dice que las personas deben olvidarse de la ciencia. Dice que deben disfrutar de la belleza del cielo. Asimov afirma que las personas pueden disfrutar más del cielo cuando saben de ciencia.

Lasyans ak santiman mèvèy
Isaac Asimov

Rezime Isaac Asimov di konsa li pa dakò avèk yon powèm Walt Whitman te ekri. Nan powèm li an, Whitman fè konnen moun ta dwe bliye zafè lasyans. Li di konsa moun ta dwe admire bote syèl la. Asimov fè konnen moun vin admire syèl la plis lè yo gen konesans sou lasyans.

Ang Agham at ang Pandamá ng Pangyayaring Kataka-taka
Isaac Asimov

Buod Ayon kay Isaac Asimov, hindi siya sumasang-ayon sa isang tula na sinulat ni Walt Whitman. Sabi ni Whitman sa kanyang tula, dapat kalimutan ng mga tao ang agham. Sabi rin niya na dapat ikalugod ng mga tao ang kagandahan ng langit. Sabi naman ni Asimov na mas ikalulugod ng mga tao ang langit kapag nauunawaan nila ang agham.

SUMMARY TRANSLATIONS

Kev Kawm Txuj Science Kev Xav Paub Txog Ntau Yam

Isaac Asimov

Lub Ntsiab Isaac Asimov hais tias nws tsis pom zoo nrog ib zaj pajhuam uas Walt Whitman tau sau tias neeg yuav tsum txhob nco txog science lawm. Isaac hais tias neeg yuav tsum nyiam txog lub ntuj dav uas zoo nkauj. Asimov hais tias neeg yuav nyiam tau lub ntuj txoj kev zoo nkauj heev tshaj yog tias lawv paub txog science.

《科學與驚奇感》(Science and the Sense of Wonder)

Isaac Asimov

摘要 作者描述自己對於一首由沃爾特·惠特曼寫的詩不表認同的原因。惠特曼在詩中描寫人類應該忘卻科學。他認為人類應該盡情欣賞天空的美麗。作者卻認為，當人類瞭解科學時，他們即更能欣賞天空的美景。

Khoa Học và Khả Năng Cảm Nhận Điều Kỳ Diệu

Isaac Asimov

Tóm Tắt Isaac Asimov nói rằng ông không đồng ý với một bài thơ của Walt Whitman. Trong bài thơ đó, Whitman nói rằng mọi người nên quên khoa học đi và nên thưởng thức vẻ đẹp của bầu trời. Asimov cho rằng mọi người có thể thưởng thức vẻ đẹp bầu trời càng nhiều hơn khi họ hiểu biết về khoa học.

과학과 경이로움 ((Science and the Sense of Wonder)

Isaac Asimov

요약 작가 아이작 아시모브는 월트 휘트먼의 시에 동의하지 않는다. 휘트먼은 그의 시에서 과학에 대해서는 잊어 버리고 하늘이 주는 아름다움이나 만끽해 보라고 사람들에게 말한다. 그러나 아시모브는 과학을 알면 하늘이 주는 아름다움을 더욱 만끽할 수 있다고 주장한다.

UNIT 4: SUMMARY TRANSLATIONS

Describe Somebody • Almost a Summer Sky

Jacqueline Woodson

Summaries In "Describe Somebody," a teacher asks her class to write a poem that describes someone. This poem describes Lonnie's thoughts as he thinks about the assignment. In "Almost a Summer Sky," Lonnie and his brother Rodney walk to the park. This poem shares Lonnie's thoughts as the two boys walk.

Describe a alguien • Casi un cielo de verano

Jacqueline Woodson

Resúmenes En "Describe a alguien" una maestra le pide a sus alumnos que escriban un poema que describa a alguien. Este poema describe los pensamientos de Lonnie mientras piensa en la tarea. En "Casi un cielo de verano", Lonnie y su hermano Rodney caminan en el parque. Este poema comparte los pensamientos de Lonnie mientras ambos niños caminan.

Dekri yon moun • Syèl ete a prèske rive

Jacqueline Woodson

Rezime Nan "Dekri yon moun," yon pwofesè mande klas li a pou l ekri yon powèm ki dekri yon moun. Powèm sa a dekri panse Lonnie pandan l ap reflechi sou asiyasyon l lan. Nan "Syèl ete a prèske rive," Lonnie ak frè l Rodney ap mache pou al nan yon pak. Powèm sa a pataje panse Lonnie pandan de ti gason yo ap mache.

Maglarawan ng Isang Tao • Halos Isang Langit sa Tag-Init

Jacqueline Woodson

Mga Buod Sa "Describe Somebody," o "Maglarawan ng Isang Tao," pinasulat ng isang guro ang kanyang klase ng isang tulang naglalarawan ng isang tao. Inilalarawan ng tulang ito ang mga naiisip ni Lonnie habang pinag-iisipan niya ang takdang gawain. Sa "Halos Isang Langit sa Tag-Init," si Lonnie at ang kanyang kapatid na si Rodney ay naglalakad patungo sa liwasan. Ipinamamahagi ng tulang ito ang mga naiisip ni Lonnie habang naglalakad ang dalawang batang lalaki.

SUMMARY TRANSLATIONS

Piav Txog Ib Tug Neeg • Yuav Luag Txog Lub Ntuj Ntawm Caij Ntuj So

Jacqueline Woodson

Cov Ntsiab Hauv "Piav txog Ib tug neeg," ib tug xib fwb hais rau nws cov menyuam kawm ntawv kom sau ib zag pajhuam uas piav txog ib tug neeg. Zaj pajhuam no piav txog Lonnie cov kev xav tias nws xav li cas txog qhov ntawv uas yuav tsum ua no. Hauv "Yuav Luag Txog Lub Ntuj Ntawm Caij Ntuj So," Lonnie thiab nws tus kwvtij Rodney mus taug kev tom lub chaw ua si. Zaj pajhuam no qhia txog Lonnie cov kev xav thaum ob tug tab tom taug kev uake.

《描寫某人》 (Describe Somebody) • 《像是一個夏日天空》 (Almost a Summer Sky)

Jacqueline Woodson

摘要 《描寫某人》中有一名教師要求她的班上學生寫一首描述某個人的詩。這首詩描述了羅尼苦思這個作業時的內心想法。《像是一個夏日天空》中羅尼和弟弟走路到公園。這首詩描寫當兩個小男孩在走路時羅尼的想法。

Miêu Tả Một Ai Đó • Gần Giống Bầu Trời Mùa Hạ

Jacqueline Woodson

Tóm Tắt Trong bài "Miêu Tả Một Ai Đó", một giáo viên yêu cầu lớp học viết một bài thơ miêu tả một ai đó. Bài thơ này miêu tả suy nghĩ của Lonnie khi cậu nghĩ về bài tập phải làm. Trong bài "Gần Giống Bầu Trời Mùa Hạ", Lonnie và em trai Rodney dạo bộ đến công viên. Bài thơ này chia sẻ những suy nghĩ của Lonnie khi hai cậu bé đi cùng nhau tới đó.

누군가를 묘사하기 (Describe Somebody) • 거의 여름 하늘 (Almost a Summer Sky)

Jacqueline Woodson

요약 "누군가를 묘사하기"에서 선생님은 반 아이들에게 누군가를 묘사하는 시를 써 오도록 과제를 낸다. 이 시는 그 과제를 생각하며 느끼는 론니의 생각을 쓰고 있다. "거의 여름 하늘"에서 론니와 남동생 로드니는 공원으로 산책을 간다. 이 시는 두 소년이 산책할 때 론니가 느끼는 생각을 적어 놓은 것이다.

UNIT 4

SUMMARY TRANSLATIONS

Poetry Collection 1

Summaries "Cat!" uses fun language and sounds to describe a frightened and angry cat. The speaker in "Silver" creates a silvery image of a moonlit night. "Your World" challenges the reader to push past life's limitations.

Colección de poemas 1

Resúmenes "¡El gato!" utiliza lenguaje y sonidos divertidos para describir un gato asustado y enojado. El narrador de "Plateada" crea una imagen de una noche de luna. "Tu mundo" desafía al lector a dejar atrás las limitaciones de la vida pasada.

Koleksyon pwezi 1

Rezime "Chat !" itilize langaj ak son amizan pou dekri yon chat ki efreye epi ki fache. Oratè nan "Ajan" kreye yon imaj ajante yon nuit ki klere ak lalin. "Monn ou an" bay lektè yo defi pou yo depase limit lavi a.

Koleksyon ng mga Tula 1

Mga Buod Ang "Cat!" o "Ang Pusa!" ay gumagamit ng mapaglaróng pananalita at mga tunog upang ilarawan ng isang pusang takót at galít. Ang nagsasalita sa "Silver" o "Pilak" ay nagbibigay ng anyong pilak sa isang gabíng maliwanag ang buwan. Ang "Your World" o "Ang Iyong Mundo" ay nanghahámon sa mga mambabasa na pilitin nilang lampasán ang mga limitasyon ng buhay.

Phau Ntawv Paj Huam 1

Cov Ntsiab "Cat!" siv cov lus thiab suab lom zem heev coj los piav txog ib tug miv uas ntshai thiab chim. Tus neeg hais lus hauv "Silver" siv cov lus kom cov uas nyeem xav tau txog ib hmo uas lub hli ci ntsa iab. " World" ua rau cov uas nyeem kom lawv xav mus tob thiab deb tshaj li tej yam ua tau nyob hauv lub neej.

《詩歌大全第一集》(Poetry Collection 1)

摘要 《貓!》利用趣味性的語言及聲音描寫一隻受到驚嚇的憤怒貓咪。《銀》的敘述者營造出一個月明之夜的銀色畫面。《你的世界》則要求讀者推開過去生活的限制。

Chùm Thơ Số 1

Tóm Tắt Bài thơ "Chú Mèo!" sử dụng âm thanh vui nhộn và ngôn ngữ hài ước để miêu tả một chú mèo giận dữ và đầy sợ hãi. Nhân vật trong bài "Ánh Trăng Bạc" vẽ lên hình ảnh một đêm trăng sáng như bạc. Bài thơ "Thế Giới Của Bạn" thách thức độc giả vượt qua những hạn chế của cuộc sống.

시 모음집 1 (Poetry Collection 1)

요약 '고양이!'에서는 재미있는 단어와 소리를 사용하여 겁에 질렸지만 화가 나 있는 고양이의 모습을 그리고 있다. '은빛'에서는 달 밝은 밤의 은은한 이미지를 그리고 있고, '당신의 세상'에서는 독자에게 과거에 느꼈던 한계를 극복하여 도전해 보도록 권하고 있다.

SUMMARY TRANSLATIONS

Poetry Collection 2

Summaries The speaker in "Thumbprint" is glad that no one is exactly like her. The speaker in "The Drum" describes different people in terms of drums. The speaker in "Ring Out, Wild Bells" wants the bells to ring out the bad and ring in the good.

Colección de poemas 2

Resúmenes A la narradora de "La huella digital" le agrada que nadie sea exactamente como ella. El narrador de "El tambor" describe a diferentes personas comparándolas con tambores. El narrador de "Suenen, furiosas campanas" desea que las campanas despidan lo malo y reciban lo bueno.

Koleksyon pwezi 2

Rezime Oratè nan "Anprent pous" kontan dèske pa gen pèsòn moun ki egzakteman menm jan avèk li. Oratè nan "Tanbou a" dekri diferan kalite moun an tèm tanbou. Oratè nan "Sonnen, klòch sovaj" vle pou klòch yo sonnen pou mal pati epi pou byen vini.

Koleksyon ng mga Tula 2

Mga Buod Ang nagsasalita sa "Thumbprint," o "Limbag ng Hinlalakí," ay masaya dahil walang tao na lubos na katulad niya. Inilalarawan ng nagsasalita sa "The Drum," o "Ang Tambol" ang iba't-ibang tao gamit ang paghahambing sa mga tambol. Sa "Ring Out, Wild Bells," o "Kumililing, Mga Mailap na Kampana" nas ng nagsasalita na kumililing ang mga kampana para palayasin ang masamâ at papasukin ang mabuti.

Phau Ntawv Paj Huam 2

Cov Ntsiab Tus neeg hais lus hauv "Thumbprint" zoo siab tias tsis muaj ib tug neeg twg uas zoo ib yam nkaus li nws tus kheej kiag li. Tus neeg hais lus hauv "The Drum" siv cov nruas coj los ua lus piav txog ntau hom neeg. Tus neeg hais lus hauv "Ring Out, Wild Bells" xav kom cov tswb nrov thawb tawm tej kev phem thiab rub tej kev zoo los.

《詩歌大全第二集》(Poetry Collection 2)

摘要 《指紋》的敘述者對於沒有一個人的指紋和她一模一樣覺得很慶幸。《鼓聲》的敘述者則以不同的鼓聲形容不同的人。《響起瘋狂的鐘聲》的敘述者則希望鐘聲響起時可以將壞運驅走，並帶來好運。

Chùm Thơ Số 2

Tóm Tắt Nhân vật trong bài thơ "Dấu Lăn Ngón Tay Cái" thấy thật vui vì không ai thực sự giống mình. Nhân vật trong bài "Chiếc Trống" miêu tả những người khác nhau trong mối tương quan với những cái trống. Nhân vật trong bài "Hỡi Những Chiếc Chuông Cuồng Nhiệt, Hãy Ngân Vang Xua Tan Tà Khí" mong muốn những cái chuông xua đuổi được những điều xấu và đem đến những điều tốt đẹp.

시 모음집 2 (Poetry Collection 2)

요약 "엄지손가락 지문"에서 화자는 아무도 자기와 똑같은 지문을 갖고 있지 않다는 사실에 기뻐한다. "드럼"에서는 여러 종류의 사람을 여러 종류의 북과 비유하고 있다. "종을 울려라"에서는 종을 울려서 나쁜 것은 내치고 좋은 것은 안으로 들어오길 바란다.

UNIT 4
SUMMARY TRANSLATIONS

Poetry Collection 3

Summaries Concrete mixers and elephants are compared in "Concrete Mixers." The speaker of "The City Is So Big" feels frightened by the city at night. The speaker in "Harlem Night Song" invites a loved one to enjoy the beauty of the night sky over the city.

Colección de poemas 3

Resúmenes En "Las hormigoneras" se comparan las hormigoneras con elefantes. El narrador de "La ciudad es tan grande" le tiene miedo a la ciudad cuando está de noche. El narrador de "Canción nocturna de Harlem" invita a un ser querido a disfrutar de la belleza del cielo nocturno sobre la ciudad.

Koleksyon pwezi 3

Rezime Yo konpare malaksè beton ak elefan nan "Malaksè beton." Oratè "Vil la sitèlman gran" santi vil la efreye l lèswa. Oratè nan "Chante denui Harlem" envite yon moun li renmen pou apresye bote syèl la leswa sou vil la.

Koleksyon ng mga Tula 3

Mga Buod Pinaghahambing ang mga pang-halo ng konkreto at mga elepante sa "Concrete Mixers" o "Mga Panghalo ng Konkreto." Ang mananalita sa "The City Is So Big" o "Napaka-lakí ng Siyudad" ay nakararamdam ng takot sa siyudad sa gabi. Ang nagsasalita sa "Harlem Night Song" o "Panggabing Awit sa Harlem" ay nangungumbida sa kanyang minamahal na magalak sa kagandahan ng langit ng siyudad.

Phau Ntawv Paj Huam 3

Cov Ntsiab Zaj "Concrete Mixers," muab cov neeg ua haujlwm tov xis mas piv rau ib co ntxhw. Tus neeg hais lus ntawm zaj "The City Is So Big" ntshai lub nroog heev rau thaum yav tsaus ntuj. Tus neeg hais lus hauv "Harlem Night Song" caw ib tug neeg nws hlub los muaj kev lom zem nrog txoj kev zoo nkauj ntawm lub ntuj hauv nroog thaum sijhawm tsaus ntuj.

《詩歌大全第三集》 (Poetry Collection 3)

摘要 《水泥攪拌器》則比較水泥攪拌器和大象間的差異。《這個城市過於遼闊》的敘述者對於夜晚的城市感到害怕。《哈林夜之歌》的敘述者則邀請一位摯愛的人與其一同欣賞城市上空美麗的夜景。

Chùm Thơ Số 3

Tóm Tắt Hình ảnh máy trộn xi măng và con voi được so sánh trong bài "Những Cái Máy Trộn Xi Măng." Nhân vật trong bài "Thành Phố Quá Lớn" cảm thấy sợ hãi khi thành phố về đêm. Nhân vật trong bài "Bài Ca Đêm Harlem" mời một người thân thưởng ngoạn vẻ đẹp của bầu trời đêm trên thành phố.

시 모음집 3 (Poetry Collection 3)

요약 '콘크리트 혼합기'에서는 커다란 콘크리트 혼합기를 코끼리에 비유하고 있다. '도시는 정말 커요'에서는 도시 밤 풍경에서 느껴지는 무서움을 이야기하고 있다. '할렘의 밤에 부치는 노래'에서는 사랑하는 사람과 함께 도시의 아름다운 밤하늘을 보며 느끼는 행복감을 노래하고 있다.

Summary Translations

Poetry Collection 4

Summaries The speaker of "Ode to Enchanted Light" enjoys the beauty of nature. A thunderstorm at the beach is described in "Little Exercise." The speaker of "The Sky Is Low, the Clouds Are Mean" humorously describes a dark winter day.

Colección de poemas 4

Resúmenes El narrador de "Oda a la luz encantada" disfruta de la belleza de la naturaleza. En "Poco ejercicio" se describe una tormenta en la playa. La narradora de "El cielo está bajo, las nubes son avaras" describe con humor un oscuro día de invierno.

Koleksyon pwezi 4

Rezime Oratè nan "Lwanj pou limyè anchante" apresye bote lanati. "Ti egzèsis" dekri yon tanpèt loraj sou plaj la. Oratè nan "Syèl la ba, nyaj yo pa janti" dekri avèk imè yon jou ivè ki sonb.

Koleksyon ng mga Tula 4

Mga Buod Ang nagsasalita sa "Ode to Enchanted Light," o "Tula Para sa Engkantadong Ilaw," ay nagagalak sa kagandahan ng kalikasan. Isang bagyó na may kasabay na kulog at kidlat sa tabing-dagat ang inilalarawan sa "Little Exercise" o "Munting Ehersisyo." Ang nagsasalita sa "The Sky Is Low, the Clouds Are Mean," o "Ang Langit ay Mababâ, Ang mga Ulap ay Masungit," ay katawa-tawang naglalarawan sa isang madilim na araw sa panahong taglamig.

Phau Ntawv Paj Huam 4

Cov Ntsiab Tus neeg hais lus ntawm zaj "Ode to Enchanted Light" muaj kev lom zem txog txoj kev zoo nkauj ntawm ntiaj teb sab nraud. Kev los nag xob nag cua tom ntug hiav txwv yog zaj uas muaj sau nyob rau hauv "Little Exercise." Tus neeg hais lus ntawm zaj "The Sky Is Low, the Clouds Are Mean" siv kev txaus luag coj los piav txog ib hnub tsaus ntuj heev ntawm lub caij ntuj no.

《詩歌大全第四集》(Poetry Collection 4)

摘要 《迷人光線之頌》的敘述者描述大自然的美景。《小運動》則描寫海邊的一場大雷雨。《天空很低，雲層不懷好意》的敘述者則以幽默的口吻描述一個陰暗的冬日。

Chùm Thơ Số 4

Tóm Tắt Nhân vật trong bài thơ "Bài Thơ Ca Ngợi Ánh Sáng Thần Tiên" thưởng ngoạn vẻ đẹp của thiên nhiên. Một cơn mưa bão trên bờ biển được miêu tả trong bài thơ "Một Cuộc Đấu Sức Nhỏ". Nhân vật trong bài thơ "Bầu Trời Thật Thấp, Đám Mây Thật Hèn" miêu tả một cách hài ước một mùa đông u ám.

시 모음집 4 (Poetry Collection 4)

요약 "마법의 불빛에 바치는 노래"는 자연의 아름다움을 노래하고 있고, "작은 운동"에서는 해변에서 본 천둥 비를 그리고 있다. "하늘은 낮고 구름은 고약하다"에서는 어두운 겨울날을 익살스럽게 묘사하고 있다.

UNIT 4 — SUMMARY TRANSLATIONS

Poetry Collection 5

Summaries In "Runagate Runagate," the speaker describes a frightening escape. "Blow, Blow, Thou Winter Wind" uses images from winter to describe a false friendship. In "Old Man," the speaker celebrates his grandfather.

Colección de poemas 5

Resúmenes En "Fugitivo, fugitivo" el narrador describe un aterrador escape. "Sopla, sopla, tú, viento de invierno" utiliza imágenes del invierno para describir una amistad falsa. En "El viejo" el narrador conmemora a su abuelo.

Koleksyon pwezi 5

Rezime Nan "Runagate Runagate," oratè a dekri yon moun ki chape yon fason ki efreyan. "Kout van, kout van, ou menm van ivè" itilize imaj nan sezon ivè a pou dekri yon fo amitye. Nan "Ti granmoun," oratè a selebre granpè l.

Koleksyon ng mga Tula 5

Mga Buod Sa "Runagate Runagate," ang mananalita ay naglalarawan ng isang nakasisindak na pagtatakas. Ang "Blow, Blow, Thou Winter Wind" o "Ihip, Ihip, Ikaw Hangin ng Taglamig" ay gumagamit ng mga larawan ng panahong taglamig para ihambing ito sa isang hindi tunay na pagkakaibigan. Sa "Old Man" o "Matandang Lalaki," ipinagdiriwang ng mananalita ang kanyang lolo.

Phau Ntawv Paj Huam 5

Cov Ntsiab Hauv "Runagate Runagate," tus neeg hais lus piav txog ib txoj kev khiav dim kom tau uas txaus ntshai heev li. "Blow, Blow, Thou Winter Wind" siv tej duab pom thaum lub caij ntuj no los piav txog ib txoj kev phooj ywg uas tsis muaj tiag. Hauv "Old Man," tus neeg hais lus muaj kev zoo sib rau nws yawg.

《詩歌大全第五集》(Poetry Collection 5)

摘要《逃亡者》的敘述者描述了一場驚心動魄的逃亡過程。《吹呀吹，冬天的風》利用冬日的景象來描寫一段錯誤的友誼。《老人》的敘述者則稱頌自己的爺爺。

Chùm Thơ Số 5

Tóm Tắt Nhân vật trong bài "Chạy, Hãy Chạy" miêu tả lại một cuộc chạy trốn đầy sợ hãi. "Thổi Đi, Hỡi Gió Đông" sử dụng các hình ảnh mùa đông để miêu tả một tình bạn giả. Nhân vật trong bài "Ông" ca ngợi ông mình.

시 모음집 5 (Poetry Collection 5)

요약 '탈주자'에서는 도망가면서 느끼는 공포를 묘사하고 있다. '불어라, 불어라, 그대 겨울 바람이여'는 겨울과 관련된 이미지를 사용하여 거짓된 우정을 그리고 있으며, '노인'에서는 화자가 자신의 할아버지를 찬양하고 있다.

SUMMARY TRANSLATIONS

Poetry Collection 6

Summaries In "The New Colossus," the speaker describes the Statue of Liberty. In "Paul Revere's Ride," the speaker tells the story of Paul Revere's Ride. In "Harriet Beecher Stowe," the speaker praises Harriet Beecher Stowe, who helped people understand the fight against slavery.

Colección de poemas 6

Resúmenes En "El nuevo coloso" la narradora describe la Estatua de la Libertad. En "La cabalgata de Paul Revere" el narrador cuenta la historia de la cabalgata de Paul Revere. En "Harriet Beecher Stowe" el narrador elogia a Harriet Beecher Stowe, quien ayudó a muchas personas a entender la importancia de la pelea contra la esclavitud.

Koleksyon pwezi 6

Rezime Nan "Nouvo estati jeyan an," oratè a dekri Estati Lalibète a. Nan "Pwomnad Paul Revere la," oratè a rakonte istwa pwomnad Paul Revere la. Nan "Harriet Beecher Stowe," oratè a fè lwanj pou Harriet Beecher Stowe, ki te ede moun konprann batay kont esklavaj la.

Koleksyon ng mga Tula 6

Mga Buod Sa "The New Colossus," o "Ang Bagong Colossus," inilalarawan ng tagapagsalita ang "Statue of Liberty" o ang "Istatwa ng Kalayaan." Sa "Paul Revere's Ride," o "Ang Pagbiyahe ni Paul Revere," kinukuwento ng nagsasalita ang Pagbiyahe ni Paul Revere. Sa "Harriet Beecher Stowe," pinupuri ng nagsasalita si Harriet Beecher Stowe, na siyang tumulong sa mga tao na maunawaan ang kilusan laban sa pang-aalipin ng mga tao.

Phau Ntawv Paj Huam 6

Cov Ntsiab Hauv "The New Colossus," tus neeg hais lus piav txog tus Statute of Liberty. Hauv "Paul Revere's Ride," tus neeg hais lus tells piav zaj dabneeg txog thaum Paul Revere caij nees mus qhia pejxeem txog kev tsov rog. Hauv "Harriet Beecher Stowe," tus neeg hais lus hais lus zoo siab txog Harriet Beecher Stowe, uas yog ib tug neeg pab tau kom sawvdaws to taub txog kev tawm tsam txoj kev muab neeg yuam ua qhev.

《詩歌大全第六集》(Poetry Collection 6)

摘要 《新巨像》的敘述者描述自由女神像。《保羅・瑞威爾的乘車之旅》的敘述者描述保羅・瑞威爾乘車的故事。《荷莉葉・畢丘・史托》的敘述者讚揚幫助民眾瞭解對抗奴隸制度之奮鬥過程的荷莉葉・畢丘・史托。

Chùm Thơ Số 6

Tóm Tắt Nhân vật trong bài "Tượng Khổng Lồ Mới" miêu tả Tượng Nữ Thần Tự Do. Nhân vật trong bài "Hành Trình của Paul Revere," kể lại Hành Trình của Paul Revere. Nhân vật trong bài "Harriet Beecher Stowe," ca ngợi Harriet Beecher Stowe, nhân vật đã giúp mọi người hiểu được cuộc đấu tranh chống lại chế độ nô lệ.

시 모음집 6 (Poetry Collection 6)

요약 "새로 생긴 동상"에서는 자유의 여신상을 묘사하고 있으며, "폴 리버리의 라이드"에서는 폴 리버리가 말을 타고 가는 이야기를 들려주며, "해리어트 비쳐 스토우"에서는 노예제도 폐지 이유를 사람들에게 설파한 해리어트 비쳐 스토우를 칭송하고 있다.

UNIT 4: SUMMARY TRANSLATIONS

Poetry Collection 7

Summaries In "January," the speaker describes images connected with winter. "New World" shares different parts of the day in nature. In "For My Sister Molly Who in the Fifties," the speaker talks about her relationship with her sister.

Colección de poemas 7

Resúmenes En "Enero" el narrador describe imágenes relacionadas con el invierno. "Un mundo nuevo" presenta diferentes momentos del día en la naturaleza. En "Para mi hermana Molly quien en los años cincuenta" la narradora describe cómo es su relación con su hermana.

Koleksyon pwezi 7

Rezime Nan "Janvye," oratè a dekri kèk imaj ki konekte ak ivè. "Nouvo monn" pale konsènan diferan pati jounen an nan lanati. Nan "Pou sè m Molly ki nan senkantèn," oratè a pale konsènan relasyon l avèk sè li.

Koleksyon ng mga Tula 7

Mga Buod Sa "January," o "Enero," inilalarawan ng nagsasalita ang mga larawan na konektado sa panahong taglamig. Ipinamamahagi ng "New World," o "Bagong Daigdig" ang ibat'-ibang bahagi ng araw sa kalikasan. Sa "For My Sister Molly Who in the Fifties," o "Sa Aking Kapatid na si Molly, Na Noong Ika-Limang Dekada," tinatalakay ng nagsasalita ang relasyon niya sa kanyang kapatid.

Phau Ntawv Paj Huam 7

Cov Ntsiab Hauv "January," tus neeg hais lus piav txog tej yam duab uas muaj nrog lub caij ntuj no. "New World" qhia tawm txog ntau lub sijhawm nyob rau hauv ib hnub ntawm txhua yam hauv lub ntiaj teb. Hauv "For My Sister Molly Who in the Fifties," tus neeg hais lus tham txog nws txoj kev phoojywg nrog nws tus viv ncaus.

《詩歌大全第七集》(Poetry Collection 7)

摘要《一月》的敘述者描述了與冬天有關的景象。《新世界》則描寫一天當中不同時間的大自然。《致我五十幾歲的姊姊茉莉》的敘述者描述自己與姊姊之間的關係。

Chùm Thơ Số 7

Tóm Tắt Nhân vật trong bài thơ "Tháng Giêng" miêu tả những hình ảnh mùa đông. Bài "Thế Giới Mới" khắc họa những khoảnh khắc khác nhau trong ngày của tự nhiên. Nhân vật trong bài thơ "Dành Cho Em Gái Molly Của Tôi Trong Thế Kỷ 50," kể về mối quan hệ của mình với cô em gái.

시 모음집7(Poetry Collection 7)

요약 "1월"에서는 겨울과 관련된 이미지를 묘사하며, "새로운 세계"에서는 자연 속에 비친 하루의 여러 단면을 그리고 있다. "오십 대인 우리 언니 몰리"에서는 화자와 언니와의 관계를 이야기하고 있다.

SUMMARY TRANSLATIONS

Poetry Collection 8

Summaries In "Grandma Ling," the speaker travels to Taiwan to meet her grandmother. She and her grandmother do not speak the same language. They still feel close to each other. In "Drum Song," the lines flow like the beat of a drum. The speaker tells how a turtle, a woodpecker, a snowhare, and a woman move through the world to their own beat. The speaker in "your little voice/Over the wires came leaping" talks to a special person on the telephone. Her voice makes him dizzy. He thinks of flowers. He feels as though he is dancing.

Colección de poemas 8

Resúmenes En "La abuela Ling" la narradora viaja a Taiwán para conocer a su abuela. Ella y su abuela no hablan el mismo idioma. Pero aún se sienten muy unidas. En "Canción con tambor" las líneas fluyen al ritmo de un tambor. El narrador cuenta cómo una tortuga, un pájaro carpintero, una liebre y una mujer se mueven en el mundo a su propio ritmo. El narrador en "Tu vocecita/vino brincando por el cable" habla por teléfono con una persona especial. La voz de la persona a quien llama lo marea. Él se imagina flores. Se siente como si estuviera bailando.

Koleksyon pwezi 8

Rezime Nan "Granmè Ling," oratè a vwayaje al Taywann pou l rankontre granmè l. Limenm ak granmè l pa pale menm lang. Malgre sa yo toujou santi yo pwòch youn ak lòt. Nan "Chanson tanbou," liy yo koule tankou batman yon tanbou. Oratè a rakonte ki jan yon tòti, yon pik, yon lyèv d Amerik ak yon dam deplase atravè lemonn avèk vitès pa yo. Oratè nan "ti vwa w/sote sou liy telefòn nan" pale avèk yon moun espesyal nan telefòn. Vwa l fè tèt li vire. Li panse ak flè. Li santi tankou l ap danse.

Koleksyon ng mga Tula 8

Mga Buod Sa "Lola Ling," ang nagsasalita ay nagbiyahe papuntang Taiwan upang makilala ang kanyang lola. Magkaiba ang wika nila ng kanyang lola. Gayunpaman, malapít sila sa isa't-isa. Sa "Drum Song," o "Awit ng Tambol," ang mga taludtod ay umaagos tulad ng kumpas ng tambol. Sinasabi ng nagsasalita kung paano kumikilos sa mundo ayon sa sarili nilang kumpas ang isang pagong, isang ibong "woodpecker", isang konehong "snowhare" at isang babae. Ang nagsasalita sa "your little voice/Over the wires came leaping" o "ang Iyong Munting Tinig/Dumatíng na lumulundag mula sa mga kable" ay nakikipag-usap sa telepono sa isang kakaibang táo. Para siyang nahihilo sa boses ng babae. Ang naiisip ng lalaki ay mga bulaklak. Pakiramdam niya na para siyang sumasayaw.

UNIT 4
SUMMARY TRANSLATIONS

Phau Ntawv Paj Huam 8

Cov Ntsiab Hauv "Grandma Ling," tus neeg hais lus ncig tebchaws mus rau Taiwan mus ntsib nws pog. Nws thiab nws pog tsis paub sib txuas tib hom lus los nkawd yeej tseem muaj kev hlub heev. Hauv "Drum Song," cov kab lus sau raws li kev ntaus nruas. Tus neeg hais lus hauv zaj no qhia txog tias ib tug vaub kib, ib tug noog thos ntoo, ib tug luav, thiab ib tug pojniam ua lub neej nyob hauv ntiaj teb raws li lawv siab xav tau. Tus neeg hais lus hauv "Your little voice/Over the wires came leaping" tham nrog ib tug neeg tshwj xeeb heev nyob hauv lub xov tooj. Tus ntawd lub suab ua rau nws kiv kiv tob hau. Nws xav txog tej paj ntoos. Nws hnov zoo li nws twb tab tom seev cev lawm.

《詩歌大全第八集》(Poetry Collection 8)

摘要《林奶奶》的敘述者飛到台灣見她的奶奶。她和奶奶說不同的語言。她們卻仍然覺得彼此極為親近。《鼓歌》的每行字排列得像擊鼓時的節奏。敘述者描述一隻烏龜、啄木鳥、雪兔、以及一名女子如何依各自的節奏行進。《你的微弱聲音/跳躍著傳過電話線》的敘述者則對某個特別的人講電話。她的聲音使得他目眩神迷。他想到了花朵。他覺得自己像在手舞足蹈。

Chùm Thơ Số 8

Tóm Tắt Nhân vật trong bài thơ "Bà Ling," đi tới Đài Loan để gặp bà mình. Cô và bà mình không cùng chung ngôn ngữ nhưng họ vẫn cảm thấy gần gũi nhau. Trong "Bài Ca Tiếng Trống," các dòng thơ tuôn chảy giống như tiếng trống đập. Nhân vật trong bài kể lại chuyện một con rùa, một con chim gõ kiến, một con thỏ tuyết, và một người phụ nữ đi lại giữa thiên hạ theo nhịp điệu riêng của mình. Nhân vật trong bài "giọng nói nhỏ nhẹ của em/Rộn ràng trên đường dây điện thoại" nói chuyện với một người đặc biệt trên điện thoại. Giọng cô làm anh ngất ngây. Anh ta nghĩ đến những đóa hoa. Anh ta cảm thấy như mình đang khiêu vũ vậy.

시 모음집 8 (Poetry Collection 8)

요약 "할머니의 반지"에서 화자는 할머니를 만나보러 타이완으로 여행을 간다. 비록 할머니와 화자는 말은 통하지 않지만, 서로에게 친근감을 느낀다. "드럼의 노래"에서는 시 한 줄 한 줄이 마치 북 치는 소리에 따라 흘러가는 것처럼 느껴진다. 거북이와 딱따구리와 산토끼와 한 여인이 각자 북 치는 소리에 따라 어떻게 움직이는지를 그려내고 있다. "전화선을 타고 온 네 작은 목소리가 뛰어오르기 시작한다"에서 화자는 누군가와 전화 통화를 하고 있다. 그런데, 그 여자의 목소리가 화자를 현기증 나게 만든다. 화자는 꽃을 생각하게 되고 마치 자기가 춤을 추고 있는 듯한 기분을 느끼게 된다.

SUMMARY TRANSLATIONS

from Anne Frank & Me
Cherie Bennett

Summary An American teenager named Nicole travels back in time to Paris in 1942. Her family is arrested for being Jewish. They are put on a train going to a prison camp. Nicole recognizes Anne Frank on the train. She tells Anne details about Anne's life. Both girls are shocked by what Nicole knows.

de Ana Frank y yo
Cherie Bennett

Resumen Una adolescente estadounidense llamada Nicole viaja a París a través del tiempo, más precisamente hasta el año 1942. Su familia es arrestada por ser judía. Los llevan en un tren hasta un campo de prisioneros. Nicole reconoce a Ana Frank en el tren. Ella le cuenta a Ana los detalles sobre la vida de Ana. Ambas muchachas se sorprenden de todo lo que sabe Nicole.

yon ekstrè nan Anne Frank ak mwen menm
Cherie Bennett

Rezime Yon adolesan ameriken ki rele Nicole vwayaje nan lepase a Pari nan ane 1942. Yo arete fanmi l paske yo se jwif. Yo mete yo nan yon tren ki ta pral nan yon kan prizon. Nicole rekonèt Anne Frank nan tren an. Li rakonte Anne kèk detay sou lavi Anne. Toulède ti fi yo choke akoz sa Nicole konnen.

mula sa Si Anne Frank at Ako
Cherie Bennett

Buod Isang Amerikanang tinedyer na nagngangalang Nicole ay naglakbay sa nakaraang panahon, pabalik sa Paris noong 1942. Ang kanyang pamilya ay dinakip dahil sila ay mga Hudyo. Sila ay pinasakay sa isang tren patungo sa isang kampong bilangguan. Namukhaan ni Nicole si Anne Frank sa tren. Sinabi niya kay Anne ang mga detalye ng buhay ni Anne. Kapwa silang nabiglâ sa mga nalalaman ni Nicole.

UNIT 5

SUMMARY TRANSLATIONS

los ntawm zaj Anne Frank thiab Kuv

Cherie Bennett

Lub Ntsiab Ib tug menyuam Meskas hu ua Nicole mus rov qab rau lub nroog Paris thaum xyoo 1942. Nws tsev neeg raug txhom lawm vim tias lawv yog hom neeg Jewish. Lawv raug yuam caij ib lub tsheb nqaj hlau mus rau ib lub chaw kaw neeg. Nicole pom thiab paub Anne Frank nyob saum lub tsheb nqaj hlau. Nws qhia Anne txog tej yam nyob hauv Anne lub neej. Ob tug ntxhais tib si yeej ntseeg tsis tau li tias Nicole paub npaum li ntawd tiag.

改編自《安・法蘭克與我》(Anne Frank & Me)

Cherie Bennett

摘要 一位名叫妮可的美國少女跨越時空回到 1942 年的巴黎。她的家人因為身為猶太人而被捕。他們被安置在一輛開往一個集中營的火車上。妮可在火車上認出安・法蘭克。她告訴安有關安一生故事的細節。兩個女孩對於妮可知道的事都驚訝不已。

trích từ Anne Frank và Tôi

Cherie Bennett

Tóm Tắt Một thiếu niên người Mỹ tên là Nicole quay ngược dòng thời gian trở về Paris năm 1942. Gia đình cô bé bị bắt giữ vì họ là người Do Thái. Họ bị đưa lên tàu để đến trại tù. Nicole nhận ra Anne Frank trên chuyến tàu. Cô kể cho Anne một cách chi tiết về cuộc đời Anne. Cả hai cô gái đều hết sức kinh ngạc vì những điều Nicole biết.

안네 프랑크와 나 중에서 (Anne Frank & Me)

Cherie Bennett

요약 니콜이라는 이름의 한 미국 십대 소녀가 1942년 파리로 시간 여행을 떠나게 된다. 소녀의 가족은 유대인이라는 이유로 체포되고 수용소로 가는 기차를 타게 된다. 기차 안에서 니콜은 안네 프랑크를 알아 보고서 안네에게 안네의 삶을 자세히 가르쳐 준다. 하지만 니콜이 알고 있는 사실에 둘 다 충격을 받는다.

SUMMARY TRANSLATIONS

The Governess
Neil Simon

Summary A wealthy mistress plays a joke on her shy employee, Julia. The mistress subtracts money from Julia's pay. Julia is left with much less money than she is owed. The mistress hopes that Julia will become angry and stand up for herself.

La institutriz
Neil Simon

Resumen Una adinerada señora le hace una broma a Julia, su tímida empleada. La señora sustrae dinero del sueldo de Julia. A Julia le queda mucho menos dinero de lo que le corresponde. La señora espera que Julia se enfade y se defienda por sí misma.

Gouvènant lan
Neil Simon

Rezime Yon metrès rich fè yon jwèt avèk anplwaye l Julia ki timid. Metrès la retire nan lajan li dwe peye Julia. Julia vin gen mwens lajan pase sa yo dwe l. Metrès la espere Julia pral vin fache epi defann tèt li.

Ang "Governess"
Neil Simon

Buod Isang mayaman na donya ang nakaisip magbirô kay Julia, ang kanyang mahiyaing empleyado. Binawasan ng donya ang pera na isusuweldo kay Julia. Ang suweldong natanggap ni Julia ay higit na kulang sa kanyang takdang suweldo. Umaasa ang amo na magalit si Julia at panindigan niya ang kanyang sarili.

Tus Niam Zov Menyuam
Neil Simon

Lub Ntsiab Ib tug pojniam muaj nyiaj heev tso dag nrog nws tus ntxhias txib uas txaj muag heev hu ua Julia. Tus pojniam ib sij rho nyiam me me tawm ntawm Julia cov nyiaj them haujlwm. Julia cov nyiaj them cia li tsawg lawm ntau tshaj cov nyiaj uas yuav tsum muaj them nws. Tus pojniam muaj nyiaj vam hais tias Julia yuav chim heev thiab yuav hais lus tiv thaiv pab nws tus kheej.

《女家庭教師》(The Governess)
Neil Simon

摘要 一位富有的情婦對她羞怯的員工茱莉亞開了個玩笑。這位情婦從茱莉亞的薪水中扣了些錢。茱莉亞拿到的錢比她應得的少了許多。情婦希望茱莉亞會因此發火，挺身而出捍衛自己的權益。

Nữ Gia Sư
Neil Simon

Tóm Tắt Một bà chủ giàu có trêu chọc cô nữ gia sư hay thẹn của mình là Julia. Bà ta trừ tiền công của Julia. Julia nhận được ít tiền hơn số tiền lẽ ra được hưởng. Bà chủ hy vọng rằng Julia sẽ nổi giận và đấu tranh vì quyền lợi của mình.

여자 가정 교사 (The Governess)
Neil Simon

요약 부잣집 마나님은 자신이 고용한 줄리아에게 늘 농담하며 장난을 친다. 줄리아의 월급에서 돈을 삭감해 버리기도 하여 줄리아는 받아야 할 돈보다 훨씬 적은 돈을 받게 된다. 마나님은 줄리아가 화를 내며 자신과 맞서기를 바란다.

UNIT 5: SUMMARY TRANSLATIONS

The Diary of Anne Frank, Act I

Frances Goodrich and Albert Hackett

Summary World War II is over. Anne Frank's father returns to Amsterdam to say goodbye to a friend, Miep Gies. Gies gives him his daughter's diary. Mr. Frank open the diary and begins reading. Anne's voice joins his and takes over. The story goes back to 1942. Anne's family and another family are moving into the space above their friends' business. There they will live and hide from the Nazis for two years.

El diario de Ana Frank, Acto I

Frances Goodrich y Albert Hackett

Resumen Terminó la segunda guerra mundial. El padre de Ana Frank regresa a Amsterdam para despedirse de un amigo, Miep Gies. Gies le entrega el diario de Ana. El Sr. Frank abre el diario y empieza a leerlo. La voz de Ana se une a la de su padre y la absorbe. La historia regresa a 1942. La familia de Ana y otra familia se mudan al piso que se encuentra arriba del negocio de sus amigos. Allí vivirán y se esconderán de los nazis durante dos años.

Jounal Anne Frank, Ak I

Frances Goodrich ak Albert Hackett

Rezime Dezyèm Gè mondyal la fini. Papa Anne Frank retounen Amstèdam pou l di yon zanmi, Miep Gies, orevwa. Gies ba li jounal pitit fi mesye Frank lan. Mesye Frank ouvri jounal la epi li kòmanse li. Vwa Anne kontre ak vwa papa l epi Anne kontinye lekti a. Istwa a te pase an 1942. Fanmi Anne ansanm ak yon lòt fanmi ap demenaje nan espas ki aletaj biznis zanmi yo a. Se la yo pral abite epi kache pou Nazi yo pa wè yo pandan dezan.

Ang Talaan ni Anne Frank, Ika-I Akto

Frances Goodrich at Albert Hackett

Buod Tapós na ang Ikalawang Digmaang-Pandaigdig. Ang ama ni Anne Frank ay bumalik sa Amsterdam upang magpaalam kay Miep Gies, isang kaibigan. Ibinigay ni Gies sa kanya ang talaan ng kanyang anak na babae. Binuksan ni Gg. Frank ang talaan at nagsimula siyang magbasá. Sinalihan ng boses ni Anne ang kanyang boses, hanggang ang tinig na lamang ni Anne ang siyang naririnig. Ang kuwento ay nagsimula noong 1942. Ang pamilya ni Anne at ang isa pang pamilya ay lumilipat sa isang silid sa itaas ng lugar-pangangalakal ng kanilang mga kaibigan. Dito sila titira at magtatago mula sa mga "Nazi" nang dalawang taon.

SUMMARY TRANSLATIONS

Anne Frank Phau Ntawv Sau Lus Cia, Tshooj Ib

Frances Goodrich thiab Albert Hackett

Lub Ntsiab Tsov rog World War II xaus lawm. Anne Frank txiv rov qab mus ntsib ib tug phooj ywg, Miep Gies, nyob rau hauv Amsterdam Gies muab Anne phau ntawv sau lus cia rau Anne txiv. Mr. Frank qhib phau ntawv sau lus cia thiab piab nyeem. Anne lub suab nrov nyeem nrog nws txiv lub thiab nyeem ib leeg tauj ntxiv mus. Zaj no rov qab mus rau xyoo 1942. Anne tsev neeg thiab lwm tsev neeg tab tom tsiv mus nyob rau ib chav saum lawv cov phooj ywg lub chaw haujlwm. Lawv yuav nyob ntawd thiab khiav nkaum cov Nazis ntev li ob xyoos.

《安‧法蘭克的日記，第一幕》(The Diary of Anne Frank, Act I)

Frances Goodrich 與 Albert Hackett

摘要 二次大戰已經結束。安‧法蘭克的父親返回阿姆斯特丹向一位朋友邁波‧吉斯道別。吉斯將他的女兒的日記交給他。法蘭克先生打開日記讀了起來。安的聲音融入他的聲音，然後變成了主要旁白。故事回溯到 1942 年。安的家人和另一家人正搬入位於朋友公司上面的閣樓。他們將在那裡居住並躲避納粹長達兩年的時間。

Nhật Ký của Anne Frank, Hồi I

Frances Goodrich và Albert Hackett

Tóm Tắt Thế Chiến Thứ Hai kết thúc. Cha của Anne Frank quay lại Amsterdam để từ biệt một người bạn tên là Miep Gies. Gies đưa ông cuốn nhật ký của con gái mình. Ông Frank mở cuốn nhật ký và bắt đầu đọc. Giọng kể truyện của Anne nổi lên từ các trang nhật ký và cuốn ông đi theo. Câu truyện lần trở về năm 1942. Gia đình Anne và một gia đình khác dọn vào sống ở gác xép phía trên cửa hàng của bạn họ. Họ sống ở đó để trốn bọn Phát Xít Đức trong hai năm.

안네 프랑크의 일기, 제 1막 (The Diary of Anne Frank, Act I)

Frances Goodrich 및 Albert Hackett

요약 제 2차 세계대전이 끝나고 안네의 아버지는 친구 미에프 기스 씨에게 작별 인사를 하러 암스테르담으로 돌아온다. 기스 씨는 프랑크 씨에게 안네의 일기를 건네주고 프랑크씨는 일기장을 펴고 읽기 시작한다. 안네와 아버지의 목소리가 겹쳐지다 안네의 목소리로 넘어간다. 이제 이야기는 1942년으로 거슬러 올라간다. 안네의 가족과 또 다른 가족은 친구의 사업장으로 이사를 온다. 거기서 2년 동안 나찌를 피해 숨어 지내게 된다.

UNIT 5 SUMMARY TRANSLATIONS

The Diary of Anne Frank, Act II

Frances Goodrich and Albert Hackett

Summary The Franks, the Van Daans, and Mr. Dussel have been hiding for a year and a half. The eight of them have managed to live together, but they do not always get along. Food is scarce, and they are constantly afraid. Anne and Peter have become close friends. Soon, they learn that the Allies have invaded Europe, and they become excited.

El diario de Ana Frank, Acto II

Frances Goodrich y Albert Hackett

Resumen Los Franks, los Van Daans y el Sr. Dussel han estado escondidos por un año y medio. Las ocho personas se las han arreglado para vivir juntos, pero no siempre se llevan bien. La comida es escasa y siempre tienen miedo. Ana y Peter se han hecho muy amigos. Pronto se enteran de que los aliados han invadido Europa y se ponen muy contentos.

Jounal Anne Frank, Ak II

Frances Goodrich ak Albert Hackett

Rezime Frank yo, Van Daan yo ak mesye Dussel te nan kachèt pandan ennan edmi. Toulè uit te reyisi viv ansanm, men yo pa t toujou antann yo. Manje ra, epi yo toujou ap viv nan laperèz. Anne ak Peter te vin bon zanmi. Anvan lontan yo aprann twoup alye yo te anvayi Ewòp, epi yo te vin kontan anpil.

Ang Talaan ni Anne Frank, Ikalawang Akto

Frances Goodrich at Albert Hackett

Buod Ang pamilyang Frank, Van Daan, at si Gg. Dussel ay isa't-kalahating taon nang nagtatago. Nagawa nilang walo na mabuhay nang magkakasama, ngunit 'di sila palaging nagkakasundo. Kulang ang pagkain, at palagi silang takót. Si Anne at Peter ay naging matalik na magkaibigan. Maya-maya pa ay nalaman nila na ang "Allies" ay lumusob na sa Europa, at sila ay tuwang-tuwa.

SUMMARY TRANSLATIONS

Anne Frank Phau Ntawv Sau Lus Cia, Tshooj Ob

Frances Goodrich thiab Albert Hackett

Lub Ntsiab Tsev neeg Frank, tsev neeg Van Daans, thiab Mr. Dussel twb tau nkaum ntev li ib xyoos thiab ib nrab lawm. Lawv yim leej tau sib swm nyob ua ke, tiamsis lawv yeej muaj tej lub sijhawm tsis sib haum thiab. Zaub mov los muaj tsawg lawm xwb, thiab lawv ua neej nrog txoj kev ntshai txhua lub sijhawm. Anne thiab Peter tau ua phooj ywg zoo heev. Tsis ntev, lawv hnov txog tias cov tub rog Allies tau nkag los txog Europe lawm, thiab lawv zoo siab heev li.

《安‧法蘭克的日記，第二幕》(The Diary of Anne Frank, Act II)

Frances Goodrich 與 Albert Hackett

摘要 法蘭克一家、凡‧達恩斯一家、以及杜索爾先生已經躲了有一年半的時間。他們八個人勉強辦到共同生活，但卻不是一直都相處得很和睦。食物極為匱乏，而他們無時無刻不在恐懼。安和彼特已經成為親密的朋友。不久，他們得知同盟國的軍隊已經攻入歐洲，他們因此極為振奮。

Nhật Ký của Anne Frank, Hồi II

Frances Goodrich và Albert Hackett

Tóm Tắt Gia đình Frank, gia đình Van Daan, và ông Dussel đã sống ẩn náu được một năm rưỡi nay. Tám người bọn họ dẫu có thể cùng chung sống nhưng không phải lúc nào cũng thuận hòa. Lương thực thiếu, và họ thường xuyên sống trong lo sợ. Anne và Peter trở thành những người bạn thân thiết. Chẳng bao lâu sau, họ biết được rằng Quân Đồng Minh đã bắt đầu xâm chiếm Châu Âu, vì vậy rất phấn khởi.

안네 프랑크의 일기, 제 2막 (The Diary of Anne Frank, Act II)

Frances Goodrich 및 Albert Hackett

요약 프랑크 씨 가족과 반단 씨 가족과 뒤셀 씨는 일년 반을 숨어서 지내고 있다. 이 여덟 명은 서로 같이 근근이 살아가고 있는데, 항상 사이가 좋은 것만은 아니다. 음식은 부족했으며 항상 두려움에 떨어야만 했다. 안네와 피터는 친한 친구가 된다. 그들은 연합군이 유럽을 침공했다는 소식을 듣고 기쁨을 감추지 못한다.

UNIT 6: SUMMARY TRANSLATIONS

Water Names
Lan Samantha Chang

Summary Three girls sit on a back porch on the prairie. Their grandmother Waipuo reminds them of how important China's longest river was in the lives of their ancestors. She tells them a story in Chinese about a girl who falls in love with a water ghost.

Nombres de agua
Lan Samantha Chang

Resumen Tres niñas se sientan en la galería trasera que da a la pradera. Su abuela Waipuo les recuerda lo importante que era el río más largo de China en la vida de sus antepasados. Les cuenta una historia en chino acerca de una niña que se enamora de un fantasma de agua.

Non dlo
Lan Samantha Chang

Rezime Twa ti fi chita sou galri pa dèyè yon kay nan yon preri. Granmè yo ki rele Waipuo raple yo enpòtans larivyè ki pi long nan Lachin te genyen nan lavi zansèt yo. Li rakonte yo yon istwa an chinwa konsènan yon ti fi ki te tonbe anmoure avèk yon fatòm dlo.

Mga Pangalang Tubig
Lan Samantha Chang

Buod Tatlong batang babae ay nakaupo sa likurang porch o batalán sa kapatagan. Pinaalala sa kanila ng kanilang lolang si Waipuo ang kahalagahan ng pinaka-mahabang ilog sa Tsina para sa kanilang mga ninuno. Sa wikang Tsina, nagkuwento siya tungkol sa isang babaeng umiibig sa isang multo sa tubig.

Cov Npe Dej
Lan Samantha Chang

Lub Ntsiab Peb tug menyuam ntxhais zaum sab nraum lub xas las. Lawv pog Waipuo qhia lawv txog tias Tebchaws Suav tus dej ntev tshaj plaws tseem ceeb npaum li cas rau tej poj koob yawm txwv ib txwm dhau los. Nws hais lus Suav piav ib zaj dabneeg rau lawv txog ib tug ntxhais uas muaj txoj kev hlub nrog ib tug ntsuj plig dej.

《水的名字》 (Water Names)
Lan Samantha Chang

摘要 三個小女孩坐在一座牧場後面的門廊上。她們的外婆提醒她們中國最長的一條河在祖先生活中有多麼重要。她告訴她們一則發生在中國有關一個女孩愛上一個水鬼的故事。

Những Cái Tên Sông
Lan Samantha Chang

Tóm Tắt Ba cô gái ngồi ở thềm phía sau của một căn nhà trên thảo nguyên. Bà Waipuo của họ nhắc nhở họ về tầm quan trọng của dòng sông dài nhất Trung Hoa đối với cuộc sống của tổ tiên họ. Bà kể cho họ nghe câu truyện về một cô gái đem lòng yêu một con ma dưới sông.

물의 이름 (Water Names)
Lan Samantha Chang

요약 대평원에 있는 집 뒷마당에 세 명의 소녀가 앉아 있다. 할머니 와이푸오는 중국 선조들이 중국에서 제일 긴 강을 굉장히 중요하게 여겼다고 이야기해 준다. 그러면서 물 유령과 사랑에 빠진 한 소녀의 이야기를 중국어로 시작한다.

SUMMARY TRANSLATIONS

Coyote Steals the Sun and Moon

Zuñi Myth, Retold by Richard Erdoes and Alfonso Ortiz

Summary This myth tells about how the sun and the moon got into the sky. Coyote and Eagle team up to steal the sun and moon to light up their dark world. Coyote's curious nature causes them to lose both. The sun and moon escape into the sky.

El coyote se roba el sol y la luna

Zuñi Myth, adaptación de Richard Erdoes y Alfonso Ortiz

Resumen Este mito habla acerca de cómo el sol y la luna llegaron al cielo. El coyote y el águila trabajan juntos para robar el sol y la luna a fin de iluminar su oscuro mundo. La naturaleza curiosa del coyote hace que pierdan a los dos astros. El sol y la luna escapan hacia el cielo.

Kòyòt vòlè solèy ak lalin

Zuñi Myth, Rakonte ankò pa Richard Erdoes ak Alfonso Ortiz

Rezime Mit sa a rakonte ki jan solèy la ak lalin lan te fè rive nan syèl la. Kòyòt ak èg mete ansanm pou yo vòlè solèy la ak lalin lan pou ka klere monn an tenèb yo a. Nati kirye kòyòt lakoz yo pèdi toulède. Solèy la ak lalin la sove al nan syèl la.

Ninakaw ng Coyote ang Araw at Buwan

Zuñi Myth, Sinabi muli Richard Erdoes at Alfonso Ortiz

Buod Isinasalaysay ng alamat na ito kung paano napunta sa langit ang araw at ang buwan. Si Coyote at si Eagle ay magkasabwat para nakawin ang araw at buwan, upang ilawan ang kanilang madilim na mundo. Dahil sa pagka-mausyoso ni Coyote, nawala nila itong pareho. Ang araw at ang buwan ay tumakas at pumunta sa langit.

UNIT 6
SUMMARY TRANSLATIONS

Hma Nyiag Lub Hnub Thiab Lub Hli

Zuñi Myth, Rov qhia dua los ntawm Richard Erdoes thiab Alfonso Ortiz

Lub Ntsiab Zaj dabneeg no qhia tias lub hnub thiab lub hli mus nyob tau rau saum ntuj li cas. Coyote thiab Dav sib koom mus nyiag lub hnub thiab lub hli los ua kom nkawd thaj chaw pom kev. Coyote tus cwj pwm xav paub txog ntau yam ua rau nkawd plam ob yam tib si. Lub hnub thiab lub hli tawm tau thiab ya mus nyob puag saum ntuj.

《土狼偷了太陽和月亮》(Coyote Steals the Sun and Moon)

入尼族神話，重述者：
Richard Erdoes 與 *Alfonso Ortiz*

摘要 這則神話描述太陽與月亮升上天空的經過。土狼和老鷹結夥竊走太陽與月亮，想用來照亮他們黑暗的世界。土狼好奇的天性造成他們弄丟了這兩種寶物。太陽和月亮因此逃了出來，並飛上天空。

Sói Đồng Cỏ Đánh Cắp Mặt Trời và Mặt Trăng

TruyệnThần Thoại của Bộ Tộc Zuñi, Theo Lời Kể Của Richard Erdoes và Alfonso Ortiz

Tóm Tắt Câu truyện thần thoại này kể lại việc làm thế nào mặt trời và mặt trăng có trên bầu trời. Sói Đồng Cỏ và Đại Bàng hợp lại đánh cắp mặt trời và mặt trăng để chiếu sáng thế gian tối tăm. Bản tính tò mò của Sói Đồng Cỏ đã khiến chúng mất cả hai. Mặt trời và mặt trăng trốn thoát lên trời.

코요테가 태양과 달을 훔치다
(Coyote Steals the Sun and Moon)

주니족 신화, *Richard Erdoes* 와 *Alfonso Ortiz* 가 어린이를 위해 고쳐 쓰다

요약 이 신화는 태양과 달이 어떻게 하늘로 올라가게 되었는지를 이야기해 준다. 코요테와 독수리는 함께 태양과 달을 훔쳐 그들의 어두운 세상을 환하게 비추려고 한다. 그러나 코요테의 호기심으로 모든 일은 수포로 돌아가고 태양과 달은 하늘로 달아나 버린다.

SUMMARY TRANSLATIONS

Why the Waves Have Whitecaps
Zora Neale Hurston

Summary The story is an African American folk tale. Mrs. Wind brags about her children. Mrs. Water grows tired of it and drowns the children. Mrs. Wind looks for her children but sees only white feathers on the water. That is why there are whitecaps. Storms at sea are the wind and water fighting over children.

Por qué las olas tienen cabrillas
Zora Neale Hurston

Resumen Esta historia es una leyenda popular afroamericana. La Sra. Viento hace alarde de sus hijos. La Sra. Agua se cansa de escucharla y ahoga a los niños. La Sra. Viento busca a los niños pero sólo observa plumas blancas sobre el agua. Es por eso que en el mar existen las cabrillas. Las tormentas en el mar no son más que el viento y el agua peleando por los niños.

Poukisa vag yo fè kim
Zora Neale Hurston

Rezime Istwa a se yon kont tradisyonèl afriken ameriken. Madan Wind ap fè lwanj pou timoun li yo. Madan Water vin fatige ak lwanj yo epi li nwaye timoun yo. Madan Wind chèche timoun li yo men se plim blan li wè sèlman sou dlo a. Se poutètsa vag yo fè kim. Tanpèt sou lanmè yo se van ak dlo k ap goumen pou timoun yo.

Kung Bakit may Puting Tuktok ang mga Alon
Zora Neale Hurston

Buod Ang kuwentong ito ay isang Aprikano-Amerikanong kathang-salaysay. Si Gng. Hangin ay nagyayabang tungkol sa kanyang mga anak. Nagsawa na si Gng. Tubig dito, at nilunod niya ang mga bata. Hinanap ni Gng. Hangin ang kanyang mga anak ngunit ang nakita lamang niya ay ang mga puting balahibo sa tubig. Iyan ang dahilan kung bakit may puting tuktok ang mga alon. Ang mga bagyó sa dagat ay ang paglalaban ng hangin at tubig dahil sa mga bata.

UNIT 6 SUMMARY TRANSLATIONS

Vim Li Cas Cov Nthwv Dej Thiaj Li Muaj Hau Dawb

Zora Neale Hurston

Lub Ntsiab Zaj dabneeg no yob ib zaj ntawm haiv neeg Meskas Dub. Mrs. Wind khav txog nws cov menyuam. Mrs. Water laj laj mloog lawm thiaj li muab cov menyuam ua poob deg tas. Mrs. Wind nrhiav nrhiav nws cov menyuam tiamsis tsuas pom cov tis dawb dawb nyob rau saum npoo dej xwb. Vim li ntawd thiaj li muaj tej hau dawb dawb tawm. Thaum ntuj los nag hlob heev hauv tej pas dej ces tsuas yog thaum cua thiab dej sib ntaus txog cov menyuam ntawd.

《海浪為何有白浪頭》(Why the Waves Have Whitecaps)

Zora Neale Hurston

摘要 這是一則非洲裔美國人的民間傳說。風夫人到處吹噓自己的孩子。水夫人聽得很厭煩，於是溺死了這些孩子。風夫人於是著急著尋找自己的孩子，但卻只看到海水上的白泡。這也是白浪頭的由來。海上的暴風雨則是風與水為了孩子在爭鬥。

Tại Sao Sóng Có Đầu Bạc

Zora Neale Hurston

Tóm Tắt Đây là câu truyện dân gian của người Mỹ gốc Phi. Bà Gió hay khoe khoang về các con mình. Bà Nước nghe đến chán nên dìm chết bọn trẻ. Bà Gió đi tìm các con nhưng chỉ nhìn thấy những chiếc lông trắng trên mặt nước. Đó là lý do vì sao có sóng đầu bạc. Các cơn bão biển chính là cuộc chiến giữa gió và nước biển giành sự sống chết cho lũ trẻ.

왜 파도의 물결 끝은 하얀 색일까 (Why the Waves Have Whitecaps)

Zora Neale Hurston

요약 이는 미국 흑인들 사이에 전해져 내려오는 이야기이다. 바람 아주머니는 자기 아이들 자랑을 너무 심하게 한다. 자랑 듣는 것이 싫어진 물 아주머니가 바람 아주머니의 아이들을 물에 잠기게 한다. 바람 아주머니는 아이들을 찾아 나서지만 물 위에 떠 있는 하얀 깃털만을 볼 수 있을 뿐이다. 그 하얀 깃털이 바로 파도 물결의 하얀 끝이다. 바다에서 폭풍이 이는 것은 바람과 물이 아이들을 사이에 두고 싸움을 벌이고 있기 때문이다.

SUMMARY TRANSLATIONS

Chicoria • *from* The People, Yes

Summaries In "Chicoria," a rancher invites a poet to dinner. The poet is asked to share poetry, but not to eat. The poet uses a folk tale to point out the rancher's rude behavior. In the selection from The People, Yes, the speaker talks about his love for America. He describes the adventures of famous characters from American folklore, and such as Paul Bunyan and John Henry.

Chicoria • *de* "El pueblo, sí"

Resúmenes En "Chicoria" un ranchero invita a cenar a un poeta. Le pide al poeta que comparta poesías con él, pero que no coma. El poeta utiliza una leyenda popular para remarcar el grosero comportamiento del ranchero. En la selección de El pueblo, sí, el narrador habla acerca de su amor por América. Describe las aventuras de personajes famosos del folclore estadounidense, como Paul Bunyan y John Henry.

Chicoria • *yon ekstrè nan* Pèp la, wi

Rezime Nan "Chicoria," yon pwopriyetè ranch envite yon powèt vin dine. Li mande powèt la pou li resite pwezi, men piga l manje. Powèt la ititlize kont tradisyonèl pou l fè remake konpòtman enpoli pwopriyetè ranch lan. Nan ekstrè seleksyon Pèp la, wi, oratè a pale konsènan lanmou ki genyen pou Amerik. Li dekri avanti pèsonaj selèb nan kilti ameriken, tankou Paul Bunyan ak John Henry.

Chicoria • *mula sa* Ang mga Tao, Oo

Mga Buod Sa "Chicoria," isang ranchero ay nangumbida sa isang manunulá para sa hapunan. Hiniling niyang magbahagi ng mga tulá ang manunulá, ngunit hindi niya pinakain ito. Gumamit ang manunulá ng isang kathang-salaysay para ipakita ang kabastusan ng asal ng ranchero. Sa pinili mula sa Ang mga Tao, Oo, pinag-uusapan ng nagsasalita ang kanyang pagmamahal sa Amerika. Inilalarawan niya ang mga nangyari ng mga tanyag na tauhan mula sa mga kathang-salaysay ng Amerika, tulad nina Paul Bunyan at John Henry.

UNIT 6: SUMMARY TRANSLATIONS

Chicoria • *los ntawm* Cov Neeg, Yog Lawm

Cov Ntsiab Hauv "Chicoria," ib tug tswv teb caw ib tug neeg txawj pajhuam tuaj koom rooj hmo. Tus neeg txawj pajhuam raug caw tuaj hais pajhuam, tiamsis tsis yog tuaj noj hmo. Tus neeg txawj pajhuam siv ib co dabneeg coj los piav kom pom tau tias tus tswv teb coj tau tus cwjpwm tsis zoo npaum li cas. Hauv cov zaj sau ntawm Cov Neeg, Yog Lawm, tus neeg hais lus tham txog nws txoj kev hlub rau lub Tebchaws Meskas. Nws piav txog cov kev ua si ntawm cov neeg muaj npe hauv cov dabneeg Meskas thiab tej co xws li Paul Bunyan thiab John Henry lawv.

《奇可里亞》(Chicoria) • 改編自《人民，是的》(*from* The People, Yes)

摘要 《奇可里亞》描寫一名牧場主人邀請一位詩人晚餐。詩人被要求分享詩作，否則不能用餐。詩人於是利用一則民間傳說來指出牧場主人的無禮行為。在取自《人民，是的》的文選中，敘述者描述自己對美國的熱愛。他描述美國民間傳說裡的著名人物以及諸如保羅・班揚以及約翰・亨利等人的冒險傳奇。

Chicoria • *trích từ* Đúng, Ta Là Dân

Tóm Tắt Trong bài "Chicoria," một chủ trang trại mời một nhà thơ tới dùng bữa tối. Nhà thơ được yêu cầu ngâm thơ nhưng không được mời ăn. Nhà thơ dùng một câu truyện dân gian để chỉ rõ hành vi thô lỗ của chủ trang trại. Trong đoạn trích từ Đúng, Ta Là Dân, nhân vật trong bài thơ thể hiện tình yêu của ông dành cho nước Mỹ. Ông miêu tả những cuộc phiêu lưu của các nhân vật nổi tiếng trong kho tàng văn học dân gian Mỹ, như Paul Bunyan và John Henry.

치코리아 (Chicoria) • 예스 라고 말하는 사람들 중에서 (*from* The People, Yes)

요약 "치코리아"에서는 한 목장주인이 시인을 저녁 식사에 초대한다. 그런데, 주인은 시인에게 식사는 주지 않으면서 시를 들려 달라고 부탁한다. 시인은 한 옛날 이야기를 들려주며 주인의 무례한 행동을 비꼰다. "예스 라고 말하는 사람들" 중에서 뽑은 이 이야기에서 화자는 자신의 미국 사랑을 언급하며, 미국 옛날 이야기에 나오는 폴 번연과 존 헨리와 같은 유명한 인물들의 모험을 그리고 있다.

SUMMARY TRANSLATIONS

Brer Possum's Dilemma • John Henry

Summary In "Brer Possum's Dilemma," Brer Snake asks Brer Possum for help. "John Henry" is a ballad, or song, that tells the story of an African American hero who races a steam drill.

El dilema de la zarigüeya Brer • John Henry

Resumen En "El dilema de la zarigüeya Brer" la serpiente Brer le pide ayuda a la zarigüeya Brer. "John Henry" es una balada, o canción, que cuenta la historia de un héroe afroamericano que le juega una carrera a un taladro de vapor.

Dilèm frè oposòm • John Henry

Rezime Nan "Dilèm frè oposòm," frè koulèv mande frè oposòm pou l ede l. "John Henry" se yon balad oswa chanson, ki rakonte istwa yon ewo afriken ameriken k ap fè kous ak yon pèsez a vapè.

Ang Problema ni Brer Possum • John Henry

Buod Ang ahas na si Brer Snake ay humingi ng tulong kay Brer Possum sa "Brer Possum's Dilemma," o "Ang Problema ni Brer Possum." Ang "John Henry" ay isang "ballad," o awit, na nagkukuwento tungkol sa isang Aprikano-Amerikanong bayani na siyang nangarera gamit ang isang "steam drill."

Brer Possum Qhov Teeb Meem • John Henry

Lub Ntsiab Hauv "Brer Possum Qhov Teeb Meem," Brer Snake hais kom Brer Possum pab nws. "John Henry" yog ib zaj nkauj uas qhia zaj dabneeg txog haiv neeg Meskas Dub tus phaj ej nrov npe uas tau sib xeem nrog ib lub cav khawb qhov.

《布瑞爾負鼠的困境》(Brer Possum's Dilemma) • 《約翰·亨利》(John Henry)

摘要 《布瑞爾負鼠的困境》描寫布瑞爾蛇向布瑞爾負鼠求救。《約翰·亨利》是一首民謠（即歌曲），內容描寫一位與蒸氣鑽孔機競賽的非洲裔美國英雄的故事。

Chuyện Khó Xử của Anh Ôpôt • John Henry

Tóm Tắt Trong truyện "Chuyện Khó Xử của Anh Ôpôt," Anh Rắn nhờ Anh Ôpôt giúp đỡ. "John Henry" là một bài ca kể truyện về một anh hùng Mỹ gốc Phi tham gia cuộc đấu sức với một máy khoan chạy bằng hơi nước.

브레르 쥐의 딜레마 (Brer Possum's Dilemma) • 존 헨리 (John Henry)

요약 "브레르 쥐의 딜레마"는 브레르 뱀이 브레르 쥐에게 도움을 청하는 이야기이다. "존 헨리"는 발라드 풍의 시로서 증기 동력 드릴(증기엔진의 힘으로 바위를 깨는 기계)과 경쟁을 벌인 미국 흑인 영웅에 관해 노래하고 있다.

UNIT 6 SUMMARY TRANSLATIONS

from Out of the Dust
Karen Hesse

Summary "Out of the Dust" includes three poems. The speaker in "Debts" describes the faith her father has that it will rain again. "Fields of Flashing Light" describes a dust storm on the prairie. In "Migrants," people leave their dried-up farms behind.

de Lejos del polvo
Karen Hesse

Resumen "Lejos del polvo" incluye tres poemas. La narradora de "Las deudas" describe la convicción que tiene su padre de que volverá a llover. "Campos de luz destellante" describe una tormenta de polvo en la pradera. En "Los emigrantes", las personas abandonan sus granjas por causa de una gran una sequía.

yon ekstrè nan Andeyò pousyè a
Karen Hesse

Rezime "Andeyò pousyè a" genyen twa powèm ladan l. Oratè nan "Dèt" dekri lafwa papa l genyen lapli pral tonbe ankò. "Chan limyè kliyotan" dekri yon tanpèt pousyè sou yon preri. Nan "Migratè," moun yo kite eksplwatasyon agrikòl yo ki fin sèk dèyè.

mula sa Mula sa Alikabok
Karen Hesse

Buod May kasamang tatlong tulá ang "Out of the Dust," o "Mula sa Alikabok". Ìnilalarawan ng nagsasalita sa "Debts," o "Mga Utang, " ang paniniwala ng kanyang ama na uulan muli. Inilalarawan ng "Fields of Flashing Light," o "`Mga Bukid ng Kumikislap na Ilaw, " ang isang bagyó ng alikabok sa kapatagan. Sa "Migrants," o "Mga Mandarayuhan," iniwanan ng mga tao ang kanilang mga natuyóng bukid.

SUMMARY TRANSLATIONS

los ntawm zaj Tawm Hauv Cov Hmoov Av Los

Karen Hesse

Lub Ntsiab "Tawm Hauv cov Hmoov Av Los" muaj peb zag pajhuam. Tus neeg hais lus hauv "Nuj Nqis" piav txog txoj kev ntseeg uas nws txiv muaj tias yuav rov los nag dua. "Ib Hav Teeb Ntsais" piav txog ib nthwv cua muaj hmoov av ntau heev nyob sab nraum thaj chaw hav nyom. Hauv "Neeg Tsiv Raws Kev Ua Teb," cov neeg tseg lawv tej teb nyob rau tom qab qhuav qhawv.

改編自《風兒不要來》(Out of the Dust)

Karen Hesse

摘要 《風兒不要來》包括三首詩。《債務》的敘述者描述自己的父親對於雨水將再度降臨的信念。《閃光的牧場》描述牧場上的一場沙塵暴。《移民》描寫人民離開自己乾涸的農場，遠走他鄉。

trích từ Cát Bụi

Karen Hesse

Tóm Tắt Chùm thơ "Từ Cát Bụi" có ba bài thơ. Nhân vật trong bài "Nợ Nần" miêu tả lòng tin của cha mình rằng chắc chắn trời sẽ lại mưa. Bài "Cánh Đồng Chớp Giật" miêu tả một cơn bão cát trên đồng cỏ. Trong bài "Những Người Di Cư", mọi người rời đi, để lại những trang trại khô cằn sau lưng.

먼지에서부터 중에서 (Out of the Dust)

Karen Hesse

요약 "먼지에서부터"는 세 편의 시로 구성되어 있다. "빚더미"에서 화자는 다시 비가 올 것이라는 아버지의 믿음을 묘사하고 있으며, "번개가 치는 들판"은 대평원 위에 불어 닥친 먼지 폭풍을 그리고 있다. "이주자"는 바짝 말라버린 농장을 뒤로하고 떠나는 사람들을 그리고 있다.

UNIT 6
SUMMARY TRANSLATIONS

Ellis Island
Joseph Bruchac

Summary The poet imagines his Slovak grandparents as they arrive in the United States. Their first stop in the land of their dreams was Ellis Island in New York. He then writes of his Native American grandparents. He points out that they had always lived in America. Their way of life was destroyed when the Europeans came.

La Isla Ellis
Joseph Bruchac

Resumen El poeta se imagina a sus abuelos eslovacos cuando llegan a los Estados Unidos. La primera parada que hizo en la tierra de sus sueños fue en la Isla Ellis en Nueva York. Luego, él escribe sobre sus abuelos estadounidenses nativos. Señala que siempre han vivido en los Estados Unidos. Sus costumbres fueron destruidas cuando llegaron los europeos.

Ellis Island
Joseph Bruchac

Rezime Powèt la imajine granparan slovak li yo lè yo te fèk rive Ozetazini. Premye estòp yo nan tè rèv yo a se te Ellis Island nan Nouyòk. Ansuit li ekri konsènan granparan endyen ameriken l yo. Li fè remake yo te toujou viv ann Amerik. Lè ewopeyen yo te debake yo te detwi fason yo te konn viv.

Ang Isla ng Ellis
Joseph Bruchac

Buod Ginugunita ng manunulá ang kanyang mga lolo at lolang Islovak nang sila ay dumating sa Estados Unidos. Ang una nilang pinagtigilan sa lupa ng kanilang mga pangarap ay ang Isla ng Ellis sa New York. Pagkatapos ay sumulat siya tungkol sa kanyang mga lolo at lolang Katutubong Amerikano. Sinasabi niya na ang mga ito ay mula`t-mula pa ay nakatira na sa Amerika. Ang paraan ng kanilang pamumuhay ay nasira noong nagsidatingan ang mga taga-Europa.

SUMMARY TRANSLATIONS

Ellis Island
Joseph Bruchac

Lub Ntsiab Tus neeg sau pajhaum xav txog tias thaum nws pog thiab yawg uas yog haiv neeg Slovak nyuam qhuav tuaj txog rau Tebchaws Meskas zoo li cas xwb. Thawj qhov chaw lawv tuaj poob rau hauv lub tebchaws uas lawv npau suav toog txog yog lub chaw Ellis Island hauv nroog New York. Tom qab ntawd nws sau txog nws niam tais yawm txiv uas yog haiv neeg khab. Nws sau txog tias lawv yeej ib txwm yog neeg nyob hauv daim av Tebchaws Meskas. Lawv txoj kev ua neej raug rhuav puam tsuaj tag thaum cov neeg European tuaj txog.

《愛麗斯島》(Ellis Island)
Joseph Bruchac

摘要 詩人想像自己來自斯洛伐克的祖父母初抵美國時的情景。他們到達自己夢想之土的第一站就是位於紐約的愛麗斯島。他接著描寫自己身為美洲原住民的外祖父母。他指出他們一直以來都居住在美國。他們的生活方式在歐洲人來了之後卻遭到破壞。

Đảo Ellis
Joseph Bruchac

Tóm Tắt Nhà thơ tưởng tượng ông bà mình—những người Slovakia khi họ đến nước Mỹ. Chặng dừng chân đầu tiên của họ trên mảnh đất trong mơ của mình là Đảo Ellis ở New York. Rồi ông viết về ông bà người Thổ Dân Mỹ của mình. Ông cho biết họ đã sống cả đời mình trên đất Mỹ và lối sống của họ đã bị mất đi khi những người Châu Âu đến.

엘리스 섬 (Ellis Island)
Joseph Bruchac

요약 시인은 슬로바키아 태생의 조부모가 미국에 처음 도착했을 때를 상상해 본다. 약속의 땅에서 조부모가 처음 정착한 곳은 뉴욕의 엘리스 섬이었다. 그리고 나서 시인은 이번에는 아메리카 인디언인 조부모에 대해 글을 쓴다. 인디언들은 오래 전부터 미국에 살고 있었으나 유럽인들이 들어오면서부터 삶은 파괴되었다.

UNIT 6: SUMMARY TRANSLATIONS

Choice: A Tribute to Martin Luther King, Jr.

Alice Walker

Summary The author describes Dr. King's successes with the civil rights movement. She explains how Dr. King inspired African Americans to appreciate their heritage.

Elección: Un tributo a Martin Luther King, Jr.

Alice Walker

Resumen La autora describe los triunfos del Dr. King que dieron lugar al movimiento por los derechos civiles. Ella explica cómo el Dr. King inspiró a los afroamericanos para que valoren su patrimonio.

Chwa : Yon omaj pou Martin Luther King, Jr.

Alice Walker

Rezime Otè a dekri siksè doktè King te genyen avèk mouvman dwa sivil la. Li eksplike ki jan doktè King te enspire afriken ameriken yo pou yo apresye eritaj yo.

Pagpili: Isang Parangál kay Martin Luther King, Jr.

Alice Walker

Buod Inilalarawan ng manunulat ang mga tagumpay ni Doktor King sa kilusan para sa mga karapatang sibil. Ipinaliliwanag niya kung paano binigyang-diwa ni Dr. King ang mga Aprikano-Amerikano para ikalugod nila ang kanilang lahing-pamana.

Kev Xaiv: Ib Zag Sau Hawm Txog Martin Luther King, Jr.

Alice Walker

Lub Ntsiab Tus sau piav txog Dr. King txoj kev vam meej ua haujlwm nrog txoj kev txhawb kom muaj vaj huam sib luag. Nws piav tias Dr. King tau ua ib tug qauv zoo kom haiv neeg Meskas Dub muaj kev zoo siab hawm txog lawv keev kwm thiab.

《選擇：向馬丁・路德・金致敬》 (Choice: A Tribute to Martin Luther King, Jr.)

Alice Walker

摘要 作者描寫金博士在民權運動方面的成就。她描述了金博士如何鼓勵非洲裔美國人欣賞自己的傳統文化。

Sự Lựa Chọn: Tưởng Nhớ Martin Luther King, Jr.

Alice Walker

Tóm Tắt Tác giả miêu tả những thành công của Tiến Sĩ King trong phong trào đấu tranh vì quyền công dân. Bà miêu tả Tiến Sĩ King đã truyền nhiệt huyết của mình cho những người dân Mỹ gốc Phi như thế nào để họ có thể biết được giá trị di sản của mình.

선택: 마틴 루터 킹 주니어에게 바침 (Choice: A Tribute to Martin Luther King, Jr.)

Alice Walker

요약 작가는 인권 운동가로서 성공한 킹 박사에 관해 쓰고 있다. 킹 박사가 미국 흑인들에게 어떻게 영감을 불어넣어 자신들이 물려받은 것을 고마워하도록 만들었는지 설명하고 있다.

T78 **English Learner's Notebook**

SUMMARY TRANSLATIONS

An Episode of War
Stephen Crane

Summary A Civil War lieutenant is shot by a stray bullet. The other soldiers are worried for him. The doctors and medical staff act as if he is a bother. The lieutenant is ashamed that he was not shot in battle. His armed is removed. The lieutenant tells his family that missing an arm does not really matter.

Un episodio de guerra
Stephen Crane

Resumen Un teniente de la Guerra Civil es herido por una bala perdida. Los demás soldados se preocupan por él. Los médicos y el equipo de asistencia actúan como si el teniente fuera una molestia. El teniente se avergüenza por no haber sido herido en combate. Y le amputan un brazo. El teniente le explica a su familia que tener un solo brazo no es realmente importante.

Yon epizòd lagè
Stephen Crane

Rezime Yon bal aksidantèl frape yon lyetnan Lagè Sivil la. Lòt sòlda yo enkyete pou li. Doktè yo ak pèsonèl medikal la fè kòmsi li se yon nwizans. Lyetnan an wont dèske se pa nan batay la li te pran bal la. Yo retire bra l. Lyetnan an di fanmi l konsa manke yon bra pa tèlman gen enpòtans.

Isang Kabanata ng Digmaan
Stephen Crane

Buod Ang isang tenyente sa Digmaang Sibil ay nabaril ng isang balang ligaw. Ang ibang mga sundalo ay nag-aalala tungkol sa kanya. Ang mga doktor at ang kanilang mga taga-tulong ay kumikilos na parang nakakaabala siya. Ang tenyente ay nahihiya dahil hindi siya nabaril sa labanan. Ang braso niya ay pinutol. Sinabi ng tenyente na hindi na bale kahit nawalan siya ng braso.

UNIT 6
SUMMARY TRANSLATIONS

Ib Zaj Hais Txog Kev Ua Tsov Rog
Stephen Crane

Lub Ntsiab Ib tug tub rog qib siab ntawm kev tua rog Civil War raug mob los ntawm ib lub mos txwv. Lwm cov tub rog txhawj txog nws heev. Cov kws kho mob thiab cov pab neeg raug mob sawvdaws ua li nws yog lawv ib tug kwv tij. Tus tub rog qib siab no txaj muag heev tias nws tsis yog raug mos txwv tua rau nraum tshav rog. Tagnrho nws txhais caj npab raug txiav tawm lawm. Tus tub rog no hais rau nws tsev neeg tsis muaj ib sab tes lawm los tsis ua li cas.

《戰爭的一件插曲》(An Episode of War)
Stephen Crane

摘要 南北戰爭中一名中尉被一顆流彈擊中。其他士兵極為擔心他。醫生和醫護兵都將他視為兄弟般的照顧他。這名中尉對於自己並不是在作戰時受傷感到羞愧。他的手臂被割除。中尉告訴自己的家人，喪失了一隻手臂其實沒甚麼大礙。

Một Câu Truyện Về Chiến Tranh
Stephen Crane

Tóm Tắt Một trung úy trong Cuộc Nội Chiến bị thương bởi một viên đạn lạc. Các quân nhân khác thấy lo lắng cho anh ta. Các bác sĩ và y tá lấy làm phiền hà khi phải chăm sóc cho anh ta. Viên trung úy cảm thấy xấu hổ vì không phải mình bị thương trên chiến trường. Cánh tay của anh ta bị cắt bỏ. Viên trung úy nói với gia đình mình rằng mất một cánh tay thực sự không là vấn đề gì cả.

전쟁에서 생긴 한 에피소드 (An Episode of War)
Stephen Crane

요약 남북전쟁 당시 한 대령이 빗나간 총알에 맞는다. 병사들은 그를 걱정해 주고 의사와 의료병들도 마치 형제처럼 잘 대해준다. 그러나 전투 중이 아니라 그냥 빗나간 총알에 맞은 것이 대령은 창피하다. 결국은 팔 한쪽을 잃게 되나 대령은 가족에게 팔을 잃은 것은 아무런 문제가 되지 않는다고 이야기한다.

PART 3: TURBO VOCABULARY

The exercises and tools presented here are designed to help you increase your vocabulary. Review the instruction and complete the exercises to build your vocabulary knowledge. Throughout the year, you can apply these skills and strategies to improve your reading, writing, speaking, and listening vocabulary.

Word Roots	V2
Prefixes	V4
Suffixes	V6
Using a Dictionary	V8
Word Study Cards	V10
Unit 1: Academic Vocabulary Words:	V12
Unit 2: Academic Vocabulary Words:	V14
Unit 3: Academic Vocabulary Words:	V16
Unit 4: Academic Vocabulary Words:	V18
Unit 5: Academic Vocabulary Words:	V20
Unit 6: Academic Vocabulary Words:	V22
Words in Other Subjects	V24
Vocabulary Flash Cards	V25
Vocabulary Fold-a-List	V29
Commonly Misspelled Words	V33
Word Attack Skills: Phonics	V35
Mnemonics	V37
Communication Strategies	V39
Vocabulary Bookmarks	V40
Vocabulary Builder Cards	V42
Personal Thesaurus	V44

WORD ROOTS

The following list contains common word roots with meanings and examples. On the blank lines, write other words you know that have the same roots. Write the meanings of the new words.

Root	Meaning	Example and Meaning	Your Words	Meanings
-brev-	brief; short	*brevity:* the quality of lasting for a short time		
-cede-	go	*recede:* move or go away or move or go back		
-dict-	say or tell	*predict:* tell what might happen next		
-fac-	make	*factory:* place where things are made		
-fer-	bring; carry	*reference:* something you say or write that mentions another person or thing, something that brings or carries more information		
-ject-	throw	*eject:* push or throw out with force		
-manu-	hand	*manual:* operated or done by hand		

Root	Meaning	Example and Meaning	Your Words	Meanings
-phon-	hearing; sound	*telephone*: a device that brings sound over long distances		
-port-	carry	*support*: carry or hold something up		
-scrib-	write	*scribble*: write something quickly in a messy way		
-sequ-	follow	*consequence*: effect that follows a cause		
-similis-	same	*similar*: alike in some way		
-spec-	look; see	*inspect*: look carefully at something		
-sum-	take; use	*assumption*: something that you think is true or take as true		
-tele-	far; distant	*telescope*: instrument that makes distant objects look larger		
-vali-	strong; worth	*valid*: true, based on strong reasons or facts		
-ver-	truth	*verify*: make sure something is true		

Word Roots

PREFIXES

The following list contains common prefixes with meanings and examples. On the blank lines, write other words you know that begin with the same prefixes. Write the meanings of the new words.

Prefix	Meaning	Example and Meaning	Your Words	Meanings
anti-	against	*antisocial*: not liking to meet and talk to people; against friendliness		
aud-	hearing; sound	*auditorium*: a room for hearing concerts or speeches		
con-	with; together	*concur*: agree with		
de-	down; from	*decrease*: become less		
dis-	not	*disorganized*: not organized		
in-	without; not	*incapable*: not able		
inter-	between	*intermission*: short period of time between the parts of a play or concert		
ir-	without; not	*irregular*: not regular		

Prefix	Meaning	Example and Meaning	Your Words	Meanings
mis-	wrong; bad	*misspell*: spell wrong; spell incorrectly		
multi-	many	*multicolored*: having many colors		
non-	without; not	*nonfat*: without fat		
ob-	against	*obstacle*: something that works against another, something that makes it difficult for you to succeed		
post-	after	*post-test*: a test given after instruction		
pre-	before	*preview*: look before		
re-	again	*remake*: make again		
sub-	below, under	*submarine*: a ship that moves under the ocean		
super-	above; over	*superior*: better than another		
un-/an-/a-	not	*unbelievable*: not believable		

Prefixes

SUFFIXES

The following list contains common suffixes with meanings and examples. On the blank lines, write other words you know that have the same suffixes. Write the meanings of the new words.

Suffix	Meaning	Example and Meaning	Your Words	Meanings
-able/-ible	able to be	*movable*: able to be moved		
-al	relating to	*financial*: relating to money		
-ance/-ence	act of; state of; quality of	*assistance*: act of giving help		
-ate	make	*motivate*: make someone feel eager to do something		
-en	make	*weaken*: make something less strong		
-er/-or	one who	*actor*: person who acts		
-ful	filled with	*joyful*: filled with happiness		
-hood	state or quality of	*manhood*: the state of being an adult male		

V6 English Learner's Notebook

Suffix	Meaning	Example and Meaning	Your Words	Meanings
-ic	like; pertaining to	*heroic*: like a hero; brave		
-ish	resembling	*foolish*: not sensible		
-ist	one who	*violinist*: person who plays the violin		
-ize/-yze	make	*publicize*: make public; tell people about		
-less	without	*powerless*: without power		
-ly	in a way	*quickly*: done in a short amount of time		
-ment	act or quality of	*excitement*: feeling of being excited		
-ness	state or quality of	*kindness*: friendly and caring behavior		
-ous	having; full of	*famous*: having fame; known and recognized by many people		
-sion/-tion	act or process of	*persuasion*: act of convincing someone		

Suffixes V7

USING A DICTIONARY

Use a **dictionary** to find the correct spelling, the meaning, the pronunciation, and the part of speech of a word. The dictionary will show you how the plural is formed if it is irregular. You can also find the word's history, or *etymology,* in a dictionary. Etymology explains how words change, how they are borrowed from other languages, and how new words are invented, or "coined."

Here is a sample entry from a dictionary. Notice what it tells about the word. Then, follow the instructions.

> **lemon** (lem´ ən) **n.** [ME *lymon* < MFr *limon* < Ar *laimūn* < Pers *līmūn*] **1** a small, egg-shaped, edible citrus fruit with a yellow rind and a juicy, sour pulp, rich in ascorbic acid **2** the small, spiny, semitropical evergreen citrus tree (*Citrus limon*) bearing this fruit **3** pale yellow **4** [slang] something, esp. a manufactured article, that is defective or imperfect

1. Circle the *n.* in the dictionary entry. It stands for *noun.* Write what these other parts of speech abbreviations mean: *v.* _____, *adv.* _____, *adj.* _____, *prep.* _____.

2. Underline the origins of the word *lemon.* ME stands for Middle English, Ar stands for Arabic, and Pers. stands for Persian. What do you think MFr stands for? _____

3. Put a box around the pronunciation.

4. How many noun definitions does the entry have? _____

5. Which definition is slang? _____

6. Which definition of *lemon* is used in the following sentence? _____
The car that my dad bought turned out to be a lemon.

Activity: Use a dictionary to learn about the origins of these words.

Activity: Use a dictionary to learn about the origins of these words.

1. literature _____ / _____ / _____
                pronunciation   main part of speech   original language(s)

   _____ / _____
      1st meaning   other meanings

   _____
   _____
   _____

2. language _____ / _____ / _____
              pronunciation   main part of speech   original language(s)

   _____ / _____
      1st meaning   other meanings

   _____
   _____
   _____

Activity: Look up each of the following words in a dictionary. Then, write a definition of the word and a sentence using the word.

moment _____
_____

popular _____
_____

remedy _____
_____

blur _____
_____

lazy _____
_____

Using a Dictionary

WORD STUDY CARDS

Use these word study cards to break big words into their parts. Write the word at the top of the card. Then, divide the word into its prefix, root, and suffix. Note that not all words have prefixes and suffixes. List the meaning of each part of the word. Next, find three words with the same root and write them on the card. Finally, write the word's part of speech and its definition. Use a dictionary to help you. One example has been done for you.

Word: invisible

Prefix	**Root**	**Suffix**
in: not	**vis:** see	**ible**-able to be

Root-related Words
1. vision
2. revise
3. visibility

Definition: invisible *adj.* not able to be seen

Word:

Prefix	**Root**	**Suffix**

Root-related Words
1.
2.
3.

Definition:

WORD STUDY CARDS

Word:

| Prefix | Root | Suffix |

Root-related Words
1.
2.
3.

Definition:

Word:

| Prefix | Root | Suffix |

Root-related Words
1.
2.
3.

Definition:

Word:

| Prefix | Root | Suffix |

Root-related Words
1.
2.
3.

Definition:

UNIT 1: ACADEMIC VOCABULARY WORDS

achieve (uh CHEEV) *v.* succeed; accomplish
analyze (AN uh lyz) *v.* study the parts of something
anticipate (an TIS uh payt) *v.* look forward to, expect
determine (dee TER muhn) *v.* figure out
establish (uh STAB lish) *v.* show or prove
formulate (FOHR myoo layt) *v.* make a statement, form an idea
intention (in TEN shuhn) *n.* purpose; goal
modify (MAHD uh fy) *v.* change
predict (pree DIKT) *v.* make a logical assumption about future events
revise (ri VYZ) *v.* correct, improve, or change

A. True/False For each of the following, mark T or F to indicate whether the italicized vocabulary word has been used correctly in the sentence. If you have marked F, correct the sentence by using the word properly.

1. _____ If you *modify* your answer, you leave it exactly the same as it is.

2. _____ You can *predict* how a story will end by paying attention to the author's clues.

3. _____ Based on reliable evidence, the scientist will *formulate* a new theory.

4. _____ Rita *anticipates* the trip that she went on last week.

5. _____ Most students *achieve* their goals in school by failing tests.

6. _____ When you *analyze* a story, you look at the plot details.

7. _____ Roger uses the blinker on his car to *determine* where he is going to turn.

8. _____ When you *revise* an essay, you usually try to make it incorrect.

9. _____ The author's *intention* is to bore readers.

10. _____ Use facts to *establish* what is true.

B. Use each word pair in an original sentence that illustrates the meaning of the academic vocabulary word.

achieve/goal _____

_____

analyze/situation _____

_____

anticipate/party _____

_____

determine/truth _____

_____

establish/rules _____

_____

formulate/idea _____

_____

intention/persuade _____

_____

modify/answer _____

_____

predict/conclusion _____

_____

revise/errors _____

_____

Academic Vocabulary Words

UNIT 2: ACADEMIC VOCABULARY WORDS

aspect (AS pekt) *n.* the specific part that you are observing or studying
conclude (kuhn KLOOD) *v.* decide by reasoning
differentiate (dif uhr EN shee ayt) *v.* show how things are different
evidence (EV uh duhns) *n.* facts that serve as clues or proof
examine (eg ZAM uhn) *v.* study carefully
indicate (IN di kayt) *v.* show; hint at
infer (in FER) *v.* draw conclusions based on facts
logical (LAHJ i kuhl) *adj.* reasonable; sensible
similar (SIM uh luhr) *adj.* alike
unique (yoo NEEK) *adj.* having nothing that is similar or equal

A. True/False For each of the following, mark T or F to indicate whether the italicized vocabulary word has been used correctly in the sentence. If you have marked F, correct the sentence by using the word properly.

1. _____ It is *logical* to think that monkeys can fly.

2. _____ What can you *infer* about the main character from the way he dresses?

3. _____ Ben can *differentiate* between books by describing how they are the same.

4. _____ Two pens that look exactly alike are *unique*.

5. _____ The left blinker in the car is used to *indicate* a left turn.

6. _____ Jason found *evidence* to support his theory.

7. _____ Facts *examine* the author's purpose.

8. _____ What can you *conclude* from the details in the story?

9. _____ *Examine* the tent carefully for leaks.

10. _____ How *similar* was the movie version to the book?

B. Use each word pair in an original sentence that illustrates the meaning of the academic vocabulary word.

aspect/character _____

_____

conclude/detail _____

_____

differentiate/novels _____

_____

evidence/prove _____

_____

examine/details _____

_____

indicate/correct _____

_____

infer/details _____

_____

logical/answer _____

_____

similar/traits _____

_____

unique/characteristic _____

_____

UNIT 3: ACADEMIC VOCABULARY WORDS

accurate (AK yuh ruht) *adj.* free from error; correct; exact
bias (BY uhs) *n.* unfair preference or dislike for someone or something
cite (SYT) *v.* refer to an example or fact as proof
credible (KRED uh buhl) *adj.* believable; reliable
focus (FOH kuhs) *n.* the central point of a work
focus (FOH kuhs) *v.* concentrate on one thing
imply (im PLY) *v.* hint at; suggest
implied (im PLYD) *adj.* suggested
pertinent (PERT uhn uhnt) *adj.* relevant; having a connection
suggest (suhg JEST) *v.* show indirectly; imply
support (suh PORT) *v.* provide evidence to prove or back up an idea
topic (TAHP ik) *n.* the subject

A. Code Name Use the code to figure out each vocabulary word. Each letter is represented by a number or symbol. This exercise will help you learn how to spell and recognize the vocabulary words.

%	5	•	*	2	#	!	7	^	&	9	¶	£	$	3	¥	+	=	?	÷	4	¢	6	§	«	ç
a	b	c	d	e	f	g	h	i	j	k	l	m	n	o	p	q	r	s	t	u	v	w	x	y	z

1. # 3 • 4 ?   _____ focus
2. ¥ 2 = ÷ ^ $ 2 $ ÷   _____ pertinent
3. ^ £ ¥ ¶ ^ 2 *   _____ implied
4. % • • 4 = % ÷ 2   _____ accurate
5. • = 2 * ^ 5 ¶ 2   _____ credible
6. ? 4 ¥ ¥ 3 = ÷   _____ support
7. ÷ 3 ¥ ^ •   _____ topic
8. 5 ^ % ?   _____ bias
9. • ^ ÷ 2   _____ cite
10. ? 4 ! ! 2 ? ÷   _____ suggest

B. Answer each question. Then, explain your answer.

1. Would drama be a good *topic* for a science paper? _____
   _____

2. If an answer is *accurate*, are there mistakes in it? _____
   _____

3. When you are trying to *focus* on homework, is it a good idea to watch television? _____
   _____

4. If a suggestion is *implied*, is it generally stated aloud? _____

5. Would a *pertinent* comment have anything to do with the topic being discussed? _____
   _____

6. Would you expect someone with a *bias* to always be fair? _____
   _____

7. Is it a good idea to *support* your ideas with facts and examples? _____
   _____

8. If someone you knew told a lot of lies, would she be *credible*? _____
   _____

9. If an article *suggests* that there is life on Mars, would it be directly stated? _____
   _____

10. If the author *cites* the work of someone else, does she mention the work? _____
    _____

Academic Vocabulary Words   V17

UNIT 4: ACADEMIC VOCABULARY WORDS

adapt (uh DAPT) *v.* change something to make it more suitable
clarify (KLAR uh fy) *v.* explain; make clearer
confirm (kun FERM) *v.* make certain; prove to be correct
context (KAHN tekst) *n.* text surrounding an unfamiliar word
convey (kuhn VAY) *v.* carry meaning; communicate
emphasize (EM fuh syz) *v.* stress
reflect (ri FLEKT) *v.* mirror an image; express or show
restate (ree STAYT) *v.* express the same idea in a different way
restatement (ree STAYT muhnt) *n.* expressing the same idea in different words
synonymous (si NAHN uh muhs) *adj.* having the same, or nearly the same, meaning

A. Completion Complete each sentence that has been started for you. Your sentence completion should be logical and illustrate the meaning of the vocabulary word in italics.

1. Some words that are *synonymous* with happy are _____

2. The teacher tried to *clarify* _____

3. A smile can *convey* _____

4. A writer might *adapt* a story to _____

5. It is a good idea to *restate* a poem so that _____

6. You can *confirm* a fact by _____

7. If you look at the *context* surrounding an unfamiliar word, you may be able to _____

8. One way to *emphasize* an important idea in writing is to _____

9. A good reason for a *restatement* of an idea is _____
_____

10. A restatement should *reflect* _____
_____

B. Using the word pair, write an original sentence that illustrates the meaning of the academic vocabulary word.

reflect/image _____
_____

convey/meaning _____
_____

emphasize/main point _____
_____

restate/words _____
_____

adapt/story _____
_____

synonymous/words _____
_____

restatement/idea _____
_____

confirm/report _____
_____

context/unfamiliar _____
_____

clarify/difficult _____
_____

Academic Vocabulary Words

UNIT 5: ACADEMIC VOCABULARY WORDS

assumption (uh SUMP shuhn) *n.* something one supposed to be true, without proof
connect (kuh NEKT) *v.* show how things are related
consequence (KAHN si kwens) *n.* result; outcome
evaluate (ee VAL yoo ayt) *v.* judge; determine the worth or strength of something
factor (FAK tuhr) *n.* something that helps bring about a result
impact (IM pakt) *n.* the power to produce changes or effects
influence (IN floo uhns) *n.* ability to affect results
rational (RASH uhn uhl) *adj.* based on reason; logical
reaction (ree AK shuhn) *n.* response to an influence or force
valid (VAL id) *adj.* based on facts and strong evidence; convincing

A. Completion Complete each sentence that has been started for you. Your sentence completion should be logical and illustrate the meaning of the vocabulary word in italics.

1. One *consequence* of a heavy rain might be _____
_____

2. Do not make *assumptions* if _____
_____

3. A *valid* conclusion would _____
_____

4. A strange *reaction* to a scary movie would be _____
_____

5. One *factor* in success in school is _____
_____

6. A *rational* reason to go to bed early is _____
_____

7. If you *connect* all the facts, you will _____
_____

8. One way that teachers *evaluate* students is _____
_____

English Learner's Notebook

9. The event that has had the biggest influence on my life so far is _____
_____

10. Books can have an impact on _____
_____

B. Using the academic word pair, write an original sentence that illustrates the meaning of the words.

factor/influence _____
_____

consequence/impact _____
_____

reaction/rational _____
_____

assumption/valid _____
_____

evaluate/connect _____
_____

Academic Vocabulary Words V21

UNIT 6: ACADEMIC VOCABULARY WORDS

critique (kri TEEK) *v.* write a critical essay or review
disorganized (dis OHR guh nyzd) *adj.* not arranged in a logical order
essential (uh SEN shuhl) *adj.* necessary
extract (ek STRAKT) *v.* deduce; obtain
focus (FOH kuhs) *v.* direct one's attention to a specific part of something
identify (y DEN tuh fy) *v.* recognize; find and name
organized (OHR guh nyzd) *v.* arranged in a logical order
revise (ri VYZ) *v.* change; adjust
sequence (SEE kwuhns) *n.* order
skim (SKIM) *v.* read quickly, skipping parts of the text

A. True/False For each of the following, mark T or F to indicate whether the italicized vocabulary word has been used correctly in the sentence. If you have marked F, correct the sentence by using the word properly.

1. _____ A telephone book should be *organized* in alphabetic order.

2. _____ If you *skim* a book, you read every single word.

3. _____ When you *revise* an essay, you should not change anything.

4. _____ We will *identify* the dishes after dinner.

5. _____ Please, *critique* my essay for me before I turn it in.

6. _____ A dictionary is an *essential* tool for an English student.

7. _____ If something is out of *sequence*, it is in the correct order.

8. _____ A *disorganized* desk would be very neat and orderly.

9. _____ If you are supposed to *focus* on a reading, you should sit in a quiet place.

10. _____ To *extract* important information from a text, only read every other word.

B. Answer each question. Then, explain your answer.

1. Is a television *essential* for life in the United States? _____
   _____

2. How would you *extract* information from an encyclopedia? _____
   _____

3. Will a *disorganized* summary help you remember key ideas? _____
   _____

4. Should words in a dictionary be *organized* in order of importance? _____
   _____

5. What would be a logical *sequence* for events in a story? _____
   _____

6. Why might you *revise* your essay? _____
   _____

7. If you were asked to *skim* a magazine article, would you read it slowly and
   carefully? _____
   _____

8. Could you *critique* a novel without reading it? _____
   _____

9. If you are asked to *focus* on a sentence, should you flip through the whole
   book? _____
   _____

10. If you were asked to *identify* the main character in a story, what would you do?
    _____

Academic Vocabulary Words

WORDS IN OTHER SUBJECTS

Use this page to write down academic words you come across in other subjects, such as social studies or science. When you are reading your textbooks, you may find words that you need to learn. Following the example, write down the word, the part of speech, and an explanation of the word. You may want to write an example sentence to help you remember the word.

dissolve *verb* to make something solid become part of a liquid by putting it in a liquid and mixing it

The sugar *dissolved* in the hot tea.

_____
_____
_____
_____
_____
_____
_____
_____
_____
_____
_____
_____
_____
_____
_____
_____

VOCABULARY FLASH CARDS

Use these flash cards to study words you want to remember. The words on this page come from Unit 1. Cut along the dotted lines on pages V25 through V32 to create your own flash cards or use index cards. Write the word on the front of the card. On the back, write the word's part of speech and definition. Then, write a sentence that shows the meaning of the word.

lurking	burdened	finery
innumerable	preliminary	descendants
virtuous	retribution	unobtrusively

VOCABULARY FLASH CARDS

verb ready to spring out, attack; existing undiscovered The man was lurking in the shadows so we did not see him.	*adjective* weighted down by work, duty, or sorrow The old man seemed to be burdened with worry.	*noun* fancy clothing and accessories The girls felt glamorous in their borrowed finery.
adjective too numerable to be counted There are innumerable stars in the desert sky.	*adjective* introductory; preparatory The dinner began with a preliminary appetizer.	*noun* children, grandchildren, and continuing generations The old man willed all of his possessions to his many descendants.
adjective moral; upright A virtuous man respects the rights of others.	*noun* punishment for wrongdoing The victim wanted retribution from the man who robbed him.	*adverb* without calling attention to oneself She slipped out of the room unobtrusively.

V26 English Learner's Notebook

VOCABULARY FLASH CARDS

Use these flash cards to study words you want to remember. Cut along the dotted lines on pages V25 through V32 to create your own flash cards or use index cards. Write the word on the front of the card. On the back, write the word's part of speech and definition. Then, write a sentence that shows the meaning of the word.

VOCABULARY FLASH CARDS

VOCABULARY FOLD-A-LIST

Use a fold-a-list to study the definitions of words. The words on this page come from Unit 1. Write the definition for each word on the lines. Fold the paper along the dotted line to check your definition. Create your own fold-a-lists on pages V35 through V38.

sinister _____

compliance _____

tangible _____

impaired _____

rigorous _____

inexplicable _____

celestial _____

exertion _____

maneuver _____

ascent _____

Fold In ←

VOCABULARY FOLD-A-LIST

Write the word that matches the definition on each line.
Fold the paper along the dotted line to check your work.

threatening harm or evil   _____

agreement to a request   _____

able to be perceived by
the senses   _____

made weaker or less useful   _____

very harsh or strict   _____

not possible to explain   _____

heavenly   _____

energetic activity; effort   _____

series of planned steps   _____

the act of climbing or rising   _____

Fold In ←

English Learner's Notebook

VOCABULARY FOLD-A-LIST

Write the words you want to study on this side of the page. Write the definitions on the back. Then, test yourself. Fold the paper along the dotted line to check your definition.

Word: _____

_____

Word: _____

_____

Word: _____

_____

Word: _____

_____

Word: _____

_____

Word: _____

_____

Word: _____

_____

Word: _____

_____

Word: _____

_____

Word: _____

_____

Fold In ←

VOCABULARY FOLD-A-LIST

Write the word that matches the definition on each line.
Fold the paper along the dotted line to check your work.

Definition: _____

Definition: _____

Definition: _____

Definition: _____

Definition: _____

Definition: _____

Definition: _____

Definition: _____

Definition: _____

Definition: _____

Fold In ←

COMMONLY MISSPELLED WORDS

The list on these pages presents words that cause problems for many people. Some of these words are spelled according to set rules, but others follow no specific rules. As you review this list, check to see how many of the words give you trouble in your own writing. Then, add your own commonly misspelled words on the lines that follow.

abbreviate	auxiliary	census	deficient
absence	awkward	certain	definitely
absolutely	bandage	changeable	delinquent
abundance	banquet	characteristic	dependent
accelerate	bargain	chauffeur	descendant
accidentally	barrel	chief	description
accumulate	battery	clothes	desert
accurate	beautiful	coincidence	desirable
ache	beggar	colonel	dessert
achievement	beginning	column	deteriorate
acquaintance	behavior	commercial	dining
adequate	believe	commission	disappointed
admittance	benefit	commitment	disastrous
advertisement	bicycle	committee	discipline
aerial	biscuit	competitor	dissatisfied
affect	bookkeeper	concede	distinguish
aggravate	bought	condemn	effect
aggressive	boulevard	congratulate	eighth
agreeable	brief	connoisseur	eligible
aisle	brilliant	conscience	embarrass
all right	bruise	conscientious	enthusiastic
allowance	bulletin	conscious	entrepreneur
aluminum	buoyant	contemporary	envelope
amateur	bureau	continuous	environment
analysis	bury	controversy	equipped
analyze	buses	convenience	equivalent
ancient	business	coolly	especially
anecdote	cafeteria	cooperate	exaggerate
anniversary	calendar	cordially	exceed
anonymous	campaign	correspondence	excellent
answer	canceled	counterfeit	exercise
anticipate	candidate	courageous	exhibition
anxiety	capacity	courteous	existence
apologize	capital	courtesy	experience
appall	capitol	criticism	explanation
appearance	captain	criticize	extension
appreciate	career	curiosity	extraordinary
appropriate	carriage	curious	familiar
architecture	cashier	cylinder	fascinating
argument	catastrophe	deceive	February
associate	category	decision	fiery
athletic	ceiling	deductible	financial
attendance	cemetery	defendant	fluorescent

foreign	minuscule	proceed	_____
fourth	miscellaneous	prominent	_____
fragile	mischievous	pronunciation	_____
gauge	misspell	psychology	_____
generally	mortgage	publicly	_____
genius	naturally	pursue	_____
genuine	necessary	questionnaire	_____
government	neighbor	realize	_____
grammar	neutral	really	_____
grievance	nickel	recede	_____
guarantee	niece	receipt	_____
guard	ninety	receive	_____
guidance	noticeable	recognize	_____
handkerchief	nuisance	recommend	_____
harass	obstacle	reference	_____
height	occasion	referred	_____
humorous	occasionally	rehearse	_____
hygiene	occur	relevant	_____
ignorant	occurred	reminiscence	_____
immediately	occurrence	renowned	_____
immigrant	omitted	repetition	_____
independence	opinion	restaurant	_____
independent	opportunity	rhythm	_____
indispensable	optimistic	ridiculous	_____
individual	outrageous	sandwich	_____
inflammable	pamphlet	satellite	_____
intelligence	parallel	schedule	_____
interfere	paralyze	scissors	_____
irrelevant	parentheses	secretary	_____
irritable	particularly	siege	_____
jewelry	patience	solely	_____
judgment	permanent	sponsor	_____
knowledge	permissible	subtle	_____
lawyer	perseverance	subtlety	_____
legible	persistent	superintendent	_____
legislature	personally	supersede	_____
leisure	perspiration	surveillance	_____
liable	persuade	susceptible	_____
library	phenomenal	tariff	_____
license	phenomenon	temperamental	_____
lieutenant	physician	theater	_____
lightning	pleasant	threshold	_____
likable	pneumonia	truly	_____
liquefy	possess	unmanageable	_____
literature	possession	unwieldy	_____
loneliness	possibility	usage	_____
magnificent	prairie	usually	_____
maintenance	precede	valuable	_____
marriage	preferable	various	_____
mathematics	prejudice	vegetable	_____
maximum	preparation	voluntary	_____
meanness	previous	weight	_____
mediocre	primitive	weird	_____
mileage	privilege	whale	_____
millionaire	probably	wield	_____
minimum	procedure	yield	_____

WORD ATTACK SKILLS

When you are reading, you will find many unfamiliar words. Here are some tools that you can use to help you read unfamiliar words.

Phonics

Phonics is the science or study of sound. When you learn to read, you learn to associate certain sounds with certain letters or letter combinations. You know most of the sounds that letters can represent in English. When letters are combined, however, it is not always so easy to know what sound is represented. In English, there are some rules and patterns that will help you determine how to pronounce a word. This chart shows you some of the vowel digraphs, which are combinations like *ea* and *oa*. Two vowels together are called vowel digraphs. Usually, vowel digraphs represent the long sound of the first vowel.

Vowel Diagraphs	Examples of Usual Sounds	Exceptions
ee and *ea*	steep, each, treat, sea	head, sweat, dread
ai and *ay*	plain, paid, may, betray	plaid
oa, ow, and *oe*	soak, slow, doe	now, shoe
ie and *igh*	lie, night, delight	friend, eight

As you read, sometimes the only way to know how to pronounce a word with an *ea* spelling is to see if the word makes sense in the sentence. Look at this example:

The water pipes were made of *lead*.

First, try out the long sound "ee." Ask yourself if it sounds right. It does not. Then, try the short sound "e." You will find that the short sound is correct in that sentence.

Now try this example.

Where you *lead*, I will follow.

Word Patterns

Recognizing different vowel-consonant patterns will help you read longer words. In the following sections, the V stands for "vowel" and the C stands for "consonant."

Single-syllable Words

CV – go: In two letter words with a consonant followed by a vowel, the vowel is usually long. For example, the word *go* is pronounced with a long *o* sound.

In a single syllable word, a vowel followed only by a single consonant is usually short.

CVC – got: If you add a consonant to the word *go*, such as the *t* in *got*, the vowel sound is a short *o*. Say the words *go* and *got* aloud and notice the difference in pronunciation.

Multi-syllable words

In words of more than one syllable, notice the letters that follow a vowel.

VCCV – robber: A single vowel followed by two consonants is usually short.

VCV — begin: A single vowel followed by a single consonant is usually long.

VCe — beside: An extension of the VCV pattern is vowel-consonant-silent *e*. In these words, the vowel is long and the *e* is not pronounced.

When you see a word with the VCV pattern, try the long vowel sound first. If the word does not make sense, try the short sound. Pronounce the words *model, camel,* and *closet*. First, try the long vowel sound. That does not sound correct, so try the short vowel sound. The short vowel sound is correct in those words.

Remember that patterns help you get started on figuring out a word. You will sometimes need to try a different sound or find the word in a dictionary.

As you read and find unfamiliar words, look the pronunciations up in a dictionary. Write the words in this chart in the correct column to help you notice patterns and remember pronunciations.

Syllables	Example	New words	Vowel
CV	go		long
CVC	got		short
VCC	robber		short
V/CV	begin open		long long
VC/V	closet		short

MNEMONICS

Mnemonics are devices, or methods, that help you remember things. The basic strategy is to link something you do not know with something that you *do* know. Here are some common mnemonic devices:

Visualizing Create a picture in your head that will help you remember the meaning of a vocabulary word. For example, the first four letters of the word *significance* spell *sign*. Picture a sign with the word *meaning* written on it to remember that significance means "meaning" or "importance."

Spelling The way a word is spelled can help you remember its meaning. For example, you might remember that *clarify* means to "make clear" if you notice that both *clarify* and *clear* start with the letters *cl*.

To help you remember how to spell certain words, look for a familiar word within the difficult word. For example:

Believe has a *lie* in it.

Separate is *a rat* of a word to spell.

Your *principal* is your *pal*.

Rhyming Here is a popular rhyme that helps people figure out how to spell *ei* and *ie* words.

<u>i</u> before <u>e</u> — except after <u>c</u> or when sounding like <u>a</u> as in neighbor and weigh.

List words here that you need help remembering. Work with a group to create mnemonic devices to help you remember each word.

_____   _____

_____   _____

_____   _____

_____   _____

List words here that you need help remembering. Work with a group to create mnemonic devices to help you remember each word.

COMMUNICATION STRATEGIES

Use these sentence starters to help you express yourself clearly in different classroom situations.

Expressing an Opinion
I think that _____
I believe that _____
In my opinion, _____

Agreeing
I agree with _____ that _____
I see what you mean.
That's an interesting idea.
My idea is similar to _____'s idea.
My idea builds upon _____'s idea.

Disagreeing
I don't completely agree with you because _____
My opinion is different than yours.
I got a different answer than you.
I see it a different way.

Reporting a Group's Ideas
We agreed that _____
We decided that _____
We had a different approach.
We had a similar idea.

Predicting
I predict that _____
I imagine that _____
Based on _____ I predict that _____

Paraphrasing
So you are saying that _____
In other words, you think _____
What I hear you saying is _____

Offering a Suggestion
Maybe we could _____
What if we _____
Here's something we might try.

Asking for Clarification
I have a question about that.
Could you explain that another way?
Can you give me another example of that?

Asking for a Response
What do you think?
Do you agree?
What answer did you get?

Communication Strategies

VOCABULARY BOOKMARKS

Cut out each bookmark to use as a handy word list when you are reading. On the lines, jot down words you want to learn and remember. You can also use the bookmark as a placeholder in your book.

TITLE		TITLE		TITLE	
Word	Page #	Word	Page #	Word	Page #
_____	_____	_____	_____	_____	_____
_____	_____	_____	_____	_____	_____
_____	_____	_____	_____	_____	_____
_____	_____	_____	_____	_____	_____
_____	_____	_____	_____	_____	_____
_____	_____	_____	_____	_____	_____
_____	_____	_____	_____	_____	_____
_____	_____	_____	_____	_____	_____
_____	_____	_____	_____	_____	_____
_____	_____	_____	_____	_____	_____

VOCABULARY BOOKMARKS

Cut out each bookmark to use as a handy word list when you are reading. On the lines, jot down words you want to learn and remember. You can also use the bookmark as a placeholder in your book.

TITLE	TITLE	TITLE
Word — Page #	Word — Page #	Word — Page #

© Pearson Education

VOCABULARY BUILDER CARDS

Use these cards to record words you want to remember. Write the word, the title of the story or article in which it appears, its part of speech, and its definition. Then, use the word in an original sentence that shows its meaning

Word: _____ Page _____

Selection: _____

Part of Speech: _____

Definition: _____

My Sentence _____

_____

Word: _____ Page _____

Selection: _____

Part of Speech: _____

Definition: _____

_____

My Sentence _____

_____

Word: _____ Page _____

Selection: _____

Part of Speech: _____

Definition: _____

_____

My Sentence _____

_____

VOCABULARY BUILDER CARDS

Use these cards to record words you want to remember. Write the word, the title of the story or article in which it appears, its part of speech, and its definition. Then, use the word in an original sentence that shows its meaning

Word: _____ Page _____

Selection: _____

Part of Speech: _____

Definition: _____

_____

My Sentence _____

_____

Word: _____ Page _____

Selection: _____

Part of Speech: _____

Definition: _____

_____

My Sentence _____

_____

Word: _____ Page _____

Selection: _____

Part of Speech: _____

Definition: _____

_____

My Sentence _____

_____

© Pearson Education

Vocabulary Builder Cards

PERSONAL THESAURUS

Using the Personal Thesaurus
The Personal Thesaurus provides students with the opportunity to make connections between words academic words, familiar words, and even slang words. Students can use the Personal Thesaurus to help them understand the importance of using words in the proper context and also avoid overusing words in their writing.

Use the following routine to foster frequent use of the Personal Thesaurus.

1. After students have read a selection or done some writing, have them turn to the Personal Thesaurus.

2. Encourage students to add new entries. Help them to understand the connection between their personal language, which might include familiar words and even slang, and the academic language of their reading and writing.

3. Call on volunteers to read a few entries aloud. Point out that writers have many choices of words when they write. Help students see that audience often determines word choice.

N

- nice
- admirable
- friendly
- agreeable
- pleasant
- cool
- phat

V44 English Learner's Notebook

PERSONAL THESAURUS

A

PERSONAL THESAURUS

B

PERSONAL THESAURUS

C

PERSONAL THESAURUS

D

PERSONAL THESAURUS

E

PERSONAL THESAURUS

F

PERSONAL THESAURUS

G

PERSONAL THESAURUS

H

PERSONAL THESAURUS

PERSONAL THESAURUS

J

V54 English Learner's Notebook

PERSONAL THESAURUS

K

PERSONAL THESAURUS

L

PERSONAL THESAURUS

M

PERSONAL THESAURUS

N

PERSONAL THESAURUS

O

PERSONAL THESAURUS

P

PERSONAL THESAURUS

Q

PERSONAL THESAURUS

R

PERSONAL THESAURUS

S

PERSONAL THESAURUS

T

PERSONAL THESAURUS

U

PERSONAL THESAURUS

V

PERSONAL THESAURUS

W

PERSONAL THESAURUS

X

PERSONAL THESAURUS

Y

PERSONAL THESAURUS

Z

(Acknowledgments continued from page ii)

Dramatic Publishing
From *Anne Frank & Me* by Cherie Bennett with Jeff Gottesfeld. Copyright © 1997 by Cherie Bennett. Printed in the United States of America. CAUTION: Professionals and amateurs are hereby warned that *Anne Frank & Me*, being fully protected under the copyright Laws of the United States of America, the British Empire, including the Dominion of Canada, and all other countries of the Universal Copyright and Berne Conventions, are subject to royalty. All rights, including professional, amateur, motion picture, recitation, lecturing, public reading, radio and television broadcasting, and the rights of translation into foreign languages, are strictly reserved. All inquiries regarding performance rights should be addressed to Dramatic Publishing, 311 Washington St., Woodstock, IL 60098. Phone: (815) 338-7170.

Farrar, Straus & Giroux, LLC
"Charles" by Shirley Jackson from *The Lottery*. Copyright © 1948, 1949 by Shirley Jackson and copyright renewed © 1976, 1977 by Laurence Hyman, Barry Hyman, Mrs. Sarah Webster and Mrs. Joanne Schnurer.

Florida Holocaust Museum
Florida Holocaust Museum Press Release from *www.flholocaustmuseum.org*. Copyright © Florida Holocaust Museum, 2001, 2005.

Richard Garcia
"The City is So Big" by Richard Garcia from *The City Is So Big*.

Harcourt, Inc.
"Choice: A Tribute to Martin Luther King, Jr." by Alice Walker from *In Search Of Our Mothers' Gardens: Womanist Prose*. Copyright © 1983 by Alice Walker. "For My Sister Molly Who in the Fifties" from *Revolutionary Petunias & Other Poems*, copyright © 1972 and renewed 2000 by Alice Walker.

HarperCollins Publishers, Inc.
From *An American Childhood* by Annie Dillard. Copyright © 1987 by Annie Dillard.

Hill and Wang, a division of Farrar, Straus & Giroux
"Thank You, M'am" from *Short Stories* by Langston Hughes. Copyright © 1996 by Ramona Bass and Arnold Rampersad.

Holiday House
"January" from *A Child's Calendar* by John Updike. Text copyright © 1965, 1999 by John Updike. All rights reserved.

Georgia Douglas Johnson
"Your World" by Georgia Douglas Johnson from *American Negro Poetry*.

The Estate of Dr. Martin Luther King, Jr. c/o Writer's House LLC
"The American Dream" by Dr. Martin Luther King, Jr. from *A Testament Of Hope: The Essential Writings Of Martin Luther King, Jr.* Copyright © 1961 Martin Luther King Jr.; Copyright © renewed 1989 Coretta Scott King.

Alfred A. Knopf, Inc.
"Harlem Night Song" from *The Collected Poems of Langston Hughes* by Langston Hughes, edited by Arnold Rampersad with David Roessel, Associate Editor, copyright © 1994 by The Estate of Langston Hughes. "The 11:59" by Patricia C. McKissack from *The Dark Thirty* by Patricia McKissack illustrated by Brian Pinkney, copyright © 1992 by Patricia C. McKissack. Illustrations copyright © 1992 by Brian Pinkney.

Liveright Publishing Corporation
"Runagate Runagate" Copyright © 1966 by Robert Hayden, from *Collected Poems of Robert Hayden*, edited by Frederick Glaysher.

Robert MacNeil
"The Trouble with Television" by Robert MacNeil condensed from a speech, *November 1984 at President Leadership Forum, SUNY*. Copyright © 1985 by Reader's Digest and Robert MacNeil.

Eve Merriam c/o Marian Reiner
"Thumbprint" from *A Sky Full of Poems* by Eve Merriam. Copyright © 1964, 1970, 1973, 1986 by Eve Merriam.

N. Scott Momaday
"New World" by N. Scott Momaday from *The Gourd Dancers*.

National Public Radio
"Profile: World War II veterans who founded the Paralyzed Veterans of America" from *National Public Radio, November 11, 2003*. Copyright © 2005 National Public Radio.

Naomi Shihab Nye
"Words to Sit in, Like Chairs" by Naomi Shihab Nye from *911: The Book of Help*. "Hamadi" by Naomi Shihab Nye from *America Street*.

Harold Ober Associates, Inc.
"Cat!" by Eleanor Farjeon from *Poems For Children*. Copyright © 1938 by Eleanor Farjeon, renewed 1966 by Gervase Farjeon.

Oxford University Press, Inc.
"Summary of The Tell-Tale Heart" by James D. Hart from *The Oxford Companion To American Literature*. Copyright © 1983.

Pantheon Books, a division of Random House Inc.
"Coyote Steals the Sun and Moon" by Richard Erdoes and Alfonso Ortiz from *American Indian Myths and Legends*, copyright © 1984 by Richard Erdoes and Alfonso Ortiz.

Pearson Prentice Hall
"The War in Vietnam" from *The American Nation* by Dr. James West Davidson and Dr. Michael B. Stoff. Copyright © 2003 by Pearson Education, Inc., publishing as Prentice Hall.

G.P. Putnam's Sons
"Describe Somebody," and "Almost a Summer Sky" from *Locomotion* by Jacqueline Woodson, copyright © 2003 by Jacqueline Woodson.

Random House, Inc.
"Raymond's Run" by Toni Cade Bambara from *Gorilla, My Love*. Copyright © 1971 by Toni Cade Bambara. "The Diary of Anne Frank, Act I" by Frances Goodrich and Albert Hackett. Copyright © 1956 by Albert Hackett, Frances Goodrich Hackett and Otto Frank.

Marian Reiner, Literary Agent
"Concrete Mixers" by Patricia Hubbell from *8 A.M. Shadows*. Copyright © 1965 Patricia Hubbell. Copyright renewed © 1993 Patricia Hubbell.

Reprint Management Services—A/R
"Hands-free Law Won't Solve the Problem" by Mike Langdon Nov. 14, 2006 from *http://www.mercurynews.com/mld/mercurynews/business/column*. Copyright 2007 San Jose Mercury News.

Maria Teresa Sanchez
"Old Man" by Ricardo Sanchez from *Selected Poems*.

Savannah International Trade & Convention Center
Savannah Belles Ferry Schedule from *http://www.catchacat.org*. Copyright © 2007 Chatham Area Transit Authority.

Scholastic Inc.
From *Out of the Dust* ("Debts", "Fields of Flashing Light" and "Migrants") by Karen Hesse. Published by Scholastic Press/Scholastic Inc. Copyright © 1997 by Karen Hesse. "An Hour with Abuelo" from *An Island Like You: Stories of the Barrio* by Judith Ortiz Cofer. Published by Orchard Books/Scholastic Inc. Copyright © 1995 by Judith Ortiz Cofer.

Argelia Sedillo
"Gentleman of Rio en Medio" by Juan A.A. Sedillo from *The New Mexico Quarterly, A Regional Review*, Volume IX, August, 1939, Number 3.

The Society of Authors
"Silver" by Walter de la Mare from *The Complete Poems of Walter de la Mare 1901–1918*.

Thomson Higher Education
"Summary of The Tell-Tale Heart" from *Short Story Criticism: Criticism Of The Works Of Short Fiction Writers, Short Story Criticism Vol 34 34th Edition* by Anna Sheets Nesbitt (Editor). Copyright © 1999.

Estate of Jackie Torrence
"Brer Possum's Dilemma" retold by Jackie Torrence from *Homespun: Tales From America's Favorite Storytellers*. Copyright © 1988 by Jackie Torrence, published in *Homespun: Tales from America's Favorite Storytellers* by Jimmy Neil Smith.

Vallejo Baylink
Baylink Ferry Schedule and Logo from *http://www.baylinkferry.com*. Copyright © 2007.

Vital Speeches of the Day
From *Sharing in the American Dream* by Colin Powell from *Vital Speeches, June 1, 1997, V63 N16, P484(2)*.

W. W. Norton & Company, Inc.
"Water Names" from *Hunger* by Lan Samantha Chang. Copyright © 1998 by Lan Samantha Chang.

Walker & Company
"The Baker Heater League" by Patricia and Frederick McKissack from *A Long Hard Journey: The Story of the Pullman Porter*. Copyright © 1989 by Patricia and Frederick McKissack.

Water Taxi, Inc.
Fort Lauderdale Water Taxi™ Schedule from *http://www.watertaxi.com*. Copyright © 2002–2007 Water Taxi, Inc.

Richard & Joyce Wolkomir
"Sun Suckers and Moon Cursers" by Richarad and Joyce Wolkomir. Copyright © 2002 by Richard & Joyce Wolkomir.

Note: Every effort has been made to locate the copyright owner of material reproduced on this component. Omissions brought to our attention will be corrected in subsequent editions.